KILLING BABIES

An Australian Digger Recalls His Vietnam War

DARRYL. A. BISHOP

Published in Australia by Sid Harta Publishers Pty Ltd,
ABN: 46 119 415 842
23 Stirling Crescent, Glen Waverley, Victoria 3150 Australia
Telephone: +61 3 9560 9920, Facsimile: +61 3 9545 1742
E-mail: author@sidharta.com.au

First published in Australia 2018
This edition published May 2018

Cover design, typesetting: WorkingType
(www.workingtype.com.au)

Bishop, Darryl A.
Killing Babies: An Australian Digger
Recalls His Vietnam War
ISBN: 978-1-925230-24-6
pp510

REVIEW

This engaging personal story by a stockman greatly appeals to veteran Diggers and those aficionados with an interest in military history. The narrative provides valuable insight into the world's most advanced jungle training school at Canungra. And the extraordinary exploits of 4RAR/NZ (ANZAC) battalion at Nui Dat. Expressed in rollicking Oz vernacular, the story takes the reader into the jungle tracks of the Phuoc Tuy Province.

The author recalls his adventures with Eight Platoon 'outside the wire': avoiding ambushes, 'Jumping Jack' Mines, Claymore booby traps, dodging "Whooshers", helo insertions, pinned down by friendly artillery, and assaulting enemy bunker systems. Infrequent and elusive contact with the VC, apart from a light skirmish with 3 Battalion 33 North Vietnamese Army Regiment and D445 Local Force Battalion, underwrites the futility of the Vietnam War.

Recreational compensation from the rigours of wartime patrols was found among the notorious teenage bar girls in the Vung Tau brothels: 'boom boom', escaping the 'White Mice' and consequent visits to the doctor at the Base to avoid the dreaded "Black Jack". Swimming and surf board lessons at Back Beach, sporadic rugby union, sightseeing Budda statues, and listening to the Melbourne Cup on a wireless set in the remote jungle were other means to briefly forget the war.

The expression "killing babies" was coined by those back home in Australia and the U.S. It does not relate to Diggers in the field of combat. The surge of anti-war public opinion coupled with political events at the White House eventually forced Australia and the U.S. to abandon Vietnam to its fate. The main body from 4RAR—the last Australian infantry battalion in South Vietnam—sailed for Australia on board HMAS *Sydney* on 9 December 1971. The author was flown home to Sydney via Darwin by Hercules aircraft in the same month. Australia's participation in the war was formally declared at an *end* when the Governor-General issued a proclamation on 11 January 1973.

CAPT David L O Hayward (Retd),
former ARES Officer, RACT

ABOUT THE AUTHOR

Darryl Bishop is a stockman. He is a jack-of-all-trades who laughingly says he is a master of none.

He broke in a lot of horses at Brewarrina while moving mobs of sheep and cattle along the stock routes and contract mustering in that district of north-west New South Wales, worked in shearing sheds in the north and south of the state as a roustabout and woolroller and was at one time an Opal Miner. He worked as a labourer on construction sites and as an Iron Worker (Tradesmen's lackey) at Dunlop's Tyre Factory in Sydney in 1974 and was in Tennant Creek, Northern Territory, as a Backhoe Operator when Cyclone Tracy went through Darwin on Christmas night of that year. Apart from the short time spent in Sydney, eight months in Townsville and the time he was away in Vietnam, he has lived all his life west of the Great Dividing Ranges.

He hung up his stockwhip, spur and saddle in 2003 and moved to the western Darling Downs with his little mate, Midge, where he and she now live the quiet life of retirement; however, he still likes to keep his hand in by doing occasional work in the cattle and sheep yards of friends in the district at mate's rates.

He is a passionate advocate for solar power, promoting it when and wherever he is able, be that at universities or to university students at his local hall, and as such is equally passionate about the defeat of dirty, stinking coal mines and coal seam gas industry in his area, and when and where he can he will malign these industries, seeing it as a duty to protect his country and its people for the generations to come.

He enjoys night bowls in the summer months and would like to play more golf. Although he said he would never write again when he left school at the end of 1966, he has recently stated that creative writing is an enjoyable and addictive activity and now feels compelled to add his compositions to the rich written history of our great land.

Firstly, I must thank my little mate, Midge, my best mate, for having the fortitude to put up with me these past thirty odd years of our entwinement and her unflinching support of me at all times.

I dedicate these pages to all those gallant Infantrymen who have served in the armed forces of all armies of all time, but most particularly the men of Five Section, Eight Platoon, Charlie Company, Fourth Royal Australian Regiment/New Zealand (4RAR/NZ Anzac) Second Tour and, in particular, Jim, Andy, Bob Denholm, Smithy, and most especially my mate, Muzzy — may your beer always be cold. Thank you, gentlemen.

AUTHOR'S NOTE

To gain a more complete knowledge of the Battle of Nui Le it would be advisable to read one of or both of the books written by people who were there on the ground at the time. One of these books is called *DELTA 4* by Garry McKay the other is by Jerry Taylor called *LAST OUT.* Both these men are holders of the Military Cross. Another source of information is the official record of 4RAR's second tour called *THE FIGHTING FOURTH* which contains maps and photos and can be obtained at your local libraries or by contacting the 4RAR association bookstore via the Association's website 4rarassociationsaustralia.com.au

“*Killing Babies* is a memoir.
If the truth hurts — so be it.
I can only show you to the best of
my ability the events as I perceived
them unfolding before me at the time.”

CONTENTS

FOREWORD

When people find out that I'm a Vietnam Veteran, they never ask me what it was like to fight in a war in that uncertain place, instead they nearly always say, 'I knew a bloke called Ted Reynolds or Jack Smith or Joe Blog (or whoever). He was over there. Did you know him?'

My answer to them is always the same question, 'Who was he with?'

I invariably hear, 'Aw, I dunno, but he was there.'

That is of little help when you consider that around sixty thousand Australians were involved in the Vietnam conflict in one station or another during the period in which Australia was committed to it.

I was a boarder at Red Bend Catholic College in Forbes in Central New South Wales when it started and I remember seeing pinned to the notice board outside the office the newspaper clippings featuring photographs of the "Burning Buddhist Monk" on a street in Saigon.

In 1967 I was working for a Roo Shooter spotlighting and trimming dead kangaroos and in '68 or '69 when Ted Reynolds and his mates were doing their bit "over there" I would have been breaking in a Yang or tearing through Lignum as tall as a man on a horse in wild pursuit of runaway scrubber cattle, or perhaps simply poking along a stock route somewhere in the Lower Barwon River area with three-and-a-half thousand head of shorn wethers in front of me.

So, no, I didn't really know Ted Reynolds, Jack Smith or Joe

Blog. All I can do is tell you to the best of my recollection what it was like for me — just an ordinary bloke from the bush — and my mates while we were doing our duty to our country when we were over there. This then is my story which starts when I leave Brewarrina in the north-west of New South Wales to hitch-hike down to Temora to spend Christmas with my family on our farm at the end of 1969. While on this break I received my Call Up papers in the mail.

The first thing I had to do was to report to a quack in Temora for a check-up. He picked up the murmur in my heart as soon as his stethoscope hit my skinny, bare chest, but I assured him I wasn't about to keel over in his rooms right there and then. I'd had the bloody thing since the local Brewarrina doctor, Tony Lopes, first found it when he'd put me in hospital with Hong Kong Flu in 1957, my first year at boarding school at that town's Convent of Mercy. Nevertheless, the Temora MO (Medical Officer) insisted on sending me to a specialist over at Wagga Wagga where the bright young man told me I was alright and that I could go and run in the upcoming Munich Olympic Games in Germany if I liked. My mother country, however, had something else in store for me.

1
IN TRAINING

I should not have been there. I should have been away droving on the Plains where the waters of the Condamine River overflow out of Queensland into New South Wales. Instead I was ushering my family's 1963 model *Humber Super Snipe* estate wagon quietly towards Kapooka Army Camp just a few kilometres south-west of the large regional town of Wagga Wagga in the Riverina District of southern New South Wales.

It is nearly three in the afternoon of a cool, clear Tuesday on the 7th of the 7th, 1970. The following day I was to start my two-year stint as a National Serviceman.

Thick shadows lay across the narrow, tarred road ahead of us; however, the shadows outside of the car were nothing compared to the shadows that showed on my fifty-three-year old father, Ray's wrinkled brow as he sat glumly in the front passenger's side seat of the wagon. He'd seen service at Milne Bay in New Guinea in 1942 during World War II. My guess is that he was hoping against hope that his number two son would never have to face the same horrors of war which he himself had faced around twenty-seven years ago, but of that I cannot be sure. He never said. He kept those sorts of things entirely to himself. For my part, now that I was going to be an Australian soldier, I hoped I would not let him down and that

I'd be able to walk tall beside him, not in his shadow, when I eventually got out.

So it was, that at precisely 3 o'clock on that day I presented my papers to the Sergeant of the Guard in the red brick building just inside the gates of Kapooka as I'd been ordered to do by the Australian Liberal Government of the day. He checked and confirmed my appointment and told me to go on up. I drove past the single sentry manning the stripped flat, stick barrier and along a slowing winding road to find a car park and as I drove up the rise towards the brick buildings on the left I was struck by the thought, *It'll be just like going back to school*. These red brick buildings remaindered me so much of the College I'd finished attending at Forbes just three-and-a-half years before.

After Dad and I said our goodbyes, I watched him drive away in his wagon before setting off to find someone who'd tell me where I was to go and what was expected of me next.

By the following morning all the other Recruits of the Second Round, Twenty-First Intake into compulsory National Service from New South Wales and Queensland were installed in the barracks, which would be our home for the next ten weeks. For us in 1RTB (1 Recruit Training Battalion) Basic Training would begin this very morning. First though, the new intake of forty-eight raw personnel in Eight Platoon had to be formally introduced to our NCOs (Non-Commissioned Officers) — the blokes with stripes on their upper arms — not pips on shoulders — who would be looking after us from now until we "passed out".

Sergeant Phillips was a lean man of about one hundred and eighty centimetres tall, with an eveready, built-in smile on his slightly ruddy face, probably in his late thirties. He was an Artillery Sergeant. His junior was Corporal Lyons, short, thickset, of dark complexion, with shiny, jet-black, brushed-backed hair and slow, droopy eyes, who was not long back from a stint with the Infantry in Vietnam. They were both quiet sort of blokes who it seemed to me were assigned to us, to soften the stuff the drill people were going to deal out to us in the days and weeks to come.

Then there were the hair cuts and photos. I was a bit peeved when I was ordered to have another hair cut. One week before this day I was a "long haired lout" like the greater majority of the young blokes of the time. On that day, the Sergeant of Police in Temora had instructed his daughter, whom I'd been going out with for the past six months to inform me that I couldn't come visiting her anymore if I didn't get a hair cut and clean up my face — most likely because of an incident with "the law" in the town of Parkes a couple of days prior when I'd just happened to drop his name in an attempt to avoid a traffic infringement fine.

Three days before arriving at Kapooka I went into Temora from the family farm and paid two dollars fifty for a "short back and sides" that I thought would surely have to be good enough for the Army, but before attending the barber I had my second eldest sister take a photo of the scruffy me for prosperity. I also paid one dollar fifty for a pair of hair-cutting scissors and another few dollars for a new razor and blades. At home on the farm I cut most of my beard off with the scissors, lathered up and took off the remainder with the razor — my first shave in eight months. Now they expected me to fork out again, this time for a hair trim that could have yielded them no more hair than you'd find on a new born baby's bum. The photo was so good that it would do the mob at Pentridge proud — number plate held at chest height and all. Don't know why they did that? I have never looked like that again.

Basic Training was as one would expect. There were lots of NCOs yelling at us as they marched us from one place to another to the very foreign sound of 'Urt-urt-urt, art urrrrt'. First it was down to the Q-store (Quartermasters Store) to collect our kit, which consisted of hand-me-down greens (our work cloths) an olive green Yank windcheater, a new slouch hat, AB boots and gaiters — not the small gaiters like the soldiers of the Second World War and the cadets at the College wore, but the longer ones with a strap under the boot and three buckles down the outside.

Then to the place they called the RAP (Regimental Aid Post) where all the doctors and such hung out, for the usual stuff like, drop your daks, bend over and show them your bum so that they can see that you haven't got piles, then cough while in that vulnerable position to see if you're herniated or not, show your hands, top and bottom, perhaps to see if you've got any abnormalities, and check your eyes to see if you're showing signs of hepatitis.

I don't know how many recruits there were in the Twenty-First Intake for National Service at Kapooka in July 1970, but there seemed to be platoons of blokes being marched all over the place. Nobody really knew each other so there were no shenanigans between Platoons as we passed each other going here and there.

Around ten o'clock on the second morning we were marched up the road around the back of the indoor swimming pool carrying our Phys-Ed (Physical Education) clothes in bum-packs. We were told to change into our whites, leave our other stuff on the ground and run down the grassy slope to the place that looked like an unfenced tennis court. This area had a high gallows-type structure at its eastern end from which hung thick ropes that seemed about twenty feet long.

We were met there by a loud, sinewy, small man in whites who soon made it be known to one and all: 'I'm your Phys-Ed Instructor — and I don't like you mummy boys coming onto my patch — I'm not here to like you little squirts — I'm here cause it's my job to make yah hurt'.

He put us through a series of callisthenics, sorted us into four groups — complete with leaders — before torturing us some more. Then he lined us up with the chin-up bars. After each man in the four teams had done as many chin-ups as he could possibly do, we were introduced to the ropes. Firstly, we were given an expert demonstration on the art of rope climbing by some fit instructors and then they let us loose on them.

When the last man of the teams struggled to the ground being ever so mindful not to just slip straight down as this would result in very painful rope-burned palms, the little torturer in white yelled at us to line up quickly. He pointed up the rise towards the road where another Platoon was just arriving near our discarded gear, and roared at us, 'I want you to disappear from here and appear up there dressed'.

As exhausted as some of us were, we nevertheless bolted up that slope and dressed again into our greens as fast as we could, but of course it was never going to be fast enough for this man's Army and we were told as much as soon as we were lined up on the roadway ready to be marched away to something else.

In this case "something else" was an hour of drill on a parade ground with left turns and left wheels until we could do them in our sleep for years to come.

Army life wasn't too bad for me for a trifecta of reasons. Firstly, communal living with blokes alone I'd done before. Almost all my ten years of schooling had been spent locked up in boarding schools, starting with the nuns at the Convent of Mercy, Brewarrina, in 1957, then five years with the Marist Brothers at Red Bend Agricultural College, Forbes, from '61. The novelty was four men to a room. There'd been eight boys in the dormitory at the Convent and thirty-eight or so up in the top dorm at the College and when we moved down to the junior high school dorm under Brother Leonard (aka "Tank") there was upwards to eighty lads lined up beside each other with just a stout, wooden locker sixty centimetres wide to put our cloths in between the old steel frame beds. In July '70 I was only three-and-a-half years removed from that environment.

Secondly, I was already reasonable fit. In my final year at Forbes I'd been my age Athletic Champion and from September 1968 until December 1969 I'd been up in Brewarrina working for Darby Neale the drover and had spent most of that time living rough on boiled meat and spuds, mutton chops grilled on the camp oven lid for breakfast, or drover's stew, and drinking black tea whilst droving and breaking in horses. I'd been doing farm stuff around the one thousand-acre family farm twenty-seven kilometres south-sou-east of Temora for the past six months while waiting to come into the Army, having received my Call Up notice while home from droving for a break over Christmas '69.

Thirdly, I'd learnt all the drills already with the College

Cadets. The main difference between this Army gig and school was that in the Army they only yelled at us when we stuffed up, they didn't wallop us with a cane.

I shared room one of twelve that opened onto a hall which led out onto a square of tar they called a Parade Ground, with a little bloke who was also from Temora. According to my Army records, I'm only five foot, seven-and-a-half inches (172 cm) tall. He was even shorter than I. He worked on the railways and had an absolutely "drop dead gorgeous" girlfriend who incidentally lived on the same small farm just out of Temora on the Young Road that my Nanna and Pop owned until a few years back when they moved out to a five hundred-acre farm which was beside the place we were now paying off.

Then there was Stassy, a big bloke with a happy face and short, curly, light-coloured hair. He was a tuna fisherman working out of Eden on the southern coast of New South Wales. The other bloke in our room was only slightly taller than me with light red hair and a pale complexion. He was an extremely talented graphic artist from Sydney.

After two weeks of doing not much more than parade ground drills, phys-ed and weapons training centred around the 7.62 mm Self Loading Rifle (SLR), the basic Infantry weapon used by the Australian Army at this time, we came in for a real treat — our first pay.

For this we had to have special instructions on the proper protocol of receiving one's pay from a Pay Officer in this man's Army. The procedure was spelled out to us and woebetide anyone who stuffed it up.

When your name is called by the Pay Officer, you march up

to a desk with him seated behind it and he hands you your pay book with some money in the middle of it. You step back one pace, chuck a brisk and proper salute and say loud and clear, 'Pay correct sir'. You do a right or left turn, march a few paces to a Pay Master, usually a Corporal, and you hand back your pay book, less the money, so that he can immediately start working on your next fortnight's income. We were not allowed to check if the contents of our pay packets were indeed correct until we were outside or at least out of sight of the Pay Officer. It was all based on blind faith that the office clerks would get nothing wrong and that the Australia Army under the control of the Australian Government for which we served would not rip us off. There were no arguments and no comebacks.

Sometime in week four they took us down to the south of the camp to the twenty-five-metre rifle range to fire the SLR for the first time. They had been mollycoddling us so much to date that I fully expected they'd have us shooting out of SLRs fitted with .22 calibre barrels the same as they did with 303s converted to .22s for the Cadets; but no, this was the real thing sure enough.

Firstly, we lined up in alphabetical order and numbered off. Then we were lined up ten abreast a metre or two behind small mounds onto which we would drop and rest our elbows in the lying position when ordered to. Once we were there the instructors fussed about a fair bit getting us into the correct posture so that we were in the most comfortable place to fire into the high mounds of loose dirt with the small dugout at their base, twenty-five metres from our prone bodies. When they felt we were properly settled in, the Senior Weapons Instructor of the day bellowed at us in a very loud, gruff voice,

'When I give the order to fire–you will fire one roun', and one roun' only at the target — in your own time — one roun' only — fire.'

I did so; but judging by the spasmodic shots to my right that followed, some of the boys had not had a lot to do with rifles up until now. In fact, I'd say that most of them had just fired a weapon of any significance for the very first time. They may have had a go at the slug guns at the local show, but this thing bucked and went off with a loud bop and understandably some of the boys were a little nervous and, by the look of some of the Weapons Instructors, they too were rather anxious.

I must say I was pleasantly surprised at the first shot. There didn't seem to be much go in the gat (rifle) at all, certainly not as much as the .303 that the men in the last wars had used. This disappointed me somewhat; however, that lack of apparent punch can be explained by the fact that the SLR is a gas-operated semi-automatic. A portion of the gas usually reserved to push the lead out of the barrel is sent back along a small tube on top of the barrel to force a breach block and slide back far enough to eject the spent shell whereupon the breach block and slide are shoved forward again by a strong, narrow spring located inside the wooden butt, which culminates in the reloading of another round into the breach of the weapon making it ready to fire again almost instantly. There was a movable gas setter just behind the sight just in front of the wood which regulated the amount of gas returning to the breach block and slide. Set on six, it was fine; however, if inadvertently set at one or two, it would just about break your unsuspecting shoulder, believe me, I've been there.

It was about this time that we started to lose a few of our

number. Firstly, there was the tall, ginger- headed bloke who out of the blue one day after lunch stood in front of our barracks door and utterly refused to pick up his pack and load it onto his back. Sergeant Phillips tried to stare him down and while getting redder in the face by the minute he ordered him time and time again to pick up his pack. The bloke stood to rigid attention and although he had tears streaming down his cheeks he did not move. Guts or not I'm not sure, but resolve, one hundred percent.

Eventually, after about a quarter of an hour, he was marched away to face the consequences of his actions and he was never seen nor mentioned in our ranks again.

A week later, a rough-looking, little bloke with thick, black hair, who appeared a lot older than the rest of us twenty-year-olds, started having some really bad nightmares. It turned out that he could not sleep under the deliberately roughened ceilings in our rooms, because it reminded him of his father coming into his room to give him his nightly hiding when he was growing up. I can't say that I'd even noticed the ceilings to this point, but, yes, they were a bit rough. His initial psyche test had found nothing wrong with him. He was discharged on psychological grounds, and we never laid eyes on him again.

I had a sneaky feeling that both these blokes got away with something that had been pulled before by their fathers, uncles or even grandfathers to avoid being sent away to one of the last two world wars or even the Korean do. The next bloke to go was a week or so later. He was found by the guards at three o'clock on a freezing cold morning, running naked around the parade ground between our lines and our HQ (Headquarters).

He was shipped out immediately with absolutely no further contact with us.

The other bloke to go went for an entirely different reason. We'd been marched down to what appeared to be a very weak obstacle course and "stood easy". We were then asked, 'Do any of you have a uni degree, or is there anyone among you currently doing a uni course?'

A strapping, good-looking lad with light-coloured hair put his hand up and meekly announced that he was in the Police Academy prior to coming here. He was told, 'That'll do,' and was then sent across the obstacle course which he bolted in. He was immediately marched away from us. I asked, 'Hey, Corp, can we all 'ave a go at that? It donn look too ard!' It certainly didn't look too hard for the majority of us, but we were told in no uncertain terms, 'No, this is only for those men who are going into Officer training.' Then we were promptly marched away ourselves.

Everybody in the Army from Junior Officers, like Lieutenants, down to the lowest of Other Ranks (ORs) had to do some form of "duties". Around week five I copped my first Guard Duty. A couple of blokes from each platoon in our intake made up the detail. We were given a boondi (a stick), and an area to patrol for a set amount of time that night. At one point, we seemed to all come together around behind a boozer where a big bloke from another platoon who had a head full of tight blond curls and went by the name of Fox suddenly decided that we all should go to the back door of the establishment and get a beer. Now I'm no wowser, I like a drink the same as most hot-blooded, young Aussies worth their salt, but there is a time and place for everything and being on guard duty as a recruit at 1RTB was definitely the wrong place and the wrong time to be hitting the piss. Foxy was nearly two metres tall and had rather broad shoulders; nevertheless, I persuaded him that he was to desist in such actions whenever I was on duty with him.

Another day I was sent down to the Gate for a stint as a guard there for the day and I presumed I'd be standing to attention at the gate all day checking visitor IDs and such. Instead I was given the job of guarding the only prisoner they had in the brink at the time. He was a thin, small, pale-faced, blonde bloke who one evening had gone down around the back and into the kitchen under our big Mess Hall, grabbed up an unattended meat clever from a bench and smartly lopped off his trigger finger. They had to take the bones behind his knuckle as well as his knuckle out to fix it up. He was a seventeen-year-old Regular Soldier (Reg) who simply said he 'could not take the Army any more'. After cleaning him up, the Army naturally charged him with self-inflicted wounds and penned him up for a bit.

I had to watch over him while he shaved and stand guard on him outside the dunny and then escort the poor prick back to his cell after he'd finished his ablutions. I felt sorry for him in a way to stuff up his hand for the rest of his life just to get out of this shit even though he'd signed up for it willingly just a short time back when he could have just as easily pulled something like the blokes in our lot had done and got away with it too.

We were all given a go at the *Owen* gun down at the twenty-five metre range. This gun looked like it was not much more than a piece of perforated pipe with a bit of wood attached at the back, a trigger under the middle and a long thin magazine sticking straight up out of it. It had been invented by an Australian during

World War II to be used in the thick jungles in the islands to our north. The bloody thing kicked like a mule up and away to one side.

You had to stand with your hand on top of it with your arm braced straight. It was almost impossible to hit the intended target more then once or twice before it rattled off line. Quick, short bursts were the answer, but it was so slow that you could virtually watch the lead travelling all the way to its target. The nine-millimetre rounds used in this weapon could also be used in the Army-issue, fourteen-round, automatic pistols some Officers carried around, so I suppose that was one good thing about it.

Marching back from the twenty-five-metre range that day we were suddenly wheeled off and lined up along the left-hand side of the road overlooking the Phys-ed court and its high ropes for that day's weapons training. At the end of each hour of such training we were to lean over and look into the open breech of the SLR in our mate's hands beside us and visually verify that there was no round still in the chamber and yell out, 'Clear'. I happened to be "marker" on this day. The Marker is the first person on the left of the front row of any section of personnel assembled to be marched or drilled. All others fall in to the right of the Marker to form a rank usually described as a squad. When the squad grows to include one Lieutenant, a Sergeant, three Corporals, three Lance-Corporals and twenty-four men, it's referred to as Platoon. Three Platoons plus Company Headquarters Group is then Company and so on. As Marker of a Weapons Training Squad, I had to check out the Weapon Instructor's weapon at the end of this session. I looked in and seeing nothing but the black hole of the empty chamber, I roared out the obligatory, 'Clear'. He walked briskly around to the rear of the squad and BANG, a rifle shot split the air behind us making us all jump out of our skins.

Next thing he was in my face — which was pretty hard for him as he was about two metres tall and about two axe-handles across the shoulders and me all of one hundred and seventy-one-and-a-half centimetres. He leaned in towards me until our noses were no more than twenty-five millimetres apart and staring daggers at me with his black snake like eyes, he bellowed, 'You miserable, useless little turd. Don't you ever say a weapon is clear when it's not clear, no matter who's weapon it is. Do you hear? Never ever! Do you hear me?'

He continued ... but I had already switched off. I knew full well that there was nothing up the spout of his gat when I cleared him and would have said something if there had been. Dad was always up us kids about never leaving a bullet in a weapon that was coming indoors at home, so I knew what was required here. To this day I reckon he slipped a blank into the breach and fired it off. I just happened to be the Marker and as such I was the one to get blasted this day. As "right is might", I had no trouble standing my ground and meeting him square in the eye, coldly staring right back at him and not conceding a fraction of a millimetre as I endured his tirade.

About two weeks later, this same bloke got the shits with us sissies and the manner in which we were corrupting the use of the SLR. When he could take no more of the slow bop-bop as we shot at the targets in the mound of the twenty-five-metre range, he said savagely to one of our lot, 'F'chrice sake, 'ere giv'us that thing 'ere, wilya'.

He stepped up to the edge of the recline where the dirt had

been pushed away to make the mound and with his left hand held firmly over his left ear, the pistol grip of the gat hidden by his huge right hand, the weapon itself fitting snugly on his hip, he proceeded to chase an empty beer can up the mound from the bottom to the very top with round after round. Bop-bop-bop; in quick bursts the can was made to hop up to the rim whereupon he'd wait for it to roll all the way back down to the bottom and go bop-bop-bop; and it would fly to the top again.

It was exhilarating to watch him in action. I was awestruck at how much he was at one with this weapon. After he'd emptied the twenty-round mag in quick time and did his clearing procedure, he handed the recruit back his weapon to clean and said gruffly, 'There, that's 'ow yur use that bloody thing'.

I told myself then and there that only when I could use this beautifully-balanced, slim-line, Belgium-designed weapon with that same grace would I say that I was truly proficient in the use of the 7.62 SLR.

Everybody who has been in the Forces knows there will be Barrack Inspections at sometime or another. Our first inspection began with a shout of, 'Stand to', from our red-headed room mate, which was the signal for us to stand to attention by our beds as the Inspecting Officer invaded our space with the stern-faced Sergeant Phillips in tow. No sooner had the Officer performed the "white glove treatment" on the architrave above the inside of our door, they marched out without a backward glance. I don't think he really wanted to be there in the first place.

On his next visit in about week six, he waltzed in, did a sharp right turn, then right again, so that he was looking into the cupboard of the little bloke from Temora, where a photo of his gorgeous girlfriend held pride of place on the top shelf. The young, skinny Officer stared at the photograph for a moment before he demanded, 'Who owns this?'

'I do, Sir,' answered Temora.

'Struth, she's one hallava sort, yur wanta keep yur eye on that one. Carry on gentleman!' Then he was gone before Temora could even say, 'Sir'.

Somewhere around this time we all had dental work done on us. I think the Army dental technicians were apprentices because when bean pole-like Peter Minchinton (Mincho) from Sydney had to have an extraction, they stuffed it up somehow. They had to cut into his gum to get to the lost bottom portion of his tooth leaving poor Mincho with a wing of stitches to close the hole in his gum to stay the bleeding they'd started.

At the end of six weeks we were granted a four-day "stand down", during which time we could go home to be with our loved ones, and as the time approached the boys started getting pretty excited. I couldn't see what all the fuss was about at first, but I then realised that the greater majority of these lads had not been away from their family home for anything like six weeks in the twenty years of their lives thus far. It must have been a bit tough on them poor things. Some were probably itching to get home to reassure themselves that their girlfriends weren't shagging someone else while they were away.

Personally, the longest time I'd spent at our family home since I first started boarding school at Bre as a seven-year-old was about eight months on Beefwood Downs, our sheep station, whilst attending Goodooga School for two terms in 1966 and eight months of '68 on the Clear Hills farm over at Temora before leaving again to work with Darby Neale the drover. Going home for a couple of days was no big deal for me and, besides, the Police Sergeant had by now been promoted to a new position in Singleton, taking his daughter with him.

The day before leave we were marched down to the RAP for yet another needle. This one was different though. A small amount of serum was smeared into our forearms and a small apparatus with six needles was placed over it and when pressed the apparatus clicked and the needles shot out penetrating the skin, thus allowing the serum to seep into our arm via shallow punctures which looked like a neat circular bite from a six-fanged snake.

The four-day "stand down" was uneventful in the main. I found out that six-year-old Jenny, the ninth of my mother's brood and number five of my six sisters, had cried for four days straight when I first left for Recruit Training six weeks ago. She may not have fully known what war was all about at that tender age, but seemed to understand that something could go amiss with this soldiering lark.

It snowed the first morning we were back at camp; not a lot, but enough to leave a good dusting of white on the slopes of Mt Kapooka just to the west of our barracks. To make the experience more memorable for us, they sent us on an early morning run right up to the edge of the snow and back. Not only was it bloody cold, but the air was really thin up there and, consequently, we were all panting like winded horses when we got back. The rotund George Pisani of Kogarah in Sydney who had jet- black hair, pale olive skin and laughing, almond-coloured eyes was especially slow and we ribbed him mercilessly as he staggered in with his head down, for fear that the whole Platoon would get punished for his tardiness.

'Carn Pisser, get a wriggle on, yur holden us all up.'

Sergeant Phillips lined us up against the north wall of our barracks to bawl us out about being so soft after the break when some of the boys began complaining about feeling a bit crook. One of our lot, a huge hairy Greek bloke who's name and place I've forgotten, stepped forward exposing his inner forearm saying, 'It might have somethin ta do with this, do yur think, Sarge?'

His whole left forearm was very red and was swollen to twice its normal size. About seventy-five millimetres down from the crease of his elbow were little grey mounds with black spots at their centre.

Phillips was horrified and angrily asked as he grabbed the mate's arm to investigate, 'What's this? Has anyone else got these?'

Half the Platoon rolled up their khaki jumper sleeves to expose the same weird markings. Some of us had four lumps, some even six. Others had odd numbers back from five back to one. I only had two though my left arm was now sore, swollen and stiffening fast.

'Stay here, I'll be right back,' ordered Phillips, and he was gone.

We stood about waiting and compared notes with growing anxiety.

'Or shit, I've just been with my missus all weekend I mighta given et ta 'er!'

'I've been rooten my favourite girlfriend all weekend. What if I've given this t'her?'

By the time Phillips returned, some of the boys were getting really irate.

'All you recruits that are showing signs of this are confined to Barracks until further notice,' growled the Sergeant. 'We'll soon get to the bottom of this. Dismissed!'

It turned out that the Orderly who'd selected the serum to smear on our arms that day had taken the wrong bottle down off the shelf and that we'd been given Smallpox. Except for the better part of a week confined to Barracks and a snake-bite scar which I carry to this day, no real harm was done. As soon as we were fit enough we were promised we'd make up for lost time.

On the Thursday of that week Stassy, another of the confined, and I witnessed an extraordinary scene up on the footpath just to the east of our rooms. A Recruit marched past two high-ranking Officers and threw them a standard salute, knowing full well that it was near enough to a death sentence if he did not acknowledge them by doing so. The trouble was he was carrying his SLR in the "shouldered arms" position and therefore could not salute them with his right arm. Upon seeing the recruit revert to his left arm instead, the two Officers wheeled on him in a flash.

'Recruit, don't you know how to salute an Officer whilst on the march and carrying a weapon?'

'Sir, err no, Sir,' answered the confused recruit.

'Here, hand me that weapon, Recruit, and I'll show you,' said the larger of the two Officers.

Apparently, as you approach the oncoming Officer, you

transfer your weapon from your right arm to your left, then you bang off the salute and once past the offending Officer you proceed to work your weapon back to your right arm, all being done in perfect sync with your step, of course. They stood there and made the poor, young bugger go over and over it for a good ten minutes or so until they were satisfied and until it was so deeply imprinted on his brain that I am sure he can do it in his sleep to this very day and most likely does.

With all large groups of people, there are always furphies going around and Kapooka was no exception to this rule. One person who always seemed to be getting a mention was a bloke called O'Connor. I think they said he was on his third attempt to make it through Recruit Training at Kapooka. He must have been a Reg, voluntarily signed up to three, six, or nine years' service in the Australian Army, as they would have most certainly bushed him by this time if he'd been a Nasho (National Serviceman) like us. One morning, he was reported to have thrown himself bodily out of the window of his room on the first floor of the building opposite ours and landed head first on the concrete footpath outside. There was talk of a crash helmet being in the mix but I can't say for sure — it was a second-hand story after all.

Around week eight we were asked to nominate which Corps we would like to go into and were given space on the written form for two choices. I, along with about fourteen other blokes including Shoemaker, my best mate at the time, chose Infantry. My reasoning was simple. Firstly, I'm an outdoors man and secondly this Australian Army wanted numbers for the shit that it was involved in up in Vietnam at the time, hence the

Nasho Call Up. So as not to get disappointed by making another choice only to be told later, 'No, you're in the Infantry, son,' I got to make that choice myself and thus I took with me the satisfaction that I'd had at least the say in the matter.

Funnily enough, Phillips was ropable with me, stating that I should have gone for Artillery (Arty).

'You would have got it,' he told me, earnestly. 'You would not have to be out in all sorts of weather. You would have been all warm an' dry at night in your own little dugout and all.'

'It's awright, Sarge.' I assured him, grinning; after all I'd already been out in all sorts of weather for the last two-and-a-half years. Even Corporal Lyons, an Infantryman himself, was not impressed with my choice.

We were into the assessment period of our training now. Snow fell again on the very morning we were to do our swim assessment, and even though they said the indoor pool was heated to 70 degrees Fahrenheit (21 degrees Celsius) for anyone growing up where I came from, that's almost as cold as the coldest days of winter and most definitely still jumper temperature.

Chlorine fumes near choked me as soon as we entered the closed space around the pool, but what made our two-minute swim worse was the sight of the snow packed up thirty centimetres deep outside the bottom of the glass outer walls of the large building housing the pool. You might say mind over matter, but I can tell you it was bloody goose-bump cold in the water that morning.

Just after the swim, we were taken around the back of the pool area to a place set up to do lectures on Contour Lines associated with map reading. The young Officer conducting the course waited until we were all sitting up on the wood-and-steel-stepped seating, then said with glee, 'I've always wanted to do this.' He then scooped up a handful of snow and chucked it at us. Suddenly, most of the boys were on the ground and peppering him with snowballs in return. He had to threaten us with being put on a charge to bring us under control again.

One day in the middle of the week Eight Platoon was lined up outside our barracks just after lunch, when Sergeant Phillips said, 'We want some volunteers. Everyone from here down, stay where you are, the rest of you go with Corporal Lyons.'

We "volunteers" were marched away full of questions, especially as we headed up onto the high road that ran past the red brick buildings I'd noted coming in on that first day and which we now knew as "God's country", as it was where all the big wig Officers hung out.

'You'll see, now silence in the ranks, urt-urt ...' was all we could get out of Lyons. Just as we wheeled in off the road, right into God's country itself, in reality not much more than one of the large, red-brick buildings that reminded me so much of the College at Forbes — a big, busty blonde sheila in a green, tight-fitting Army uniform stepped out of a dark green Army kombi van near us. The boys went wild with cat-calls and wolf-whistles, but the rebuke was swift.

'Fuck off boys, yer wooden know what ta do with someone like me,' she said, unashamedly, instantly putting the boys in their place.

We waited restlessly at what looked like the back door of the Officers' Mess until we were eventually stood down and told to follow a Corporal who had been sent outside to escort us in. Once indoors, we were told that we would be waiters for a big function that night, and no, none of us had ever done any waiting on tables before in our miserable little lives but, 'Never mind, we'll teach you, that's my job,' said the bright, skinny young Corporal. By the time we left the building at three o'clock that afternoon we could all "give to the right and take from the left", knew the size of the table we were to attend, where the guest of honour would be seated, and who was to pamper him.

With the rest of the arvo off to make sure we were tubbed and spiffed up, we arrived back at "God's country" at six-thirty. Dinner was served at seven sharp and the guest of honour was none other then the Right Honourable Mr Andrew Peacock, Minister for Defence in the McMahon Federal Liberal Government of the day. Wifey was along as well.

Dinner was a very drawn-out affair with lots of "be up standings" and toasts to Queen and Country. Eventually, they all left the big dining hall and we were sent in to clear away their mess. Having boarded almost all my schooling days, I always take advantage of opportunities when they present themselves and so, of course, I got stuck into whatever I could, as I worked my way along the two long rows of half empty glasses of spirits and Champers left on the tables. Some of it was all right too!

As soon as everything was cleared away, we were hunted out of the dinner hall to the bar area and all the Officers traipsed back in. The busty blonde we'd heckled earlier in the day closed herself in with them, pulling shut the large double doors in on herself as she disappeared.

I have no idea what went on in there, but for ten minutes or more all we could hear was loud cheering, cooeeing and whistling. None of the Officers' wives out around the bar took a blind bit of notice as they talked merrily to each other like they were at a CWA (Country Women's Association) meeting. I was given the task of walking among them with a silver tray loaded up with small glasses of Sweet or Dry Sherry. I held them aloft as waiters do and, when asked what I was toting, I'd swivel them down in a very professional style to a more presentable level and say with a most disarming smile, 'Sweet and Dry, love'.

Every time I was asked by a little old lady, 'Which one is the Sweet and which is the Dry?' I'd say, 'Dunno love, just try one an' see wotcha think.'

They'd select one, and if they screwed their noses up, I'd say with a cheeky grin, 'Can't be that one then, try the other one.'

Given that there were only two choices on my tray; the next one was usually the right one.

I even got to serve the exquisitely-dressed Mrs Susan Peacock, who without the slightest doubt had the sexiest legs in the whole place that night. When the Officers emerged from their shenanigans in the Mess Hall and re-joined us in the bar area, I was put behind the bar to help. I think I was supposed to just wash up, but took great delight in serving drinks as well, when suddenly this fresh-faced young Officer asked me for a Milky Way. I tugged on the overworked barman's right jacket sleeve and leaning towards him asked, 'E said 'e wants a Milky Way, wotsa Milky Way?'

He hurriedly pushed me aside, saying, 'I'll do that,' then proceeded to concoct a brew of milk, cream and a drop of something in a liqueur glass, inspecting it closely while handing it over the bar. It must have been quite a drop because after only three of these, the "wet behind the ears" Lieutenant was inebriated almost to the point of being a falling-down drunk. I'd never seen anything work that fast before!

Meanwhile, in between serving drinks, I kept swigging away at a half-glass of beer which I kept on the shelf under the bar and topped up when necessary. Eventually it caught up with me. Having been on the dry for the last eight months, and not having eaten before coming into work that night, I was eventually forced to go and chuck in the toilet reserved for the bar staff. Don't remember much more of the night after that, but I'm sure a good time was had by all.

Even with all these interruptions, we still had to carry on with our training to get ready for the big day, our Passing Out Parade. One stinking hot afternoon I came down with a migraine headache and whatever the Drill Instructor hollered at us I heard, but failed to execute on time. Because of the pain in my head, he seemed to be a long way away and by the time my brain digested his command and I acted on it, I was way behind what everyone else had done. The Instructor got so mad with me he chucked me off his parade ground in utter frustration.

'Not that way, you moron,' he yelled at me as I — by this time feeling thoroughly nauseous -attempted and extricated myself from his presence.

'Go straight to the closest side, left, right, left, right!' he roared.

'Arr, get fucked,' I heard myself saying.

The pain in my head had put me beyond caring about the consequences of ripping it back into one of these jokers who thought they were some sort of god and whom we had to completely kow-tow to. Like everyone else who has never had a migraine headache, he could never understand the pain that was throbbing through my head at that moment.

'What? What did you just say?' his horrified, high-pitched voice reached me as I got to the edge of the square.

I ignored him and made a beeline for our lines. All I wanted to do right then was to lie down and keep still. For as long back as when I was about four years of age I'd had these terrible headaches and even though mum used to give me little pink pills back then, it was always the sleep that stopped the pain. The Instructor roared something else about staying right there, he'd deal with me later, but I just moved off. What were they going to do? Kick me out of the Army. Not likely!

Sergeant Phillips met me on the footpath half way to our front door.

'What's going on? What's wrong with you?' he asked, with concern written all over his face.

'I've got a splitting headache an' that cunt down there is given me a 'ard time about it,' I answered accusingly, tears of pain and frustration in my eyes.

'Why can't no one understand the pain that goes with migraine headaches?'

'Wait here,' Phillips replied. Down he went to the popular Instructor, calling him off his parade ground where he told him he'd deal with me, then coming back to where I now sat on the grass near our lines, he told me to go and lie down for the afternoon. Maybe Phillips himself understood migraines because no further action was taken.

A few days later, we were up on a parade ground east of our

barracks, which incidentally looked a lot like the quadrangle at the College where I'd done the drill with the Trainee Cadets. This day our Drill Instructor was trying very hard to get us to do an "about turn" but only a few of us could get it. All the while the Instructor kept looking fearfully at someone off to the side of the square. He finally became so frustrated with us that he swore at us before breaking down in tears. Only then did another bloke come to relieve him. The poor bastard should not have been there in the first place as he'd only just come home from Vietnam.

Then, of course, we got the obligatory Sheet Parade. This came one morning around four o'clock, with us being woken by loud yelling, 'HEADS EIGHT, come on, you lazy lot of blighters, on parade NOW, with yur sheets, MOVE, MOVE, MOVE.'

By the time we'd stumbled out to the Parade Ground, there was no one there. We stood as a Platoon and looked across the dark, empty and very cold, tarred square to the warm inviting lights of the Headquarters building which seemed a long way off, wearing nothing but our night gear and a sheet around our shoulders as we waited for someone to come out and dismiss us. The person on "duty" that night, be it Corporal, Sergeant or Officer, must have been real pissed off with having scored or perhaps not scored, for he made us stand and grumble for ages until our fingers and feet were numb. Finally, someone marched across the square to tell us, 'OK, you can go now. Piss off,' and it wasn't even the dope who'd ordered us out in the first place.

The Mess Hall was as big as a gymnasium and capable of comfortably seating a thousand personnel at the same time.

A gaping hole in the north wall with a large room behind it worked as a servery from which the cooks served us up the grub as we moved past them with empty plates, craning to see what was in the big, stainless-steel or aluminium pots. Some of the boys had the hide to complain about Army tucker, but after the boiled mutton and spuds diet I'd been on while I was "on the road" with Darby and the stuff I had to push down at my two boarding schools just to survive, I thought it was grand. Probably the best part in this whole deal was that the bloody Government was forking out for the lot.

There was one Catering Corps Corporal, who store-walked the place during each sitting asking if everything was to our satisfaction, which I thought was a bit queer because even if it wasn't who the hell in this place was going to do anything about it anyway.

'You're in the Army now, son, no one to blow yer nose for yer here.'

Every morning this Corporal was really put through his paces by the boys. They'd stack up the toast-making machines, one near each end of the great hall's southern wall, then deliberately leave them unattended. The toasters were little more than pie-heating trays stacked about five high accommodating about eight slices of bread on each tray. When one toaster caught on fire at one end of the hall, he'd bolt over to it and contain the flames himself, but no sooner he would have the first one out than the other one would erupt at the other end. We'd laugh as he'd sprint the full length of the place to save it and us.

Then one evening we were all in the midst of dinner when a bus load of new recruits streamed into the east end of the hall. They were still in their civvies, sporting long hair of all descriptions, wearing pointy-toed shoes and an array of different coloured and types of clothing. As these newcomers were ushered into empty seats, the whole Mess erupted with wolf-whistles and coo-ees as the boys welcomed them into our fold with calls of, 'Get a hair cut! Give us a kiss! Hey, who's yer boyfriend?' and such like. I think they must have been Regs as there was only the one busload of them and it wasn't time for another intake of Nashos yet. Whatever the case, we knew that the following day they'd be getting busted into shape anyway and by lunchtime they'd all look just like the rest of us.

A day or two later, about mid-week of week eight, we were standing on a small track with puddles on it from overnight rain overlooking the torture chambers (the court to our south with the chin-up bars and the dreaded ropes), when Corporal Lyons suddenly asked, 'Who wants to go to Townsville?'

'Townsville! Why, wot's good about Townsville?' I wanted to know.

'4 RAR. Nine weeks crash course in Infantry, no duties, 'an' you'd be next in line for Vietnam,' he answered.

'But I thought 3 RAR were next in line for over there, Corp?' I put in.

'Well, they're having a bit of trouble with them, so 4 RAR gets the nod,' he informed us.

Mincho, who had crimped blonde hair, laughter lines at the corner of his eyes and was always smiling, the more serious board-shouldered, short-necked, black-brushed-back haired Bob Reid, myself, and an ordinary looking bloke with light hair, about my size, called Mullen, put our hands up. My reasoning was simple: Let's get this shit over and done with. The sooner I get over there the sooner I get back and, anyway, I'd never seen Townsville. Dad had been there loading ships with supplies for New Guinea during the war when the Japs bombed her. Fortunately, they were too high up and missed leaving their load of bombs to blast the hills at the back of town.

With that sorted, we stood about awaiting our next assignment, when Lyons suddenly piped up with, 'All those fools stupid enough ta want ta go inta Infantry, line up out 'ere.'

Next thing we know, the Townsville four and the other ten "fools" were running along the wet and slippery track with orders to hit the deck fast, when Lyons called 'DOWN!' It was fun, but I had a feeling that the rest of Eight Platoon were laughing at us rather than with us as we slipped and slid while getting ourselves covered in red mud from head to toe.

As I've already told you, Lyons was a bit mad at me for choosing to go into Infantry. Well, one day he really ripped the piss-and-pick handles out of me after bayonet practice when I inadvertently left the sling for my rifle where we'd been waiting our turn to stick it up the hanging strew-stuffed chaff bags. Not once so far had we slung our rifles over our shoulders as we always carried them at the ready, so the sling was really just a useless bit of web strap that had to be blackened to within an inch of its life like the rest of our web gear. We carried it everywhere, but in fact it seemed to serve no real function and I therefore could not see the point when Lyons stood me out in front of the others and bellowed at me before setting me a time limit to go fetch it, or else. Maybe he was using me as an example to the others about not leaving equipment behind.

In about the middle of week nine, a couple of SAS (Special Air Service) blokes turned up from Western Australia. They showed us flicks of the training they were doing in the Western Australian desert and of their current operations over in Vietnam, including pictures of their "you beaut" lightweight radio sets. I decided then and there that that was the sort of soldier I wanted to be. I could just see myself going out as part of a five-man group, doing lightning strikes on the enemy, then disappearing into the jungle like a shadow, only to turn up somewhere else soon afterwards to rip it into them again hard and fast. At the first opportunity, I put it to the slightly-built, gaunt, snake-eyed, light-skinned, mousy-haired Sergeant in charge of the team that I'd like to be one of them.

'You're a National Serviceman, aren't you?' he asked, mildly.

'Yeah,' I agreed, probably too quickly.

'You're no good to me, son. It would take me two years to train you then you'd leave us,' he announced. There was no real feeling in his voice, but I'm sure I could feel the contempt in his delivery.

'What are yur doing here, filling us with all this bullshit if yur don't want us?' I found myself thinking. I was extremely disappointed that he'd dismissed me so offhandedly. Stranger still, we were all Nashos in Eight Platoon, so it seemed to me he was just wasting our time.

On Thursday, we went for a walk down the back fence of Kapooka. It was supposed to be some sort of forced march, but it was a piece of cake really, and at around five o'clock we turned back. We headed up a hill at the back of the twenty-five-metre range where we were to spend the night outdoors and Lyons got the shits with me again because I seemed to be having such a good time of it; in fact, I was in my element. While droving with Darby I'd spent a lot more nights camped out under the stars then I had indoors.

Week ten and you could see that it was getting real close to the big day. In our rooms at night everyone was spit-polishing boots, shining brass so bright that you could see yourself reflected in it and buffing webbing and gaiters to a dull shine. This night time activity was so infectious that even I was laughingly pulled into it to some extent.

One night mid-week, we were on our way back to our lines from a lecture or something and Sergeant Phillips was marching us along the road which ran around the back of the Mess. For some time now he'd stopped barking at us like a seal, so we marched silently along in the clear, night air when suddenly he piped up, 'Listen,' and again, all enthused, 'Listen to yourselves!' and there it was — crunch, crunch, crunch.

We were so in sync with each other that it sounded as if just one man rather than forty odd marched along the gravel on the edge of the roadway that night. Yes, it was something to be proud of. I'm sure Sergeant Phillips was proud, having been responsible for moulding us Eight Platoon, Second Round, Twenty First Intake, into a cohesive unit at last? It did sound good!

During this final week, we made our last trip out to the big range for our shooting assessment. The first time we were out here back in about week five, we recruits had been made to hold the targets up ourselves. We were told not to worry and the crack we'd hear overhead was not the bullet actually hitting the target, but the sound barrier breaking as the projectile passed us. It had been fun standing in the pit behind the mound and copping heaps of stones falling on us as the 7.62 full-metal jackets struck the dirt above and just a little behind us. On our second trip out, we moved across to a spiffy range where we shot up olive-green, oblong, one-and-a-half-metre tall, fall-down targets. They were great because when we hit them, they slowly fell over backwards so you knew for sure you had a "kill".

This time we were given five rounds at the twenty-five-metre fall-downs, five rounds at the one hundred-metre ones and ten rounds at the ones three hundred metres out. The order was given by the big, gruff voice of the Weapons Man for the day, 'In yur own time, fire'.

The closer ones were a piece of cake and the ones at one hundred metres fell like nine pins; however, I was still coming to grips with the confounded peep sight with its circle at the back and the post between two bent sticks at the front, so I missed low on my first shot at the three-hundred-metre target. Peeved with myself, I aimed a little higher, but still hit the ground just short of the target; however, the target fell as the plume of dust dissipated around it. Apparently, the stones and dirt my round had kicked up caused enough of an impact on the fall-down to drop it. 'This is good,' I told myself and proceeded to get a kill on each of my next shots by aiming low, so that even if I hit the dirt, I scored a "kill". I passed that assessment with flying colours.

The day before the big parade, Stassy and I were alone in our room making last minute improvements to our already sparkling gear, when we heard footsteps coming along the footpath below our window. As they passed, Stassy raced to the window and sticking his head out he yelled in an elevated gruff voice, 'Swing those arms, Recruit.'

I was beside him in a flash and we nearly killed ourselves laughing as we watched this bloke march away from us down the path that ran along the north side of our building: back rigid, hands clenched, thumbs straight ahead, and swinging his arms as never before, not game for an instant to look back in our direction to find out who'd scolded him. Still laughing, we heard another unsuspecting rabbit coming from the same direction. Wanting to get in on the fun, I made towards the window with the intent of repeating Stassy's trick, but was soon stopped dead in my tracks. I watched opened-mouthed and as still as a statue as the red, braided caps of two very senior Officers appeared in front of me. They strolled by totally unaware of my intent or my presence just sixty centimetres above them. Phew, that was close!

Then it was upon us, the Big Day. The day when all that blundering around and sweating on hot parade squares was going to pay off. The day of the Passing Out Parade. All personnel in all three branches of the Armed Forces get to do at least one of these in their illustrious careers.

So, there we were all done up to the nines in our never-before-worn battle dress, spit-polished AB boots, blackened gaiters and web belt and, of course, our distinguished slouch hats bashed to the exacting style — left side of the brim hooked up, with that little polished hook and square copper chinstrap buckle lined up exactly parallel with the mouth.

Never mind all the other stuff like "shouldering off" at the beginning of the Parade to get all the ranks in exact lines and all squared up, for me the most enjoyable part of any parade like this is always the March in Review Order. First there is the order by a very loud battalion 2IC (2nd in command) to prepare to open order march, then, 'OPEN ORDERRRRR MARCH', whereupon the rear ranks of all the Platoons on parade take three paces backwards at the same time as the front ranks take three paces forward and crunch to a standstill at the same time. Thus "open order" is formed and a new order prepares the assembled intake to fix bayonets, followed seconds later by the cry, 'FIIIIX BAYONETS!'

With one very small click, all bayonets are attached to the pointy end of our rifles and, after a slight delay for effect, the next order is to shoulder arms, being quickly followed with, 'PRESEEEEEEENT ARMS.'

Our weapons are now held at an angle, not quite forty-five degrees away from the front of our bodies, the bolt about waist high and the bayonets out in front a bit above our heads. The best part now comes as the 2IC delivers the following order, 'The parade will advance in review order. PARADE –ADVANCE IN REVIEW ORDER, BY THE LEFT, QUIIIIIIICK MARCH.'

All the soldiers on parade step off on the left foot and stride briskly towards the big nob and his companions on the podium out front — boom, boom, boom, boom. To the single beat of a bass drum we advance exactly nine steps and then all halt as one, with a very audible CRUNCH.

I don't know if that movement is supposed to intimidate the Reviewing Officer or his entourage or not, but its always fun pretending for a moment that it makes them a little uneasy to have nearly five hundred soldiers march straight at them so boldly with bayonets fixed. It's just a pity we had to stop.

The next order is to Close Order March where we all close back to normal ranks one arm's length apart from each other. Now at least we are closer to the mob sitting on the chairs next to the top bloke, who is standing to attention behind the little stand so we can scan those in attendance to see if any good-looking sorts have come along to see us off.

The whole show went off without a hitch and it was during this ceremony that the Reviewing Officer of the day presented the big, blonde bloke, Private Fox (Foxy), with an award for being the Most Outstanding Recruit for this particular intake of National Servicemen from New South Wales and Queensland.

After we'd been dismissed and marched off the Parade Ground, I went to see my family members who'd come over from Temora to watch the show. There was my Mum, Dad, all my six sisters — Judy, Susy, Cathy, Margy, Jenny and Lizzy — Mum's mother, Nanna Kavanagh, and Mum's cousin, Betty, along with Carolyn (my older brother, John's, wife-to-be) and John O'Connor, sister Judy's betrothed. It was really good to see them, but we hardly had time for a photo shoot before we had to get back to Barracks to prepare for the next instalment of this Army caper; Corps Training. It was also time to say goodbye to our training mates, most of whom we'd never see again.

2
TO TOWNSVILLE

The morning we left Kapooka, it was a typical September day in southern Australia. Light rain swept up into the Riverina from the south-west on a real chilly, lazy wind. Wearing our Battle Dress uniforms for the second time in a few days, the four of us from Eight Platoon who were going to 4RAR along with about twenty or so other blokes from the other Platoons were transported to Wagga Wagga Airport in a light, covered-in, sickie green, pug nose Bedford truck.

Upon arrival, we were marched out onto the bleak tarmac, bypassing the Terminal. Heavy grey cloud hung low over a very large silver aircraft which stood some distance away facing away from us at a slight angle with its four big engines still revving madly. Beneath a huge tail structure a gaping black hole led into the back of the large rounded belly of the aircraft and here an airman in a light green overall-type suit and helmet waved frantically at us to hurry up and join him where he stood just inside the opening.

We double marched across the strip through clear, rippling, wind-blown puddles and into the high- pitched scream of the plane's massive engines, and got soundly buffered by the four giant propellers rotating at supersonic speed before charging up the tail ramp into the comfort of the bowels of the RAAF's C140 Hercules Transport Aircraft.

There were already other blokes on board. They were the boys from the other recruit training facility, 2RTB, down at Puckapunyal in Victoria, which took its intakes from Western Australia, South Australia, Victoria and Tasmania. They occupied the right side of the interior, so we were hustled into the other. The crewman from the craft hurriedly checked that each of us new arrivals was properly harnessed into the red canvas webbed seating. These seats ran along the side and along an aluminium panel structure rigged up in the middle so that the boys faced each other. Hydraulics noisily drew the tail ramp up at an angle to close off the back. This done, the Crewman again spoke into the tiny, round microphone that was suspended just in front of his mouth. The breaks were released, the engines changed pitch and the big machine began to roll along.

The speed and assent of the take-off was exhilarating. I love flying, but to add to this particular free flight was the prospect that at the other end of it was Townsville, a large seaside town in tropical north Queensland. All the fresh-faced young blokes on that plane that morning, though, were sullen and withdrawn. No one spoke to us or even offered a smile, just stony blank stares. It was my guess that none of them had ever contemplated moving this far from their families and homes before this.

Disregarding their ashen expressions, I occupied myself by watching a beam of sunlight which shone in through one of the portholes on the fuselage as soon as we breached the fluffy white tops of the thick blanket of cloud. From the sunbeam's movements, I knew I would be able to ascertain in which direction we were going first.

Rumours back at Kapooka as to where we would refuel

on the trip north had mentioned Singleton, which suited me as I might have a chance to see my girlfriend, the Police Sergeant's daughter, while others had heard talk of Eagle Farm in Brisbane. I'd never been to Brisbane, so again this was OK by me; however, having spent most of my schooling locked away in boarding schools, I'd long ago learnt to place very little worth on hearsay and speculation and resigned myself to whatever outcome lay ahead of us.

When the spot of sunlight finally stopped on the inner wall of the plane above me, I was able to confirm that we were indeed flying in a northerly direction. Singleton was most definitely out. *Must be Brisbane*, I concluded and settled in for the long wait as the big plane found its full height, whereupon the engines toned down and we levelled out.

At a time when I felt we must be somewhere over the New England area of northern New South Wales, I got up to look out of the porthole which was directly above me. I had to stand and lean over the seat to see that we were flying really high, higher than I'd ever flown before even in the *Fokker Friendships* that I'd been on in the past. Instead of tree-clad mountain ranges and small, green, square patches of New England farms, though, I saw a black flat land stretching to the horizon below us.

I sat back down in the webbing seat confused. *So, where are we now, then?* I asked myself. Then, as if in answer to my unspoken question, at that moment someone from the aircrew up front spoke to us over a crackling intercom system.

'Some of you might be wondering where we are. We'll be passing over a town called Walgett in just a few minutes.'

WALGETT! My home town until a few years ago and of all

things we were now flying right over it. I was beside myself. *Walgett? That explained the great expanse of flat black ground I'd witnessed a few minutes ago as the black soil plains between Coonamble and Walgett in the north-west slopes and plains of upper New South Wales don't come much flatter.*

I was on my feet in a flash. However, looking from the porthole on the port side of the craft, I was to be somewhat disappointed. I could see the Barwon River winding its way west and the formed roads which ran along each side of the river with the one on the south side leading to a station called Brewon and the other on the north side which ran out towards Booramah Station and on to Brewarrina, but I could not see Walgett directly under the plane. Then the Narran Lake came into view and despite measuring forty-eight kilometres long and sixteen kilometres wide from this altitude, it looked no more than a pothole of a weird, murky, pale green colour.

The ground below changed to red and I knew we were now over the red sandy ridge country, so I strained to pick up the Grawin Opal Fields, but nothing showed of them. I traced the path of the Narran River by following the dark, winding line of its studded river gum trees along its banks. When it started to slip away under the plane and I could not yet see the Cumborah Road running northwest to meet up with the Brewarrina-Goodooga Road, I suddenly realised that I was going to miss out on seeing what I most wanted to see. I ran around the back of the partition to the starboard side of the plane where I hastily asked the bloke sitting under the nearest porthole I could see if he wouldn't mind moving for a bit. 'I grew up down there!' I yelled at him over the din, answering his bewildered look, by pointing at the floor of the aircraft, and after giving me another strange, wide-eyed look, he reluctantly gave up his seat, allowing me to stand on its frame for a better look.

Now I could see it! Stretched out like a giant map below us was the 14500-acre soldier settler's block Beefwood Downs, the sheep and cattle station that my family and I had called home until three-and-a-half years back and I could see it all as clear as anything. The fences were thin, straight, black lines as if drawn in by Indian ink, pen and ruler. The roads were almost white and they appeared as winding threads connecting the various buildings within the picture while even the bore drains showed up as white ribbons traversing the black soil through which they flowed.

It was such a thrill to bear witness to my boyhood playground stretched out beneath us and with it a myriad of my fondest childhood memories came flooding back to me.

As the river portion of our old place slipped away beneath the plane and I lost sight of it, I deflated. Reflectively, I made my way back to my original seat. Suddenly, just past Goodooga, the plane's portwing dipped and we changed direction slightly to the west.

'*Where to now?*' I asked myself, and was on my feet again. Looking out the porthole, I could see only endless red ground below us. '*Out of my territory,*' I mused, and was forced to sit silently once more like my comrades and wait whatever was to come.

A little further on, the pilot made another identical adjustment to our course and soon afterwards an announcement came over the crackling intercom system that presently we would be landing at Charleville to refuel.

My fellow passengers were a bit disconcerted when the

back door of the aircraft slowly descended to within fifteen centimetres of the tar and they were confronted with the very unfamiliar site of a single, tarred runway on red dirt surrounded by thick Mulga scrub and a small unoccupied glass- fronted Terminal.

It was a glorious spring day in south-west Queensland this day; a clear, blue sky and a moderate, twenty-six-degree temperature with no wind; the kind of day you just wish would last all year around. As I walked to the front of the plane to ask one of the ground crew how long we'd be here, another bloke ahead of me enquired in a very anxious tone, 'How far from the sea are we?'

'I dunno. I only fly this thing!' was the reply from the bemused pilot.

Smiling to myself, I asked the same crewman, 'Ow long 'ave we got 'ere? 'ave I got time furra smoke?'

Receiving 'half an hour' for an answer, I wandered over to the Terminal with a small bloke, whom I was not yet acquainted with, in tow. I rolled a smoke and got talking to a lean man with a weathered face, sharp eyes and light hair who was leaning on the galvanized-pipe-and-netting fence beside the lone building. From in town he'd seen the big, four-engine transporter fly in and had decided on spec to bring his kids out to see it. We were strolling back to the aircraft at the end of our break when my weedy shadow asked me, quite seriously, 'Do you two know each other?'

'Nar mate. Why?' I replied, in surprise.

'How can you just go up to him an' talk to him like that?' he questioned me.

'We're bushies, mate, yur know, bushie t' bushie,' I answered, grinning to myself and knowing full well that he'd never understand it.

A few hours later we landed in Townsville. We must have been pretty important people to someone up there by the look of it because when the *Hercules* came to a halt on the tarmac we were serenaded by these blokes in a Bugle and Drums band. They played loudly outside for a time while we waited for the back door to drop and for the first time that day the rest of the blokes on board started to show a bit of enthusiasm. They gathered at the portholes and poked fun at the boys in the band, or, more precisely, at the way they were dressed.

They wore light cotton, short-sleeved, khaki shirts, shorts that came to just above their knees and were a rayon mix of a slightly darker colour than their shirts, long khaki socks pulled up to a point below their knees, and highly polished, flat black shoes.

However, the moment we stepped off the back of the tailgate onto the tarmac, we understood exactly why they were dressed so, as a shockwave of heat wrapped itself around us so forcefully that it almost physically knocked us to the ground. 'Welcome to the Tropics, gentlemen!'

We were immediately bundled into the back of six-wheeled, flat-nosed, olive-green *International* open cattle trucks with hard, wooden, fold-down seats on either side of the back and driven across to the other side of Townsville where we were duly delivered to Lavarack Barracks. This would be our home for the next eight months.

Lavarack Barracks was built on the North Queensland style of building, up on stilts, with the ground floor reserved for the laundry and a sizeable shaded area. Two floors of four-man rooms shared a common back wall and fronted out onto a full-length verandah, at one end of which were the communal showers. The ORs Boozer was just across the road at the eastern end of our lines while the Mess Hall and the Q-Store were situated to the south. These were the only buildings on the eastern side of the area at ground level. BHQ (Battalion Headquarters) to the west of our lines was a two-storey building which stood across a road behind the flat Guard House which fronted the main road running right along the front of the place.

Between BHQ and our lines were Administration, Bravo, Charlie, and Delta Company Headquarters. All these building were two stories as well with offices on the top level and storerooms and our rifle racks underneath. Further south again was the Officers and Sergeants Mess with its built-in Boozer to keep them happily disassociated from the riff-raff. The Officers Quarters was a little to the west of their Mess and there was a huge, tarred Parade Ground between them and the BHQ. Another two grassed Parade Grounds lay between our Lines and the Company HQs. There were no trees or shrubs within the entire complex as the whole camp had only recently been constructed.

A CSM (Company Sergeant Major) greeted us there with a frown, saying, 'This will never do,' as he eyed our woollen Battle Dress uniforms.

'Straight down to the Q Store with you lot,' he said, adding, 'Follow me,' as he turned and marched off down a footpath that took us past the brand new, light grey buildings. In the Q Store, we quickly discarded the Battle Dress for jungle green shirts and shorts (Greens) a new giggle hat and best of all, a pair of General Purpose boots (GPs). These boots laced up to roughly fifteen centimetres above our ankles doing away with the tiresome gaiters we had been using thus far.

As soon as we were kitted out, we were lined up outside our new Mess. They were going to sort us out into three Platoons that would be commanded separately by Officers and NCOs from the Company into which we would go as soon as we finished this phase of our life in the Green Machine.

Within minutes Mincho, Reedy, Mullen and I were so clinically separated that it was breathtaking to behold.

'When I call your name from this list, you will answer in the affirmative and move to your respective Platoon at once. No talking, that clear? Bishop–C Company, Minchinton–D Company, Mullen–C Company, Read–B Company,' and so it went until all the new blokes were sorted. 'Right, now off yer go with your NCOs and they'll show yuh yur barracks.' I never got to associate with Readie or Mincho again from that afternoon 'til this.

One of the first things I noticed at the Townsville Camp was the casual attitude of those in charge of us, as gone was all that bellowing from Recruit training. This mob seemed downright human and normal and the contrast was remarkable and evident from the very beginning. It was as if they were going to quietly coax us through the next nine weeks of this crash course in Infantry Corps training. Right from the start they were saying things like, 'Come on, ladies, we haven't got all day, yur know,' with broad grins on their faces.

And another thing to go with this cheek was, 'There'll be no more saluting of Officers from now on.'

We were bound for Vietnam soon and the last thing any self-respecting Officer wanted over there in the "J" (Jungle) was for a bloke to salute him if there was an enemy sniper within the vicinity. We still had to address them as "Sir" and show respect with a polite nod of acknowledgement and if we met one of them in town we'd have to stiffen our arms by our sides and bring our feet smartly together before moving on, but out in the field it would be nothing but a quiet, 'Sir'.

The morning after we arrived at Lavarack, we new blokes were loaded again onto those six- wheeled *International* trucks and taken on a grand tour of Townsville. The highlight for me was the lookout on the top of Castle Hill. Getting there involved a laborious climb starting from the base at the front up and up around the north side of the hill, winding up the back spine in an anti-clockwise direction to be facing north-west in the car park at the summit.

Castle Hill is a giant, light-red rock that stands sentinel over the CBD of Townsville and faces out to sea and which is about a metre short of being high enough to be called a mountain. From the paved circular lookout at the top you can see way up the coast to Palm Island and across the five nautical miles to the big Magnetic Island. We were told that during the Second World War the Yanks wanted to push Castle Hill into Cleveland Bay and use it to build a causeway across the Bay to the Island, but the good people of Townsville would not let them do so. It's a good thing too — an island linked to the mainland by a causeway is no longer an isolated piece of land and as such loses its status as an island, by my reckoning.

A brass plaque on a concrete pedestal up there tells the visitor that Magnetic Island is due north from this spot on Castle Hill. Captain Cook himself was supposed to have named the Island "Magnetic" because of this fact.

On the way back, we passed a round-shaped restaurant perched just off the narrow, tarred road about half way down the rear southern slope of the hill. From there we could see the full extent of Lavarack Barracks Army Base about eight kilometres south of us at the bottom of the rugged, cream-coloured cliffs which form the north face of Mount Stuart.

As we rattled along between sites of interest, one Terry (Donks) Donnelly, a short, square-set, blond-haired bloke with wickedly keen eyes and a forever grin who hailed from Western Australia and was one of the Puckapunyal boys, kept trying to lead us in song with such refrains as "In the Store" and "He Jumped from Forty Thousand Feet", but it became a very long morning and enthusiasm waned as it wore on. We arrived back at camp in time for lunch with the top of our legs burnt red raw from exposure to the harsh, tropical sun, the painful burns emphasised by neat straight lines where the hem of our shorts ended.

Soon after our midday meal, we were paraded, only to be told, 'OK, you lot, yur time's yur own from now til Mundee mornen.'

This meant that from then, which was Thursday afternoon, we could do whatever we wanted; go wherever we wanted, just as long as we were back in Barracks by six o'clock on the following Monday morning. The only other stipulation was that no one was allowed on leave wearing a uniform.

'You must wear civvies at all times while you're in town

except if on official duties,' they insisted, which suited me just fine because it was not going to be like at College and it would feel fresh after being constantly clad in an army uniform of one sort or another for the past ten weeks.

It was a bit overwhelming at first. Where to go? What to do? However, as the afternoon wore on we got our act together and away we went into town. We hit the pubs and night clubs of Townsville, got pissed and taxied back to Barracks somewhere in the early hours of the morning.

Next day, slightly under the weather, I joined a big mob of the boys heading out to Magnetic Island. We boated over in the little wooden ferry and by around ten o'clock we'd arrived at the long, wooden jetty that constituted the wharf at Picnic Bay on the Townsville side of the Island. Not knowing the set-up, we all got off the ferry there and made our way to the pub, which was not too far inland from the end of the bright white jetty. There was a very big tree — a Moreton Bay Fig Tree, I think — out the back of the flat-roofed pub. The tree cast a large, cool shade in which the owners had made a beer garden.

'*What a place to spend a day*,' I told myself, as I thirstily downed my first of many a beer on Magnetic Island.

It wasn't long before someone discovered that we could hire brightly-coloured, canvas-covered Mini-Mokes here and that we could tour the entire Island in one of these. So off some of the boys went to gain access to one. Excited by the prospect of more to discover, I left the shade of the big tree and boarded a small bus going somewhere else on the Island with a mob of others. After a picturesque journey on a narrow, tarred road that wound its way through small hills where lush green foliage comprised of tropical trees palms and grasses covered the ground in the spaces between giant granite boulders which seemed themselves to have grown right up out of the hillsides, we came down into a settlement where most of the buildings were hidden in among the greenery.

The pub at Acarida was very tropical North Queensland as I had always imagined it should have been. Having been a "inlander" all my life thus far, and this being the first time I'd been anywhere near a tropical island, I only had my limited imagination to go by, but it just had that feel about it. The main bar was spacious and cool with low ceilings and louvres running the length of the western wall. Most of all, it had very friendly staff. Just across a road to the east of the pub we found a quaint, little, crescent-shaped beach with reasonably soft sand bounded on both sides with hills of the implanted big boulders. We could sit under the swinging coconut palms and face the Pacific Ocean on the crescent-shaped, concrete sea wall that ran the entire width of the little bay or lie on our towels on the hot sand and worship the sun god.

After a little scouting, some of us soon came across a really cool shade around the back of a large boulder that was some five metres across and three metres high, which was sticking up out of the sand at the top of the south side of the beach. In a narrow gap between that rock and another, we also found a flat area of smooth sand bounded on all sides by more large rocks, except where it looked seaward. That very night was to be the first of many cosy nights spent in that secretive place curled up on a towel in drink-induced bliss.

Having had a great evening at the main bar, we were all well and truly bushed by closing time. Sunday morning found some of us sitting with a squad of four "long-hairs" who had shared the beach with us through the night. We laughed with them as one of their number, Murf the Surf, a tall, well- defined bloke with mottled, shoulder-length, blonde hair and an all-over tan, tried in vain to ride the wee, thirty-centimetre waves which lazily attacked the shore of our little bay.

After a very heavy, long weekend, late Sunday afternoon found us heading down past the tree with the yellow-and-blue, polka-dot bikini top playfully painted over a pair of rounded lumps protruding from its trunk about one-and-a-half metres from the ground which looked like the breasts of an over-endowed woman. From it, we followed a gravel track leading to the wharf amidst a throng of happy, day visitors. They needed to get back to Townsville that afternoon, as much as we did.

3
CORPS TRAINING

Corps training started in earnest next morning when at the break of dawn we were called out, platooned up in our green singlets and shorts and taken on a run along the interior roads at the back of the Camp. The still morning air had a noticeably warmth feel about it even before sunrise, warning of a hot tropical day to come and the sun had only just risen by the time we arrived back at our lines blowing and sweating. Some of the old boys who were leaning on the top rails of our rooms gave us shit as we trotted in and this ritual was to become a daily event for the next seven weeks.

We had a quick breakfast with a few of our tormentors before being readied to go in our greens. Our new instructors got really pissed off with many of us though as most of us who'd spent the weekend at Magnetic Island, myself included, had blisters on our shoulders and could not possibly put a pack on our backs. Some of the poor bastards, especially those from the southern states like Victoria and Tasmania, had blisters upon blisters bigger than fifty-cent pieces. My own were relativity small in comparison. There was angry talk of charging the lot of us for self-inflected wounds, but seeing as the weapons training could be conducted without having us roaming around out in the bush at the back of the camp fully packed, this option was never taken up.

We'd been issued the same type of backpack we'd be carrying in Vietnam. It was an American pack which sat snug on our back held up by two lightly padded straps over the shoulders. We'd carry our bedding in the bottom half which was sectioned off from the top. The top half was just big enough to accommodate five of our one-day ration packs. A wide, tie-down flap stopped rain from getting into them. There were two small pouches at the sides of the top section in which to put other things. A tie-down flap covered each of them. Around our waist hooked onto a thick woven web (webbing) belt, were two basic pouches that were used primarily to carry six fully-laden, twenty-round magazines for the SLR. Also hooked on at the back of the belt were four dark green plastic water bottles nestled snugly in their own pouches. These had a thin layer of woollen insulation in them and press-studs on both sides of the flap at the top to hold the bottles in place when we ran about or went to ground. This belt was to become part of our very being for months to come.

Infantry training was all about the things we had to know to become thoroughly effective foot soldiers. With that in mind we trained a great deal with the personal weapon of the day, the SLR. I was stoked when they handed us our rifles telling us quite solemnly that this was to be our weapon from now on until we got back from Vietnam. The inside of barrel of my gat had small pitholes in it and the wood showed signs of bruising and small dints. I reflected that, by the looks of it, this weapon had seen service in Vietnam already and survived. This to me was a good omen. She'd serve me well too, I felt. I called her Bessy.

We also had to be proficient in the use of both the M16

Armalite and General Purpose Machine Gun (GPMG) M60. Proficient meant that when tested at the end of seven weeks we'd all have to be able to strip down and re-assemble all three weapons within strict time limits. We also had to be able to unload and reload a SLRs magazine of twenty rounds in next to no time flat. We seemed to do our weapon drills for hours until we had mastered "mag off cock — mag on cock and keep on firing" to the point that we could do them in our sleep — and most likely will still be able to do them in our sleep right up until the day we ourselves pull the pin.

Most of this training took place underneath our barracks. By the end of the first hectic week all of us could indeed strip down an M60, name its parts, expertly re-assemble it and change its barrel in case of a "cook off"— which is when a bullet jams in the barrel and has its back end ripped off by the extractors, causing the next round to be rammed up hard on the empty backless casing of that previous damaged round and the whole thing stops firing its two hundred and sixty rounds a minute. The bloke beside "the gunner" had to swap this extremely hot barrel with one he'd be carrying with him in a small bag we called a golf bag. He'd have to don an asbestos glove which came in the bag to perform this feat so as not to get his hand badly burnt. We all had to learn this action so that if ever we got into trouble "over there", we'd know how to keep the M60 going no matter what, "to bring to bear as much firepower as possible on the enemy for as long as possible". We could also quickly and expertly link the belts of bullets so that those rattling into the thing would continue as one long belt until there were no more belted rounds left in the platoon to fire. Of course, when that happened, we'd be near enough to "had it".

We studied the ins and outs of the M16 Armalite in detail as some of us might well be carrying one of them in the not-too-distant future. With the "mag off, mag on" stuff we became very efficient at dropping the empty magazine into our basic pouch, retrieving a full one from it and whacking it into the underside of our weapon quickly and smoothly.

I don't know about the other blokes, but I was really starting to warm to this phase of our life in this man's army. Our instructors — most of who had been to Vietnam before and therefore could be considered as old soldiers — didn't look down on us at all, treating us more as their mates than as their inferiors. Their camaraderie toward us I believe made it easier for us to learn.

At the same time, we were getting to know the blokes we'd be serving with "over there" this time around. Blokes like the ever-smiling Corporal John McKinley and our Chief Instructor, the lean, clean, more serious Jim Pollard. Tall, thin, light-haired Lieutenant (Lt) Paul Andrews was our Boss. We didn't get to know those further up the chain at this stage.

Come Friday night of the first weekend of actual training they let us go at five o'clock. I'd no sooner alighted from the taxi in town when I ran into a girl from a not-so-distant past. As I hurried past a pub directly across the wide main street from the Railway Station, I glanced in to see a girl from Richmond, a small town 500Ks west of Townsville working behind the bar. I was astounded by the sight of her there, but bolted in to say hello anyway. The last time I'd seen her I was at the Richmond Swimming Pool with the Carrigan kids (fellow roo-shooters) the day before I left town to go home to my family in southern

New South Wales for Christmas of nineteen sixty-seven. She'd asked me to come and join her and her family at Mass that afternoon in the little Catholic Church which stood on the rise just on the edge of town. I'd declined, laughingly telling her I'd seen enough of the inside of churches during my boarding school days to last me a life time. It was refreshing to connect with her though, however briefly.

Saturday morning found a heap of us once again out on the Island despite the blisters of the previous weekend. After a great two days of partying and camping on the beach on Saturday night most of us caught the last boat back over to the mainland. This was known as The Drunks Boat. We were indeed a very merry crew as we made our way past the bikini-clad tree with the day trippers towards the wharf. Somehow I'd managed to knock a bit of skin off one of my right knuckles and as we stepped aboard the vessel I branded the clean white T-shirt in front of me with a neat triangle of little red dots of my blood.

Half way back to Townsville the wind got up and the boat began to heave a little in the gathering swell. I sat back on a box-like structure in the middle of the back deck, and spurred at it with my size eight, black, R. M.Williams, Santa Fe, high-heel riding boots as if I was riding a mad, bucking bronco out of the chute at a rodeo. Stretch Salinovich, the two-metre plus, thin-as-a-rake-handle blonde headed Croat from Western Australia who'd come up with the southern contingent in the Herc, walked to the back of the boat and urinated over the corner. Meanwhile, O'Connor of Kapooka fame, who had somehow ended up on the same flight with us, now went mad mid-deck. From the back wall of the steering room he plucked a small, white life-buoy, pulled it over his head so that it sat loosely on his shoulders and then started to run around the deck shouting, 'Where's the plug? I'm gunna pull the plug an' sink this bloody tub. I'm gunna sink us all.'

Suddenly he was standing on the railings that run along the side of the deck just ahead and to the right of me. The boat gave a heave as a larger wave caught her underside and O'Connor was falling overboard. I sprang towards him and grasped a handful of loose clothing, and then we were rolling around on the deck laughing. We laughed all the way back to camp.

Mullen, my fellow Eight Platooner from Kapooka, wasn't with us on Monday morning. After a polite inquiry as to his whereabouts, we were told that he was in Townsville Base Hospital with Rheumatic Fever. Sadly, he never re-joined us.

Week two became a week of learning about patrolling in Sections. They split us up into typical ten man sections and we moved about out the back of the camp under the brow of the towering cliffs of Mount Stuart. The daytime air tended to be still here so it became very hot. Sweat ran freely, soaking our shirts, the conditions being made more challenging by the weight of the full packs, web belts and the SLR we were carrying.

Three Sections plus Platoon HQ made up an Infantry Platoon in the Australian Army at this time and we were all given a turn in the various components that make up a Section. In a Section, you have two Scouts followed by the Section Commander, who is usually a Corporal. These three are followed by the Machine Gunner, his number two who carries the bag, then the Second-in-Command (2IC) of the Section, usually a Lance Corporal, who also assists with the gun. Behind them come four Riflemen, the last one being known as "Tail-end Charlie". At one time we might be a Rifleman, then next a 2IC or a Scout.

We had to acquaint ourselves with all the hand signals we'd use over there. This was to be our major form of communication once in the confines of the jungle as it was imperative to remain as silent as possible in enemy territory. We practised this over and over until the Jubie Juice Man (Salvation Army Officer) turned up in a *Land Rover* about mid-morning to give us a boost with his lolly water. Then after a small break we'd be away again using only hand signals to communicate with each other until lunch after which we'd be at it again.

On Wednesday afternoon, we were paraded facing our CHQ building, whereupon a very angry and very vocal CSM scolded us most vehemently from up on the second-floor verandah starting his tirade with, 'It has been reported to me by members of the public that there has been some unseemly behaviour by members of you people on the boat returning from Magnetic Island last Sunday night.'

He went on about giving his Army a bad name in town and adversely affecting the good relations built up over time with the public and all that and he ended by informing us that, 'None of you will be allowed to travel over to the Island from now on — Dismissed.'

Wanting to get to the bottom of this quickly, we soon found out that a pair of little old ladies had witnessed our loutish shenanigans — including one young man fully exposing himself to them whilst relieving himself at the back of the boat — and had reported us to the Army. God knows how high up they went, but it came right back down to us. We protested with promises of far better behaviour if they'd let us go back over. By Thursday afternoon they had relented a little with the proviso that we could only go over if we had accommodation over there. O'Connor made a few phone calls and by Friday afternoon thirteen of us who really wanted to go over were booked in to stay in some joint at Acadia.

After they let us go on Friday evening, some of us went to see how Mullen was getting on. The boys found a pub near the front of the hospital called The Allens, grabbed a couple of stubbies from there and smuggled them into the grinning Mullen. As I have an aversion to hospitals, that was the last I ever saw of him. We ended up back down at The Allens after our visit to find that it had a dance floor deep inside, so we stayed until closing time at around two on Saturday morning.

The thirteen mates with accommodation on the Island were ensconced by ten that day. Our digs were a small, stuffy, ground-floor room in a two-storey, brick building about a block north-west of the pub. We spent the rest of the day down on the beach. That night a very rowdy crowd of young people lined up ten deep to harass the frustrated bar staff at a small window on the south end of the bar at closing time. Among them was a very happy, tall, dark-haired bloke with glasses, Private Kiss. He exuberantly slapped me on the back saying, 'Good on yer Bisho,' just as I was handed my good-night stubby of VB. I went down to the beach and was darn right surprised to find that I was the only one of the boys from the Army ("Short Hairs") who was there, so I settled down for my night's kip with the long-haired builder mates at the base of the big rock.

The next thing I know I'm being kicked hard in my back. I tried to curl up as in my grog induced state I didn't comprehend what was happening. Thump! The boot connected again sharply striking my kidney region, then I could hear the smallest of the "Long Hairs" calling to me earnestly, 'Wake up mate, wake up, they'll kill yur if yur don't.'

I responded, staggering to my feet, to be confronted by two burly cops shining a torch down on me.

'Do you know a bloke named Kiss?' one of them asked, forcefully.

'Hurr?' I came back to them — I'd dealt with cops before!

'Bloody 'ell, the only night we want to talk to someone who's sober and all we get is a drunken little shit like you. There's usually heaps a youse down 'ere. Where's the rest of yuh?' the other one demanded.

I pointed into the night towards our digs and immediately set off across the sand towards them saying as I went, 'They're up there.'

One of the cops called me to a halt before I got to the concrete seawall. 'Hang on a minute, we'll drive yuh.'

I directed them to the double-story, brick building where I was supposed to have put up for the night and as the three of us made our way along the concrete path to the door at the very end I caught a glimpse of someone sitting beside us knees up with his back against the wall asleep. One of the cops must have spotted him too and suddenly he swung his torchlight. The beam lit upon O'Connor who awoke a little quicker then I had done when the cops confronted him.

'Hey, you, d'you know one of your blokes called Kiss?' they

put it to him, as he struggled to his feet before them under the glare of their torchlight.

'Yeah,' he answered at once.

'Good, come with us,' the boss cop ordered him and they whisked him away leaving me to my own devices.

I crashed on an empty bunk in the humid, stuffy little room to surface around eight o'clock in the morning. In the cold light of day, it was left to O'Connor to relate to us the story of what had occurred through the night.

Sometime after I'd last seen them, Privates Kiss and Bugg — who had grown up across the street from each other in a suburb of Melbourne and had been childhood friends — were returning from Picnic Bay in their hired Mini Moke when it left the road on a corner at the top of a hill and hit the flat face of a giant rock head-on. Private Kiss lost his life instantly. Private Bugg had severe facial injuries from being thrown forwards out of the vehicle, and hitting the actual rockface.

The cops had taken O'Connor to identify Kissy, after which he went with them by police launch over to Townsville with Kissy's body and a severely-injured Private Bugg. He returned to the Island with the cops sometime before daybreak.

After a couple of heartstarters, a bloke we called Pinky and I decided we'd go pay our respects to Kissy at the very spot he'd come to grief; however, it very quickly become apparent to us that we'd taken on a real ordeal. As we rose out of Acadia, it grew extremely hot and in our dehydrated state from the session the night before we were soon tonguing for a snort. We had no idea how far we had to go to the place so we just kept on going anyway. We struggled past Nelly Bay — not much more than a large expanse of mud flats — and climbed up the next ridge. As we rounded a bend at the very top we came across the place. We loitered a while taking in the enormity of it all, then bowing our heads and looking at the base of that rock, we stood stock still, hands clasped in front of us and afforded Kissy a minute's silence for a fallen comrade. God Bless yuh, Kissy!

On Monday morning O'Connor was missing from First Parade and we never saw him again and after a subdued start to week four we slowly got back into it. Acting Sergeant and Chief Instructor, Jim Pollard, shook us out into what he considered might well be our roles once we got into the Battalion and we began learning ambush procedures in Section formation as well as getting into a little map reading or more precisely navigating by compass.

Most nights we were dismissed just in time for our evening meal. Then we were free until five the next morning and it wasn't long before a lot of us found the Chinese Restaurant and Night Club called The Raymonds, which stayed open until two in the morning, seven nights a week. We'd dance till then on the little square of polished, wooden floor in front of the resident band, where I swear I must have danced to Proud Mary just about every night that I attended that venue in the time I was stationed in Townsville.

It was very early in the piece that I started drinking what I referred to as "fifty fifties". On about the second night in The Raymonds when I asked for a Bacardi and Coke, I watched the bartender who was serving me give the glass she held a squirt of Bacardi Rum, then fill the glass up with big blocks of ice and slop a small portion of Coke into it. I was peeved that I was paying a heap of money for what amounted to not a lot and ice, so when she put the glass down in front of me I dipped my fingers into the mixture and hooked the ice out, leaving a very small dose of the Bacardi and Coke in the bottom of the glass.

'I arsed yur fur a Bacardi an' Coke, love,' I told the girl, 'Do yur reckon youken get me a full glass a Bacardi an' Coke without the ice?'

'It'll cost yuh,' she smiled at me.

'No sweat,' I told her, and from then on I drank only "fifty fifties" while I was at The Raymonds.

Getting going in the mornings was a bit of a drag and every morning at First Parade someone always covered for Ray Graham who'd be out cold on the upper story verandah of our Lines. One morning, we could actually see one of his arms and a leg hanging over the edge, but as long as someone said the obligatory "Urt" when his name was called, to all intents and purposes he was on board, and someone always responded at the appropriate time.

Some nights mid-week, we'd be held back for further training, the first of these nights being a date with the Radio set. Someone in each Platoon would be carrying one of these brutes with us while "over there". It was called the Twenty-Five Set. First we had to learn the international code for the Alphabet: A for Alpha, B-Bravo, C-Charlie, D-Delta and so on. Then, when they were convinced that most of us had grasped the gist of it, they let us loose on the sets with only a wall between ourselves and the bloke on the other set. Now we had to quickly master the "Rogers" and "Overs" in their rightful places and all the stuff that's called "protocol". By the end of the night's session we were all "sort of all right" at it.

Navigating by compass proved very difficult for me. I can take you anywhere using the sun during the day and the stars at night just as long as I can see The Cross, but getting all my back references right was a mathematical problem and I was never much good with maths. I can read a contour or topography map like the back of my hand having been subjected to so many mud maps scratched onto the ground with a piece of stick each time we entered a strange paddock to muster back out at Bre, but I never conquered the compass stuff.

On one of the nights "in camp" we were sent up into the undulating ground at the bottom of Mount Stuart to try out our night navigating skills. We had a small torch between each group of three personnel, but were only supposed to use them sparingly and under cover to line up the markers on the maps. It proved to be a very dark night and the long, dry grass came up to our waists, so about half-way through the exercise our group of three stumbled into a low-slung, rusty, barbed-wire fence and inadvertently ripped small holes in ourselves. It was, 'Stuff this,' and we decided immediately to find our way back down towards the lights of civilization and safer ground.

On another of these evenings of "confined to Barracks for training purposes" we were introduced to one Dusty Miller, a huge, dark-haired man seemingly of a gentle nature. Dusty was our Medic Sergeant and was there to tell us all about the various and numerous tropical diseases which we would have to avoid at all cost whilst overseas. I knew about Malaria, of course, seeing as my Dad had been pretty crook after contracting it in New Guinea during the Battle for Milne Bay in World War II. Old Claudie, our man on the place back in '62 til '65, had told my brothers and I how crook you can get from Cholera and how half the men had perished from it in a camp he was in on the infamous Burma–Thai Railway Line when he was a P.O.W. to the Japs there.

This big bloke, Dusty, started talking of things like Typhoid, Yellow Fever, Rabies and such, so that before the night was out I was forced to interrupt him by putting my hand up high and waving it about.

'Yes?' he asked, pointing a large finger at me.

'Wot in hell are we going over there t'fight Sarge? Diseases or Noggies? There seems t'be more diseases than nogs t'me!'

'Both,' he replied forcefully. No one laughed.

By the third week Pollard had me entrenched as First Scout and Ralf Bodsworth — a mate thinner than I, about my height with very light red hair, light skin and of a quiet disposition — as my Second Scout. He was from Redcliffe, a seaside suburb of Brisbane. Together we made a fair team and we were to stay in this combo until the end of Corps training.

There was a chopper mock-up near a track out the back of the Camp. It was no more than a box-like structure, open in the middle, with a bench across its back wall. It was meant to represent a *Bell Iroquois* helicopter's mid-drift with a sectioned-off bit at the front of this for where the pilot would sit. It was here that we got to practice the proper procedure of boarding and disembarking the said craft. These marvellous machines were the utilities and the run-a-bouts of the war business in Vietnam.

Each chopper, affectionately known to all who travelled in

her as a "Huey" could carry only seven fully laden personnel into battle: five across the seat and two sitting crossed-legged on the floor looking out to either side. The first bloke in the line of seven facing the chopper at an angle out to the front of the machine would give the thumbs-up to an imaginary pilot who'd just given an imaginary thumbs-up signalling that it was safe to board him and with our "giggle hats" (floppy hats made of cotton with a small, stitched brim) firmly tucked inside our shirts to avoid them being blown away by the down draught from the imaginary blades of our transport, we'd rush across — stooping so as not to get beheaded — and scramble into the mock-up. Once settled, it was everybody out, do a couple of steps and hit the deck, literally.

Then there was the "hot insertion" drill, where the incoming troop-filled choppers are landing under enemy fire. We had to leap out, cocking our weapon while still in mid-air, and land prone on the ground — three personnel to one side, four on the other in a flared pattern ready to fight — just feet from the skids of the chopper. This one really hurt due to the exposed gravelly area we were expected to land on. By the end of the two-hour practice session we all had blood oozing through our greens at our knees and elbows. The ever-present flies just loved us for it.

Week four saw us out on Angus Smith Drive, on the east side of Ross River at the back of Mount Stuart doing "ambush of convoy" drills. The trucks with us on board would drive slowly along and when the "Wizzbang" — a round cracker that was nearly the size of a grapefruit — was set off, it would let out an almighty, elongated scream before exploding with a loud BOOM that shook the whole area. White smoke would erupt up the slope from the road and we'd have to jump out of the "hit" truck, shake out in the table drain beside the vehicle in attack formation, then rise in extended line and attack the unseen enemy with our trusty, black, plastic blanks. That afternoon we did a map-reading exercise as well, locating hidden objects, the last of which we found under a studded tree which grew out of the hot, white sand in the bed of the then dry riverbed.

Week five was huge. On Monday we were taken out across the back road past the Q Store and shown this awesome Tank Killing Gun which was new to the Australian Army from Sweden and could knock out a tank from as far away as you could see it through the telescopic sight. It was like a long-barrelled bazooka on wheels which could be towed anywhere by a Land Rover and we only had to make sure we didn't stand behind its open fluted rear end while it was firing or we'd be blown away by its back-blast.

The "tracker dogs' were there to see us as well that morning and we got to meet the two beautiful, happy, shining, black Labrador dogs, Milo and Marcian, who our Trackers of the Battalion would be taking with them to Vietnam.

Then they showed us how to build a real decent barbed-wire entanglement with rolls of concertina wire and star pickets. This made me laugh — it was the first time I'd ever heard of a black Waratah iron fence post being call a fancy name like "star picket". After constructing a section of "wire" we indulged in a fun game of getting a band of marauding Infantrymen across it. I, being scout — and suppressing the thought that the rusty tips of the light barb could very well give me Tetanus — had to run full tilt at it and throw myself spreadeagle over it, after which my mates got to race in and, using one foot on my back as their springboard, bounced clean over the wire. The last two over stopped on the other side, took me firmly by the ankles and reefed me off the barb. It was interesting and fun and absolutely amazing to me that no one got a scratch on them while doing it.

On the way back up to the lines for dinner camp, this little bloke suddenly pulled me up. 'You're the one!' he exclaimed with a triumphant tone in his voice. 'You did it an I got the proof!'

I was perplexed. I burred up immediately and readied myself for a stoush with him.

'Wottayur on about?' I snarled at him.

'You put blood on me shirt geten on the boat out at the Island that day, an' I got the proof,' he put it to me in a friendlier manner.

'Yeah, 'ow?'

"Someone took a photo of yur doen it.'

'Nar, fair dinkim? Where's it at?' I found myself asking in disbelief.

'Up in me room. Carn, I'll show yah.'

In his digs he did indeed produce the undeniable proof that I was the one who'd done it. In the photo I could be seen clearly, my right fist clenched just inches back from one of three red dots on the back of his white T-shirt and he oblivious to my covert actions. Unbelievable! Talk about being caught in the act. I apologised profusely and asked if I could buy him another white shirt, knowing the type of stain dried blood can leave on such absorbent material. He, however, just waved my offer aside with a grin, saying, 'Nar, shit no. Donn worry about et.'

Come Tuesday we were down at the Lavarack Barracks

indoor swimming pool located near the middle of the complex on the Mount Stuart side of the rear road. We were there to do our Water Efficiency Test. First, we all had to bundle a heap of stuff up in our "hutchies", tie the four corners into the middle, then with rifle on top swim it across the pool and finish on the other side with every thing bone dry. It worked! Our next test was to tread water for five minutes fully clothed, boots and all. The bloody boots made this pretty hard, but I found that if I lay back a little and kicked away, moving a little but keeping within the same region, it provided the required result for me.

Wednesday brought the Weapons Efficiency stuff, which we passed with flying colours, and then on Thursday, pay day, we were taken out to Angus Smith Drive to do our Seven Mile Forced March. It was flat strap without our packs or rifles — just swing your arms and go — however, we still had to wear our web belts, which by now felt like they were getting welded to our hips. About halfway back to Camp the CSM caught me having a swig out of one of my full water bottles and hurried up beside me.

'Wot the fuck do yur think yur doen?' he roared at me, all red-faced and flustered from the stroll in the heat.

'Just lightening me load, Sir,' I beamed at him.

'Put that away at once, yuh moron,' he growled at me. I did so, although for the life of me I could not understand what all the fuss was about.

A little further on and with all of us soaked through from sweat, he was all smiles as we rounded an easterly bend in the road from which we could see the outskirts of town in the distance and he called out to us with glee, 'Keep going, lads, not long t'go now. Just think of wot that first beer'll taste like t'night when yur get it.'

We were in such a good swing by this time, travelling fast on a slight downhill grade that we actually kicked up dust around us, which rose lazily from our crunching boots up through us like a creamy mist as we bustled along in the customary still hot, dry, afternoon air.

That night the entertainment at The Raymonds was none other than the legendary, one-and-only Johnny O'Keefe. Being pay night, the place was packed and had a real buzz about it from the start. Then "he" was on the stage doing his thing. People were singing along and clapping and cheering. The place was going off. About three quarters of the way through his routine the crowd was hushed a little as he made this announcement. 'Now I know this place is full of Army tonight, and I know that a lot of you will shortly be going overseas and I don't want any of you wives or girlfriends to believe any of this, but this is the theme song for the lads while they are over in Vietnam.'

The band strummed a short introduction and he started, 'Uc da loi, him cheap Charlie ...'

The Raymonds erupted in an ungodly noise the likes of which I'll never hear again. The roar that went up completely drowned out everything else and must have loosened the fasteners on the roof above us, I swear. I was standing at the table closest to the bar at the back of the night club where I'd stopped with an empty glass in my hand to see what he was going to say. When the crowd went off, people started climbing into the tables to sool him on, but I was too slow and within seconds the tables and chairs in front of me were full, so I hooked it to the bar and swung up onto it with a couple of others. The din was such that not a single soul in that place that night — other than perhaps Johnny himself — heard anything past those first few words, even though he went right through the entire rendition despite the hullabaloo. The rest of the night had an electric pulse about it that you could literally feel in your being.

Next morning, a little worse for wear, we were taken up to the west end of the Camp where the Engineers lived and worked. They were going to teach us some stuff about booby traps and mines. The "Gingerbeers", as they were affectionately known by Infantrymen, had set up a scenario whereby if you put a foot wrong on a little track leading into a small mock-up which represented a village, you stepped on a supposed mine, thus setting off an awful, stinking, purple, red, or yellow-coloured smoke bomb. This was to show us that we were dead and that at least two or three blokes around us were dead or seriously wounded as well. The survivors of the blast then had to go through the laborious task of securing our spot by prodding the ground around us with the end of our bayonets to see that there were no more mines near us. We then had to sit and wait until the Gingerbeers come in with metal detectors and, after sweeping the place, declared it safe for us to move on. It was painstaking work, but necessary for us to keep our hides. In the "village" there were things like strategically placed North Vietnamese flags and swords and suchlike that one could grab and take home as souvenirs; however, they'd been booby-trapped with hidden devices and, if lifted, set off the foul smelling, coloured smoke again. It was a great practical demo.

On the Sunday night of the beginning of week six, Pinky

wanted to go into town to see Johnny O'Keefe again. He said he knew Johnny personally. Pinky and I had been hanging around together for a couple of weeks by this time. He had eyes that turned down a bit at the sides, an ever-ready smile and a head of light hair that looked as if it might well recede in the not-too-distant future and always wore his giggle hat to one side. There was a definite larrikinism about him and to me he could have been a dead ringer for old Claudie, when he, Claudie, was our age and was desperately trying to stay alive at the hands of his sadistic Japanese captors.

A little short on cash, we turned up together for Johnny's last show at The Raymonds, where we sat right up the front crossed-legged on the floor in front of him and when Pinky thought the time was right he jumped up and sprinted across the little dance square to talk to Johnny directly, asking for one of his favourite songs from the star. Johnny smiled a great, big, red-faced smile and immediately went into the soppy love song that Pinky had requested. Pinky was rapt.

The more the night went on, the more trips Johnny made to the bar at the back of the club for another glass of Scotch, until by the end of his gig he could barely stand up — but he could still sing.

When around midnight we got out of the taxi back at Camp, Pinky baulked at going in, then suddenly he was off in the opposite direction as fast as he could walk, across the expanse of lawn that separated the perimeter road of the Camp from the main road which ran the length of Lavarack Barracks Army Base.

'What in fuck's name are yuh doen?'I called to him in dismay, as I hurried to catch up with him.

'I'm going 'ome. I've 'addanuff of this shit. Gotta catch that taxi.'

Fortunately for us, the taxi went west from the turn-off onto the main road near our Guard House and I was pleased with this as now I'd have time to talk some sense into him, so we sat in the gutter like a pair of swaggies and talked for half an hour or more. He had a woman back down on the southern outskirts of Sydney and it was to her he was going. He went on and on about how good she was to him and about how well she looked after his every need, but never having been tied up with a woman as yet, I just could not begin to relate.

'Yeah, but they'll get yur mate, yuh know this. An' when they do, what's the bloody gooda that to yuh. They'll lock yur up, yur know they will, yur fucken idiot.'

'No, they won't, mate,' he insisted, 'I won't let'um. I'll be right. I'll get a job somewhere, you'll see. I'll be right.'

I somehow managed to get him to his feet, telling him it would be best all round if he'd 'Come up n 'ave a good night's sleep, 'n' youkin go in the mornen if yur really wanna.'

We headed back towards our lines again. Halfway across the lawn he hauled up as if hit by something.

'Yur tryen ta trick me,' he accused, about-turning and striding off again in the wrong direction, so I ran at him, crash-tackling him to the ground from behind, and we rolled around a bit until he managed to get free and scramble unsteadily to his feet whereupon he took a wild swing at me.

'Yur wanna fight, yuh bastard? Carn then, 'ave a go,' he said, shaping up to me and dancing around a bit.

'Nar, mate, I donn wanna fight yuh, yur fucken deadshit,' I

assured him earnestly and then with arms around each other's shoulders and laughing we made our way over to sit once more in the gutter of the main road.

Twenty minutes or so later a taxi came towards us from the Charters Towers Road turnoff which was east of Lavarack. Pinky jumped up to stop it, but it went straight past us to swing in at the Guardhouse and continue on to dump its cargo deep inside the Camp.

Pinky was cursing and accusing when the taxi came back out, turned our way and drove quietly down to pulled up beside us.

'Well, see yuh, mate,' he said solemnly, as he shook my hand firmly.

'Yeah, see yuh, mate. Look after yourself, 'ay?' I answered, returning his hand shake just as firmly. Then, as he hopped into the car, I learned in and said to the driver quite seriously, 'You look after me mate, 'ay? En make sure 'e gets away OK, 'ay?' And suddenly they were gone. As I watched the tail lights of that taxi disappear towards the east I knew that Pinky was being spirited out of my life forever and that we were now another good man down in the Platoon.

There was a bit of a stink at First Parade, but there was nothing they could do now that he was gone and even though I thought I might be in for it for a bit as they knew we were mates, nothing was said.

By mid-day Monday, we'd been trucked out to the top of High Range. The Army maintained a huge training ground and shooting ranges out there and for the rest of week eight we would be having a crack at all the weapons we might be expected to use in Vietnam. We made ourselves as comfy as possible in a well-used, static camp by constructing stretchers out of our blow-up mattress covers. To achieve this, poles were pushed along each side of them and wedged over x-shaped lengths of round timber at each end to keep us up off the ground and we strung our hutchies over the top of us to keep out the sun and rain and by Monday night, after a good feed from a camp kitchen, we were ready for a start bright and early Tuesday morning.

We had a go at everything! There was a place in a gully where that Recoilless Rifle Tank-Killer from Sweden had been drilling neat round holes through fifty-millimetre-thick steel slabs, which were about two-and-a-half metres square and set in the ground at weird angles. There we were shown how to open and operate the M72 Rocket Launcher and then we lined up to send rockets down the slope into the same slabs of steel. M72s were heavy, olive-green cylinders about sixty centimetres long which then became roughly double that length when we pulled the caps off each end and extended them out. In so doing we caused the sights to pop up, one at the front and a see-through plastic one with red lines across it to indicate distances a little over thirty centimetres in front of our eyes.

The trigger was a small, squishy, grey rubber rectangle which was raised about six millimetres above the top of the tube just behind the back sight when the whole thing rested on your shoulder. There was a bit of a bang when you squeezed on the trigger patch and a whoosh and then, with smoke trailing from the rear end of the rocket from inside it, it flew away from us to explode with a loud crash into the plate steel target.

The M72 wasn't as hard to use as I'd expected, except that it did have a tendency to dip its nose a bit when I pressed down on the trigger pad. The last bloke on the second wave to have a go at firing it must have not been listening to Chief Weapons Instructor Sergeant Barry Filewood or he might have been a little nervous about having to let loose with such a powerful weapon, I don't know, but I can tell you that when it came to his turn, there was a BANG-WHOMPER as his round failed to exceed twenty metres before hitting Mother Earth and exploding in a plume of dark brown dirt right in front of us.

Filewood, at his position in about the middle of the line and some five or so metres back to avoid the back-blast of the weapon and being taken completely unawares, stumbled two or three startled paces backward before quickly regaining his composure.

He was livered. 'You useless, fucken little twerp, whattaya think yuh fucken doen?' he roared at the offender.

The culprit turned, a bewildered look on his face, and in doing so swung the still shouldered M72 side-on facing down along the line of his mates. Having just been emptied, it was harmless enough; nevertheless, it was not good weapons protocol to do so and Filewood reminded him of it. 'Don't point that fucken thing at me yur stupid, fucken idiot. Get off my range an' don't come back near me again,' he bellowed.

When the firing was done, we were told that in Vietnam we would be expected to jump all over the fibreglass cylinder which remained after expanding the rocket so that our enemy the VC (Viet-Cong) could not fill it up with explosives and use it back on us as a booby-trap.

We were educated on the workings of the Claymore Anti

Personnel Mine which we, as Infantrymen, would be using over the other side primarily as night perimeter defences and as ambush initiators. The Claymore was a dull olive-green, moulded, hard-boiled, plastic case, a bit over twenty centimetres wide by twelve centimetres high and about thirty-five millimetres thick. Inside the case was a slab of white PE (Plastic Explosive). In front of the PE were seven hundred ball bearings embedded in a dark brown, hard-wax-type substance. The case was slightly bent so that when stood on its two pairs of thin, scissor-type, fold-down, spin-around legs, about seven-point-five millimetres off the ground, it projected the ball bearings at a sixty-degree angle up, down, and to each side of the blast site. On top of the case could be found two detonator (DET) wells with screw in caps over them to hold the DET in place. Between these DET wells there was an aperture sight. The operator of this deadly weapon held a small, weighted block, which looked like a shortened office stapler with a flat leaver on top of it. This small, hand-held dynamo was called the "clacker" and when its lever was pressed it initiated the device by sending an electric current to the elect-DET in the DET well.

Using the white, instantaneous detonator cord known simply a DET-cord, with an explosive DET on each end, we could effectively connect any number of the mines together, making a bank of them. The operators had to stay at least fifteen metres back from them to avoid their back blast. We were shown how to carry the DETs, so that if one of them inadvertently went off we would only lose a finger, a thumb and a bit of our bum, but not the family jewels.

We were told stories of their use in Vietnam, such as when

the South Vietnamese Army wanting to stop the enemy from ambushing their supply convoys strapped a whole heap of them to the sides of their trucks, but when they pressed the "clacker" they blew their own convoy away; and how the VC woman, who not knowing what it was, walked up to inspect one that our Diggers had tied to a tree at head height with the inevitable consequence. Then we all had a go at lying on the ground and sighting the mine up with someone inserting the DET while someone else again set it off with the "clacker". Wow, the back-blast was nearly as bad as the front blast, less the ball bearings, but, all in all, the Claymore was a mighty defensive/offensive weapon for us to have at our disposal.

There was night firing of the GPMG-M60 during which all that first lot of training came into good use since we had to load the thing in the dark. We'd then wait for the imaginary enemy to get close enough to set off the trip flares, whereupon a whole line of ten of us would open up at once. What a racket, but, best of all, every fifth bullet was a tracer so that the space in front of us now had a couple of thousand mini red lights streaking away from us into the darkness, beyond the bright light cast by the flares. Because of the way the M60 is built, it shoots ten rounds in a small circle, which land in a cone shape at the intended target, and this caused the tiny streaking lights to go off in different directions out in front of us, crossing paths with hundreds of others to turn on a spectacular sight.

The M79 was like a very short shotgun to look at, breaking in the middle to accept a round that resembled a very short .22 round about forty millimetres thick. The projectile was called an "ogive", but I'd be more inclined to call it a bright yellow golf ball full of little case-hardened ball bearings. It had to travel a distance of at least thirty metres to arm itself via its own spinning motion and had a killing range of five metres or so. It had a sight mounted ten or twelve centimetres back along the barrel which had to be lifted so the user could sight up the intended target with a fixed blade sight at the end of the muzzle. It made a loud TOONK sound when fired and had the same type of kick as a shotgun. If the "ogive" didn't go far enough to arm itself, the VC would pick up the unexploded device and drill it out to make a snatch grenade out of it, whereupon a Bar Girl could drop it at the feet of an unsuspecting hero out from between her legs — hence the name — and slip away before it went off, seriously wounding the legs of the intended target. Nasty little blighters over there!

When we arrived at the range where we were to have a crack at the Nine Millimetre Automatic Pistol, the stern, stony-faced Sergeant Filewood was there already and instructed us on the workings of the weapon before giving us a go at firing it. Our targets were a mob of brightly coloured balloons tied to a small tree and, after taking very careful aim at them, I squeezed off the first shot of a full magazine of fourteen rounds. The bloody thing snapped back with tremendous force unexpectedly, jarring my forearm smartly upwards. 'Fuck!' I exclaimed, surprised by the reaction of this small, hand gun, so I placed my left hand over my right wrist and, holding on tight, attempted to take down my first balloon. This time, both hands were bounced upwards.

'Stuff that,' I thought to myself. Raising the little black gat so that it pointed straight up, I threw it down flat and fired indiscriminately at the target tree allowing the recoil to bounce my arm back up after each shot before dropping again to fire with only hope that I might pop a balloon. When I heard the hammer click on an empty chamber, I turned immediately towards Filewood all smiles and handed him the now inactive gun.

'Yer hit fucken nuffen, now fuck off,' he growled at me.

Before dinner on day two at Camp at another place just off the road we'd come in on, we had a go at blasting grenades off the end of our rifles into some thick scrub. This was done via an olive-green attachment which went over the muzzle of the SLR and which held a M25 Mills grenade lightly in place. It had a raised sight that we were to use to line up the target by lowering the butt of the rifle and looking from it to the grenade stuck out on the front. A special round called a balastite cartridge — more or less the standard 7.62 round with the lead extracted and folded in on itself like a shot gun cartridge without the shot in it — was used to send the grenade on its way.

The first one I sent off shocked the shit out of me. I dropped my arms, lined up the bunker and let go. What seemed like beach sand blasted back into my face at the same time as the brass end on the butt of my gat whacked hard against the front of my hip bone? Because I'm naturally lean, that bone sticks out and, man, it fairly drove me; however, I did hit the target despite my shocking introduction to the bloody thing. I loaded up and went again, this time making damn sure that my throbbing hip was well and truly out of line with the butt of my gat which jarred back with twice the force of a shotgun. Again, I struck the target. All in all, this setup was not a bad weapon; however, it might be a bit hard to conceal oneself from the enemy while standing up to fire off a grenade. I suppose we could place the butt of the rifle on the ground, but then how would we sight it up?

In the early afternoon of Thursday, we were sent down a track along a creek bank to do something called "instinctive firing". Unfortunately for me, I turned my left ankle as I jumped across a small gutter while running with "rifle at the ready" to the venue. It wasn't too bad so I picked myself up off the ground and carried on. This was the first time we'd came across Major Ron Boxall. He was a man who looked like he came out of a good paddock with light ginger hair atop a smiling, rounded baby face that showed a hint of freckles. He was keen as mustard to show us how to get off the quickest shot possible from an SLR which was what this "instinctive fire" stuff was all about. 'Eye your target, then with both eyes open lift your weapon to your shoulder as fast as you can point and shoot.' It was fun and this time around I managed to bust quite a few balloons which were tied to a line strung between two thin sticks in the creek.

That night after tea we were taken around the small knoll just east of our camp where we sat and listened to the sounds of the night, with a few man-made ones chucked in. It was our job while sitting in the total darkness to identify and name the man-made sounds such as an aluminium mug or bayonet coming into contact with a rock, or someone moving about close at hand.

When it was time to go back to Camp, no sooner had I stood up than my left leg gave away under me and I came crashing down on the craggy rock which scraped and bruised my left shinbone while ripping skin off the soft bit under my wrist and off my forearm just below my elbow. My gat and I made quite a bit of noise as one went rattling onto the rock, the other cursing. I was growled at by someone out of the dark as I tried to scramble to my feet again, but it was to no avail. I just could not for the life of me put the slightest bit of weight on my injured left ankle which had just spent the best part of an hour sitting around resting and now it seemed had every intention of keeping the status quo from this point on. Someone took my gat from me — which I must say right here that I was very reluctant to relinquish at first — and a couple of seconded blokes carried me back to camp by linking hands to make a seat for me. It was most embarrassing!

At Camp, a young Medical Officer bandaged a very swollen and blue ankle and told me I'd have to stay off it for a while.

'Well, dur, no shit,'ay?' I thought to myself. At that point in time I couldn't even put the slightest bit of weight on it.

Friday morning started off all right when I discovered to my relief that I could put my left foot on the ground without crumbling in a heap. The ankle was tender, but I managed to make my way up the slight slope to the soup kitchen without mishap; however, it all went downhill from there except for the smokes. By this time none of the boys in camp had any smokes left and that morning there was talk of rolling tea leaves and the like. I was ordered to attend the Medic as soon as I got back from breakfast. Upon arrival, I spied two unopened dark-blue pouches of Drum Tobacco on the dirt just inside the front flap of the Medico's tent.

'You bastard,' I cried in dismay, 'there's not a smoke to be 'ad by any of these blokes in this entire camp and yur got this lot stashed away in 'ere, 'owbout yuh sell us a packet?'

'I don't think so,' he said bluntly, 'you should have thought an' made sure you had enough with you before you came out here. Now what can I do for you?'

'Gotta show yur me foot,' I grouched.

He re-bandaged it, told me to keep it elevated and once again told me to stay off it.

'Wottayer mean stay offet, 'ow'um I spos'ta do that when I'm on me Nine Mile Route March t'day, ay?'

'You won't be marching anywhere on that foot today or for a few days yet. I'm putting you on light duties,' he said, without emotion.

'But I gotta do et. If I don't, they won't pass me,' I harrassed him further. The Nine Mile Route March fully-packed was the last of the tests to gaining Infantryman status which took us up a pay level. Minute though it was, I still desired it.

He dismissed me then, but as I was about to leave I spotted those half-hidden pouches of Drum again.

'Yude betta sell us a packet of that backie, mate.'

'No way, now piss off,' he said.

'What do yuh think will appen when I go back over there 'n' tell them blokes yur got a stash of t'backa over 'ere, mate? There'll be a riot, that's what,' I growled, looking across to where the rest of the boys were packing up their gear for the big march.

He snatched up one packet of the precious brown weed and shoved it towards me.

'Here,' he said quickly, 'now piss off.'

I hobbled away as best I could on my bung leg to my camp site and called to the blokes closest to me.

'Look wot I got.'

'Gees, whereja get that? Can we 'ave some?' they asked, enthusiastically.

'From one of them Officers over there,' I informed them, 'but there's none left. 'ere,' I offered them the packet so that they too could make a smoke from its contents. Being grateful enough for what we'd already scored, I didn't want to let on that the Officer had another full pouch over in his tent. I gave away half a packet of Drum Tobacco in minutes flat, but what the heck, easy come, easy go.

Jim Pollard arrived on the scene then and wanted to know what the Medico said.

'Told me I couldn't go on the march, but fuck 'im, I'm goen anyway,' I reported to him.

'If he said yur not goen, yur not goen,' Jim growled. 'Pack up this shit an' go an' report t'one of them truck drivers over there, they'll take yuh out.'

'But, Jim, if I donn go I donn pass, an' I won't get me pay rise,' I pleaded to his better nature.

'You'll get it, I'll make sure of ut,' he assured me. 'Now shift this mess.'

I was pretty disgruntled as the others broke camp and started to tramp away down the track that would take them off High Range and home. Thank Christ that MO gave me the tobacco to smoke, I sure as hell needed it right then.

I shuffled about attempting to give the Cooks and such a hand at striking the full-blown tents and generally packing up the trucks, but I think I was more a hindrance than a help.

Finally, one of the drivers said, 'Righto, git in, we're goen.'

With an effort, I managed to haul myself up over the front

wheel of the flat-nosed Inter, onto the hard seat and away we went down the gravel road that took us off the top of the Range passing the blowing, sweating mates about half way through their ordeal. As we left them in a veil of dust, I began to feel pretty smug that I'd managed to miss out on that walk with the promise of no detriment to my future pay rise, until the driver of the angry-sounding truck got too close to the edge of the road on a sharp bend. It gives the confidence a dint to feel like you are swinging out over the edge of a road looking almost straight down to the valley floor far below and you have no control over what's going on.

After the last few days, it was over to Acadia for a quiet weekend. This was shattered around eight o'clock Sunday morning by raised voices coming from where the Long Hairs were always camped at the base of the big rock with their backs towards the sea. I got to their area just in time to see the smallest of them put big Foxy (of Kapooka fame) on his arse. Foxy jumped up and made another attempt to assert his dominance, but when the little, brown-haired bloke smacked him as clean as a whistle on the point of his chin from his low position and the big blonde went down again. That was it, all over, Red Rover! The Fox had to pick up his towel and shift camp with his tail between his legs. It served him right as he should never have tried to use his size to stand over a much smaller bloke, especially someone who'd been using this beach for years before we'd even been sent up here.

Week nine — the last week of our Corps training — was called "in the filed training". Again, loaded into the trucks, it was away over towards the airport, then north-west up the

Ingham Road. We travelled along at a reasonable pace in the shadow of a mountain range that was to our left. About 60 kilometres along the road we turned off and headed west and after a short stretch we started to climb up into the Paluma Range. On a narrow, tarred road we snaked our way up and around some pretty sharp bends which made for slow going for the six wheeled *Internationals* laden as they were with their human cargo. The trees growing beside the road began to take on a more tropical look the higher we rose; then suddenly turning north on a bend we were afforded an almighty panoramic view of Palm Island out to the east off the coast. From here we could see all the way back down to Magnetic Island and way up to the unknown north as well as down to the neat patches of the canefields below us. It was a truly breathtaking scene for a real "bush-boy" like me.

Just before midday we were on the top of the range and after a short journey to the west beyond a small village we came across a fair-sized clearing in the tropical forest. There was a large, dilapidated, rusty, tin shed across to the south-west of us as we turned right here onto an old logging track and plunged northward back into the greenery. It was hot sitting as we were in the back of the open trucks, exposed to the overhead sun and so it was with some relief to be told to disembark the vehicles when next they stopped and to go sit in the shade at the side of the seldom-used, leaf-covered dirt track.

I was in raptures the moment I entered the rainforest. It was cool. There was green everywhere. The pungent smell of decaying leaves when disturbed filled my nostrils with a scent that wheat farmers can only dream about in their wildest fantasies. Even though I had been a heavy smoker of roll-your-owns for the past five years, it could not dilute the richness of the aromas all around me. The calls of unknown and unseen birds sounded from everywhere. The early afternoon sun only made it to the forest floor in long lit columns to alight in occasional small, bright patches where it lit up large scattered patches on dense clumps of dark green leaves at varying heights all the way up from where we sat on the damp, shaded forest floor to the canopy high above us. A few steps in from the track and we could not see that it was even there — and who would want to anyway? It would only diminish the splendour of this paradise. I felt like I wanted to go exploring immediately being sure there must be much more to be discovered just over the rise at our backs. Alas, we were here to work and almost as soon as the trucks had backed out of there we were formed up on the track and marched further north deeper into the green wilderness.

For the next three days we practiced ambush drills of all categories up and down that track which ran beside a small creek. To do this, one of the mates would go off on his own, plant himself as best he could and wait in his hideout to fire on the Section when they came by. I used a lip over the bank of the creek once and they went back past me five times before they found me, whereupon I was asked not to make it so difficult for the boys to find me in the future. Gees, I don't know, I thought that's what it was all about.

This was also a great venue to practise our hand signals, so we did a lot of that as well, but when that handy, black, plastic blank went off it was 'Ambush left — ambush right — ambush rear or ambush front' at the tops of our voices, followed by the appropriate manoeuvre to savagely counter-attack the aggressor.

About ten-thirty Thursday morning Jim Pollard told me that Pinky was here.

'Pinky? Here? Where?' I asked in disbelief. I hadn't seen him. However, he confided in me that he was here on the mountain with some Sergeant or another.

'Can I see 'im?' I asked excitedly, yet half believing that he was having a go at me.

'No. We've been told ta keep you two away from each other,' he answered me, dryly.

'Well, wots the pointa yuh tellen me 'es 'ere if yur not gunna let me see 'im then,' I replied, angrily.

I harrassed Jim for a couple of hours until he gave up and around dinner camp said that I could go see Pinky for only five minutes or so.

'Right, well where do I go then?' I threw at him, more convinced than ever that they were gamming me.

'You'll see them just up along this track and down by the creek,' he said, pointing north. I went, emerging at last into a rather large break in the canopy where the track seemed to crash right into the creek at a sweeping bend and until I die I will never forget the picture presented to me there.

Two Australian soldiers sat motionless on a giant granite boulder worn smooth by years of cascading water where they looked for all the world like they were trying to figure out how to catch their dinner in the crystal clear waters that they were staring at as it flowed gently past them amongst the rocks. The heavier one sat on his behind, his arms resting on his knees, hands hanging loose, while the slimmer one sat on his haunches beside him. They could have been in any of a number of jungles in the islands to our north straight out of the pages of World War II history. I stood unnoticed watching this pair of Diggers for two minutes, not wanting to break the magic of this surreal scene, hearing only the tinkling of the mountain waters and the call of the unseen birds before I made my presence felt.

As soon as I was sitting at Pinky's side, after shaking his hand I scolded him.

'Yur stupid bastard! 'Owja git caught? 'Ow farja get? Didyur get ta see yur woman or not? Yur stupid bastard.'

Pinky grinned at me with his now familiar lopsided grin, as if to say, *yeah good to see you again too, mate*, and proceeded to tell me how he'd got all the way home and spent a night with his woman. He then went over to his brother's place of work at the Wollongong Steel Works to get a job the next day and was in his office teeing it up when in walks two cops on a totally unrelated mission and bang, they clicked immediately that he was AWOL and he was gone. How unlucky can you get?

All too soon the burly Sergeant said, 'Right, times up, now piss off back to your own lot, you.'

Pinky and I shook hands and said our good byes and then I melted away back into the forest to re-join my mob. We have not seen each other since.

The last night we were there we had a go at setting up a Platoon harbour site, the likes of which we'd be expected to camp in whilst in Vietnam, night gun duties and all. The harbour is a circle with the three machine guns — one to each Section — spaced out to form a triangle on the perimeter.

Riflemen were spaced in pairs between the guns, the Scouts and Section Commander half way back to where Headquarters sat in the middle of the "wagon wheel" as it were. In this case, Lieutenant Andrews was in Platoon HQ.

A little while after dark one of the boys called out, 'Hey, look, someone's comen.'

Sure enough, to the north of our harbour site something or somebody appeared to be walking through the forest with a lantern and we could see the light flick on and off as it passed by the big trees between us and them. It reminded me of car headlights coming through the scrub towards our home when we lived at the "old place" on Beefwood Downs when I was a kid growing up there. The excitement was shattered almost immediately when a wise voice told us out of the darkness, 'Nar they're just fireflies.'

Fireflies? Dad had told me all about them. He said a big mob of them put the wind up a whole heap of battle-hardened Diggers up at Milne Bay by congregating around one little tree at the end of the airstrip there and lighting it up in a big ball.

Soon more fireflies joined the one we had seen and, while concentrating really hard, I noticed that they were not way out there in front of our harbour but right in front of my very eyes. I whacked at one and it dropped to the ground almost in my lap so I picked it up by its wings and brought it right up to my eyes so as to study it more closely. I discovered that it was indeed a small fly whose abdomen was its light bulb and all too soon I found that if you hold them for too long in one spot their light slowly shuts down because they are not using the wings. The poor little thing!

Someone found me at some ungodly hour of the night to inform me that it was my turn to go man the gun for my two-hour shift and I rolled out of my camp into oblivion. It was as black as the inside of a closed coffin. I had space but could see absolutely nothing so down on my hands and knees I started to crawl to where I was sure the gun was situated and suddenly came across somebody lying prone, so I poked him.

'Hay mate, are you the gun?' I whispered. There was no immediate answer, so I prodded again and repeated my question a little louder.

'No, I'm not the fucken gun, I'm Lieutenant Andrews. Now piss off, I'm trying to get some fucken sleep here.' He snapped at me. I'd liked him up to this point.

I was a little shocked that he was so mad at me. Shit, it was dark! I crawled away from him and ran head first into the spikes near the bottom of a Wait-a-while bush and was speared right between my eyes. We were told before we came up here that the worst two bushes we had to worry about was the Wait-a-while and the Stinging Bush which has a large, flat, rounded leaf with hairs on it like Stinging Nettles and so was to be avoided at all cost when making clean after disposing of one's body's waste.

The Wait-a-while bush has palm-type leaves which make it look innocent enough but also grows long, thin, strong, bamboo-type runners that have sharp thorns much like small rose thorns on them at the join of each section. We'd been informed that if we got tangled in them we couldn't do much more than back out of their clutches, disentangling ourselves slowly; and as the name of this nasty vine suggests, it can take a little while to extricate one's self from their grasp. No one, however, had said anything about these bloody seventy-five-millimetre spikes that grow by the hundreds straight out from the base of the Wait-a-while and which are as sharp as sewing needles.

By the time I got over the shock of being speared in the forehead and down the bridge of my nose by these killer spikes, I'd had enough of bush-bashing without eyes for the night, so I dropped down where I was and went back to sleep. 'Fuck the gun; it could stay where it was for mine.'

At ten o'clock the next morning we were all sitting patiently along the side of the track when the trucks came to take us off the mountain. Again, we experienced the great vista of the coastline, Palm Island and beyond, way, way out into the expanse of the sparkling Pacific Ocean. We descended slowly to the flats and canefields and onto the Ingham Road, then south-east towards Townsville.

No sooner was I back in camp and unpacking my gear than I was pining for Mount Speck and her cool, secretive greenery. For someone who'd spent all his life living west of the Great Dividing Range in New South Wales, those tropical mountains held a mystical magic about them that I had never experienced until now. Perhaps I felt heavy of heart because just then I believed that I'd never again venture into that wonderland which was only a stone's throw away. It wasn't long, however, before I — like all my mates — was revelling in the fact that we were now fully fledged Infantrymen, having passed all tests and spent time playing about in the field.

The crossover from Infantry Corps training to Infantry Battalion was conducted in such a manner that this upheaval to our lives caused not the slightest bit of stress at all. With absolutely no fanfare to mark this momentous occasion, we simply changed our sleeping arrangements. For myself, I emerged on Monday morning from my room of three new mates, two stories up facing Townsville on the north side of our lines as the third Rifleman (Tail-end Charlie) of Five Section, Eight Platoon, Charlie Company of the Fourth Royal Australian Regiment.

Sergeant Filewood (Reg), who the week before last was Chief Weapons Instructor and Safety Officer, was now our acting Platoon Commander. This was because our actual Platoon Commander had not yet joined the Battalion. Filewood was a boilermaker by trade from Newcastle in New South Wales. He was about one hundred and seventy-eight centimetres tall and in reasonably good shape with curly, light-brown hair on a squarish head.

Corporal Jim Pollard (Nasho turned Reg), who only yesterday was my acting Sergeant of the Corps Training Platoon, was now Five Section's Section Commander. Thick-set, black-haired Territorian cattleman Lance Corporal Ian (Andy) Anderson (Naito) was our 2IC and Commander of the Gun Group. First Scout was the ruddy, thin-faced, sharp-nosed, blue-eyed blond Colin Mullen (Nasho) from Redcliffe. His Second Scout was twenty-one-year old Bob Coggins (Nasho), a little heavier built than the skinny First Scout, Coggins had an olive complexion, an easy grin emanating from a rounded face under receding, brushed-back black hair and he was a shearer from Western Australia who had a slight Pommy accent. Our Gunner was nineteen-year-old Steve (Clarkey) Clarke (Reg), a great, strapping boy with Ginger Megs looks and a ready smile under thin, blonde eyebrows that matched the colour of his short, spiky hair. He was South Australian born and bred. Curly, light-haired Robert (Bob) Denholm (Nasho) from Hobart Tasmania was his number two on the Gun and the bloke who carried the "golf bag" with the spare barrel and asbestos glove in it. Bob had bright, laughing eyes in a thin, kind face that hid his intellect and spirit.

The three Riflemen were Dogsbody Moody (Reg), Greg (Muzzy), Musgrove (Nasho), and I (Nasho). Dogsbody, as his nick name suggests, was lean to the point that his clothes simply hung on his person. He had light skin and very light, fawn hair and he carried a worried expression about him at all times. He too hailed from a suburb of Hobart.

Muzzy was a tall, gangly Victorian with a Grecian nose in a slightly elongated face who was quietly spoken and seemed to be a serious type of bloke despite his ready smile, which suggested that he relished life. In his younger days, he'd carried "The Bag" for his father at Country Race Meetings all over the back-blocks of Victoria and there seemed to be a tangible gentleness about Muzzy, who had a wife and an infant girl just weeks old waiting for him down in Melbourne; and then there was yours truly. We were one short of a full Section but that didn't seem to matter at this stage.

That first morning Sergeant Filewood lined us all up just out from under our buildings facing the Mess where he stood looking carefully at us for a minute or so. 'You; you'll do,' he said to me.

'Sarge?'

'Come 'ere,' he said again, pointing at the ground in front of him. When I was at attention before him, he asked. 'Can you drill men?'

'Yes Sarge,' I answered, brightly.

'OK then, drill these men,' he ordered.

I faced them up — my new fellow Platoon members, all of whom I did not yet know.

'Righto you blokes, attention, er ... Platoon, stand at ease,' I told them, politely but seriously. To my relief, they all responded and performed the drill as instructed. Suddenly there was a light tap on my left shoulder. I glanced behind me to find Filewood right there on top of me.

'Yes Sarge?'

'Have you got balls son?' he asked, mildly.

'Yes Sarge,' I answered, confused.

'WELL, FUCKEN WELL USE THEM THEN,' he bellowed, at the back of my head, 'These men are animals. They don't know what to do. Yur've gotta tell 'em in a way that they can understand yuh.'

'But Sarge, they're me mates,' I protested, not wanting to get off-side with these blokes who I'd only just met and with whom I hoped I was going to be working harmoniously with from now on, all of them being my senior.

'Yur've got no mates. You're a Drill Instructor. Now drill these men,' he roared at me again.

I couldn't look directly at anyone in particular as I pulled myself together. It was my turn to make myself heard to all and sundry within cooee. I let them have it.

'Platoon! Platoon attennnnhon! Platoon, riiight turn,!

Platoon, quiiiick march! Righto you lot, lift yur feet, yur ain't got lead in'em — urt-urt-urt-art urrrt — come on, get wiffet.'

I hussled them around bellowing at the top of my voice for half an hour or more with the boys responding to my every call and Filewood never too far away watching on like a hawk.

Once stood down as their Drill Instructor I tried to keep a low profile for the rest of the day hoping the boys would forget as quickly as possible the harsh workout I'd put them through all be it at the behest of one Sergeant Barry Filewood. I don't know why he'd singled me out as their first up Drill Instructor — maybe he still had me in his sights from the pistol shoot two weeks back?

In the afternoon we newcomers to the Battalion — that is, we who had just graduated up from Corps Training- were introduced to a real treat that was the norm in this man's Army, but which had eluded us to date: Four o'clock Stand Down.

'Yeah mate, yuh time's yur own n'till First Parade at 0.800 t'morra.' And this was going to happen every day from now on.

A tall, skinny, red-headed, freckled-face, incessantly-happy bloke, who in that time-honoured Australian tradition was called "Blue" and who seemed to treat Army life as some sort of joke, arranged during the day that we all should meet at a pub on the road into town via Kerwin for 'get-to-know-you drinks'.

We arrived en masse at the appointed place and he led us out to the open dance floor space on the west side of the main bar area. There were a few patrons drinking quietly here at the time of our entry, but as soon as Blue got up on the small square dais where the abandoned microphone sat snug atop the long stand and announced that the Army was here to entertain them, everyone immediately got up and hastily vacated the room. I don't remember how or when I got home to Lavarack that night so I put that down to a real good night had by all.

Around ten the next day when we'd assembled under our building to start our day's work at whatever, the boys started to sort themselves out. A scuffle broke out between Clarkey and Andy. When Andy crouched and let go a long right that missed Clarkey's moosh by mere millimetres, Clarkey was wise to back down as quickly as he did. Andy was most definitely not one to come to grips with by the look of his cat-like action and intent.

Next day Clarkey messed up again. Filewood said something to him, but Clarkey just laughed. Filewood then told the teenager, 'If you're not careful, boy, you'll find yurself doen laps around the Battalion Parade Ground at the double.'

Clarkey just laughed again.

'What's so funny, Private?' Filewood asked him in a dangerously quiet voice.

'If I'm out there runnen roun, then you'll be out there runnen roun in the heat with me, Sarge.'

Filewood shot back at him. 'No, I won't, boy. I'll stand in the middle an' every time you get to a corner I'll call, left turn.' Shut the young fellow up real quick that did.

No sooner were we endorsed as fully-fledged members of 4RAR, then some of us, including my good self, copped Duties. From this we were to find out first-hand why our CSM was called Mother. Done up in our Sunday best greens we — the Guard Detail — were paraded on the little Parade Ground between our lines and the HQ buildings for finial inspections by Mother.

'No, this won't do. Get a lighter an' burn those threads off the flap of yuh pocket there. Yeah, that one there, half way down yur left leg. Yes, yes, that one! 'ere, straighten up this chin strap, son,' and so on until he finished fussing around us like an old hen. Only when he was completely satisfied that we were presentable by his strict standards did he march us over to the Guard House for our shift.

There was a small innocuous ceremony of the Changing of the Guard and by six o'clock or so we were fully installed as the night's Guards, two hours on, four hours off. All we had to do was roam around the Battalion area keeping both a low profile and a wary eye on things.

The Guard House was a large room fitted out with a mob of bunks. At the end of each two-hour shift, as the new detail ventured out into the night, we'd crash on one of these and sleep as well as could be expected for the next four hours. The night Guard Duty usually finished around eight in the morning when the blokes who'd be manning the gates for the day would take over.

* * *

4
JUNGLE TRAINING CENTRE

Now that 4RAR was almost at full strength with the latest infusion of us Twenty-First Intakers, we were destined to take our turn at the world's toughest Jungle Training Centre, Canungra. This place was so tough that visiting high-ranking staff from the American Armed Forces were quoted as saying that it was far too harsh a regime to put their Marines through. When Charlie Company's turn came in early November, we were flown to Brisbane in *Hercules* transport aircraft, trucked south through the hinterland to Beaudesert and then a little south of east to the camp in the hills west of Surfers Paradise.

There was nothing of note in the appearance of the place to suggest its fearsome reputation. Large, dark-green, tarpaulin tents were scattered about in what appeared at first glance to be a haphazard manner much as you'd find in a lot of Army camps. This, however, was to be our home for the next two weeks. Our Training Program was to be conducted in two halves: two weeks at Canungra and two weeks down over the border in New South Wales.

Everything we did here was going to be assessed by Instructors to see if we had what it took to get through a tour of duty in Vietnam as a unit, but not just any unit: as Charlie Company of the Fourth Battalion, Royal Australian Regiment. The training became so full-on from day one that I cannot in all honesty describe to you the events as they took place in chronological order during that two weeks; however, I will relate as best I can the things that I do recall in detail.

There were some shenanigans as the various Platoons passed each other going to one place or another with shouts of joyful jibes such as, 'NOBODY'S a Naito!'

And comebacks like, 'And you were stupid enough ta sign up fer this!'

It didn't matter one iota to the tough-arse Vietnam Veteran Instructors whether we were Reg or Naito. We were just Viet Cong bate to them and they were going to change that quick smart or kill us trying.

On a cleared piece of ground just east of the camp, we were instructed on the finer points of re-organising a Section for a straight-line frontal attack in the case of a front or rear ambush whereupon we practised these procedures over and over until they were satisfied with our efforts.

In the same area they showed us how to assemble our night time gear; that is Hutchie, mozzie net, ground sheet and silk. The silk was in essence a top sheet and, as we were going to be in the tropics, there would be no need for the Army-issued, thin, khaki blanket. Dogsbody Moody made the sloppiest camp imaginable with the middle of his tent almost touching the ground and, even though he was scolded by our NCOs, he failed to improve his overall attitude, bringing us all down in the eyes of our aggressive assessors.

We were taught how to tie the drab olive-green string line from tree to tree around the perimeter of our harbour so as to find our way to the Gun at night by using it to help guide ourselves along small cleared tracks; thus, avoiding being spiked between the eyes by those nasty needles at the bottom of the Wait-a-while bush. 'Well, there yer go! So, it isn't a fishing line after all.'

Then there was the setting up of a bank of Claymores across the bows of the Section, after which came the clearing patrols out and around in front of each Section between the guns, covering one third of the Platoon while we were harboured up, in order to ensure that our immediate area was free of spying enemy, who may have followed us into our harbour site and who were now lying in wait ready to pounce on us at or after nightfall or even first thing in the dull light of early morning; hence the need to adhere to "Stand to" procedures just as daylight receded to dark and at the coming of light each and every day that we were "out" from then on, no matter what.

They also showed us the best use for the black plastic, blow-up mattress we'd all been given, which we'd found were too noisy to use as intended, especially out in the jungle at night. When cut down the seams, each Section made a great cover to keep mud out of the belts of M60 rounds. These linked belts of two hundred rounds each were distributed throughout the men in the Section — excluding the Scouts -thereby lightening the load of the Gunner who would have one hundred rounds attached to the gun ready to go with the loose end of the belt slung over his shoulder. Another two hundred rounds joined up would hang from each side of his neck crossing his chest.

At a place that I'd hesitate to call a range, we had a go at chucking M25 hand grenades, eight in all, two to each throwing pit. Actually, one of these pits was a fair-sized log which was big enough to hide both the instructing Sergeant and the 4RAR thrower at the same time. The procedure was that each of us were to throw two grenades from one pit — yelling 'grenade' after each throw to let our mates know that we'd let one go — following which we'd run to the next pit on our right, jump in, pull the pin of one grenade, throw, yell, watch where it landed (in case it failed to detonate and we'd need to retrieve it to stop the enemy from making a booby trap out of it), duck, wait for it to explode, pull the pin on second grenade, throw, yell, watch, duck, wait, then as soon as it went off jump up and run to the next pit, repeat action, then run to the next place. Of course, while all this was happening the rest of us watched on at a safe distance in arrears.

At the middle pit about halfway through our turn, one of our mob threw and ducked. The burly Sergeant in the pit with him grabbed the poor unfortunate with two huge hands around his upper ribcage, held him aloft and shook him yelling. 'Did you see where that bloody grenade landed?'

At first the little bloke seemed to dangle like a rag doll as he was being shaken, then as the precious seconds sped by, he started to fight violently while still suspended in mid-air screaming. 'Let me down, let me down.' Just in time to avoid the grenade's blast he was whisked down into the depths of that pit.

At a sturdy steel structure by a creek known as the "The Tower", we were all required to jump off a high board into the water ten metres below. When I finally climbed to the top of the Tower's ladder, I was met by the well-fed and fit-looking Major Boxall, Charlie Company's Commander. 'Can you swim?' He asked me, seriously.

Now I ask you — remembering that we had to pass two water safety tests to get this far — if you could not swim, would you be standing high up in the air on a thirty-centimetre wide board about to throw yourself off to plunge ten metres down into the murky green waters below, even if there were two Safety Officers down there somewhere waiting to save you should you appear to them to be drowning?

I threw Boxall a hearty, 'Nuh,' then walked boldly past him to the end of the board even as he leaned over and put a cupped hand to the side of his mouth and called in a loud voice to the blokes in the frogman suits below, 'This man can't swim.'

The Safety Officers had been keeping back from each jumper thus far so as not to get their heads wet, but as I leapt from the end of the board and plummeted, they swam in to where they expected me to hit the water and sink. At the very last moment I lifted my left knee and grabbed it with both hands, spread my elbows wide and leant back as the sole of my left boot hit the surface of the water. I think it was my best ever "bomb". The extra height from whence I'd come might have had something to do with it, but whatever, I felt it thump in on my chest so I knew it was a good'un. I was laughing even before I surfaced, but more so when I did and my would-be rescuers swore at me.

'Yur fucken, little bastard, we've bin keepen dry up until now, yur fucken prick.'

I playfully splashed water in their direction and swam — as best I could whilst fully clothed and in boots — away to the bank under The Tower to haul myself out.

We were taken into a hut and shown a great array of enemy booby traps and how they were built. One that really caught my attention used an ordinary bread knife as a push/pull switch, while another — which we could quickly make ourselves — was a grenade pushed up by a piece of bamboo and connected to a trip-wire stretched across a track. There was also a demo of how to make a switch that could be used to activate a bank of claymore mines so that they would go off as intended wherever the operator wanted. This set-up could be used against pinpointed targets around the outside of a large static position such as a Base Camp or Fire Support Base. We were also shown a movie on RPG7s and 9s (Rocket Propelled Grenades) and how the enemy might be expected to use them against us. It was a Yankiee demo movie and I can tell you the sand-bagging depicted in their flick left a hell of a lot to be desired.

I remember it rained every day for the first week we were at Canungra. At any given time from mid-morning on it would suddenly turn dark like a veil was being drawn over us. A different type of air would envelope us and then it would pour down. We'd don camouflage-coloured, nylon raincoats that did little more then keep us warm — certainly not dry — wait until it stopped and remove them, only to find that within minutes of doing so our shirts would be soaked through again with our sweat.

Late one morning about the beginning of the second week, we were lined up facing a cargo net which had been draped over a wooden A-frame structure falling from the top to the ground on both sides. It was about 3 metres to the top, I'd say. We were instructed to start on the west side of the structure, climb the net, come down the east side, run as fast as we could across the road on which we now stood, up into the hillside of low scrub through the barbed-wire entanglements, and then diagonally across the ridge top to a set point. From there we were to descend the hill, cross the road again and climb up and over the cargo net once more to finish off on the ground on the other side.

Away we went with much gusto; however, no one said anything to us about the loud-mouthed bloke and how he would be screaming abuse at us from somewhere within the confines of the scrub as we struggled our way through the course.

'Come on, hurry up yer useless mob'a bastards, fucken move. The Vietcong will 'ave yer fucken arses if yer move as slow as this, yer useless mob'a pricks. Come on, move, move, yer cunts.'

This went on the entire time we ran the course. As I approached the cargo net for the second time puffing like a winded horse, one of our lot who was sitting up atop the A-frame, with his legs on either side of the pole, announced seriously, 'Oh, I wish someone would tell that useless cunt t'shudup.'

Then he just let himself go and rolled down the backside of the net. As exhausted as we were, we all laughed aloud at him?

When the last bloke was done and we were lined up as a Platoon to be marched the three kilometres back down to the Battle Inoculation Course — which was the next thing on our agenda for that day — the Corporal Instructor said, to everyone's surprise, 'Righto! Who was the smartarse who called me a cunt? One pace step forward! March!'

No one moved. How did he know? He was too far away to hear anything anyone was saying at the cargo net, having still been up in the thick, grey-green scrub yelling his head off at the time.

'Come on,' he said again. 'Who was the smartarse bastard who called me a cunt? One pace step forward! March!'

Again, the Platoon stood motionless and expressionless.

'Well,' he stated, 'I can stand 'ere all day until I have someone out 'ere.'

'Stand here' for him meant in the shade on the east side of the roadway which he was now standing in while we wilted away out in the late morning sun.

Suddenly, one bloke broke. I cannot say for certain if he was the culprit or not, but he boldly took that one pace forward and, crunch, his right foot defiantly hit the gravel. Before anything else could happen, three more blokes to the right of me in the front row took one pace forward and, crunch. Instantaneously, we all moved as one and in unison, CRUNCH. There was a stiff-necked stillness and utter resolve in the three ranks as we reassembled as a Platoon once more.

I thought this sort of stuff was only used to embellish movies, but here I was a party to this ultimate act of mateship. It was an absolute defining moment for me. I knew right then and there without the slightest doubt that this mob of blokes was the mob I wanted to be with in Vietnam. We'd only been together as a Platoon for less than a full month and here we were so thick. It really was that "one in, all in" thing. If you're going to take one of us on, then you'll be taking us all on. We will stand together and fight you to the very last man standing. It felt to me like the essence of all that is right in this great land of ours was concentrated in on us at this one time and place. I was so very, very proud to be an Australian right then.

The Corporal Instructor did not see it this way at all, though. He just saw red.

'So,' he said, slowly, 'I've got thirty smartarse bastards, have

I? OK! Riiight turn!' We now faced down the road as a squad. 'Doubllle march!' he roared. So away we went down a slight grade on a gravel road trotting along the three kilometres to the next course. I don't know if I've mentioned this or not, but nigh on everything we did at Canungra was done fully packed and carrying rifles. The only beauty of our little run was that the useless instructor prick had to trot along with us and no matter how much more abuse he threw at us as we went, we knew in our hearts we'd won.

We arrived at the place of the next course puffing and panting a little, but with our spirits up. Here we were informed that we were now going to run another kilometre or so along a cleared piece of ground about the width of an outback station airstrip. They casually informed us, 'There'll be a few barbed-wire entanglements to negotiate and the odd little explosion going off at the sides of the course. You're not to worry about them, they won't hurt you. They're just blocks of TNT. You will be attacking an enemy weapons pit with two enemy in it.'

This last obstacle was so far away that we couldn't even see it yet.

'The main idea of this exercise is that you will attack the enemy as a Platoon in extended line using fire and movement under battle conditions, which means you have to listen to your individual Section Commander's orders and advance in groups: that is, Scout Group, Gun Group and Rifle Group. Piece'a cake.

We shook out, steadily moving forward in extended line. Suddenly, the first blocks of TNT went off at both sides of us at once. THUMP! The air around us shook. It was on. We started running forward and then someone yelled 'DOWN.'

The NCOs began calling their instructions through the din of intermittent explosions going off on either side of us, while large clods of dirt rained down upon us. 'Gun Group, GO.'

They'd run in a dodging run for about twenty metres or so with the rest of us giving covering fire before they'd get the 'DOWN'. Then it would be, 'Rifle Group, GO ... 'DOWN', and so on until all three groups were back in line and the process was repeated. It seemed like chaos reigned supreme for a bit, but we did make it to the first of the very low barbed wire entanglements still in our line. It was a real pain trying to wriggle through under the wire as fast as possible with packs on in order to get out to a point where we could cover our mates as they advanced, so a lot of swearing could be heard above the din

About half way through the exercise I lost interest in the great clods of dirt that relentlessly bombarded us from above, suddenly becoming aware that if I concentrated my hearing solely on Pollard's voice and blanked out Corporal McKinley's — who was closest to me on my left yelling orders to his Six Section boys — then it all come together. It was so surreal that with all the noise and movement going on around us there seemed to me to be just us in Five Section floating forward yelling angrily and shooting blanks madly at our two entrenched opponents who we could now see in an exposed gun pit, then suddenly we were on them and overwhelming them.

'That was the fastest we've seen anyone complete that course correctly,' the Instructors told us afterwards and the two pretend enemy confided in us that it was actually a bit frightening to sit in their pit and watch us advance on them with such force. That was two up for Eight Platoon and both on the same day.

Next day Filewood had us on the double back to camp for lunch when I stepped on a fair size, loose stone on the gravel roadway and turned my ankle again — the same one I'd done up on High Range about a month back. I stumbled out of line as the pain drove up through my lower leg. Filewood roared at me from behind, 'Get back inta line, yer fucken dim wit, wot's the fucken matter with yer?'

I gritted my teeth as I managed to line up and carry on with the others not letting on to him as to what had just happened as I was not going to let this mob down because I could still keep going as long as it did not get too cold and stiff. I had my blue, swollen ankle bandaged up that night after stand-down.

Then around ten the following morning, Filewood lined us up at about the same place that I'd done my ankle and appealed to us. 'We've got a situation. They won't let us continue on unless I have a batman, so I need someone to volunteer to be my batman for the time we're here.'

Naturally, no one moved. We were all well aware of that old Army adage "Never volunteer for anything". Filewood calmly waited for a bit, then announced, 'Well, gentlemen, I donn care. It's not me who wants this t'happen. It has come from higher up an' youse can take all day if youse like, I'll just wait for yurs t' make up yur minds while I stand 'ere in thu shade.'

He was standing in the plentiful shade of some monstrous trees while we stood to attention in the sweltering, mid-November, mid-morning sun.

'*This is stupid,*' I told myself, '*and anyway, how hard could it be being his batman. He's all right and anyway it will get us out of this bloody sun and doing what we've come here to do sooner rather than later.'*

So, silly me, I stepped forward and said lamely, 'I'll be yur batman, Sarge.' Filewood showed no emotion as he accepted my offer and away we went again with no change to the program other then that I'd have to keep close to Filewood from then on.

The whole of Charlie Company went for a little stroll after this down to the south of the main training centre returning via the creek and at one point we came to a waterfall about five metres across and some eight to ten metres high. It was a very slippery climb up the side of it with the grass all wet from the mist and spray of the cascading water, but we made it up and over the top, albeit slowly.

Shortly afterwards — and a little further along a goat track which followed the creek from up on the side of a steep slope Bill Keenan– a tall, thin extremely mild-mannered bloke who often laughingly boasted that he came from "where men are men and the women eat their babies" (in fact, the harsh, dry country north of Broken Hill in far western New South Wales) and who, against all appearances, raced speedway bikes and by all accounts was game to the point of endangering himself — lost his footing and slipped from the track. He rolled flat out down the hill towards the four-metre drop which would take him off the bank onto large boulders in the bed of the creek below. Fully-packed and clinging to an M60, he spun out of control and beyond help and then, as suddenly as he'd started rolling, he stopped just two thirds of a metre short of the drop-off. He was on his feet in a flash and, using his free hand to help himself, climbed like a monkey back up the steep slope and not a sound was heard during the whole event save the distant tinkle of the green tinted water in the creek below us. I quickly glanced in Filewood's direction, but he was looking north with a faraway look on his face and had not noticed a thing.

'Yur wanna watch wots goen on Sarge, yur nearly lost a man jus' then,' I reported to him.

'Wot?' he said, clicking back to earth in the present and looking around behind him. 'Wot man? Where?'

By this time, Keenan had hot-footed it back onto the track and had resumed his place in the single file without to-do and it now looked for all the world like nothing out of the ordinary had occurred.

'Arr fucket, furget et,' I growled. Filewood just glared at me in bewilderment.

To get back to camp at the end of the track, we had to cross a small, suspended, swinging bridge, but, to make it more interesting for the Instructors, we had to run across the bloody thing with rifles at the ready. After our first foot hit the boards the whole thing started a waving motion causing our next foot to land lower than expected then the next foot higher and so on. It's a real wonder to me that as we all crossed it at breakneck speed that no one tripped A over T or fell over the side.

Next afternoon we were sent out to patrol away to the east of the main camp. Along the way, Doc, our Platoon Medic, and I became entangled in the same Wait-a-while bush. Instead of just backing out quietly, he began to pull and fight with the runners clinging to him and in doing so ripped a cane past my eyes and I was left with thorns embedded, one in my cheek, one in my eyelid and one in my temple. I cursed him aloud and when he turned to see what I was on about, he tried to extract the thorns from my face, but I had the shits good and proper by this time and told him so in no uncertain terms to, 'jus' fuck off, will yuh, if yur haden a'been so fucken stupid, then this woodna 'appened.'

When Filewood turned back to see how we were travelling behind him and saw the blood running down the side of my face, an appalled look came over him.

'Wot appened t'you?' he asked, concern etched in his voice.

'Arr, jus fucken Doc,' I growled.

'Wot? De'it yuh or sumthun?' his tone turning more to accusing now than concern.

'Nar 'e jus went rip tare bust in that Wait-a-while back there, en I copped somea thu thorns.'

The Sergeant turned on Doc with real menace in his normally calm eyes and spat at him, 'Fix this man up at once.'

Doc grumbled as he attended my bleeding face, which I swear looked a lot worse than it really was. He fussed until I was a tanned, white man again and I let him, to save him from getting another blast from Filewood.

After dark that evening when we were finally settled in our harbour, high on an exposed ridge top, we sat and marvelled at the sight of the lights which emanated from the entire length of the Gold Coast far down to the east of our position. As great as it might have looked from up there, we couldn't ogle this splendid sight all night for the next day we were going to simulate a full Battalion attack on an enemy position at an unknown location, without Officers leading us.

'Why no Officers, Sarge?' we asked Filewood when we heard this.

'They've been turned into an ordinary fighting Platoon. They've all been busted down to Privates and NCOs jus t' give 'em a taste of wot it's like t'be ordinary Grunts like yourselves.' Grunts are what all other Corps called us Infantrymen. Can't say whether it did our Officers much good or not?

Blue had a leach suck on his eyeball overnight and come up with a very red eye and swollen lid in the morning causing him to be taken out to the hospital straight away. As soon as he left we broke our fast and then set off to find and destroy the enemy. By late morning our forward segments located the enemy hideout in a very densely over-grown gully and a noisy mock battle broke forth. It was all over bar the shouting by the time Eight Platoon were abreast of the gully and all we got to see was smoke drifting up out of the dark green foliage as we rolled slowly by.

That night we camped out again and around eleven o'clock, when most of us were just getting to sleep on the rocky ground, some stupid prick set off a couple of wizz-bangs. Of course, it was everybody out. 'STAND TO! STAND TO!'

We lay about on our bellies on the rough, stony ground for a bit, then the "all clear" was given.

'It was just a probe,' someone informed us. We'd only just got settled down and they did it again, prompting the same reaction from the encamped Company. Around three in the morning they were at it again. '*Fuck, don't these bastards ever sleep?*'

This time the initial explosion was much closer to our quarter and we waited silently in the dark to defend our position should they attempt to penetrate the perimeter at our sector. It's a bloody good thing we were just play-acting with blanks or someone might have got really hurt that night.

That was the first two weeks down, two to go. On a bright morning, the entire C Company of 4RAR were loaded aboard open trucks and driven out to Beaudesert where we turned left and went south-west through paddocks full of pineapple in various stages of growth. To the east was a chimney- shaped mountain which fascinated me. It had vertical sides and a flat top — a real eagle's eerie if ever I saw one and the type of place I'd dreamed of living on back when I was holed up on those long, cold, winter nights in the dorm at the College at Forbes.

The convoy of Army trucks crossed the border of Queensland into New South Wales at a very nondescript gap in the fence sometime just before dinner camp and the only thing that determined the crossing was that almost immediately we were in New South Wales the unsealed road became rougher and more corrugated. There was no one here to make sure no exotic pests like fruit fly and the like could cross over to stuff up banana plantations to the north or grapevines down south.

Continuing south-west for a while, we suddenly turned south-east and onto a better road and then after travelling in that direction for a while and passing through a small village we turned north climbing a ridge where Lantana completely covered the ground on both sides of the trucks. We stopped for a bit high up on a mountainside and from our airy position we could see the thick, silver ribbon of a board river winding its way towards the sea far to our east which was the mighty Tweed. We snaked our way a little further up a logging track and when we were facing back the way we'd come, the trucks stopped. We were told to disembark at around two-thirty in the afternoon right into the Lantana. Thank you very much! Climbing westward on foot, we lost the Lantana, to be dwarfed in a forest of giant trees with vines and things hanging from them. It was reasonably open in here, but dark and dank. Unlike Canungra, it looked decisively uninhabited. It lacked the smell and comforting feel of Mt Speck now so far away. A sad place was Wiangaree National Park.

Next day we moved west again and around eleven o'clock we started to descend a pretty fair slope where the tall trees with their entanglements made it hard to ascertain how far down we had to go. We followed a goat track which wove its way ahead of us and there were dobs of red and blue paint on trees about head height, so it was obvious that man had been here before us, but this was the only sign he'd left. The rest of the wilderness all around us appeared to be untouched.

At midday we were on the valley floor, or what there was of it, and I was pleasantly surprised and delighted to see a grove of three-metre high palm trees down here. We had lunch among them before starting off again, this time in a nor-westerly direction and almost at once we began a six hundred- metre ascent up another slope as steep as the one we'd just come down. The further we went the more northerly we got, when suddenly we were confronted with a sheer cliff of about six-and-a-half metres. Someone scrambled to the top and tied toggle ropes together making them into one six-metre rope on which the rest of us could use to haul ourselves up and over the top.

When half of Eight Platoon — who were in the middle of the

Company -were on top and going to ground in dense foliage to secure the area, we were hit by the "enemy". The "enemy" in this case were in fact members of 9RAR who were based at Enoggera in Brisbane and who for the duration of this exercise were acting as our adversaries. They'd planned it perfectly because with most of us still to conquer the cliff, they'd effectively split the company.

It was a hit-and-run ambush. CRACK-CRACK-CRACK, then some black-clad figures streaking off through the shadowy undergrowth at the edge of a cleared line that could have once been a logging track — pissed some of us right off, me included. We gave chase, yelling and shouting for a hundred metres or more before being called back by Filewood and blasted for acting like undisciplined rabble.

'But Sarge, they ran. 'ow we gunna get 'em if we donn run after 'um?'

But he was right, of course. We could have run right into a well-prepared ambush site and if this happened in Vietnam we could very well have been wiped out.

Once the company was all on top and secure, we were off to the north, but hadn't gone too far when it started to rain again. It rained a lot down here and, with the constant grey skies, the temperate rainforest high up on these ridge tops never seemed to completely dry out.

For the next eleven days we operated for the most part just as we were expected to once we were over in Vietnam. We split up and moved about in Platoon-sized patrols with the "enemy" supposedly having no idea where we were and vice-versa, but I suspect that there was radio contact — albeit on a different frequency to that of the company — between the "enemy" and our Instructors who were still dogging us on a daily basis. We set up ambushes and waited silently in them literally for hours, most times with no result as no one came through our carefully prepared killing grounds to trigger us off. At other times we got lucky getting some pretend kills and taking the odd prisoner.

Talking to a couple of these bods one day, they informed us that, '3RAR will cop it when they get over there; they wouldn't train properly; they were just too slack to cope with what is coming their way.' These blokes had acted as 3RAR's "enemy" as well when they too went through Canungra.

Filewood and I sat on the edge of a track one day and watched from the dense shade as the rest of the Platoon practised the "immediate ambush" drill over and over. This is used when the scout spots the enemy coming along the same track he is on and there is no time to do anything about preparing a proper ambush. He quickly covers his eyes with his free hand and immediately follows this signal with a point to the side of the track, and then he takes a small step sideways into the bushes at the side of the track and hopes like hell that the rest of his Platoon mates have seen his signal and have mimicked his move. Under normal circumstances an "immediate ambush" is pretty neat, but when done to perfection it's almost beyond belief. Once, I blinked and suddenly a whole Platoon vanished before us. They executed the move so effectively that it actually scared me. One minute they were there and a split second later nothing but empty space where twenty odd troops had just been standing. A strange thrill chilled the length of my spine at the time.

Each Platoon had to protect itself with covering fire from

the big guns at night and once the harbour site was settled the Platoon Commander had to bring in the guns to bear on selected targets around the encampment, which were usually tracks a little way out from us and selected as targets in the hope of getting the enemy either on their way in to us or on their way out. The first night up here Filewood threw me a little book and said, 'Bring the guns in.'

'Wot?'

'Youken read, can't yuh? Yur know yur codes, donn yuh? Bring the guns in.'

There are about twenty-six different things that have to be done to successfully carry out this procedure and all had to be done using the International Code. I was flabbergasted, but attempted to carry out Filewood's orders as well as I could. I don't remember it all, but what does come to mind was the fact that I had to estimate the height of the tallest trees in the vicinity and I remember doing the "shot over" and the "shot out" thing each time the Gunners and I were happy with the selection and final set-up of targets. I must have got it right because Filewood never interfered and the Gunners on the other end of my calls didn't pull me up, letting me carry on regardless, and this became my evening ritual from then on.

Being in Platoon HQ, I was subject to the three-hour radio picket like every one else in the hub of the Platoon harbour. Remember, those on the perimeter had to man the gun in a staggered rotation two at a time for two hours a night. The one thing I learnt from this was that the radio set was our ears to the outside world and if I stayed close to the man with the set I could find out everything that was going on within the

Company, the Battalion and sometimes beyond. At night, around three or four in the morning I'd often call up CHQ just to keep myself awake.

'3 this is 3-2 over.'

'3-2 this is 3 over.'

'Roger 3 this is 3-2 time check over.'

'3-2 this is 3 — 0335 hours over.'

'Roger 3 this is 3-2 out.'

It was so good. There was always someone there.

On Thursday of the second week, we found the trucks waiting for us again on a logging track pointing down the mountain and they transported us back to Canungra by nightfall. For all intents and purposes we were now battle-ready jungle fighters fully able to go into battle immediately if called upon to do so.

As we got back to our digs after breakfast the next morning there was a wailing and a loud exchange of words out behind our tents. Upon inspection it was found that the contemptuous Four Section Commander, the rotund Corporal Ron Templeman, had for some inexplicable reason jumped all over Keith Day's snake bag and killed the three snakes within. Keith was a snake-catcher from Townsville. He kept snakes at home and used to milk these snakes for Townsville Uni who then made anti-venom out of the poison. On this trip he'd caught a fair size carpet snake, a small greenish one and a black one he said he'd never seen before. The boys told me he would suddenly break ranks and go walk-a-bout while we were moving about in the jungle, to return with a snake to put in the extra sand bag he carried — the other one being the garbage bag we all carried while in any of the National Parks we trained in. There was no bash/burn and bury while anywhere here in Australia, and rightly so.

It just so happened that my older brother, John, was getting married at Temora the next afternoon, which was a Saturday. I reasoned that, seeing as we were so close anyway, if they dropped me off in Brisbane today I'd have no trouble making it to his wedding, so I put the concept to Corporal Jim Pollard.

'You've gotta take yuh rifle back.' I was told.

'But anyone can do that,' I protested.

'Yeah, but yur bolt, only youken put yur bolt in,' is what he came up with next.

'Bullshit, 'ow much work does ut take ta 'and a bolt toah orderly,' I growled, getting hot under the collar by this time.

'Look,' he said, 'if yur got a problem, go see a padre.'

So much for Army compassion and all that shit. Once you're in they give you nothing and take you only where they want you to go– in this case right back up to Townsville so that they could load us onto a train to send us right back down here again.

At the Brisbane Airport while we waited our *Hercules* Transporters turn to taxi out to take off for Townsville, we watched an RAAF bloke start up a *Canberra Bomber* which was parked beside us and it was of some interest to see an Aircraftman walk up to the front of each of the two jet engines and shove something into them, then walk away. There followed a loud explosion and the engine was covered with smoke; next thing it was going and starting to scream to its full pitch.

5
CHRISTMAS BREAK

Townsville. Friday afternoon. Bolt and rifle stored away in the room under CHQ and onto a train first thing in the morning. Big brother John would be married by three-thirty this afternoon.

The train was plump with a rowdy bunch of mostly 4RAR soldiers and the atmosphere within was electric as we clickety-clacked our way slowly south through sugarcane fields on all sides anticipating a whole month with our loved ones and friends over the break.

As the train rolled cautiously into the large Central Queensland coastal sugar town of Rockhampton at around seven or seven-thirty that evening, there was an excited exclamation from one of the blokes, 'Hey, look at this, there's cars goen down both sides of us — we're in the middle of them!'

Anyone not familiar with the quaint uniqueness of this particular place would be understandably surprised by this; however, I'd become aware of it some two months or so before being pressed into service. John (Johnny Honk) O'Connor from Temora — who'd been at Red Bend with us in the mid-sixties to finish his schooling at an Agricultural College and who was now betrothed to my eldest sister Judy — had been up here and saw for himself what we were seeing for the first time now.

Apart from this excited bloke, most of us only took a cursory glance at the lights of the cars on the streets on either side of the train. We were scanning the buildings for something far more important to us right then: pubs. Being a trainload of soldiers, we'd long ago drunk this train dry and were looking to top her up. Some of the boys were on the toe even before the carriages actually stopped. I sprinted to a likely pub some way ahead of the stationary hook-up on the left side of the road in case it got going and I had to abandon my attempt to stock up and climb aboard as it passed me by. In the small front bar of the old fashioned establishment I asked breathlessly for a carton of VB stubbies, and with time to spare had to trot back to the train waiting patiently at the station with the two dozen little brown bottles rattling in the green box on my shoulder.

The party got into full swing now and raged on late into the night. The only drama came at around two in the morning when the question arose: 'Where is Brenda gunna sleep?'

Brenda — five-foot-one or -two tall, of slight body, wavy, brown hair, pleasant smile and good-natured — was the only girl on that packed train that night. She was a corporal in the Australian Women's Armed Forces (AWAF). These girls were often maliciously referred to as "Officers' Mattresses" but Brenda didn't fit that category as she could be often enough found in The Raymonds drinking with the likes of us of the lower ranks. The problem was solved when it was decided with much good humour, banter and raucous laughter that big Andy Bligh was going to take good care of her. Andy was a lean six-foot-something who had very clear, bright eyes, thick, shiny-black hair and a look that told you not to mess with him; however, I think he was a softy under it all and, besides, was a friend of Brenda's, so all would be alright. Poor Brenda, she had to go all the way down to Hay in the absolute west of the Riverina District of southern New South Wales to be with her folks for Christmas.

With Brenda's sleeping arrangements finalised to the satisfaction of all concerned, it was time to break camp. I went back along the train to locate the compartment that held my drab, olive-green carry-all bag and found bodies everywhere. They were sprawled out on the floor in the corridors, on the seats and in the luggage racks of most compartments on this train. The carriages were of an older style that had the corridors to one side, a double sliding door opening into the compartment with two large, dark-green, leather-covered bench seats facing each other stretching from the door to the window. The bottom portion of the two windows slid upwards to halfway where they locked into place with small, solid, brass locks at each side. Above each seat there was a luggage rack made of sturdy, meshed wire. I slept in a rack in my compartment as both seats, the other rack and the floor were taken before I got home.

I surfaced at sun-up to find we were still some two hours or so out of Brisbane. I discovered that I'd retained half a dozen stubbies from my stash and despite being very dry in the mouth I decided to forego the "hair of the dog" this morning. I'd keep them for later on.

Upon arrival at Roma Street Station — Brisbane's Central Railway Station — we were in for a surprise. Not only would we be changing trains, we would also be changing train stations! It was just as well some of our mob was clued up on the procedure and we quickly learnt that we had to make our own way from here to South Brisbane Railway Station to catch the trains to

New South Wales as this was as far as the wider gauge of the New South Wales rail lines come to in Brisbane.

As it turned out, we could have taken the day off and walked at our absolute leisure to South Brisbane Station instead of squeezing in as many bodies as possible and splitting the cost of a taxi ride because the rush across town was to no avail. We had to wait until late in the afternoon before we could board the only train out, which was a night train to parts of the south. About the only saving grace for the South Brisbane Station was that the long, narrow platform faced south so that at least we were not going to cook in the midday sun. It was a long, tiresome, dry wait. At one point some of the boys came back past us and informed all within hearing distance that there was a young sheila further along the platform wearing a very see-through blouse.

'Uken see er tits an' everything,' they told us in earnest.

About half an hour later and after just about everyone else had had a gander at the girl with the see-through top, Brenda said to me, 'C'mon let's you and I go an' see what all thu fuss is about.'

We strolled slowly down along the platform with her arm through mine like a couple from a bygone era and wandered as casually as possible past the girl seated on a hard, wooden seat and right along to the very end. She was petite with long, straight brown hair and large, doe-like eyes. She was wearing a broad-brim, floral, coloured, material hat, which was predominantly blue and, yes, a very see-through, black-tinted top which she might as well have left in the drawer at home for all that it hid. Her only possession seemed to be a sturdy looking, new acoustic guitar.

It was "all aboard" at around five in the afternoon and, after what I'd consider a long, unwarranted delay, we were away, speeding off in a westerly direction before gradually swinging south into the suburbs by six. An hour out I found the girl with the see-through top sitting alone by the window in an empty compartment and dropped in beside her on the long seat. I tried to converse with her, but she was having none of it, remaining quiet and aloof. I tried to get her to play the guitar for me, but she utterly refused. Maybe she really believed all that media shit that was fashionable at the time, that we were being trained to go over to Vietnam to kill their babies — who knows — but she was saying jack-all to any of us. At seven-thirty or thereabouts we crossed the border into New South Wales, by which time most of us had sniffed out at least one wet canteen, some more. Also, by this time some of the troops had already been cautioned for unruly behaviour and had been threatened with expulsion from the train.

'You and who's Army will do that?' Peanuts was told, amid jolly laughter.

At Cassino, a couple of neatly dressed girls joined the train. They were student teachers from the nearby Lismore Teachers College and the party went up a level as they gleefully joined our lot. One of them did this almighty version of *Hey, Big Spender*, bumping her delightful hips provocatively — first on one sliding door to jar it open then onto the other — and swagging slowly in, singing in a low, hot, husky voice to the absolutely crowded compartment.

'Hey, big spenderrrrr, come and spend a little time with me.' We'd clap and roar our approval and send her out to do it all over again until Peanuts came along, going crook about the excessive noise emanating from this sector and threatened to chuck us all off again. 'Yeah, yeah.'

By ten o'clock, things were getting pretty grim in the grog stakes. We'd near drunk this train dry too. A couple of us pressed forward a long way along the train and found a well stocked Boozer in first class.

'This'll do us,' we said, and prepared to settle in for a real session away from the rabble. It didn't take Peanuts any time at all to find us. He hunted us out even though we tried to convince him right or wrong that we were 'nothing to do with that drunken mob back there'.

'I know who you are. I've seen and spoken to you all more than once tonight. We're coming up to Grafton soon and if you don't go now and quieten down I'll have the Grafton Police board this train and they can haul the lot of you off my train.' Heads down, we reluctantly left First Class. Party pooper!

When the train arrived at Broadmeadows Railway Station near the Steelworks City of Newcastle about an hour and a half's drive north of Sydney in the morning, I made a snap decision to jump off and go see my girlfriend, the Police Sergeant's daughter, who was now living at Singleton just a few kilometres west. I had an Army Travel Warrant on me which entitled me to travel on any train at any time anywhere in Australia and therefore I didn't have to buy a ticket here for Singleton. I could return and continue my journey to Sydney and thence to Temora any time I wished. When I had told her on the phone just a few days back that I could do this, she said she'd be away down on the coast at the time so there would be no point in my coming over to see her, but what the heck, I could sweeten up her old man so as to get into the good books with him. The last time he'd seen me I was still a "long haired lout" and he was telling his girl to bush me. I was all cleaned up now!

In Singleton, I came across the girl as she was leaving their modest home to go to work. She stopped momentarily on seeing me and then, with her head bowed, she attempted to walk straight past me, saying tensely, 'What are you doing here?'

My emotions went haywire. She'd lied about not being home on this day. Why? Was there someone else on the scene? If so, why not say so? She had plenty of time to say something during one of the phone calls I'd made to her every week that I'd been up in Townsville. I had an angry conversation with her all the way to her place of work and the last thing I yelled at her as she went into the back yard of the motel was, 'I'll see you in hell.'

I must have looked a forlorn figure indeed as I stood there alone and confused, watching her walk away from me without even looking back for an instant. What to do now? Stuff it. I'd come here to give the cop some grog and that's what I'd do, even if he did try to bush me again.

At his back door, he told me that she had just gone to work and that I'd 'just missed her'. I assured him that I hadn't.

'Oh, I see,' he said sadly, looking over me and out the back gate as if to see if she was coming back in. When he looked back down at me he asked, 'Have yur had breakfast? I'm just cooking mine. Do yur want some?'

'Yeah that'ed be good,' I told him, and stepped inside the opened, wood-framed, gauze door.

We talked amicably while he fried up some bacon and eggs in a pan. Living as he did in a town with a large Army Training

Base on its doorstep, he most likely didn't fully concur with the propaganda that the Unions under Bob Hawk and the Opposition Labor Party Minister, Dr Jim Cairns, and his little side-kick were spreading through the papers and TV about Australian Troops being nothing more than "baby killers" in Vietnam — no doubt to aid their RED mates in the north of that country. Although there was nothing said to any of us along those lines in Townsville, we the troops were well aware of this "red lover" sentiment from down here in the south. After we'd eaten, I presented the cop with his Christmas present — the half dozen VB stubbies — which was the main thrust of this excursion anyway. He thanked me and then drove me to the Railway Station in his new white car, most likely very relieved to be ridding his town of me.

I arrived at Cootamundra, eighty-eight kilometres shy of Wagga Wagga at two thirty on Tuesday morning, where I had to change trains to Temora which lay some seventy-two kilometres to the west. It was cold as I sat alone on a solid wooden seat against the wall on the deserted platform. I fished a suede leather vest that had fringes dangling from it out of my bag and donned it to protect myself a little from the unfamiliar chill of the night air. At three, a bloke walked out onto the platform and as the south-bound freight train hurtled through at some ungodly speed, he held out a large ring. The train appeared to hook it up and sweep it away as it flashed noisily by, dropping another one for the bloke to retrieve as it passed. He was about to evacuate the dimly-lit platform when I called out to him, 'Hey mate, wen's the next train to Temora?'

He jumped at the voice from the shadows and turned slowly around to find me.

'There's a passenger train leaving at seven-thirty,' he told me, squinting in my direction through the gloom.

'Seven thirty!' I retorted, 'I can't sit around 'ere in this fucken cold for another four 'ours mate, 'aven't yer got sumthen betteran that?'

The man of small stature pointed to a line of freight cars across the tracks and announced quietly, 'That train over there is goen to Temora in about thirty-five minutes, but you'd 'ave ta ride with thu Guard in thu Guard's Van if yur go on that.'

'That'll do me, thanks, mate,' I said, enthusiastically, thinking to myself, *it will be like jumping the rattler.*

I jumped down off the platform. Crunching on Bantam egg-sized, rough-cut, basalt stones I crossed the main line between Sydney and Melbourne and headed towards the back of the stationary train two tracks over. Climbing up black, steel steps into the open door of the dull-red Guard's Van, I called out, 'Anybody there?'

'Yeah,' came from down a hallway which led to the back of the van.

I was met by a thirty or thereabouts-year-old, scruffy-looking bloke who had a crop of loose brown hair and was wearing faded navy-blue Railway-issued shirt and dungarees. His boots were unpolished, he had red-rimmed eyes and he smelled of grog.

'Wodda yur want?' he slurred at me, a little confronted at meeting a complete stranger on his train at this hour.

'Jus' wonderen if I could catch a lift wifyuh to Temora? The bloke over there said I could arss yuh.'

'No,' he blurted out, pointing a thick, grubby finger at my

chest while using the inside wall of the van to steady himself. 'Donn like yur jacket.'

'Get fucked then,' I growled at him. I spun around and was at the door about to climb down to the tracks before he spoke again.

'Nar, its awright, jus kidden. Yer ken come wif me. 'Ere, wanna cup a tea? No milk though.' With that he led me back to a tiny room in the rear of the van which served as his kitchen and bedroom.

'Yeah, that'ed be great,' I answered, following him up.

We chatted for half an hour or so until we were away a bit behind time and almost as soon as the train departed he was in snooze land. I crashed too and the next thing I remember I was rocking awake at sun-up as we sped by the huge Bulk Wheat Terminal a few kilometres short of Temora. I had to shake the Guard awake out of his drunken stupor as we rattled past mum's first cousin's — my uncle, Johnny O'Sullivan's — tiny house opposite the railway crossing on the Old Cootamundra Road, a bit over a kilometre from the Temora Railway Station, so that he'd not cop it from his superiors for not being on deck when the train pulled in. He thanked me, pumping my hand profusely before going to attend his duties.

I grabbed a taxi and got the driver to deliver me across town and up over the big hill to 185 Kitchener Rd where I surprised my Nanna Kavanagh and Betty who lived with her. I rang the farm from there. Within the hour I'd be in the bosom of my family. This Christmas I would spend with my loved ones, but by this time next year I'd be seven thousand miles away in the midst of a war in a foreign land.

* * * *

6
BACK IN HARNESS

Half way through the second week of 1971, I arrived back in Townsville by train on a moonless, warm night. The next morning at First Parade we were introduced to our new Sergeant: Sergeant R.C. O'Brien, known to one and all as "Boris". Boris replaced Filewood who had been transferred over to Nine Platoon during our break. Boris was rotund, to say the least, with a jolly, full-moon-shaped face, but a dry, sarcastic tongue to go with it. I've no idea where he'd been up until now.

Upon returning, I had in my possession a small, black, opal stone which I'd noodled from the side of a mullock heap on the Garwin Opal Fields during my break. These fields are about thirty kilometres west of the Lighting Ridge Opal Fields in north-west New South Wales. They are only twenty kilometres south of Beefwood Downs. Using an old mining mate's — called Gardner — cutting gear, I cut and polished the stone myself and now I was certain I could sell it around town for a reasonable sum to help prop up my next fortnight's Army pay.

With that in mind, after we'd been dismissed for the day the first afternoon back, I hit the streets of Townsville in search of a buyer for my stone. It was a lot harder then I thought it would be, trudging around the hot streets from one Jeweller's to another trying to convince one of them that this little stone was a genuine black opal and that it was indeed mine to sell, as I'd cut it myself.

My search led me to the intersection of Stanley Street and Sturt Street and, finding no more retail shops beyond this point, I started back down the left side of Stanley Street. Inside a small Material Shop I caught a glimpse of a real, good-looking sort and decided on the spur of the moment to pop in and say hello. Not being at all sure how it went on that first brief encounter, I moved on down towards the main drag (Flinders Street) and, as a result of curiosity more than anything, discovered a small Executives Bar.

I'd pushed open a very ordinary door — one back from the large inviting main doors of the Louths Hotel and, to my delight, entered this wonderful, empty haven. A small bar with six bar stools faced the entrance. On both sides of the door stood a small table and clustered around each table were four chairs. The plush, dark-blue carpet completely hushed any footfall, while soft lighting added atmosphere. The room was cooled by a hidden air-conditioner, but best of all, it was quiet, locking out the outside world. Contenting myself with just two cold beers in this place for the present, I continued to scour the town for the rest of that afternoon looking for a buyer of my stone.

During the third day back at work, Corporal Jim Pollard found me and told me that the newly installed Platoon Commander of Eight Platoon really wanted to see me. I was to go over to C Company HQ and present myself to him.

'Fuck 'im, I donn wanta see im at all,' was my immediate retort. After all, I'd only ever volunteered to be Filewood's

Batman just to get us through Canungra. I had no intention of keeping on in that position now that we were back in Townsville and back as I thought into our normal roles.

'You will go over there an' see him now,' Jim ordered, getting all serious with me.

"Ow will I know 'im?' I asked, with raised eyebrows. Most of us had not laid eyes on him as yet.

'Aw, you'll know 'im when yer see 'im, 'ez about this tall an' 'ez got blue eyes,' Jim told me, while holding his hand up, palm down about one-point-two metres off the ground. Disgruntled, I wandered over to CHQ.

At the top of the stairs there were a few blokes poking about from room to room, but as none of them took any notice of me, I proceeded to find the door that would lead me to our as yet unknown fearless new leader, the one and only Second Lieutenant Peter A. O'Brien.

Above an open doorway it read 8 Platoon, so I waltzed in. Seated behind a large desk which undoubtedly looked bigger because of his dimunitive size sat the new Boss. All I could see of him was that he had a rounded face, was wide between the eyes and had reasonably broad shoulders. I strolled up to the front of the desk and made a point of leaning on it with my left hand face down on the top. My right thumb and forefinger were spread and resting at the top of my right, cocked-up hip, the other three fingers loose.

'Yeah, yur wanna see me?' I offered by way of introduction.

He looked up from some paperwork in front of him startled and demanded. 'Who are you?'

'Bishop,' I answered, brightly.

'Stand up straight, an' you call me Sir, an' you salute an Officer when you address them,' he ordered, loud enough that the entire building could have heard him.

I stepped back, throwing him a sloppy salute, while thinking to myself, '*God, are we are gunna have some fun with this prick.*' I lent on the desk again. 'Yur wanna see me, SIR?'

'Yes, I hear that you don't want to be my Batman. Is that right?'

'That's right, Sir, I don't,' I assured him.

He stared at me with a pair of piecing, light-blue eyes that seemed to drill right through me and lock onto the top of the door behind me as if I did not exist at all, as he snarled in no uncertain terms.

'You are, whether you like it or not,' then he got louder, 'Now, get over there and wash my shirt and trousers out.'

"Over there" was over in his room in the Officers' Quarters, which were just away from the Officers' and Sergeants' Mess. I did as he ordered.

Next day I was called into his office again and, upon entering, adopted the exact same approach as the previous day.

'Yeah, yur wanna see me?'

This time there was no dressing down as expected. Someone must have got to him since my last encounter with him and told him that we were not saluting Officers in this outfit. Instead he hissed at me. 'You didn't starch my shirt and trousers out. Now, get over there an' starch my shirt and trousers out.'

I stepped back from the desk rubbing my forefinger and thumb together a couple of times before presenting an empty palm to him down low as I told him, 'C'mon, I'm not forken out forut.'

'Oh, awright then,' he said, standing to fish two dollars out of one of his pockets before handing it to me.

At the sink in the laundry, armed with the freshly bought packet of starch, I ran some water. In went his shorts and in went half a packet of starch. I then filled in half an hour of time in his room looking at the regalia that he was expected to wear for formal functions and on the parade ground. I strapped on his ceremonial sword for size, unsheathed it and swung it about. Nice balance. Finally, I went back to the sink and took his shorts out to the line where I pegged them straight onto it to dry all day in the tropical sun.

The next morning, I was called back into his office. Again, I fronted his desk with the now familiar stance and repeated. 'Yeah, yur wanna see me?'

'What did you do to my trousers? They were like boards this morning when I tried to put them on,' he roared at me, his round face red and contorted, his blue eyes fairly blazing.

'I starched them Sir. You said starch 'em, so I did.' I responded with the innocence of primary school kid.

'Get out of this office. You're not my Batman while ever we are in town again. Now get out of here,' he exploded, standing to point at the open doorway behind me.

Beaming with glee, I stepped back from the front of the deck and threw the shortarse Officer the finest stiffest most proper salute he would ever be likely to receive in his entire life, quipping as I did so, 'Thank you, Sir.'

Absolutely elated, I bolted from his presence. I'd still be his Batman while we were "out", but there'd be no more washer-woman hands for me.

I did another round of the town that afternoon endeavouring to unload my stone, to no avail, again stopping in at the little bar on the side of the Louths Hotel for a quick one before moving on. Late on Thursday I finally got rid of it at a shop that I'd been in on the first day, but for a reduced price of twenty-eight bucks. By this time I didn't care much, just as long as I got something for the bloody thing.

I went back to the little bar to celebrate my sale and stayed a little longer this time. From that time on if anyone wanted to find me after knock-off (which would have been most unusual), then on almost any weekday afternoon until around seven o'clock, this is where I'd be. I'd put a couple of dollars on the counter and tell the girl to hunt me when it was gone. When I wanted another charge, I'd tap a twenty-cent coin on the counter and the girl would appear through the door from out in the main bar with a full glass for me and dutifully take the price of it from my cash pile.

Stanley Street was almost always near deserted by the time I emerged from the sanctuary of the air-conditioned bar and as I'd cross over to the other side heading down towards Flinders Street (usually at an acute angle) the effects of exposing myself to the warm, tropical air were evident by my unsteady gait. I'd head straight down to the Broadway Café opposite the Railway Station for a nice big T-bone steak and veg for my evening meal. Having satisfied my culinary needs thus, I'd then hop two doors up to The Raymonds to fill in the rest of the night dancing and drinking.

However, there are always exceptions to the rule and these started on the first Friday night of the first week back. It was decided by our NCOs during the day that we had to give the

Boss a proper "get-to-know-you party". We were to all meet up at the Exchange Hotel down on the waterfront end of Flinders Street at seven.

By seven-thirty, all of a very merry Eight Platoon, less the new Boss, were ensconced in the back bar, which was behind the door down past the main bar of the quaint old pub. Not waiting for the guest of honour the boys got into a strange game, whereupon someone like John McKinly would begin to hum and all the seasoned soldiers gathered would follow suit, then point an accusing finger and slowly move it around the room until they all stopped on one bloke. That bloke would then be expected to recite a poem or sing a song. The funny thing was, no one ever seemed to fully get through their rendition before they were humming and pointing again amid much laughter as the beer flowed freely.

It was late before "his nibs" showed up. He was escorted into the back room by two of our number — don't know if they went and found him or not. He was all smiles as he entered. He'd only just got through the door into the back room when Mullen, with an enormous grin on his thin face, started to sing, 'Four foot two, eyes of blue, has anybody seen our boss?'

There was a howl of laughter and clapping. Every time the short bloke started to talk that night -especially when he was hummed and pointed at — we'd all break out with, 'Four foot two, eyes of blue, has anybody seen our boss?'

He did manage to tell us that he'd spent most of his induction night pissing on out in the Blue Room at the airport. Party pooper!

At the beginning of the second week back, I was sent over to

Battalion HQ running an errand for someone or another and when returning from there I walked right past a young Sub-Lieutenant (a One Pipper, also known as a "ninety-day wonder") between D and C Company HQ buildings and failed to salute him.

'Err, Digger?' He called after me, in a very authoritative tone.

I turned around slowly to face him. I had just been given the highest accolade any man in the free world could ever be given. I was a Digger; an Australian Digger. This Officer had just said so. I felt like I was three metres tall. My ego was puffed up like that of a tormented Bearded Dragon.

'Yeah?'

'Do you know what these are?' he asked, leaning towards me and pointing at the one bit of brass he carried which was attached to his epaulette.

'Pips Sir,' I answered merrily, knowing full well I was not supposed to officially call them that, while noticing for the first time just how really young he looked.

'Do you know what you're supposed to do when you see them?' he asked, staring at me.

'Yeah, salute 'em Sir.'

'Are you going to salute me then?' he demanded.

'Nuh,' I shot back at him.

'Why not?' he retorted, a look of surprise on his face.

'Cause we're be'n tort not tuh,' I told him, simply, and with that I turned about and walked away from him. There was a shocked pause. I was four metres from him when I heard him call. He was ropeable.

'Digger, Digger, come back here, Digger,' he yelled after me. Glancing over my shoulder I caught a glimpse of him repeatedly stomping the ground with one foot as he bellowed at me. Then he changed tact.

'What's your name, Digger?' He called out, as the distance between us lengthened.

'Find out.' I yelled back at him, in a loud, clear voice and kept on going. I was still laughing by the time I got back to our lines.

On the second Saturday night back at the end of January, Dogsbody and I were down at The Raymonds when we got talking to some "long hairs" who'd just arrived in Townsville from Wollongong, the Steel City, sixty-four kilometres south of Sydney. They were keen to get to know a few of the locals, but I don't think Dogsbody and I really qualified; nevertheless, we got stuck into the grog with them. When we left The Raymonds late — or early in the morning as the case was — they invited us around to where they were staying whilst in town for a few more beers.

Six of us piled into an old, dark-green '56 model *FJ Holden* Sedan. I was absolutely rapt. I love these cars and thus far I'd owned two of them: one, a ute my younger brother Paul rolled one day on the farm chasing a fox; the other, a car into which we'd put the running gear out of the ute and which I rolled on the Old Cootamundra Road on the way into Temora from our farm, on my little sister Cathy's eighth birthday. I had my youngest brother, Frank, with me as a passenger at the time. No one got hurt in either prang although both *FJs* were too bent to drive again.

When it came time to call it for that night, I ventured outside and curled up on the back seat of the *FJ* to crash. The next thing I know I'm on the back floor of the car having just been flung forward with a jolt. Instantly awake, I quickly discovered that it was around seven o'clock on a very bright, sunny morning. Dogsbody was sitting up behind the wheel laughing. We were at a big intersection of unknown streets in a part of town that was completely foreign to me. We cruised about for half an hour or so before taking the car back to where it belonged.

The small, young, long-haired bloke who owned the *FJ* did not seem too perturbed about Dogsbody's jaunt in his car when we returned to their place for breakfast, so I presumed he'd given "the body" permission to take her out for a spin while I was asleep — although, I must admit, I had grave fears at the time that we'd gone drive-a-bout without permission

The decision was made that we'd all ferry over to Magnetic Island around ten o'clock for a spot of fishing. I'm not really a fisherman of any sort, so while the *FJ* owner clambered between the huge boulders making his way along to the point on the south side of our little bay at Acadia, I went back to the pub to secure a small cargo of stubbies before following him out there.

Upon arrival at his location with half a dozen fresh mini-bottles of beer tucked under my arm, I came across a very angry little man standing on a big rock. He was in the process of throwing nigh on two pounds of green prawns into the restless, emerald-coloured waters, where they heaved against the barnacle-encrusted rock a couple of metres below him.

'Ere, yer might as well 'ave the fucken lot, yer bastards,' I heard him cry out in anguish as the bundle of prawns he'd hurled hit the water with a splash and quickly sank.

'Geeze, wottayuh doen?' I asked in surprise.

'They took all me 'ooks!' he exclaimed. 'They're got teeth. They chewed me line right off. Git a load a this?' he added, holding up the line to show me. I must have developed a real dumb look on my face by this, as I'd never heard of such a thing as fish with teeth, so he pointed to the one small fish on the white, sandy soil amid the rocks beside him, which he had managed to catch, and growled, 'ave a look at that one.'

I prised open the mouth of his catch and found a bunch of long, very sharp teeth at the front end of its pointed jaw.

'Ere, giveus one of them,' he said, in a frustrated voice and pointing at the beers.

We sat to drown our sorrows and watched the ocean do its thing for a bit until the cargo was done and then adjourned to the pub for the rest of the day. We parted company late that afternoon in Townsville with Dogsbody and I going back to Lavarack and the Southerners heading back down to Wollongong, topping the old *FJ* up with used sump oil from out the back of Service Stations all the way through.

The next week and weekend were uneventful. Then, on the Monday morning of what was the last full week of January, we were given five days of rations and being fully "brassed up", were trucked out on the first "Exercise" since Canungra. This was to last four days. I think they thought we were a bit soft after being down south for a month over the Christmas holidays and sitting around the camp since we got back, so it was time to get us fit again. We were taken up to High Range and put through a series of route marches. On the fourth day Jim Pollard came around to give us our O Group (orders for the day).

'Do yur want the good news or the bad news first?' he asked, laughingly.

'We'll take the bad news first,' we assured him.

'Well the good news is we're going home in the morning; the bad news is we've got ten thousand metres t'march t'day to the pick-up point.'

It was between three-thirty and four o'clock in the afternoon when we finished that march at a very exposed place on rough, rocky ground and that day had been the hottest day of the whole of January, I'll swear. Dogsbody and I tried to share the same small one-point-five-metre high bush as we crawled in underneath it for its diminutive shade, but Dogsbody was crook and started to spew. He was as red as a beetroot and as listless as a worn-out, near-to-death, newborn pup. We poured water on him to cool him down some, but that didn't help much so they decided to send for a chopper to take him out.

Just before dark that evening a RAAF Iroquois Helicopter left our location for Townsville Hospital with Dogsbody on board suffering from a bad case of heat exhaustion. There was not a great heap of room on the little clearing we were occupying and as the chopper lifted him out to the north of our position, it clipped the top of a big, old, dead tree, showering little bits of broken wood back down amongst us. Moody was back at base by the time we got back there.

I popped in to see the girl in the Material Shop when I got back in and asked her to come over to Magnetic Island with me on Saturday next for a first date. She was a bit unsure, but tentatively agreed. Unfortunately for me, there was a mob of our blokes over there that weekend and the day didn't go too well, with drunken louts hitting on her nearly right from the start. She left in a filthy mood on that afternoon's boat and I have not seen nor heard of her since. It wasn't meant to be, I guess.

Extracting my half-drunk self from The Raymonds one night during the week just after this, I found Obie O'Brien of Melbourne asleep on the front entrance of a shop two doors north of the Club. It was one of those old-style shops, the front of which had large display windows almost to floor level on each side, a built-up wooden walkway flanked by two more like windows running at angles leading back to the double doors which led into the business.

Obie had literally crashed on this stepped entrance way. He had a broken stubby bottle beside his outstretched hand, which lay lifeless in a pool of spilt beer. I bent down and listened to see if he was still alive. He was breathing slow and strong, so I got one of our blokes who was passing by to help me and together we dragged him to the gutter. Propping him between us, we hailed a taxi which was trawling the street and which, fortunately, stopped for us. With some difficulty because of his rotund shape and his unconscious state, we managed to manoeuvre him into the taxi and away we went out to camp.

At Lavarack I got under Obie in a fireman's lift and carried him up two flights of stairs to the floor of our digs and once in his room dumped him on his bed as was. Next morning, while I was in the process of dressing in my greens to go down to the Mess for breakfast (one pint of milk), Blue McNiven dropped into our room.

'You'd better go an' get yur mate awake, 'e'll miss First Parade if yuh don't,' he announced to me.

'My mate?' I asked in surprise, looking around at the others in the room. 'Who yur callen "me mate"?'

'O'Brien,' came Blue's answer.

'E'snot my mate,' I retorted.

'You brought 'im 'ome larss night an' carted 'im up to 'is room.'

'Yeah' well, 'e was crashed out with a broken bottle beside 'im, wodja 'spect me t'do?'

'I dunno, but e'snot up yet.'

'OK, I'll see wot I can do,' I assured him, so that he'd go away and leave me to my dressing.

Annoyed, I went along the verandah and into Obie's room to find him still fully clothed in his last night's civvies and still out cold, exactly where I'd left him around four-and-a-half hours earlier. I shook him repeatedly to no avail.

'Obie, Obie, c'mon wake up will yuh, yur'll miss First Parade, yuh prick, c'mon.'

When after a couple of minutes of this sort of stuff he still did not respond in the slightest, I pulled him off the bed into another fireman's lift and carried him into the shower room which was nearly next door to his room. I gently lowered him into one of the cubicles and, propping him up in the corner at the back and stepping to one side, I turned the cold water tap full on. Water hissed from the rose raining down on the prone O'Brien. I left him thus, and returned to my own room to finish up my own morning preparations.

Once ready for the day, I ventured back along the verandah to see how Obie was fairing.

'Es still out,' someone told me, earnestly, as I entered the shower room. 'See,' he said pointing towards the cubicle.

There was Obie still propped in the back corner as I'd left him fully dressed, soaked through from head to toe and sleeping like a baby with cold water pouring down on his midrift. I left him there. When his name was called out on the First Parade, I lowered my head, changed my voice slightly and uttered the obligatory 'urt' to cover for him.

Then, on another occasion around about this time a mob of us had gathered in the front bar of the Louths Hotel. I don't really remember the reason for the gathering — perhaps it was someone's birthday or some such thing — but at any rate the place rocked and the grog flowed freely among the Charlie Company boys who had assembled there. Suddenly, Clarkey said to a couple of us who were standing together in the middle of the large front room, 'Let's light Chaddy up.'

'Woddya mean, light 'im up?' one of the boys asked the most obvious question for all in the group.

'Youken light 'im up, c'mon I'll show youse,' said Clarkey, grinning gleefully, and with that he led us over to the long bar at the back of the room where Seven Platoon's Sergeant, Garry Chad, was holding sway with another group of Diggers in civvies.

Chaddy was a big man, about ninety-three kilos of solid muscle. He was one hundred and eighty centimetres tall, and had huge arms on very broad shoulders. His torso tapered down to his hips. Compared to the rest of him his legs looked small, but they could carry him swiftly over any terrain fully-packed; in fact his size made his back-pack look like a kid's school lunchbox on his back. I'd witnessed rough, rock-covered ground appear to give way to him as he approached it. His dark brown hair was brushed back off his wide, wrinkled brow and he always looked like he was happy enough to be just where he was at that given time. He also had a very full chest of thick, black, curly hair.

Clarkey undid the buttons of Chaddy's pale-blue, light cotton shirt all the way from the top down to belt-buckle. Then, with a wicked grin, he produced a thin, disposable cigarette lighter from his pocket and thumbed the reel. A small flame ignited at the top of the device which Clarkey then touched to the hair down around Chaddy's belly-button. Chaddy's belly hair caught on fire, and a golden flame quickly spread upwards towards Chaddy's chin.

Clarkey patted the flame out as a cloud of blue smoke that reeked of burnt hair rose into the air above us. Chaddy drank on oblivious.

'Do ut agan,' we all urged, having been privy to this spectacle for the first time. Clarkey obliged, lighting up the big Sergeant's exposed chest once again. Again, we patted him out and, as before, the "burnt hair" smelling smoke filled the air above us and wafted about the place.

Our contingent moved away from the bar area then with Chaddy, as he wandered off with a fresh full glass of beer in hand. Almost as soon as he got settled near the middle of the room, Clarkey lit him up again. We laughed and patted him out.

Of course, by this time we had attracted the attention of the Hotel's four rather large, impeccably-dressed Bouncers. In their white shirts black pants and ties they'd gathered near the bar observing us and then they advanced on us.

'You blokes will have to stop that or we'll have to put youse out,' they told us, sternly.

Within seconds and with no rehearsal Sergeants Barry

Filewood, Garry Chad, Dusty Miller and about twenty fit, battle-ready, rearing-to-go young Diggers formed a resolute half-moon around the four Bouncers.

'Yeah, an' you an' who's army's gunna do that?' came the retort from one of the Sergeants.

With black looks, the burly Bouncers turned on their heels and strode straight back to the bar where they stood eyeing us off warily.

'Quick, quick light 'im up agan,' was the response, and we did. A very merry night ensued for all of us.

I copped a Kitchen Duty along with a couple of others about a fortnight before we were due to go out bush again. Kitchen Duties wasn't much more then going over to the kitchen on the proscribed night and helping the cooks clean up and wash the place out after everyone had finished their evening meal. It was, however, a real pain because the detergent they used for this job dissolved the glue that held the sole onto one of the types of boots the Army were using at the time. So, invariably, I was now going to have to break in another pair of boots even though the ones I was wearing at the time were not all that old. Never mind; the job got done in good time and I managed to get into town early enough that night to be suitably dry in the mouth the following morning.

When we got over to the Mess, however, there were no milk cans out for us to breakfast on. A bit of a line was starting to form up around the middle of the Mess Hall where they were usually stationed. There were restless mutterings amongst the boys, but no one seemed to know what to do as we milled about waiting for the cans of fresh milk to appear.

Taking matters into my own hands, I went over to the counter at the back of the Hall that was the servery and put it to one of the cooks who was engaged in dishing up portions of greasy eggs and bacon, tomato and mash onto the empty plates of those blokes who had lined up for them, 'Ay mate, where's tuh milk?'

'Don't ask me mate, I jus work 'ere.'

'Smartarse prick. Why ain't et out?'

He turned to another cook behind him and asked, 'Where's thu milk? This bloke wants sum.'

'There sno milk,' the other replied, 'they'll have t'make do with this lot,' meaning, of course, his greasy offerings.

'Bullshit there snot, I saw some out there larss night,' I challenged him. 'We want our milk, we're dyen a thirst out 'ere.'

'Wait on, I'll go get a Sergeant,' he offered, and promptly disappeared around the stainless steel barrier which separated the serving area from the working parts of the kitchen out the back.

'Yeah, you do that,' I called after him.

The Sergeant Cook appeared around the side of the petition saying even before he got to me. 'There's no milk out there.'

'Fucken bullshit Sarge! I was on juty larss night an' I put a heapa milk in thu freezer out there.'

'OK,' he said, in annoyance. 'If youken find it, youken 'ave et.'

I turned to the assembled throng waiting at the place where the milk cans usually stood each and every other morning, and waving my hand to summon them over to me, I yelled out to them. 'If any of you blokes want sum milk, come wiff me.'

I was rushed.

'Eight of youse'll do,' I commanded. Eight of them quickly split off from the others and eagerly followed me around the partition and out the back to the big fridge door. I jerked it open and there were the four large, steel milk cans standing just inside the door where two other blokes and I had put them the previous night.

My men marched back into the Mess in triumph with the four cans of milk between them and dumped the precious cargo in its rightful place. The boys lined up with point in hand right back out through the Mess Room door that morning. Half those in Camp must have had "a really good night out" the evening before by the look of it.

As anticipated, the sole of my *Seal* boots started lifting the day after this, so it was off down to the Q Store to L and D (Lost and Destroyed) them. I returned to our rooms with a brand new pair of "*Dunlop* boots, black, GP, for the use of", which I now had to break in before our next trip out bush. I'd found the *Dunlops* tended not to lose their sole after a stint on Kitchen Duties.

Next morning in the shower what a picture I must have presented to anyone who may have looked, standing there in nothing but my birthday suit and my new boots. I'd discovered while I was droving that if you wet boots thoroughly and wear them all day until they dry to the shape and size of your feet, you will never get blisters from them.

That same morning we were informed that we might have to brace ourselves as there was a tropical cyclone brewing out to the south-east off Townsville and no one knew exactly where it was going to make landfall.

At about this same time, I turned twenty-one. I didn't tell a soul in Townsville. I didn't want a fuss; it was enough for me that my Mum, Dad and my Nanna Kavanagh had remembered and had sent me a card. When I stepped back from the desk behind which Shortarse sat as Pay Master to dutifully fire off the required salute, saying 'Pay correct, Sir', I had one hundred and sixty-eight dollars in my hot little hand. It was party time.

I hit The Raymonds at the usual hour and started with my customary fifty-fifties — which all the bar staff knew by now was my drink — with gusto, boring them into me until two-thirty closing. I was a bit pissed by that time and actually had a job to see the end of the street as I tumbled out of the Club with a mob of fellow revellers and looked north towards where the taxi rank was located about half way along the next block. It was just plain blurry. I staggered about for a bit, then deciding on a course of action, I tapped an anonymous, young, male person on the shoulder as he passed me and asked, 'Ay mate, gettus a taxi, willyuh? I'll be waiten for 'im over there.' I finished while pointing to the other side of Flinders Street directly opposite the Club door.

'Yeah, OK mate,' he replied, and it seemed to me at the time that he'd said it with genuine enthusiasm, so I knew I was right.

I strolled off the footpath and proceeded to make my unsteady way slowly across the four lanes of late-night traffic. I held my hands high and, although being temporally blinded when approached, I blocked the oncoming cars first one way and then the other until I was on the other side; whereupon I turned around and acknowledged the hecklers back from whence I'd come before decisively sitting down in the gutter to await my taxi ride home.

The next thing I recall is being awoken by a savage kick to my kidney region. I struggled to find consciousness immediately, but by the time I'd copped another two, good, hard kicks in the same place, I was aware enough to notice the gold emblem embossed on the middle of the door of the car at eye level right in front of me and that at least one of my attackers had extremely highly polished toes on wide, flat shoes. Without even looking up I said to the cop who owned the shiny shoes.

'Oh, good, you blokes 'ill take me 'ome, woncha?'

I'd been reliably informed that they would do this for Army personnel on occasions.

'Yeah mate, we'll take yur home, 'op in,' they told me as they helped me to my feet, opened the door and ushered me inside the Townsville Police patrol car.

Instead of going straight down Flinders Street and out to Camp like the taxis did, they went wandering about up some side streets into which I had never ventured and after a bit I put it to them. 'Ay, this'esnot the way 'ome! I thought youes said youes were taken me 'ome?'

They laughed. 'No mate, we've got a nice, warm cell for you for the night, round at our place.'

I became aware of being told to place my hands flat on the big, high desktop and having my legs kicked sideways apart as one of the coppers fished things out of my pockets, plonking my wallet and some loose change up on it in front of me. I perceived a glint of gold that blinked at me out of the silver. It was my onyx signet ring, but how it got up on the counter I did not know. I took it up and was putting it back on my finger where it belonged when a dire struggle broke out between one of the young coppers and I over it, leading to both of us pulling in opposite directions. 'Awe, c'mon, I won't choke meself with this thing,' I told him. Then, all of a sudden, it hit my senses like a hammer: These bastards are putting me in gaol.

I dropped everything and done a bolt out through an open door into the dark.

'Like fucken 'ell yuh'ar,' I let fly at them as I went.

They grabbed me. I had one young cop gripping an arm each on either side of me. I don't know how I managed to get rid of the one clinging to my right arm, but suddenly he wasn't there so I turned my right hand into a fist and was in the process of swinging it around my body to thump my other aggressor in the gut when in mid-swing I changed my mind, opened my hand and with fingers fully extended made contact. I squeezed hard and twisted vigorously. He let me go. I ran again, but got nowhere. I was caught almost immediately and both my arms were twisted up high behind my back — I was lifted so high that my dangling toes barely touched the ground.

'I got 'im boys,' said the olive-skinned, round-faced, fat, Italian Mafia Boss look-a-like Sergeant of Townsville Police; and he did have too. I fought with all my might. I bit, hit, kicked, rolled and twisted — I was not going quietly. With one of them lifting a leg each and the Sergeant handling my arms, they were literally forced to carry me off to the cells. It took all three of them to throw me in.

I was as mad as mad could be with myself as I lay there on the cold, hard, concrete floor. My old man was right when he'd warned me some years back that 'you can never trust a copper'.

I was also spewing about the fact that my miserable, skinny sixty-six-kilogram, wringing wet body had let me down.

I was still fuming when half an hour or so later they were at the door again. They rattled the lock; the door opened and they appeared with none other than the 2IC of our Section, Lance Corporal Ian Anderson, in tow. He was poked through the door without him giving the slightest bit of fuss. I took from his demure attitude that he'd most likely been in boob before. Once inside, he merrily asked his young gaoler, 'Hey mate, can'ya gettus a couple a blankets? It gets kinder cold in these places overnight.'

'Yeah mate, I can do that,' the cop told him, then turned to address me, sitting defiantly in the back corner. 'Wotta'bout you, you want one too?'

I glared at him, but did not utter a word. He left, to return quite quickly with two thin, tightly-woven, grey blankets. He handed one to Andy who thanked him politely. He threw the other one at me. He hadn't even finished locking the door on the outside before Andy was gleefully spreading his blanket out on the cell floor just near the door as if he were unrolling a swag an saying as he did so, 'Arr, this is thu way t'go.'

He curled up on it and inside a minute he was asleep and snoring loudly, while I fumed on in silence for a bit more, before eventually I too succumbed to my predicament and, rolling myself in the thin, dark blanket, I went to sleep.

They came to get us around seven in the morning and while I was shoving my possessions that they'd confiscated from me some hours before deep into the pockets of my "go to town" trousers, the young cop behind the counter piped up with,

'You'll be a little bit more co-operative next time we bring you in, wonjah?'

I just glared at him with a look of utter contempt; what more could I do. They drove us out to Camp and dumped us off at the gates outside our Guard House, giving us just enough time to walk in, get dressed and be ready for First Parade.

I was back in town that night and Saturday night as well. On Sunday night I was forced to retire halfway through the evening as by then I was stony broke and walking — well, not quite walking. I did manage to share a taxi home with some bloke, but I was busted after that.

On Monday morning, I was summoned to Major Boxall's office. 'About this thing with the Police in town on Thursday night, want me ta fix it up for yur?' he asked, solemnly.

'Sir,' I answered, briskly, relieved that he had some magical way to make it go away with no effort on my part. I didn't ask how; it was enough to know that he could do it.

Two days later when we were due to go out on our second excursion into the bush on Exercise Third Stab, Tropical Cyclone Gertie — which had at first gone south-east — had now turned around and was almost upon Townsville. Exercise Third Stab was going to be conducted up at Mt Spec and it was designed to show us just what we could expect to be doing in Vietnam when we got over there. The Battalion, despite being fully packed and ready to go was now confined to Barracks for the foreseeable future. A nervous anticipation prevailed among the troops as we hung about our rooms waiting it out as an eerie silence and a strained restlessness pervaded the entire area. Very low clouds completely covered the sky, looking for all the world to me like enormous running guts of sheep joined together by invisible thread. All day they rolled in menacingly from the south-east, passing quickly overhead and curving away to the north.

To keep myself fully occupied that day I pulled out my little tubes of oil paints, which I carry everywhere I go, and proceeded to paint a beautiful Crown and Anchor table on a spare Hutchie. The small Army-issue, plastic bottle of tick repellent proved an excellent replacement for thinners. My only concern was whether it was going to dry before we copped it. I didn't have to worry though as the ambient air although, laden with moisture, was still warm enough to do the job well.

As it turned out, however, during the night the storm crossed the coast at Cardwell about one hundred and sixty kilometres north of Townsville and was downgraded to a Tropical Depression which caused little or no real damage to people or their property in that region. So, around eight-thirty the following morning — only one day late — it was, 'Hurry up, the trucks will be here any minute.' These arrived at the 4RAR lines at nine o'clock and it was 'all aboard' and away we went.

* * *

7
THIRD STAB

When our transport convoy of drab, olive-green, six-wheeled *International* trucks turned north onto the Ingham Road out near the airport we saw for the first time the newly-constructed and recently opened hotel/motel on our left.

'There's a swimming pool in the roof,' someone informed everyone within earshot on the back of the exposed cattle truck.

'I wodden mine see'n that.' I mused, as the truck driver changed up another gear and we trundled by.

Shallow water ran across the tarred road in many places and at one stage a great cascade of white, foaming water could be seen high up to our left, spewing out of the top of the range and over a huge, exposed, dark-coloured rock face.

Eventually the convoy halted at a T-junction where a smaller gravel road left Ingham Road and went straight west somewhat shy of Ingham itself. It was 'everybody out', and now came the waiting part, and wait we did, literally for hours in oppressive heat and humidity that felt like a heavy blanket was wrapped around us under increasingly low, dark cloud.

While the majority of us told yarns, joked among ourselves and generally twiddled our thumbs, Charlie (Hilly) Hill from Mulgoa near Penrith, west of Sydney, and Paul (Pig) Pratt from a suburb of Brisbane — Four Sections First and Second Scouts respectively — again pulled out a pack of cards. Facing each other crossed-legged in the long grass, Hilly and Pig entertained themselves for the duration of our forced stay by the roadside playing two-handed Euchre.

As dinner camp approached, some bright spark — probably Blue McNivin — asked Boris, 'Yuh gunna lete s'go into thu pub for a counter lunch, Sarge?'

'An' wot pub would that be?' Boris came back, with a smirk on his face.

'Them 'ouses youken see just up there, that's the outskirts of Ingham, Sarge, ask Day, 'eze from round 'ere an' 'e says so.'

'Be a long walk f'nothen if eze wrong, don't yuh think? B'sides, yur got perfectly good water on yuh, drink that if yur getten dry,' was his comeback. That settled it. There'd be no pub for us today then.

At three-thirty in the afternoon, a couple of choppers whopped their way into our position and, under a blanket of very low, thick cloud, lifted us slowly high up and south-west into the Paluma Range.

It had been decided by the "powers" that Charlie Company would ambush a logging track for the night. With the "killing ground" selected, the Company went to ground up the side of a very steep slope to the north of it. Just after dark, with us all settled down in pairs, it started to rain, but this was no ordinary rain, this was a tropical downpour. It came down in torrents for what seemed like more than half the night, leaving us soaked to the skin with cool water running down the hill and through us.

The party of 6RAR blokes, who were playing our enemy on this trip, decided that this was the best time to walk through our killing ground; and walk through it they did, completely unopposed. When they got no response from their first pass, they turned around and marched right back through us again. Again, nothing happened; and anyway, I reckon the blokes down in the front manning the actual "kill" site would not have been able to see "the enemy" out there in front of them even if their lives depended on it, so heavy was the rain and so black was the night.

But ambush them we would, so on their next sweep through the "killing" ground, they actually yelled and cooeed out to attract the attention of their would-be attackers. There was a feeble attempt to engage, which we barely heard from our position up on the slope. Stuff 'em. No one for real would be out walking about on a night such as this.

Because of his greyhound-like disposition, Muzzy, who I'd been paired with, didn't have a lot of meat covering his bones and other organs. As the intensity of the rain dropped away a bit and the wind got up to roar through the treetops above us, he started to shiver uncontrollably, a little at first, then more and more. I realized that if he kept this up we'd both get no sleep at all for the night, so I suggested he lay with his back to mine so that he could at least warm up his kidneys. Eventually, in the early hours of the morning he was still; only then could we rest.

The next morning we walked a long way to the south. It was like they had dumped us in the wrong place in the dull light of the cloud-shrouded mountain last evening and now we had to make up the kilometres by route march. Around two in the afternoon, the RAAF came back with a chopper to give us a demo on how they use the winch, which is attached just above one of the doors of the aircraft for extracting personnel up out of country where it's too thick to actually get a chopper down onto the ground by them.

They put their charge on the ground and we gathered around to listen to the pilot give us a bit of a chat about how not to touch the steel mesh, basket-type litter which they'd be lowering down to us until it had touched Mother Earth so that it got grounded out, because the machine would built up static electricity while it was in flight. According to the spruiker, this build-up would be worse if the aircraft had flown through an electrical storm.

They took off to give us a practical demo then, leaving a RAAF crewman — complete with the full-frontal, zip-up, pale-green jumpsuit and obligatory dark sunglasses — as ground crew. Incredibly, as the chopper rose, buffeting the troops below with its downdraft and flew a little way to the west, it passed right through a small, fast-moving electrical scud before returning to hover just above the Charlie Company personnel. The scud then caught up with it and joined in the proceedings, so as the chopper hovered slowly lowering the mesh basket, giant drops of water were hammered down upon our upturned faces.

I was forced to turn away from the action when a supersonic raindrop powered into my eyeball causing it considerable pain. At that very moment, there was a collective cry of anguish from those assembled.

'Wot? Wot 'appened?' I asked of no one in particular, as I looked back.

'Didja see that? That bloke jus' got chucked arse over 'ed!' someone informed me.

'Nar, who? Wot 'appened?' I queried again.

'That RAAF bloke they left 'ere, 'e jus' grabbed thu basket before et 'it thu groun' an' soon as 'e touched et, et threw 'im arse over 'ed backwards.'

Some of the boys were on their feet in a flash and rushed to his assistance. They speedily strapped the injured RAAF bod into the mesh stretcher, whereby he was winched up and dragged into the bowels of the chopper and swiftly flown away to the Townsville Base Hospital for treatment. He was all right, they told us later.

That night, Muzzy was shivering again in the chill of a wet camp, so I again lay back to back with him to warn him up so that we both could get a little sleep.

Next day around ten in the morning, Charlie Company was strung out in single file, crunching down a slight, rock-infested slope, when Dogsbody slipped and twisted his ankle. A chopper was called and once again Dogsbody left the field of play early. Then, approaching dinner camp, the RAAF — flying Korean War vintage *Saber* Jets- began a mock bombing raid on a mountainside ahead of us. They flew straight at the hillside and then, smartly pulling out, would go near-vertical up the side of the slope, leaving in their wake a noise that sounded for all the world like they'd actually dropped bombs up there.

A little later we were dining out on a very damp, grassy flat with a couple of Hereford cows contentedly grazing near by when Jim Pollard came over to us to tell us, 'There'll be some high-ups coming around soon to ask us about our rations.'

'Where are they? Let me attem, I'll tell em a thing or two about 'em,' I offered, teasingly.

Jim glared at me with a look that could kill. 'You will say nothing if they come here,' he ordered.

'Yes, Sir,' I mocked, and quickly forgetting them went on nibbling at my dry biscuits that were covered with a measly, minute smear of butter and plum jam.

A chopper flew in and discharged its human cargo. After a short yarn with Major Boxall, the "high-ups" started to do their rounds. The trio had the red bands around their caps just like the Top Brass down at Kapooka so I took them to be "very high up indeed".

As I looked over my right shoulder at them — blow me down if they weren't making a bee-line for the party I was sitting with — like a magnet they seemed drawn directly to me and suddenly this tall, thin, sweet-smiling Officer of about forty-five to fifty years of age, going by the grey hair beginning to appear at his temples, was standing a metre from my back.

'G'day gentlemen, no don't get up,' he said, in a timid voice.

'*Yeah, as if we were going to anyway, especially in the middle of our hard-earned dinner,*' I said, under my breath.

'We're here to find out what you think about your rations.'

Without looking up at him, I let fly, 'There'snot enough in 'em.'

The big bloke was not the least bit perturbed even if Jim must have been, judging by the black look he threw at me when I quickly glanced his way.

'Yes, we get that all the time, but really they have all the minerals and vitamins in there for your daily requirements and besides we have to make them small so that you blokes haven't got too much weight to carry around all day,' he told us, in a seriously patronising voice.

I found myself thinking as a silence ensued around us, '*Well, if yur not gunna fix ut, wot the fuck are yur doen out 'ere asken stupid fucken questions for then?*

With no one else near me prepared to chat to him, he piped up with, 'Carry on gentlemen,' and they moved away, leaving us to finish our lunch and make ready for the afternoon's ordeal.

Suddenly there was a rushing, screaming, roaring, rumbling, thundering sound almost on top of us. We ducked. It took a moment or two to fathom out that it was the Jets. They'd snuck up on us and were conducting what seemed like a mock strafing run very low over our position. Shit, they were loud.

After this it was another hot, humid march to somewhere south. Meanwhile, I started to feel the first prangs of "prickly heat" coming on that day. I knew from what my Dad had told me that's what this was. As the week progressed it got worse and by the time we finished this stint out, it was like a million needles were sticking into my back each and every time I shouldered my pack. I never told anyone — the last thing I wanted was for the Army to use this issue as an excuse to bush me to another Corps and then maybe send me over to Vietnam without my mates. As I'd told myself before down at Canungra, these are the blokes I wanted to do my time with over there, no matter what, and to that end I would prevail.

A day or two later, we were introduced to APCs (M113 Armoured Personal Carriers) for the first time. We'd spent the intervening period patrolling along the west side of the hills that the Jets had "shot up" and had now reached a flat piece of ground which looked like it was used as a staging place for a logging operation, going by the rough piles of logs strewn about. Just after lunch there came what sounded like a distant, low, growling hum of some huge insect. I couldn't ascertain exactly in which direction they were coming at us even when they were quite close to our static position; and even when we could plainly hear the constant revving up and down of their diesel engines, it was still impossible to tell. It sounded to me like we were bring surrounded by the bloody things.

Finally, three of them appeared, coming at us from the south-east. They came in fast, zig-zagging this way and that and one of them nearly stood on its nose as it stopped abruptly and turned smartly to one side to avoid hitting a tree. It was an impressive demo of their incredible manoeuvrability for our behalf, especially considering the weight of these things.

APCs are essentially big steel boxes on small tracks. As their name suggests, their main roll is to carry troops into or out of battle safely. They are, of course, highly efficient and very mobile gun-carriers as well, due in no small part to the fifty- and thirty-calibre machine guns they carried atop of them.

After they let us have a good look over the things and gave us a little talk on their usefulness in times of war, they decided that we needed to do a "running drop out". We'd be locked up inside and when the order was given, we'd step onto one side of the lowered back door that would constitute a platform and step off the fast-moving vehicle when told. That sounded easy enough — just step to the edge, estimate the speed we are moving at and with our feet already moving to counter the sudden contact with a stationary Mother Earth, we'd step off. That's the theory anyway. It always worked back home when we were jumping off the carry-all of our little red Fergie to run past it to open a gate. The APCs went a little faster then the Fergie, but I managed to land as expected and when I stopped running I sat down on the ground and looked around to see how the others were faring.

What a spectacle. The idea was that two APCs would go in the same direction about a hundred metres apart, dropping off Diggers at intervals of ten metres or thereabouts and the other one would cross from the beginning of one line of disgorged personnel to the beginning of the other line of disgorged personnel, dropping off its ten Diggers in the same manner as the other two, forming what could be described as a rough, u-shaped cordon.

No one had thought to tell these blokes how best to dismount a moving vehicle and now I sat and watched with bemusement as the boys were going A over T everywhere. People were literally flying through the air. There were bodies with arms, legs and rifles cart-wheeling, then crashing back to earth in a cloud of dust. I've no idea how no one got hurt — a broken ankle or something — but we all survived. Finally, when we'd all settled, they said, 'Well, that wasn't much good, waset? I think we'll try that again, only this time get yur legs runnen before yur 'it the groun'.'

And away we went again. This time it came off without a hitch and as everyone seemed happy with the result, they loaded us up with some of us on top and some of us in the hulls and shifted us further south again.

Around the middle of the afternoon on the eighth day, we congregated on a small ridge which consisted of rather large, very old, irregular, rust-coloured rocks. The sky was cloud-free. It was hot and the rocks offered little to no shade. From here we could see the silvery thread of a reasonably-sized river away to the west and as we were on the west side of the range it could be presumed that it should be running in a westerly direction away from our position.

As the afternoon progressed, it cooled a little. We ate at the usual time at around four o'clock so that by nightfall we were ready to roll again. Apparently, we had to be somewhere else that night, so eastward into the gathering gloom we strolled. After two hours or thereabouts, it became extremely dark. We'd turned little by little until we were travelling south-east. To maintain contact with the bloke in front of us and to keep this conga-line from disintegrating, we were ordered to hold onto the handle of the entrenching tool (small, fold-down shovel and light pick combined) strapped to the back of the pack of the Digger ahead of ourselves.

At about eleven, as near as I could tell, and without the slightest warning, the entire place was lit up by a brilliantly powerful, blindingly white-flashing light, followed immediately by the abrasive, vibrating crash of close-quarter thunder as we unexpectedly became engulfed in yet another tropical storm. The big raindrops that began to pound us almost from the onset of this display of the storm's intent were not the least bit cold. Within minutes it was bucketing down. We must have been following the spur of a fair-sized razorback ridge. With each savage flash of lightning we could see nothing but a gaping blackness out to the north-east and indeed falling rapidly away from our feet on both sides of us. We could only trust the powers now.

After another of the frequent stops a couple of hours later when the lightning had dissipated and the rain had eased to drizzle, I was still clinging to the shovel handle of the bloke in front of me when I was dragged slap-bang into a stick about ten centimetres thick and about forty centimetres high which lay horizontal across our path.

'Fuck!' I cried loudly to the night, as the shock and pain wracked my bony shin. Next thing there was a hushed message coming back along the line from those on high and up front.

'Who was that man?' was being passed slowly from Digger to Digger and, of course, when it come to me I immediately passed it on to the bloke behind me and listened as it went back beyond my field of hearing.

Presently, a second message came back to us and 'Don't know', went on from us to a forward position. Then, yet another message made its way back past us and on down the back. 'Find out.'

However, no one ever did. In fact, you have just become the first person to "find out". The powers must have seen how fruitless their endeavours were at that point, so they decided to put a stop to all this idle chit-chat going back and forth between us. Pity, as it was the only communication we'd had with our immediate neighbours all through this otherwise dull night.

The rain was finished as daylight was about to break in a sodden, eastern sky. By this time, our column was in fact heading towards where the sun would eventually rise. There was another very tedious delay enforced upon us by those up front. In a whispered message, it was eventually revealed to us that, 'a scout has been sent down to see if we could get across the creek'.

'Half his luck.' We could clearly hear the waters of a decent sized creek on our left to the north and a long way down from where we stood in silence in the inky blackness. How he was going to find his way across a fast-flowing stream without shining a light and giving away our position was beyond me. Perhaps this scout could actually see in the dark?

Eventually, they pointed us down the steep side of the razorback in the direction of the creek and we descended slowly and carefully towards it. I was about half way down that thirty-centimetre in forty-five-centimetre grade when they told us to halt and 'rest if you like'.

As the very first, tiny light of the coming day began to reveal a dull, smoky version of what was around us, I dropped onto my bum and lay gratefully back onto my pack. I could feel warm water filling my clothes and running on past me, but I was at that moment too buggered to care, so clutching tightly to my gat where it lay across my gut, I succumbed to my fatigue and was asleep in seconds.

It was fully light when I was raised by one of the boys — well, as fully light as the heavy, low cloud would allow. The trees were a lot sparser on the steep slope than I'd anticipated and the creek was making more noise now than before and seemed to be closer to us. I was tonguing for a smoke as were, I'd say, most of the other blokes in the Company and breakfast would have gone down real well too at this juncture. No such luck? Apparently, we needed to be somewhere else right now and that fact took precedence over all else, so we were quickly shuffled off at an angle down the slope towards the north-east. We encountered the noisy creek on the east side of where it curled around to make a bend. The muddy, brown water rippled along at a great rate of knots as it rushed past the front of us on a nor-nor-easterly path. The vegetation was thicker and lusher down here closer to the stream where we were going to cross. Obviously some poor cow had been snooping about in the growing dawn trying to find this place and had succeeded.

For the first time we all got to see a small village on the other side of that creek. It consisted of huts of a kind with which I was not familiar and there was smoke rising lazily from amongst them. There were people in black clothing wearing white coolie hats — this was the recognised uniform of the Viet Cong, who would be our enemy in Vietnam. It was also the national dress code of most of the residents in the small villages that we'd be likely to encounter when we got over there. This mob was seemingly poking about around the huts doing their morning chores. It all looked so authentic. So this is what it was all about? We were doing a surprise raid on a mock-up Vietnamese village to see if the mock-up Viet Cong (Members of 6RAR) were hereabouts.

Well, it was too late, they'd have seen us standing about on the wrong side of the fast-flowing creek gawking at them and doing very little else! Eventually, one very strong swimmer from our ranks was "volunteered" to ford the creek with a mob of our toggle ropes tied together and to him. He was swept downstream a little, but eventually got across safely and coming back to where he was opposite us, he tied the connected ropes off to a stout tree. Now it was our turn to breast the stream and breast it we did, literally. The cold, fast-flowing water was as high as our packs. It tugged at our legs, pushing and shoving and threatening to rip them out from under us. One behind the other we struggled slowly across, holding tight to the wet toggle ropes with one hand, our gats in the other, while easing our way along, up to our tits in the dirty, swirling liquid.

We must have fairly pissed off someone high up in the pecking order by being late, for no sooner then we were all gathered in a gaggle on the other side of the stream, than we were hassled back around the bend on the inside of it, which was flatter, and plonked down at set intervals in a line between the "village," and with our backs to the creek.

'You can eat now,' were our instructions once we got settled and thank Christ too as I was starving.

We got stuck into our wee tin of bacon and eggs while sitting crossed-legged in the long, lush, wet grass observing the goings on in and around the "village".

Apparently we were in a "Cordon and Search" exercise and we, Charlie Company, were the Cordon bit of it. It wasn't long before a member of Bravo Company strolled into our area. One of our blokes breakfasting near me knew him.

'G'day mate! Wodda you blokes doen 'ere? Wotyer up to?'

'G'day mate! 'Ow are yuh? We're gotta check an' see if there'snowone hidden in any 'oles down along thu bank down there, an' there'snow caches around 'ere. You ain't seen no one roundear this mornen, ay?'

'Nar mate! No one roundere but us.'

'OK. Well, we'll catch yer up later, mate, 'ay?'

'Yeah mate! Seeyuh, yuh dag.' And with that he moved away to the west of our static position. We hung around a bit and in the mid afternoon we moved north-east as a Company.

They harboured us up a little later then usual in close proximity to a very noisy lot of water, which I took to be a substantial waterfall. Having never being exposed to such a sound before in my short life, it kept me awake for the biggest part of that night.

By mid-morning on the tenth day of this excursion, we were mounting up in open trucks to be extracted from the top of the range via an old logging track. These were one-lane wide and cut into the sides of the hills. All seemed good at the start, but as you know, Murphy's Law can intervene at any time and so it was this morning. Half an hour or so into our tedious trek down the mountainside, the convoy was halted by a large fallen tree which lay at an acute angle up the slope, while its exposed butt with extended twisted roots was blocking a small portion of the carriageway. There wasn't much of it in the way, but it was enough.

The ground dropped at the same acute angle down from the other side of the track into a dark-green ravine below. There was a small V-shaped gap which had been carved out by running water and had crept in onto the track, so that the actual distance between the out-thrust roots and the inner edge of the V-shaped gap was smaller than the distance between the tyres of our transport.

With no chance of turning the convoy of six-wheeler *International* Army trucks around on the narrow logging track, another solution had to be found. It looked simple enough at the start; just hook onto the lower part of the tree and tow it out of the way. This strategy was executed almost immediately. The log did not budge an inch; the roots of it that were still hidden beneath the ground were stuck fast. A second truck was tied to the first one and they tried again with the same result. There followed a lot of discussion into which our Company Commander, Major Boxall, had a great deal of input, until a decision was reached. We were ordered to disembark from our trusted transport and walk on a little way past the offending tree to the downhill side of the stationary trucks.

Once we were all safely on the other side, it was time for the trucks to follow. The first one backed up a little, halted, then roared the engine into life and gunned it. It came hurtling toward the obstacle on the roadside at full revs in first gear. Its tyres squeezed within twenty-five millimetres of the up-thrusting roots on the right. They actually glided right over the V-shaped gap in the left hand side of the track. There was less than a half of each tyre on solid ground while the bigger portion was in mid-air as they careered over it. Bits of earth fell away into the ravine with the passing of each tread. We stood captivated as one by one the remaining trucks followed their leader, keeping exactly in the same track of the truck that had preceded them.

It was by far the most incredible feat of precision driving that you would ever want to bear witness to. I take my hat off to the courage, daring and skill of those extraordinary men, the Army drivers of those trucks that day. It was an absolute miracle that no one went over the edge to end up down in the bottom of that terrible ravine.

With that out of the way, we mounted up and rolled quietly down out of the ranges onto Ingham Road and home to Lavarack.

I rang home, as I always did on Friday evenings before going into town, to let them know how I was going and to see how things were down there. However, I was told by Jenny the ever-bubbly telephonist — who I nearly always managed to get to put my interstate calls through to Temora — that Dirnaseer 27 had been cut off. This was the telephone number of the Farm. I was a bit taken aback for a second. Mum owned a house in Temora at 76 Hoskin Street, so I asked Jenny to try the number which went with that address for me. She was happy to comply.

When Mum answered, I immediately put it to her, 'Wotta you doen there? Why aren't youse out at thu farm?'

To which she replied, 'Rathnells gave us a week to get out.'

'Why?'

'They've taken over as Mortgagee in Possession.'

'They can't do that!'

'Well, yes, they can, and they already have. As soon as you turned twenty-one they had the right to take over. We still haven't finished paying them for the place yet.'

'Yes, but how do they expect us to payem if there's no one on the place worken et?' It was so galling. What could I do from up here in the Army?

Dad bought the farm in my name when I was still sixteen. The intention was that he'd work it until I became of age, meaning that when I turned twenty-one I was legally the rightful owner and as such I was also legally the largest debtor. We had no way of knowing at the time of buying that we'd run into an extremely cold winter the year we took possession in 1967, or that then we'd endure the inevitable drought that usually follows such an event. Things were dire, but with time the place could have traded itself out of the trouble. In the six months I'd spent on the place, prior to being pressed into service in the Australian Army, we were fighting back; however, Rathnells had me over a barrel right now.

By the time I got into town that night, I was, to say the very least, really pissed off. Because I'd been "pressed into service" and was being "conditioned" to take my place over in Vietnam for the sake of all Australians, I had lost the family farm in doing so. Had I been down there at Temora at the time, I may have been able to prevent the expulsion of my Mum, Dad and seven siblings from their home. As it stood, I could do nothing of the sort. Australia was training me to be an assassin and that was the most important thing for Australia right now.

That night when we'd been bushed from The Raymonds at closing time, a handful of us were making our way towards the taxi rank up in the next block when we crossed paths with a mob of 6RAR blokes coming in the opposite direction. These were the blokes who had played our "enemy" while we were out last time on Exercise Third Stab. One of them — a Junior Officer who showed signs of being very drunk — tried to pick a blue with our bunch over nothing at all. I'd been lagging behind the others, but as soon as I picked up that it could be on, I was right there, and given the phone call I'd participated in with my Mum earlier that evening and the mood I was in right then, I was rearing to get stuck into anything that moved. I was certainly right up for a "barney" with this lot.

Suddenly, someone yelled out, 'RUBBER DUCKIE.'

The middle of Blackwood Street where it joins with Flinders Street was instantly filled with 4RAR boys as they came streaming from side streets to join our mob facing off with the 6RAR crew. One of the 6RAR personnel could see what was about to happen and earnestly communicated to their leader, the reckless young Officer,' Sir, c'mon, Sir, etsnot worth ut.'

Although the drunk Officer tried to extricate himself from the grip of the intuitive one, slurring, 'Carn, I'll 'ave yer,' his arrester hung on until he and the rest of the Officer's subordinates managed to haul him off out of harm's way. Oh, such an expedient move on their part.

A week or so later I was told to go over and see Major Boxall again.

'Wot'se want this time?' I quizzed Pollard, upon receiving my orders.

'I donn know, jus go,' he told me, pointing towards the CHQ buildings.

In Boxall's office, I stood to attention. 'Sir,' I said in a manner that told him I was acknowledging him as my superior at the same time as asking him why I'd been summoned to appear before him.

'At ease Private,' he said reassuringly, as he looked at me from behind his desk. He seemed relaxed enough, so I kinda knew that I wasn't in too much strife.

'You're having a bit of trouble on the home front, Private,' he told me rather than ask. I bristled up immediately. Pollard must have found out and pimped on me. *'Yeah, thanks Jim,'* I found myself thinking, *'this is none of his business.'*

To the Officer sitting in front of me, I merely said, 'Sir,' again, which was short for, 'Yes, Sir.'

'I've got a letter from a solicitor at Temora that states that you owe a fuel company in Temora a lot of money and that if you don't pay them up by the end of the month, they are going to take you to Court to redeem it.'

'So that was it. Jim hadn't put me in at all. Sorry Jim.'

'That'snot my debt Sir. It's thu farm's!' I hastened to inform Boxall.

'What would you like us to do about it?' he asked me then, which came as a bit of a surprise.

'Well, if yuh let me go down 'ome I could fix et up, Sir,' I assured him. It was a very long shot, but I had to attempt it.

He sat in silence seemingly looking at the grain in the wood of his desk for a moment or so before coming back to me.

'I can't do that,' he told me, solemnly, 'we've invested far too much money, time and effort into your training to just let you go now. You are a very valued member of this outfit. We'll be going to Vietnam soon and you don't really need this sort of worry on your mind while you're over there. I suggest that it might be best all round if you were to sign the farm over to your father for now so that you can concentrate on what's ahead of you over there.'

I was a little taken aback. He had spoken to me in such a fatherly manner. It was as if he thought I didn't know what was ahead of us in the not-too-distant future. Notwithstanding, Dad had been running the show down on the farm all the time I'd been away with Claudie roo shooting in '67, and droving from late '68 with Darby Neale at Brewarrina, so it seemed to be a reasonable option, given the circumstances.

I don't know what Boxall wrote to the Solicitor representing the fuel company, but that day I too penned a short letter relinquishing my stake in the farm ... until, or if ... I got home.

A week or so later on the night of the 8th of March, I was in The Raymonds once again. I'd been through my usual routine, that is, time at the hideaway in the side of the Louths, tea at the Broadway Café and now the Club.

I had just met a girl and was about to buy her first drink for the night when the Bouncer of The Raymonds came to me where I stood at the bar and asked, 'D'you wanna to see that fight?'

'Yeah, bloody oath, but 'ow?' I answered and asked in the same sentence. I knew he meant the fight that was about to take place between the world's two heavyweight champion boxers of the time, Mohammad Ali and Joe Frazier.

'Come wif me down thu back in thu kitchen, we can watch it there on their TV.'

I looked at him in astonishment. 'No! We can't do that. That's their private place,' I told him.

'Nar, its awright, you're wif me,' he assured me. 'C'mon.'

I dropped everything and eagerly followed him through the door on the right hand side the bar and into the kitchen area out the back of the restaurant.

Freddie Tim So, the small Chinese owner of The Raymonds and his diminutive wife, Rae, met me with beaming smiles and nods as if they knew exactly who I was. I felt most humbled that they would accept me into their home, a place I knew only a few outsiders had ever visited.

The Sos, the Bouncer and I watched the entire fight on a

small black-and-white television set which sat on their kitchen table. It was one hell-of-a-fight which went the whole fifteen rounds. Frazier won on points by a unanimous decision. At the end of the proceedings, I profoundly thanked the Sos for allowing me the opportunity of being entertained in their home and with more bobbing from both sides, I left their gracious company. The Club was full when I got back out into it.

Still revved up by the sensational blue I'd just been privy to, I breasted the bar to get myself a fifty-fifty when I was immediately accosted by an extremely irate woman.

'Where the fuck have you been? Why in fuck's name did you leave me here alone with all these drunken Army blokes for? I've been waiten ages for my drink,' she spat at me from a distance of at least fifteen centimetres.

I blinked at her. 'I'm Army too!' was my lame retort but, of course, I did go on to explain, 'I went to watch the fight.'

That didn't cut it with her at all and she upped me again about pissing off and leaving her to watch some stupid, bloody fight and not telling her.

'I'll get yuh that drink now if yur like,' I told her, earnestly. Lead balloon?

'You can stick it, I'm going home,' she hissed at me, and as her smiling friend raised her eyebrows and shrugged her shoulders at me, the wild one turned on her heels, threw her head back and marched through the Club and out the front door. I never had the privilege of her company again.

Then, one afternoon not long after this, I was sitting quietly on my own in the little hideaway bar in the Louths Hotel when the door squeaked behind me and the small room filled with light from the outside world. I turned to see four men dressed in suits and carrying briefcases enter one after the other. They seemed a jovial crowd who it appeared to me must have worked together somewhere in town, so I gave them little heed and got back to my beer in hand.

Next thing I know the smallest and elder one of their number, a rotund bloke, was perching himself up on the barstool beside me.

'G'day, I'm Harold Phillips, mind if I sit 'ere?' he said, by way of introduction.

'Nar mate, you're right,' I answered, taking his outstretched hand and shaking it while telling him who I was.

'You're with the Army?' he told me rather than ask, which would have been immediately obvious by the cut of my hair.

'Yeah,' I answered, wearily.

'What Battalion?' This time he did ask.

'Fourth.'

'Or yeah,' he nodded, looking at me with keen, knowing eyes.

'So wotta yer do fur a liven then?' I queried; after all I seemed to be the one answering all the questions here so far.

'Awe, I'm the Mayor of Townsville,' he said, nonchalantly.

You could have knocked me down with a feather.

'Nar, bullshit! Fair dinkum? Nar!' I exclaimed.

'Arse those blokes, they're some of my councillors,' he said amused, turning to indicate the spiffily-dressed blokes sitting away from us in the corner of the little bar. They nodded solemnly back at him in agreement.

I looked him over again — wrinkled white shirt, unbuttoned

two-down, no tie, loose black dacks belted below a large gut. He somehow didn't seem to fit the bill.

'Ow come?' was my next question.

'I donn wannabe, they jus' keep voten me in,' he answered, before adding, 'I'm from out west.' And then it started to add up.

'Yeah!' I said, with enthusiasm, 'Where from?'

'Winton.'

'You're a long way from home,' I told him, with a grin.

'Yeah, I donn get back out there as much as I'd liketa these days. Came down 'ere years ago an' sorta got stuck 'ere,' he told me, with a hint of real sadness in his voice. Yes, he looked like the sort of man who would not have been out of place in a big, gidgee post-and-rail sheep yard somewhere out there, labouring under a battered, dirt-coloured, sweat-stained, wide-brimmed, felt hat complete with a tattered hole in the peak of the crown, the edges of the sides roughly curled up and the front of the brim bent down somewhat; sooling his dogs on with 'Push up, push up' while shaking a tin rattle; his upper torso barely visible in a mist of light tan dust.

His colleagues intervened then to tell him that they were off. Turning towards them, he waved his cheerios without moving off his stool beside me.

'Yeah, see yurs t'morra at work,' he told them, as they got up off their stools and disappeared out through the door. We drank and talked station stuff for ages until he suddenly piped up with, 'There's a SPU club meeting out at your place t'nigh, isen' there?'

'Yeah, there is,' I answered in astonishment, 'but owjew know about that? It's Army only.'

'Nar, well, I'm thu Patron and there's a civilian Secretary. We might go out there later.'

'Err, yeah, righto.'

We drank on way past the time I usually went for my evening meal down at the Broadway Café. At length he said with a grin, 'Well I s'pose its time ta go out ta your place. C'mon I'll take yur 'ome.'

I followed him outside to find it was already dark and there was nobody about on the warm, brightly-lit streets. We started up the slope towards Castle Hill and I'd wandered right past the brand new, white *Mercedes Benz* Sedan in the gutter without even a second glance at it until I heard him call to me, 'This is it.'

I spun around to find him at the driver's side of the car and opening the door with a set of keys. I was stunned, but why should I have been? He was the Mayor of Townsville after all.

'Op in,' he said, as he leaned across to open the passenger's side door for me. Seating myself on the plush, light-tan, leather seat as reverently as possible, the door clicked quietly as I closed it. We hadn't gone too far when he drove into an enclosed backyard of a pub.

'Yuh comen?' he asked, as he got out of the car. As we strolled in through the back door of the establishment, he said over his shoulder, 'I might know someone in 'ere.'

No sooner did we enter the back bar area when a glass of frothy beer appeared on the counter in front of him, to which he said jovially and with a wave of his hand to present me, 'An' one f'me mate from the bush.' Like magic another beer was produced immediately and plonked on the bar towel beside the initial one.

We hadn't even finished that first one when someone from the next bar was indicating to him that they would like to see him. He obliged, I followed him and the previous sequence of events ensued. Then there was someone from around in the front bar waving and inviting him to join them. Away we went and it was on again.

'An' one f'me mate from the bush.' Again the beer appeared.

There were three bars in all the nine pubs we visited on our way out to the Camp, and there was a free beer for myself and my good mate, the Townsville Mayor, at each and every one of those bars, so by the time I staggered into our Boozer behind him, I was literally blind. Just inside the door on the left, seated behind a small table was a sheila with (I think) long, straight, blonde hair, that I took to be the Secretary. Whether she was a looker or not I could not possible tell you as for to me her features were just plain blurry. 'I'm sorry, lady, but I honestly cannot remember you.' I seemed to fancy that I spoke to her before making my way to the bar but can't be real sure on that one.

Our Boozer was packed and very noisy and almost as soon as we entered, I lost the Mayor. I squeezed in at the tap and got myself another beer; however, that was it for me. I cannot remember getting home to my room — which was not too far from the back door of the Boozer — but I can assure you I was well and truly full by the time I hit the cot that night.

* * * *

8
MONARO MALL

It was time for us to go out again. This time the exercise was to be called "Monaro Mall". On the designated day, we got started in the very best of ways. We were lifted by Chopper from the Battalion Parade Ground and carried away. Once again there was that exhilaration feeling as the big, noisy, vibrating machine rose a little at first to become airborne, then dipping its nose slightly ascended under power across the Parade Ground and up and away over the rest of the buildings of Lavarack Barracks.

Gaining altitude all the while, we passed over the Engineers' end of the Camp and banked westward in a slow arc. We flew around the top shoulder of Mt Stuart, leaving the University on our right, and passed over Ross River where eight months ago some of us busted our guts on a Seven Mile Forced March. We levelled out and settled in for our short ride to somewhere out in the middle of High Range. What a way to go to work!

On the first night up there, we again had to sneak up on some poor, unsuspecting "mock-up enemy camp". We ventured east into a moonless night as quietly as was possible for a Company of fully packed Infantry Diggers to move in the dark and it was a marvel as to just how quiet that was.

When we were at the acquired distance and at as close a proximity to the enemy camp as we could get without raising them, we went to ground to wait out the rest of the night.

'You go down 'ere,' Jim Pollard whispered to me, as he moved up past me.

'Roger,' I whispered back, and went to ground at the butt of what felt like a fair sized tree. Unfortunately for me, I dropped right down on a big green ants' nest. They attacked me with much enthusiasm and venom the moment I disturbed them.

As anyone who has been bitten by a green ant will tell you, the pain is immediate and excruciating. I cannot tell you how many bites I received from those vicious little beasts that night; what I can tell you is that I ached all over, especially about my chest area where they'd somehow managed to crawl in the front of my shirt.

I couldn't move. I couldn't make a sound. I couldn't make a scene — not that anyone would have seen me do so anyway, given the state of the night. If I left this spot, I might very well have walked on one of my mates and caused a real ruckus. The pain became so acute that I thought I was going to die right then and there. I reasoned that if I did die alone through that dark night, at least having stayed put they'd find me in the morning and give me back to my parents down in Temora to bury.

I lay still and eventually the ants stopped biting me. I could only imagine the multitude of round, white welts that had emerged where they'd got me. The pain slowly consumed all parts of my body. From when they stopped biting until the pain subsided seemed to take an age, but I suspect it was only an hour or so, as this is usually how long it takes for a green ant bite to wane. Even though my head still ached, I somehow succumbed to slumber somewhere in the wee hours.

The only thing I can remember about the following morning

— apart from the fact that I still ached right down in my bones and joints — is that we rose and went due east into the morning sun without even being given the chance to chow down on a hearty breakfast from that miniature tin of scrambled eggs with its tiny bits of chopped bacon.

I wasn't much "with it" for the next few days. I certainly wasn't into their silly "catch-me-if-you-can-type war games' that we were supposed to be participating in, especially as our supposed "enemy" proved to be so damned allusive.

The fun part of this whole "exercise" didn't come until we were four or five days in. We patrolled into an area of small, rugged, rocky hills that seemed to grow up out of the otherwise flat ground. Here, the Company was split up into two halves: Eight and Seven Platoon in one, Nine and C Company HQs into the other. Then Eight and Seven were sent up into a little hill on the right, having been told to find a comfortable place to sit among the large, rounded rocks up there to await further orders.

The other half of the Company were going to attack the small hill directly in front of them in extended line. They would be firing live rounds at targets placed in among the rounded rocks about the base of that hillock. All this sounds reasonable enough, but here's the rub; while that half of the Company were advancing in extended line firing live lead at the rocks in front of them, we were ordered to open fire at the targets from seven to ten metres up in our perches on the right hand hillock. This was fun. We'd not been allowed to expand this much ammo since we were up here on High Range during Corps Training and now we'd been given orders to truly brass this place up. We sent copious amounts of hot, copper-coated lead over the right shoulders of our comrades as they passed by our static position to be halted just thirty metres short of the kill zone.

Then it was our half of the Company's turn to go down and assault the hillock while the other half assisted us from on high. We were astonished when the boys coming up the hill admonished us ever so severely with calls of, 'You fucken wait yur bastards till it's your turn. We'll give youse wot youse just give us, youse'll see, yur pricks.'

Perplexed by their outburst, but nevertheless ready to do our thing, we quickly shook out in the extended line as ordered and began our slow march towards the hillock to be attacked. The order to "load" was given to us by an NCO at one end of the line. Then it was, 'In your own time. Firing at will. Fire.'

We let fly and so did the boys up the hill to our right. What a racket. Suddenly the whole place became alive with ricocheting bullets zinging and zapping out of the rocks ahead of us. Our line faulted for a second, but the NCOs on both ends bellowed at us over the din to keep it straight and to keep it moving by keeping up with the blokes either side of us. It was scary shit and there was many nervous, sideways glances, but nobody wanted to be the one to follow his instinct and break whereby letting his mates down. Despite the noise and the anticipation of being struck by a wayward round, we kept moving as one body advancing towards the objective. There was somewhere in the vicinity of nine M60 machine guns firing two hundred and sixty rounds a minute, twenty-seven semi-automatic M16 Armalites and seventy-six SLRs, which again were semi-auto jamming that hillock at the same time with all the lead they could spit at it — and all the while we silly bastards strolling quietly along in extended line towards it.

I could see now what the boys up on the hill to our right had been so miffed about when we'd crossed paths a short time back and I bet they were having a good laugh at our expense while they too now pounded away at the "entrenched enemy" from up out of harm's way. We were halted thirty metres or so short of the rocks at the foot of the hillock and told to expand all the ammo in our remaining mags. It was a real wonder no one got hit or even killed that day, but I suppose the Army knew what it was doing.

Next day, they put us through a completely different scenario. Each of us was given two full magazines of twenty rounds. We then had to take a slow stroll with a young Officer along an allotted course dotted with pop-up targets. Twenty targets in all and we were supposed to expand no more than two rounds per target.

'The idea of this little exercise is to count your shots. You will have to be on the ball so that when you get half way through you will need to change your mag and ping the next target that pops up. The last thing you want to hear is a loud click on an empty chamber with the enemy emerging from behind a log just metres from you,' we were instructed.

A young Officer carried with him a small, green, box-like contraption that had a short joy stick protruding out of the top of it. From my peripheral vision, I could see each time he pushed it forward to control the targets, so I knew when I was up. I took my first shot on the rise and if needs be my second shot as an "instinctive" from my shoulder. I came out with three rounds left to go. I was reasonably happy with my performance.

I was getting closer to being able to "use this weapon properly", although by my own standards, I should have done better. Mind you, a couple of the targets got slugged twice in quick succession because they wouldn't go down immediately they'd been whacked.

On the morning we were due to depart for home, we were sitting about waiting for our chopper on a small, rocky outcrop in a sparsely-treed area, when Boris, our rotund Sergeant, gave us a stern and timely warning about not watching our flanks in situations just like this.

'There were these blokes over in Vietnam,' he said, 'who were sitten roun' jus' like youse are 'ere an' a little Noggie snuck up on 'em an' let go with a RPG an' whoosher, they were gone, just like that.'

'Yeah, right Boris,' we chuckled.

A chopper pulled us off High Range at around eleven in the morning, but as we came over the escarpment the machine suddenly dropped in altitude. It wasn't as bad as when you're going down in a lift and your guts gets pushed up into your rib cage, but we were going down fast and I anxiously looked at the heads of the pilots seeing only the rounded, drab, olive-green backs of their helmets, but they didn't appear to be acting up. There was no frantic looks at each other or their instruments and their hands didn't seem to be grabbing for things to tweak. As the craft still kept falling away alarmingly, I started looking for cleared ground ahead and below us that might serve as a crash landing site, spotting a small clearing which they seemed to be heading straight at.

'Goodo,' I thought, then as we came to the place, *'OK, here*

we go.' We came in fast and I braced myself for the inevitable impact ... However, it never came? This wonderful big bird merely touched the ground as if picking something up off it and was up and away again.

Chopper pilots have a special name for this manoeuvre and they are expected to practice it on odd occasions to keep their skill levels up. This must have been one such occasion. I think it's called a "skid roll" or some such where they touch the back of the skids on the ground and roll forward along them to the front before lifting off again. It's great stuff, but I wished to Christ right then that they could have done it on some other flight, or some other time, or at the very least have warned us green horns as to what they were going to get up to.

When I was just a nipper growing up on Beefwood Downs I wanted to fly like the Wedge-Tail Eagles that plied our skies in search of lambs, small roos and other pray. In this machine, I felt like one. Flying in a Helicopter is the closest man has come to being a bird; you can put down virtually anywhere except in a tree and fly straight up from that spot without the need for runways. This little demo we'd just been part of was like being a bird of prey swooping in on a ground-dwelling food source, scoring it and making off to devour it on the wing. So neat!

A short time later we deplaned on a makeshift helipad on the southern slope of Mount Stuart. Eight Platoon began gathering on a gradient of small, sharp, loose, yellow, shale-like stones a little way away from the pad while waiting for our full complement to arrive. Boris was one of the very last to fly in and as he trudged his way slowly up the slope towards us with his head down — no doubt dreaming of that first beer that was waiting for him in the Officers' and Sergeants' Mess just over the other side of this infernal mountain — Mullen and Coggins, Five Section's First and Second Scouts respectively, looked at each other and laughed out loud and without a word being spoken they sprinted down the slope in a crouched position. Arriving at a lone, small, dead bush that resembled a rollie-pollie, they threw themselves prostrate on the rough stones behind it from where they pretended to raise a RPG to their shoulders and delivered a loud 'WHOOSHER' at him. They jumped up laughing and scampered back to where we were with Boris' words following them, 'Oh, yeah, ha, ha, very droll, boys.' From that moment on Eight Platoon would forever refer to RPGs as "Whooshers".

When we got back in camp next day, we were introduced to the bloke who was going to be Five Section's Third Rifleman. G.B. (Smithy) Smith was a brow-beaten poddy whose father ran a huge prison near Perth, the capital city of Western Australia. Smithy had black hair with a decent wave at the front and he too had trouble filling out his greens. Although he displayed a tough exterior, there was a vulnerability about him that made you want to protect him at all times, but we knew he could and would do his job as well as any one of us when the time arose.

On the morning after our return, there was a real kerfuffle in Camp. Apparently after we'd handed in our rifles and assorted accessories, the Army found that they had lost a *Wizz-bang* and they wanted it back. Everybody had to stay in their rooms while a search took place. We stood to attention at the ends of our beds as an Officer and a couple of NCOs went through all our gear and our dressers. They even looked under our mattresses.

They found the Crown and Anchor masterpiece I'd painted on the hutchie up on the top of my cupboard; however, they did not find that offending, wayward *Wizz-bang*.

The Raymonds was packed to capacity when I eventually got in that night. On pay nights, all the free-loading girls of Townsville would be out in their droves sponging off the cashed-up Diggers — it was a bit of a dance, free piss all night, then scoot off home in the wee hours of the morning, leaving a very frustrated bloke in their wake once a fortnight. We fell for it every time, ever the optimists, I suppose. Believe me; these girls knew full well which day was pay day for the Army.

At any rate, I'd spotted a real good-looking blonde seated at one of the tables on the far side of the Club up near the dance floor and decided to concentrate my efforts on cracking onto her for this night. Unfortunately for me, someone else had grand designs that night as well and it wasn't the blonde. Seated beside her was this huge, young woman. Every time I tried to get a conversation going with the blonde this big piece would deliver me a vicious kick to my shin under the table and then giving me a most meaningful wink she'd flick her head towards the door. Now I have to tell you right here and now, obese women, no matter what age, frighten the living bejesus out of me and always have. Don't know why; maybe some extra-large woman grabbed me when I was quite young and squeezed me to her, lavishing me with her love. Whatever the reasons, the fact remains I don't handle big woman.

Obie O'Brian wandered past where I was sitting.

'Bisho,' he greeted me, in his usual cheerful manner, slapping me on the back. I had a brainwave.

'Hey Obie, you wanna girl for thu night?' I asked him, enthusiastically.

'Yeah, bloody oath! Why?' He answered excitedly and then a slight frown appeared on his brow.

'Look, I'm tryen t'crack onta that blonde over there.' I explained, pointing towards the blonde girl sitting at the other side of the table as he leaned closer to me to hear the plan over the din of the very crowded venue, 'an' that there big piece keeps tryen t'cut in. If youken get 'er outta 'ere, I might 'ave a chance with thu blonde.'

'OK,' he said, and with a grin strode to their side of the table, lent in close to the big one and whispered something into her ear. She immediately lumbered up out of the chair and, clutching her purse, she followed Obie out of the Club, a delighted grin on her podgy, round face. I instantly collared the chair she had just vacated to be closer to the blonde.

The night went reasonably well, I thought. We had a couple of dances and I bought her a good few drinks of her choice. At around one-thirty or so she picked up her little, gold purse and headed down the back of the Club to go to the loo. She was about half-way there when she suddenly did a sharp left hand turn, crossed over to the other side of the Club, another left and bolted for the front door. Yet another one? I know Obie scored that night, but once again I dipped out. Oh, well!

It was now nine days after our last exercise and we were up for Pre-embarkation Leave: Six days off to be with our families and to get our affairs in order before going away to war. Most of us lived away and had to fly to get home though, so it was in fact only four days with family with two days of flying there and back.

We left Townsville airport sometime through the night in a *Boeing* Seven-Two-Seven Fan Jet — so quiet and comfortable. As daylight began to show over the wing on the left-hand side of the south-bound plane, I got a real shock. Because a blanket of cloud covered the ground over which we flew, I could not tell you exactly where we were at the time, but what I can tell you is the tip of the wing was bouncing up and down by at least thirty centimetres at a time as we hurtled along. I'd noticed the red light on the wing-tip earlier in the flight, but had taken little notice of it. Now I was appalled at the sight of the end of the wing moving that much. *'Christ, the way this old crate is actually flapping its way down to Sydney, I sure hope to Christ we can make ut,'* was all I could think. I changed planes at Sydney to a smaller one for Temora and got there around two in the afternoon.

On the second night at 76 Hoskin Street in Temora, which was the address of my family's home at this time, I suddenly said to my little sisters, Kathy, now eleven years of age, Margy now nine, Jenny seven and five-year-old Lizzy, 'You kids wanna come for a drive wiff me an' 'ear a big bang?'

Well, if it was some sort of mischief that they were going to get up to with their big brother, they'd be right into it. With their eyes gleaming brightly, they carolled in unison. 'Yeah!'

'C'mon then, let's go.'

We drove eastward up Kitchener Road and over the hill at the top, then down past Nanna Kavanagh's little turn-of the-century cottage with its bull-nosed verandah and tall pencil pines at either side of the front gate. At the bottom, we turned left into Bundawarrah Road and cruised down past Players' grey fibro-house out in the paddock on the right until we came to Chifley

Street, a gum-tree-lined lane which was the back boundary of Nanna's property. Here, there was a little dam surrounded by a couple of big Yellow Box trees and large Briar bushes. This is where we stopped to throw that *Wizz-bang* that the Army could not find in the barracks in Townsville ten days or so back.

There was the usual blood-curdling scream which sounded like the high-pitched scream of a sheila who believes she is about to receive a fate worse than death. There was the sudden blinding flash of light followed immediately by an almighty chest-thumping crash. It was a resounding explosion in the still, cool night air which prevailed over Temora that night, echoing loudly around the undulating countryside at the back of town before coming back to rest with us.

Baby sister, Lizzy, stood spellbound, a stunned expression glued to her small, smooth, rounded face. The other girls were just clearly ecstatic, but, nevertheless, wanted us very much to get away from there as quickly as possible in case someone had rung the cops, who might be on their way at that very moment to investigate the source of that mysterious blast in the night.

At home our old man gave me the most disapproving look when the girls, all revved up with excitement, began explaining what we'd just been up to, but what could he do? It was done now and, anyway, I'd be going off to a war very soon. Besides, I thought I detected a glint of amusement in his eyes as well. Really, having told us some of the stuff he'd got up to when he was a guard in the RAAF during the World War II, what could he say to me at this juncture in time?

Two days later I was back at Mascot Airport in Sydney with the rest of the New South Wales contingent as we began to gather at the Domestic Departure Lounge prior to our trip back to Townsville. While we sipped at our overpriced beers, we noticed from our elevated vantage point behind the glass that every time a plane pulled in to unload it cargo of humans from places elsewhere, four MPs (Military Police) would go to the bottom of the mobile steps and wait, two on either side. The conjecture started coming thick and fast.

'Bet they're waiting for someone who's AWOL.'

'Yeah, wonder where those planes are from?'

'Do yer reckon they're waiten fer someone they know or they're jest 'ere on spec?'

'Donno, but they look like Navy blokes t'me.'

'Yeah, well 'e's a goner whoever 'e is, with two of'um on either side of him when 'e gets off.'

'Yeah, that's fer sure.'

Then a short while later, the inevitable happened.

'Hey, look, there 'e is now!' one of our mob piped up. We rushed to the large window to watch as a thin, little bloke walked down the walled, mobile steps and was immediately surrounded by the four burly cops. It was all over in seconds — he had nowhere to go. They led him off the tarmac to presumably spend the night in the stockade before being hauled up to take his medicine.

Upon arrival back at the barracks in Townsville, I quickly discovered that some mongrel bastard had nicked the hutchie on which I'd painted my Crown and Anchor design. I had my suspicions as to who that thieving bastard was, but without proof there was little I could do about it at the time. He'll get his one day!

A week or so later, it was pay day again. The Raymonds was full of revellers and the little dance floor was as packed as I'd ever seen it. Somewhere in the middle part of the evening I was attempting to dance with one of the "free loaders" — in reality merely moving up and down on the spot at the northern edge of the sweaty, heaving throng, most likely to *Proud Mary* yet again — when suddenly thick, orange smoke started to ascend slowly from the middle of the dance floor to drift up through the crowd. To the cries of 'Arr yuck' the floor emptied quickly as people tried to avoid that horrible smell that is given off by one of the smoke-bombs which the "Gingerbeers" used to simulate a walked-on mine. Alas, the stench filled the entire place and it took an age for the air-conditioners to disperse it, by which time a lot of the clientele had already left the premises and the night lost its oomph.

The next big thing on the Battalion's agenda was the 4RAR Ball. There was lots of talk around the lines about who was taking who to it. Personally, to date I had no idea who I'd be escorting to this prestigious event. On the first weekend back, I rang home for my weekly contact with my family. While the ever-friendly, bubbly telephonist, Jenny, and I were waiting for my call to get through to Temora via Brisbane and Sydney, we chatted as usual, when it struck me. I'd ask her to the Ball!

'Hey Jenny, wot are you doen Fridee nite?' I suddenly asked her.

She laughed her throaty laugh. 'Why, are you askin me out?'

'Yeah, well if yer not doen anything on that nite, we might be able t'meet up someplace. I mean, we bin talken to each other fer ages now, wot about the Allans on Fridee nite if yur not worken or anything?'

'OK,' she said, with another giggle. She sounded quite happy with the prospect.

'Ow will I know yuh?' I queried her. I was starting to get my hopes up too.

'I'll be wearing purple,' she told me, and then finished with, 'Your call is through to Temora. You can go ahead now.'

'Yeah, thanks Jen, see yuh. Hello, Mum ...'

That Friday night I arrived at the Allans early as is my wont whenever I have an appointment to keep. I strolled around the slowly filling interior of the dance area looking for the gorgeous sexy 34-24-34 five-foot-six bombshell with long, wavy hair that I knew Jenny must be, by the way she talked and laughed when we flirted on the phone.

I was beginning to think I'd been stood up having as yet not spotted anyone even remotely resembling my dream girl and was around at the bar deep inside the pub opposite the dance area when I heard it: that wonderful, throaty laugh that I knew was emanating from no one else but her. I looked around sharply.

There, seated on a chair with her back to the wall which ran along to the northern end of the bar area, sat a whale of a woman.

'No! This cannot be!'

I've already told you previously, a big woman frightens the living daylights out of me, but this big lass was not the girl I was supposed to be meeting for drinks and such, surely?

Around her in a semi-circle stood at least eight two metre-tall, fit, young blokes. She wobbled all over like a fresh-made jelly when one of them said something to her and then came that distinctive laugh again. I ventured cautiously closer to get a better look. Yes, she was wearing purple, or rather a mauve chiffon outfit. Still I was not convinced. Then he said it. One of those admirers called out aloud, 'Hey Jenny.'

I bolted. The poor girl does not know to this very day that I was there at the Allans to meet her that night. An empty seven glass with froth slowly sliding down its insides was the only sign that I even been there as, like a will-o'-the-wisp, I disappeared out into the warm night. The only consolation for her was that at least one of those strapping lads who were sniffing around her that night might very well have taken her home later on, as they did seem to be on intimate terms with her. Needless to say, I didn't escort our Jenny to the 4RAR Ball.

When the big night came around a fortnight later a team of us Charlie Company boys arrived at the Lavarack Barracks Hall in high spirits well before the band started playing. The hall was situated just off to the south side of Robert Town's Boulevard roughly in the middle of the large Army complex. Even at this early hour you could feel a real carnival-like atmosphere prevailing over the large, brightly-lit interior of the building. We quickly set up headquarters close to the bar at the north-west corner of the great hall. Some of our lot had their girlfriends with them, a couple had newly acquired consorts and some like me were flying solo for the night.

This being an Army "do", I thought it would be a pretty mundane affair with a Bugle and Drums-type Military Band providing the bulk of the music. However, I was gravely and very pleasantly mistaken; not one, but two modern rock bands from in town played throughout the entire night. It was great. One band would stop playing their bracket, get up and walk off the stage, whereupon the other band walked on took up the instruments left there and immediately start playing again — non-stop rock all night — heaven.

I had a Ball, literally. I hit the turps pretty hard initially and then danced with all the girls in our group — they were an interesting cross-section of Townsville's maidenhood, from Uni students to shop assistants and factory workers. A few of our lot had been tasked to run interference between a certain party in our group and one of our mates. This became irrelevant, however, when the sheila we were watching spewed her guts up and went home about eleven-thirty. I suspect she got crook from getting stuck into the spirits a little too heavily earlier in the evening.

As the night wore on, I ventured out from our immediate tables and danced with the wives and/or girlfriends of Corporals and Sergeants. I even scored a twirl with the partner of the odd young Officer. One or two of these women turned their noses up a little when they found out that I was of the lower ranks, but still managed to dance with me despite this inconvenience. At times I'd stay out on the floor for two straight brackets before coming off in a lather of sweat, going back to our tables and hooking into some more slops, then plunging right back into it. By doing this I danced myself sober twice in the one night, a first for me.

Eventually, I decided it was time to go for the highest prize of all, the esteemed wife of our Big Boss. I sought out Lieutenant Colonel J. C. Hughes himself, Commander in Chief of 4RAR, who was seated over in the middle of the hall. "Hughsie", as he was affectionately referred to by the majority of the lower ranks was very hard to miss. He was a small, lean, middle-aged man with dark hair, hawk-like eyes surrounded by laughter lines in a thin face with a sharp nose over a distinctive neatly trimmed, but very healthy moustache. He was smiling merrily when I sidled up his chair from behind.

'Sir, j'mind if I arse yur wife furra dance?'

'Nar take 'er away,' he laughed, turning just enough to catch a glimpse of me while waving me away with his right hand.

Mrs Hughes beamed as she gladly led me out onto the dance floor. I think she was thrilled to bits that this brash, young Digger had what it takes to ask the Boss' missus up for a jig. We danced through one bracket and into the next until she could go on no more in the stifling heat on the crowded floor, at which time I was content to formally escort the gracious lady back to her seat beside her distinguished husband. To have had the privilege of dancing with her was the highlight of the entire evening for me.

A hint of apricot merging with a smudge of soft pink, which seamlessly melted into the illuminating turquoise glow on the eastern horizon, heralded the start of another warm, dry day in Tropical North Queensland as the last of us Charlie Company boys left the hall and began to trudge slowly along Robert Town's Boulevard towards our lines at the eastern end of Camp the morning after the Ball.

At that same hour, in villages, small towns, large towns, country cities and capital cities all down the eastern seaboard of Australia, old soldiers pressing their tarnished, hard-won medals and people of all ages and all walks of life were standing quietly together at a cenotaph, looking up at an Australian flag in solemn silence listening to the strains of the Last Post and reflecting on the horrors of war. This day was Anzac Day 1971.

To mark the occasion, the RAAF out at Garbut Airbase

situated beside the Townsville Airport were bunging on an Air Show. However, I was going to miss out on that. A week back Ray Graham found out he was supposed to be on Guard Duty that day and had been in a bit of a quandary. His woman — the one he intended to marry one day — was coming up from Brisbane for the Ball and he wanted to spend the day after it with her. I made a deal with him that I'd take this duty for him if he agreed to do my next one for me. After all, I had no woman to worry about at the time, so it was that while he was off gallivanting around the town, I was going to be confined to Barracks of my own volition.

At 0800 hours, the day's Guard Detail presented to the Guard House all spruced up in our fresh pressed greens. It shouldn't have been too bad of a gig and, with luck, I might have been able to score some much-needed sleep for the first four hours before taking my place at the gate, although there was the chance that I'd only get two hours sleep then do two hours on duty before getting the four off that I needed to sleep, or worst case scenario, go straight to work on the first shift for two hours.

As soon as we entered the big, clean, airy room at the back of the building that served as the Guard's bunk house, we checked out the roster to see how each of us had fared. There was understandable cursing from those who had pulled the short straw. For myself, I was pleased to see that I was about to get four hours' rest. We were in the process of picking out our preferred bunk, when the Corporal of the Guard walked briskly into the room.

'You blokes not on guard now or the next shift, come wiff me,' he ordered.

'Wot? Why? Wear we goen?' came the anguished cries from those of us who had been about to crash.

'You'll see. Now, outside, your transport is here.'

We were delivered down to the now empty hall by an open topped *LandRover* Troop Carrier.

'What are we doen 'ere?' was the obverious question. The reply: 'Yur gotta cleanet up.'

'Wot?'

It was a mammoth task, not helped at all by the fact that most of us had been up dancing, drinking and womanising all night. It was made worse for me by the fact that I was only here because I was doing a favour for a mate.

It was about ten o'clock and we were only half-way through sweeping the now huge, empty floor space of the hall when the first of the RAAF jets flew over. I cursed aloud. I would much rather have been out there at the airport enjoying the show instead of in here slaving away. You owe me big time, Graham? With so few of us to do the job, we went a bit over time and it was eleven by the time we got back to the Guard House. A little tweaking of the roster and I was told to eat straight away as I'd be next on. I started at midday and finished at two and only now could I sleep. I hit the sack and, despite the heat of the afternoon, crashed out until six when it was time to hand over to the night shift. I took my evening meal in our Mess that night. Back in my room I again succumbed to sleep and didn't wake till the early hours of the next day.

* * *

9
EMBARKATION

Six days after the Ball, the entire Fourth Battalion was out in force on the streets of Townsville for the "Off to War" March Past. There was a stiffness about us as we gathered at a street corner in preparation for our stint down the main drag. We were going to be on show to the Australian public for the first time as a fully fledged and battle-ready outfit. Our nervousness must have been evident to the CSM who was there with us at the time. To settle us down he told us, 'Donn worry 'bout this shit boys — jus' treat ut like a sundee afternoon stroll, an' youes'll be right.'

So away we went marching down Flinders Street to the strains of our Pipes and Drums Band; we, the Queen's Own Guard all spruced up in our starched greens, spit-polished GP boots, bright-red lanyards and shiny Skippy badges on the turned-up sides of our slouch hats, carrying rifles with bayonets fixed in the shoulder-arms position, with the Returned Diggers in our ranks proudly sporting shining medals on their chests.

About halfway down Flinders Street, a middle-aged man rushed out of the crowd of onlookers and flung a red streamer over the shoulders of one of our blokes just in front of where I was marching saying, 'Carry this all the way Sonny.'

To this day I cannot figure out what that was all about. Was he trying to say that we had blood on our hands, that we were indeed nothing but "baby killers", or was he covering us with streamers in celebration of us being that proud Australian icon, the Australian Digger? I suspect it was the former. I couldn't see why, though. We had not even gone away yet. Whatever, the Digger never missed a beat. He was stiff and resolute as he marched on undaunted.

It was a good thing that no ratbags lay down in front of us like they did to the marchers down in Sydney on Anzac Day just gone because this mob would have marched clean over the top of them, I can assure you, and probably would have kicked them in the ribs for good measure as they passed.

When I got to The Raymonds that night, I got into a chinwag with the Bouncer at the front door. It was slow inside, so I was still yarning to him when Brenda Parsons showed up.

'Brenda! Owyergoen? 'Aven seen yur round 'ere fur a bit. Where yur been?'

'Oh, I've been around,' she assured me, with a tentative grin. She slipped past me and went inside. Within a minute, she was back at our sides. She seemed fidgety.

'You awright there mate?' I asked her. She was normally so upbeat when I'd seen her down here before.

'Yeah, yeah. You goen out t'see the boys off t'night?' was her reply.

By "the boys" I knew she meant the 4RAR Advance Party who'd be flying out to Vietnam on a Campaign Flight this very night and would be gathering out at the Townsville Airport as we spoke. Blue McNiven was going to be Eight Platoon's rep on this occasion.

'Hadden thought about ut really, wooden mind, though. You goen out?' I asked her.

'Yeah, bloody oath, I'm just looken to see if anyone else wants t'come. Doyawanna come?' she asked, raising her eyebrows at me.

'Yeah, I'll go wiff yuh,' I told her.

We waited on the kerb outside the Club to catch a taxi that was trawling Flinders Street. Having hailed one, the two of us were transported out to the airport.

A small but noisy crowd had already gathered in the facility's Blue Room by the time Brenda and I joined them. After buying her first drink, I quickly lost her. The crowd grew and soon the Blue Room was bursting at the seams with Army personnel, their wives and girlfriends. The place fairly hummed. It became difficult to get to the bar to refresh our glasses as the bar staff were being rushed off their feet. It also became difficult to find a place to sit down. Most of us ended up sitting on the blue carpeted floor with our backs to the wall or on the steps that led down into the room. The noise level grew until we had to shout at the person next to us to communicate with them, while having a job to hear their answers. It became quite cosy.

Around eleven o'clock or thereabouts a large Commercial Jet Aircraft taxied up to the Terminal. As the scream of the jet turbines subsided when the engines were shut down, the buzz in the confines of The Blue Room went up a notch. Boarding was called and the loud crowd of well-wishers left the Blue Room and followed the departing Diggers out onto the area by the departure gate.

It was easy to pick the soldiers among us that were about to board as they were wearing "dress uniforms" — light-green polyesters, slouch hat with brass Skippy badge on turned-up sides, bright-red lanyards, silver RAR bars on epaulettes and shiny black, flat-heeled shoes.

We cheered and coo-eed as one by one the boys broke off their last embraces with loved ones and made their way slowly to the high sided steps that lead up to the interior of the *Trans Australian Airlines* (TAA) *Boeing* 727 aircraft.

The onlookers became subdued as the large international jetliner's turbines began to spin, slowly at first, picking up speed until they screamed. We stood in silence amid the fan-forced smell of burnt kerosene, watching the machine pull steadily away from the front of the terminal and poke its way out onto the strip to ready itself for take-off. The crowd began to spill out onto the apron beyond the departure gates and press towards the runway. The jet revved to full pitch and when its breaks were released, it picked up speed smoothly and careered along the runway past us.

Suddenly, a distraught young woman broke from the crowd and was running down the darken tarmac behind the fast receding aircraft screaming, 'Come back you bastard, come back.'

Unable to foot the aircraft, she flung an empty beer glass at it in frustration. Oblivious, the jet lifted off and thundered away into the dark night sky out over Magnetic Island. Soon the little, red, blinking lights began to shrink out of sight and a very sober audience slowly made their way back into the terminal. Within minutes they were leaving to all parts of the city to drown their sorrows in ways of their own choosing, leaving the now cold, empty airport to brood in its own solitude.

Early in the evening of the second night after this, I was back out at the airport again. Someone had told me I could hire a car out there and I was looking for one to hire. I'd taken a shine to one of the girls who were in our party at the Ball. Narelle seemed to have a healthy outlook on life and had a wonderful laugh when she threw her head back and let it go. Also, I'm a sucker for long, flowing hair and this girl had a headful of that in a light, gingery colour. The bloke from our Platoon who had taken her to the Ball seemed to me to discard her as he would a piece of oily rag that had been used to wipe the dipstick clean after checking the oil in his car. I felt sorry for her, so I got her details from him and rang her to ask her out. To my surprise, she accepted my invitation with pleasure and now I was seeking a set of wheels to add a little spark to the night.

There was just the one girl working behind the bar as I entered the Blue Room. She was very absorbed in placing trays of sparkling glasses on top of each other under the counter as I approached her. She was extremely tidy in her dark, tight-fitting uniform that hugged her small, slim, neat frame and her dark hair was pulled back tight off her smooth forehead. Her face was pale and she had a smudge of light-blue eye shadow framed between her dark, thin eyebrows and her mascara-laden eyelashes. Her dark shade of red lipstick wasn't overdone.

Still in a stooped position behind the bar, she looked up momentarily and flashed me a *Colgate* grin. 'Be with yuh in a minute,' she offered.

'You're right,' I told her, and duly waited for her to finish her task.

'Now, wot can I do for yuh?' She smiled again, giving me her full attention.

'Seven,' I told her, then added, 'You on yur own t'night? Bit quiet, 'ay?' as she went about pulling me a seven-ounce glass of *XXXX* draught beer from one of the taps behind the counter.

'Yeah, bit,' she answered, concentrating on the glass of amber ale, as she placed it carefully on the bar towel before taking the small change I'd put up to cover the cost of it.

'Was you on thu other night when the boys left?' I asked her.

'Yes, I was,' she assured me, in a tone that told me that she was none too pleased with the happenings of that night.

'Yeah, sorry about that, hope we weren't too much of a nuisance.'

'Youse broke two dozen glasses! A whole tray of glasses! I've never seen anything like it before,' she informed me, before asking as I drained my glass, 'Another?'

'Nar mate, I really only came out 'ere t'get a car. I was told I could get a hire car here. That right?'

By now she'd come out from behind the bar where I could better appreciate her diminutive size and curvy shape while she fussed about with cleaning tables in the Blue Room itself. She stopped mid-swipe, damp, brightly-coloured cloth in hand and, standing statuette-like, responded, 'Well, normally yur can, but we've got none here at the moment. They've all been booked out.' She moved closer to me, then led me to the door.

'But if you go over there, they're the owners of the business and they sometimes lend people their own cars when there's none here,' she informed me, pointing towards a house maybe three hundred metres away from where we stood in the doorway.

'OK, yeah, thanks love,' I told her and started away saying softly to myself 'two dozen glasses!' I just couldn't get over it. I knew one was broken because we all heard it when the distraught girl hurled it at the plane, but two dozen, really?

The dwelling of the owners of the hire car fleet proved to be of a modern design. It was all acute angles, sharp edges and, as such, devoid of feeling and character and felt from the outside like a cold place. I knocked on the heavy, wooden door with twin frosted glass panels on its upper half and stepped back a pace or two. Presently, the door opened and there before me stood a vision straight out of a fashion magazine.

The woman, whom I took to be the lady of the house, was most likely in her mid-thirties. Her dark brown hair was pulled back into a French Roll. She stood tall and elegant in a figure-hugging, little black dress which ended in a tight cut just above her knees. She had really nice-shaped legs and wore shiny black stilettos. Around her smooth, slightly-elongated neck was a string of very shiny somethings and she was in the process of attaching something just as shiny to her right earlobe. Her warm smile of greeting just added class to the picture.

'Yes love, can I help you?' she cooed.

'The girl over there told me t' cum over 'ere an ask yuh about geten a car. She said you might ave one for me. There's none over there,' I managed to get out.

'Oh, I'm very sorry,' she started, and I immediately thought that the barmaid was having a go at me and had just set me up. However, the model continued, 'We'd normally let you have one of these, but one's already booked out and, unfortunately, my husband and I are going out tonight and we're taking this one, otherwise you could have had it.'

By 'one of these' she meant the remaining shining, black

1970 model *Ford* Fairlane Sedan with the red leather interior which stood so stately in the double garage beside the front door. I was taken aback somewhat and found myself asking, 'Ow much more iset t'get one of these?'

'Oh no, we don't charge any more,' she told me, sincerely.

Now, strictly speaking, I'm not a *Ford* man, but what the heck. You don't look a gift horse in the mouth, isn't that what they say. I could only imagine what an impression I'd have made turning up at Narelle's front door driving one of these beautiful, black machines. I'd been so close too but, unfortunately, I had to settle for a Townsville cab instead.

Narelle's home was a modest house that looked for all the world like a Housing Commission home to me. It was situated in a quiet back street of Townsville. I left the taxi driver instructions to wait and went to the front door to knock. A casually-dressed, middle-aged man of dark complexion and of about the same height as myself answered the door. Mr Watson seemed a little tight at meeting me; however, he asked me in and escorted me along the hall. The hallway carpet was dark green and there was a bronze plaque of a peacock hanging on the far wall as you walked towards the lounge room. In here I met Mrs Watson, who was a lot more relaxed than Mr Watson was. Narelle was fashionably late, of course.

When she did come out of her room, she looked very fresh and happy. We left all smiles, with her father saying to her as we went out the door, 'Remember it's a week night, girl, you don't want to be late for work tomorrow.'

When Narelle realised that the taxi had waited for us while I was in meeting the folks, she lost it.

'Why didn't yur tell me yuh had a taxi waiten? I woulda hurried up if I knew that!'

'Nar, donn worry about ut, its awright,' I assured her, but she insisted.

'No itsnot, you shoulda told me, yur coulda sent him away and we coulda went in my car.'

I got the taxi driver to drop us off at that new Hotel/Motel with the swimming pool up in the roof that I told you about before. It was very quiet when we arrived. There was no one in the big, bright, airy bar on the ground floor. The front of the bar and the stools on which we sat were made of cane. It wasn't long before I was hankering for the buzz of The Raymonds and when Narelle said she didn't want to go upstairs to see the swimming pool on the roof, we got a taxi back into town. After a reasonably quiet evening at the Raymonds, I dropped her off at her home at around twelve.

With just a week to go before we were to be shipped out to foreign shores, I copped another Guard Duty. The night would have been unremarkable except for one tiny incident that could have had dire consequences for the individual involved.

Around half ten or thereabouts, the Guard I'd been teamed up with and I were alerted to a rather noisy party which was happening up in one of the second-storey rooms at the western end of our lines. A party in itself is not that big a deal, but there were girls up there and we were prohibited from entertaining girls in our rooms at any time. It wasn't too hard to conclude by the brogue of the female participants that there were at least two Palm Island girls in the mix.

As the raucous, high-pitched laughter emanated from the lit

room, my fellow guard stood below and, craning his head up, yelled for the fourth or fifth time, 'Hoi, you up there?'

The door opened and Clarkey strode out.

'Wot, woddya yuh want?' he called down, as he approached the upstairs railing.

'You know yur not 'spose ta 'ave sheilas up there. Piss 'em off outa there right now.'

I was thinking to myself, 'Gees, that's a bit rough. We're only a few days from going off to war. Surely the boys can have a bit of fun before they go.'

Next thing there was a yellow, wriggling rope of steaming water descending from Clarkey's midriff as he urinated off the balcony. It landed right on the Guard. Clarkey let out a stupidly delighted laugh of triumph and sang out, 'Get fucked.'

The Guard got out from under the spray as best he could, but understandably he was ropeable.

'Right, you're gone yur bastard,' he called up at Clarkey, but Clarkey just laughed again and staggered back inside the room to continue the party.

By now, I was beside the unfortunate bloke who had been drenched. 'We've gotta go get 'im outta there. 'E can't do that, no matter wot. 'E can't piss on a Guard on duty.'

'Yeah, I know,' he told me in a very agitated tone, then ordered, 'You wait 'ere an watch 'em, I'll go get the Sergeant of the Guard an' see if 'e'll 'elp us. There could be a dozen of them in there an' they're all drunk by the sounds of et.'

When he arrived back at my station outside the lines where I'd kept silent vigil in his absence, he had the Sergeant of the Guard and two other Guards in tow. We tackled the stairs together, surrounded the second door along the verandah and knocked on it loudly. As soon as the door opened the Sergeant pushed his way into the room and let them have it.

'Get this lot cleaned up and get these women outta here this instant. Clarke you're with me. Now.'

I caught a glimpse of one of the dusky maidens as she recoiled away from the angry Sergeant. She wore a bright-pink mini skirt, tight yellow top, pink high-heeled shoes and a light-pink, glossy lipstick. There were howls of protest, but the Sergeant stood firm. 'You 'eard me. Now get 'em out of 'ere,' he bellowed.

One of the girls could be heard saying in a snide manner, 'Nar, it's or'rite, we know when we'snot welcome. Carn then, let's go someplace else.'

The party broke up then and the participants were leaving the room as we summarily marched the highly intoxicated, profusely apologising Clarkey away to cool his heels in the brink for the rest of the night.

Interfering in any way with a Guard whilst he is on duty is a chargeable offence. I heard later that Clarkey had been told in no uncertain terms by those on high that he was very lucky to have been joining us "on the boat", which would have been a great setback for his career in the Army if he had not, he being a Reg and all.

With the last weekend in Australia upon us, I found myself in the company of the merry, red-headed Narelle once again. This time we were going to have dinner at The Raymonds and this time she was driving her white and yellow 1966 FB *Holden* Sedan. There would be no taxis waiting for anyone.

The club was empty when we arrived to dine. That would

change, but for now we had the place and the staff to ourselves. On other occasions, whilst here early in the evenings, I'd watched as patrons had flaming steak brought out to them and this had always fascinated me, so when it came time to order I naturally asked for the flaming stake thingy. The girls laughed, but knew that I wanted a Steak Flambé. I was, in fact, very disappointed in my choice of menu, but that wasn't that they didn't bring me out my steak and then set it alight producing a weak audible explosion, it was because the steak itself was a very thick slice and it was still near enough to raw in the centre. Cannot remember at all what Narelle ordered.

We were going to spend the rest of the night living it up in The Raymonds after dinner; however, things took a turn for the worse when a very drunk and loud Obie O'Brien stopped at our table and started to carry on about Black Fellows. Narelle flew into a rage and admonished him most severely and, all flushed in the face, she grabbed up her purse and said angrily, 'Come on, I'm geten outta here.'

I was astonished at her outburst, but nevertheless reluctantly followed her out to her car.

'What was all that about?' I asked, as we walked to where it was parked.

'Your stupid mate going on and on about aboriginals. I'm aboriginal and he donn know wot the bloody 'ell 'e's talking about.'

Minutes later we tore past The Raymonds heading south-west down Flinders Street with the driver still in a foul mood.

'Where we goen?' I asked, suddenly.

'I'm taken you 'ome,' she said.

'Oh, no, you're not, this night has only just started an' I'm not goen 'ome yet. Turn roun' and take me back.'

Narelle ignored me. We sped on. I grabbed the thin-ribbed chrome inside door handle on my side of the vehicle and opened the door a little. A rushing noise greeted our ears.

'Wottdoyer think yur doen?' she screamed in panic.

'If you don't stop this fucken car now I'm jumping out,' I yelled at her.

She brought the car to a fairly sudden halt by the side of the road and, staring at me, demanded, 'Well, where do you want t'go then?'

'I donn give a shit, any way but that way,' I told her seriously.

'OK then.'

She reefed on the gear stick that stuck out from the steering column, dragging it back and down to select first gear and noisily turned around onto the other side of the broad street and we took off back towards the centre of town. She was still seething though. She went right past The Raymonds again at speed, but I didn't care just as long as we weren't going back out to Camp. Suddenly, we were on a street that I'd not been on before. It swung in a slow arc around to the right, but the girl with her blood up was driving a bit too quick for the curve. Exceeding the speed limit, we scraped past enormous trees which could have been Morton Bay Figs with millimetres to spare on my side of the FB.

Narelle sobered up immediately after this and slowed the car down somewhat.

'You weren't even scared,' she piped up after a minute or so, while looking across at me with wonderment in her voice.

'Nar, why should I be? Either you kill me here or they kill me over there. What difference does it make?'

We parked at a deserted, moonlit beach on the east side of Townsville and talked for hours. At some point I put the hard word on her, but she refused my advances, so I walked out into the water a bit to cool down. Eventually, as the sky in the east was starting to pale with the dawning of a new day, she promised me she would come down to The Strand and see me off on Thursday morning.

The morning of embarkation started before sunrise for us at Lavarack. Section Commanders Jimmy Pollard, Johnny McKinly and Ron Templeton seemed to be in unusually high spirits. They were buzzing around rousting people up and making sure we had everything on us that we needed to be taking with us. We'd leave the Barracks this morning with all our worldly possessions on or about our person. We'd be dressed in greens and slouch hats, basic pouches and water bottles about our waists, full packs on our backs, bulging carry-all bags in one hand and our rifles in the other.

The Camp had been in lockdown overnight, which meant that all those personnel who didn't have family living in Townsville had to stay in camp. This way there'd be no one choked down somewhere who might "miss the boat", so to speak. Some of us did manage to hit the clubs that one last time though?

The first thing I noticed when we alighted from the trucks at eight o'clock on a bright, sunny morning at Anzac Park on The Strand was the warship standing off shore. It looked sinister. It reminded me so much of the Japanese warship that suddenly appeared off the little island on which Deborah

Kerr and Robert Mitchum — playing the part of a nun and a US Marine — had been stranded together on in the movie, Heaven Knows Mr Allison. Even though I knew this ship was the Australian Aircraft Carrier HMAS Sydney — which had been converted to a Troop Carrier and was now known by all in the forces as the Vung Tau Ferry — I still kept a wary eye on her, half expecting her to start shelling us at any moment.

I was shuffling along gawking apprehensively at the ship when Corporal Brenda Parsons greeted me.

'Brenda!' I exclaimed, 'I didn't think I'd see you 'ere.'

'Yur didn't think I'd let my boys go without saying goodbye, did yuh?' she smiled at me. She grabbed me and pulled me into a strong embrace saying, 'Here.'

I hugged her back, of course, but even as we released each other tears glistened up in her hazel eyes.

'Oh, look at me, I promised myself I wouldn't do this when I came down 'ere this mornen,' she sniffed, then she spotted someone else in the crowd and was off to squeeze them. She looked a little bit of alright too in her neat-fitting, bottle-green uniform. I got a hug from a couple of other Army girls who were with Brenda and who I'd met on one other occasion at The Raymonds; however, I got the impression that they were doing it out of duty rather than anything else.

I was searching amongst the crowd for Narelle when the waitress from the Broadway Café appeared in front of me. I rather liked this woman, but not in a sexual sort of way. A cool, calm, collected soul of about twenty-eight or thirty years of age, she was always quietly spoken and reserved in her manner. She had a plain beauty about her and never used make-up, wearing her shoulder-length, brown hair out and her plain skirts were always modestly below her knees — not quite a maxi length. She never really got aroused even when talking to me about her artwork, which I thought was of an exceptional standard. To tell the truth, I think she was a religious type and that frightened me a bit. I felt she'd had a chequered past, but that was to remain a mystery to me.

'Ollo,' I said, blinking at her. She was most definitely the last person I expected to see among the throng this morning.

'D'ave someone 'ere?' I asked, my surprise evident by the tone of my voice. I thought this would explain her presence.

She looked at me evenly. 'No,' she said quietly, 'I came because I thought you might need someone to see you off.'

I was a little taken aback, to tell you the truth. I didn't know her that well, having met her only three or four weeks back and never having associated with her outside her work at the Broadway Café, but she put her arms around me and held me tight before pulling away and telling me earnestly, 'You be very careful over there. You keep your head down and come back safe.' She looked at me intently for a long moment. 'I've gotta be going now, I've gotta get home,' she said, then turned and walked quickly away. As I watched her leave through the crowd of Diggers and their well-wishers, I thought to myself, *Shit, I don't even know her name*.

They called for us to assemble. Still no Narelle? She had said though that she might have to work at the Fish Factory across on the other side of Ross Creek and therefore might not be able to make it. We were marched as one down to the east end of The Strand, then out along the Breakwater Wall. It was only then that I caught sight of her car over at the Factory. Oh, well, that's life.

Near the end of the Breakwater Wall, there was a wide, concrete boat ramp. We clustered around and watched as one of the two high-sided, flat-bottomed landing craft sent in to ferry us out to The Sydney edged up to the bottom of the boat ramp and lowered its front. The first wave of personnel — close to sixty blokes in total — slowly filled the open interior of this vessel. The loading ramp levitated on its hinge, closed off the front and they were off ...

Well, not quite. Black smoke billowed up out of an exhaust stack at the back of the craft as its big diesel motor roared into life; however, the fully-laden boat failed to move. There were cheers all round from the onlooking Diggers. Try as he may the Sailor in the silly cap and light-blue uniform at the helm of the Landing Craft could not dislodge her from terra-firma; well, at least the concrete boat-ramp. She was stuck fast.

With heaps of unhelpful banter being thrown his way, he slew her this way and that, but no matter how many times our Sailor boy fished-tailed his stubborn charge and revved the shit out of her, there was nothing else to it. He was bogged.

Then some bright spark decided it might be best to unload the first wave of Diggers and set the craft free. Of course, as soon as the combined weight of the Diggers and their gear was off the flat- bottomed boat, it was floating again. So as not to repeat the last attempt, it was considered best if the craft stood off a bit and lowered its ramp so that it would only just connect with the concrete at the water's edge. This way, it would be still afloat when fully laden and would be able to pull away unimpeded. As it did so, another chorus of loud approval went up from those of us still on shore.

Eventually, Charlie Company was on the two Landing Crafts and away. H.M.A.S. Sydney lay eight kilometres off shore and some five or six kilometres east of Magnetic Island. The flat-bottomed boats bobbed about a bit on the uneasy waters of the bay as we edged slowly towards their mother ship. Most likely it would have been better had we skipped along a bit.

H.M.A.S. Sydney was enormous — four stories high from the water to the top deck. Until that day the biggest vessel I'd been associated with was a Manly ferry. This British-made Aircraft Carrier saw service in World War II before being given to the Australian people by Britain at the end of hostilities — probably to make up for them having abandoned us to the Japanese at the Fall of Singapore on the fifteenth of February 1942. I was struck by the size of the anchor hooked up on the side which we approached her on, but most of all the rust.

Father (Tink) Tinkler, the 4RAR Padre, who had bestowed his blessing upon the departing Battalion down at the Lavarack Barracks Hall yesterday, was most likely not too far wrong when he said that this 'old crate might fall apart and sink seven miles off shore after we get under way'. Sydney was indeed a real rust bucket, but I would not have believed it had I not seen it with my own eyes; it was nearly as orange as it was the conventional Naval grey when we got up close.

We alighted from the Landing Craft in an orderly fashion and followed each other steadily up the steel steps that were attached in a zigzag configuration to the side of the ship. Almost as soon as I set foot on the flat expanse of the lawn-green flight deck, Jim Pollard singled me out and said, 'You're back in Five Section, come wiff me.'

I didn't argue. I was extremely happy with this sudden turn of events for now I could go to Vietnam as an Infantry soldier and not just a Louie's snotty arse runner.

We were surprised to see that the flight deck had a mob of trucks parked four abreast on it. As the rest of the Battalion personnel slowly transferred onto the ship, we, who were already on board, assembled on what was left of the flight deck to the rear of the impressive turret amidships and looked back at the distant foreshores of Townsville.

It soon became apparent as to why I'd been put back into Five Section. Dogsbody Moody was missing and I was just back in the Section to make up the numbers. Five Section again had three of the four Riflemen it was supposed to have to be a fully operational unit. Certainly it would not have looked too good turning up in "Vetters" with just two Riflemen, especially as we were being touted as being, "a full, ready-to-go Battalion".

It was asserted that Moody must have got "Gang Plank Fever" at the last minute and, by all accounts, there were at least three others who, along with Moody, didn't make the boat that morning.

At around one in the afternoon with the whole of the Battalion on board and the Landing Craft hooked up high on one side of the ship, it was time to get under way. We paraded on the hot deck where we were given our first anti-malarial pill, *Paludrine*. It was a small, round pill, the shape, size and colour of a dried-up pea and we were expected to have ten of these in our systems before entering a place like Vietnam where

Malaria is rife; and it would be a must for us to take one of these things every single day from that time on until we came home. Then we felt the vibrations of the ship as it started up and watched as seaweed and silt-laden water boiled up from around the stern and slowly the ship turned around and away we went.

And so it was, that on the thirteenth day of May, in the Year of our Lord 1971, members of the Fourth Battalion, the Royal Australian Regiment, second Tour of Vietnam, sailed away from Australian shores and off to war.

When we were dismissed from the Parade, we were immediatedly introduced to a Sailor who was to be our "Sea Daddy". He led us away to show us where we would be sleeping on the trip while explaining some of the do's and don'ts of living on board ship as we went. Ship life was a noisy world of cold, hard, grey steel and things going clang day and night, with a constant hum going on in all quarters.

As soon as that was over, Jim Pollard told us that Eight Platoon had scored the first lot of duties. We were taken down to the huge Mess on a lower deck where he pointed me to a door about midway along the eastern side and said, 'You're in there.'

I found myself in a small room with a big, stainless steel tub in a bench beneath a good sized porthole on the far wall which faced the east, out to sea. This was the Scullery. Looking around, I could see that there were a few items which needed my attention, so I got stuck into it and while the pots and pans dribbled in for the rest of the afternoon at a steady rate, I had little trouble keeping up.

However, when it came time for the evening meal, I suddenly got inundated with more pots and pans then I had seen in my entire life. They came in thick and fast and after overflowing the bench on both sides of me they started building up on the floor from the bench back out to the door. I could not believe it. I thought this sort of shit was just something they put in movies. I'd never have believed it could happen for real, but here I was surrounded by cooking utensils packed near to the ceiling, going full tack trying to get them washed up so that the Cooks could come back and get them to use for the next meal. It was well past eleven by the time I got away that night.

It very quickly became apparent to us that we would not be able to sleep in the room that had been allocated to us about two decks below the flight deck. It was stifling hot down here and there was a heap of hammocks hanging from the ceiling in which we were expected to sleep. However, none of us land lovers had ever slept in a hammock before and, of course, we were continually accosted by that very audible hum. Most of us ORs shifted our sleeping mats up onto the gangways which ran along the ship on the deck one below the flight deck where there were large, oblong-shaped holes guarded by railings. Here we found we could at least catch a breeze, although we had on-duty Sailors stepping over or around us all night.

Next morning I was back in the Scullery early, but something was wrong, really wrong! There was land passing by the porthole. There is no land on the east side of Australia. I went back to the door and looked over the other side of the Mess for another Scullery door, just in case I'd accidentally gone into the wrong one. No, there was no door over there. So what's going on? Utterly confused, I went to work on the pots and pans that had accumulated during the night. On the occasions that I had to look up from my scrubbing, I noted with increasing unease that the land was still slipping silently by outside the porthole. When the first Cook came into the room to dump a couple of pots, I put it to him,

'Wot thu fucks goen on, ow come there's land on this sidea thu ship?'

'Some bloke went overboard larsnite an' we're goen back ta get 'im,' he told me.

'One of our blokes?' I asked in surprise.

'Nar, one of ours,' he laughed.

After they'd found that the Sailor was missing, it took eleven nautical miles to stop and turn the Sydney around. Given that we were inside the Great Barrier Reef, they could not really do a big marly and go back to get him. They found him still out in the channel, stuck in the strong currents which run between the mainland and the reef, trying to swim home to see his folks in the Far North Queensland coastal town of Cooktown. Silly bastard, he'd be in some real trouble now?

My duties finished somewhere close to midnight that night and that was it for me for the rest of the trip. Some other poor bastard would have the mountains of pots and pans from tomorrow onwards.

Early on the morning of the third day out to sea, my Sea Daddy took me and a couple of other blokes in his brood way down into the bowels of the ship to the steering room. This room had two very small ship-steering wheels above which there was a fair-sized compass. From the ceiling there extended a tube about two hundred millimetres in diameter which bent out from the bulkhead at its bottom and flared a bit just above each wheel and through this the Captain gave the bloke on the wheel his directions from about ten decks above. The Sea Daddy told us that the Sydney had one propeller on one side and two on the other and when 'you're new to the wheel it's really hard to keep her going straight as she had a tendency to continually pull to one side'.

Late morning the same day, while sailing along in a slight swell on the Arafura Sea between Australia and West Papua, we had a go at shooting balloons off the back of the ship. It's a lot harder than you think with the balloons bobbing about on the unsteady water in the wake of an Aircraft Carrier, especially when its obvious that the bloke on the wheel is only new to the game and has her fishtailing all over the place.

In the afternoon I went with a mate up to the front of the ship to where the boys from Four Section were camped in the place where the anchor chain comes in. That chain was enormous. The space had a low ceiling tapering towards the front, but a beautiful sea breeze poured in through the aperture where the chain hung from. I was sound asleep while enjoying this same breeze when the boys went to get their Paludrine pill at Three O'Clock Parade. Consequently, I copped a charge of "Disobeying a Lawful Command and Neglect of the Prejudice".

Apart from this, it became a very leisurely trip. The Officers lived somewhere amidships and for the most part kept to themselves. We spent a lot of our days listening to stories of the exploits of our newly arrived CSM, Sergeant Major Tod (Toddy) Smith. He was not long back from a stint with the Montagnards as their trainer in the Australian Training Team. These wild, primitive people were the original Vietnamese people who had been bushed to the high mountains of central Vietnam centuries ago by Chinese raiders. He told us about drinking blood with them to prove his manhood and of them going on a rampage through villages to avenge one of their own that the VC had got.

The other NCOs among us who had spent time in both Vietnam and Singapore regaled us with stories of what we could expect from the girls we were likely to meet up with in Vung Tau as they looked dreamily towards the north.

It was also interesting to watch how certain people were reacting the closer we got towards our destination. I noticed one junior NCO, who was all piss and wind in Australia, always going on about how good he was when he was in SAS, get quieter and quieter as the days slip away.

Each afternoon we were given a daily ration of beer — two cans per man per day — only these were not your everyday cans; these were the large cans of *Fosters*, twice the size of your average cans. It was fortuitous for those of us who had a mate who didn't drink as we could score their ration or at least share half their ration with another mate. Most nights at sea we watched movies.

Day four and we were off Darwin. We had to wait there for a Patrol Boat to come out and pick up a small, light-blue, wooden cabin boat, which was to be towed back to Darwin for some Officer there. When the little boat was put overboard, it bobbed about on the swell like a cork and at times it actually disappeared into the troughs of the waves. While out there we stood at the railing of the ship in the bright, midday sun and heckled the Sailors who were exercising by running around the entire deck of their Patrol Boat, which would have been all of one hundred metres or so.

At four o'clock that afternoon when we were once again under way, Jim Pollard found me. 'Come wiff me,' he ordered.

He led me and another bloke he had in tow down deep into the bowels of the ship. Here, the constant hum was heightened and the narrow corridors were lit with red light. I was herded through a smallish, thick door with rounded corners to be confronted by Major Boxall who was sitting sternly behind a small desk in a very small room. It looked to me like he'd rather have been on the piss, up in the Officers?' Quarters. I was put through a drill that went: 'Accused, one pace step forward, march. Escort, one pace step back, march.'

Escort nearly ended up out through the door by which we'd just entered. In a matter of minutes my misdemeanour was read out and I was found guilty as charged. I wasn't even asked if there were any mitigating circumstances or if I had anything to say in my defence. I was sent packing with, 'Ten dollars, march him out of here,' ringing in my ears, meaning that I'd be ten dollars lighter in my next pay.

By the morning of the fifth day we were going through the Java Sea. This was the site of a major turning point in World War II when on the first of March 1942, the Australian warship H.M.A.S. Perth went out alone from what is now Jakarta and sailed right into the middle of a Japanese armada, sailing round and around sinking thousands of tons of Jap shipping before being sunk herself in the middle of what was left of the Japanese convoy. A little known, but very proud, Australian history lay beneath these waters.

That night I came back from the movies to find that some smart-arse bastard had moved my swag from where I'd set it down by the pole in the middle of the gangway and was sleeping in my camp site. I let it ride for now.

Morning six found us out in the bottom of the South China

Sea. Here we picked up two Australian Escort Ships. They were the British-built Daring Class Destroyer HMAS Duchess and the Australian- built River Class Destroyer HMAS Parramatta. They would shadow us to Vietnam.

That morning I walked out onto the flight deck in front of the bridge and accidentally walked out onto God's Country. Immediately some irate bloke told me very clearly and precisely via a loudspeaker attached to the bulkhead just below where the Captain and his mates hang out, to 'get off the turf'. Apparently, as the Captain of the Ship is also known as God, there is an invisible square on the deck in front of the bridge called God's Country and nobody — and I mean nobody — is permitted to step out onto that piece of the deck.

In my wanderings about the top deck, I came across a very dejected bloke dressed only in shorts and a blue, floppy hat using a small, hand-held jack-hammer. He was chipping away at the rust on the edges of a huge thirty-millimetre deep hole in the flight deck. So, this was the source of all that hammering? I got the distinct feeling that this poor chap was the bloke that had gone overboard back closer to home and he was now on some sort of pack duty for his crime.

We were cruising directly north now and many small fishing vessels crossed the path we were taking. They were dotted everywhere you looked on the flat, glassy sea. All day long we could hear the blokes on the bridge calling out their position and approximate speed so our ship would not collide with them. This slowed us down a bit.

What struck me most though, was the fact that all these little sampans were chugging along on motors. Not a sail to be seen anywhere. They all seemed to be heading in the general direction of Indonesia. In my mind's eye I could see a heap more of these fishing boats clumped together in ports on the south side of Java. I found myself thinking that if each one of these vessels carried just ten men and they were all issued with ten rounds apiece and they headed for Australia, they could overrun the place in one day and there be no way anyone could stop them. I had this uneasy feeling that we were indeed heading in the wrong direction.

Of course King Neptune came visiting the ship as it passed over the Equator and, to appease the Lord of the Deep, some of the men on board had to be slimed. It was great light entertainment. We cheered as the selected unfortunates got drenched under a bucket of the green goo and even more so when it was an Officer who copped it.

Around nine on the seventh morning, the Sydney actually came to a complete standstill out in the middle of the South China Sea while the Escort Ships played war games around us. They would go out and away so far that they were just specks on the horizon before returning at full steam ahead and cross paths out in front of us. Then one or the other of them would come about behind us and come in alongside of us to tear past us at speed. It was fun to watch even if we Infantry trained Diggers did not fully understand the concepts of the manoeuvres they were conducting.

Early in the afternoon a Fuel Tanker come out from Singapore to fill us up. Johnny McKinley told some of us to 'watch the colour of the smoke that will come out of the funnel of the Sydney once they start using this Singapore fuel'. The

Tanker was enormous. It came up from astern on the starboard side of the now slow-moving Sydney. When it settled in beside us and was travelling at the same speed, one third of its length was out in front of the Sydney and one third of its rear end was to the aft of us. Its deck looked like a gigantic bowling green as we looked down on it. The Tanker's crew shot lines over to the Sydney and proceeded to fill her up. Then one of the Escort ships came in on the starboard side of the Bulk Fuel Carrier and they filled her up at the same time. When the Fuel Carrier left, the Escort ship came up alongside the Sydney and they sent someone over to us on a Bosun Chair. And, yes, by now there was thick, black smoke coming out of the Sydney's stack, evidence that they were already using the Singapore-made fuel.

As I put my swag down in my preferred place that night, I asked Bill Keenan, who was camping in the same place, 'Bill, don't let that bastard take my campsite t'night, will yuh?'

'Yeah mate,' he assured me, so off to the flicks I went pretty confident all would be well when I returned. When I did get back, however, there's Bill crashed out and snoring, my swag shifted over to the bulkhead and this other bloke in my place once more.

I saw red. I squatted down beside him and rousted him up. 'Hey mate, thisis my place, shift yuh camp or I'll shiftet for yuh?'

'You can't do that! I'm in Battalion Headquarters,' he retorted, when he was disturbed enough to make sense of what I was on about.

I grabbed the side of his mat with both hands and lifting them slightly to indicate that I was about to roll him straight out under the rail and into the sea below us, I hissed at him,

'You'll be in the sea in a minute if yur donn move yurfuckenself outta 'ere.' He vacated my camp site forthwith, never to return.

Day eight was uneventful; however, they did hold a Casino Night that night, down in an empty corner of the Hanger Deck. Couldn't smoke down here as it too was full of the gifted trucks, and they were fully fuelled up, ready to drive off as soon as they got onshore.

I'm not a gambler. My position on gambling is and always will be the same: Life is a gamble. Any money I make I'd rather piss up against a wall than give away to a shonky Bookmaker, crocked jockeys or bent tables, so I only went down to their Casino Night out of curiosity. They had rigged up Crown and Anchor tables and such, but I had no interest in being fleeced by the Navy.

On the ninth morning of our cruise just as the first grey light of day appeared over the glass-like waters of the South China Sea, the first sign of the war we were about to enter showed up on the port side of the ship. Big Gun fire at the distance we were sailing from it, looked very much like a large lightning storm without the clouds to go with it. We could hear the thunder that followed the flashes of light on the horizon even above the constant hum of the ship.

When the ship noisily dropped anchor in Vung Tau Harbour that morning, the whole place stunk of nothing but rotting fish. John McKinly, who'd seen service here before told us, 'Youse'll get used t'that as time goes by over 'ere.'

There was plenty of activity around the ship to keep us occupied that day. We crowded the rails wherever possible to watch those donated trucks being off-loaded onto barges.

When each barge was full, small tugs would tow them away towards the shore. It was generally accepted by all the onlookers on board the ship that, 'The Vietcong will have the biggest part of these trucks in their control within a month.'

Whilst this unloading was in progress, some of the ship's crew were tearing about in small boats around us. One lot in a "Rubber Duckie" was dropping small Anti-Personnel Depth Charges into the water. Their explosions shook the hull of the ship and before the day was over some of us, for want of something better to do, started counting the fish which would float to the surface of the murky-green, smelly water, stunned by the blast.

In another small, wooden boat a crew of three were engaged in a barbed-wire drag. They would throw the barbed-wire out and around, then haul it back in as fishermen do with those round nets, than race to another spot and throw it out again. Unfortunately for them, they came home empty-handed. All they got for their day's work was a wet arse.

We headed back out to sea that night and linked up with the Escort Ships, who had waited patiently out there all day for their sister and charge.

* * *

10
IN COUNTRY

Next morning found us safely back in Vung Tau Harbour and the most amazing thing was about to take place: the swap of one Battalion with another by the use of the Air Force. Absolutely amazing, because not a single thing went wrong throughout the entire operation and the Army, Navy and Air Force were all involved, the Yank Air Force at that!

The 4RAR boys assembled in Company groups and waited down in the hanger deck. The big lift –normally used to hoist aircraft from here up to the flight deck — descended slowly towards us. Standing upon it opposite us were the 2RAR men who we'd come to relieve. They took a pace backwards dismounting the square and we took a pace forward stepping onto it. It ascended slowly and when it reached its zenith we were standing in brilliant sunlight. The air was filled with the near-deafening scream of large machines, the whop, whop, whop of fast, rotating chopper blades and the smell of burnt Avgas. We took a step back and the incoming veterans took a step forward whereupon the lift descended once more. The 2RAR blokes were grinning at us from the other side of the platform as they went; and under the circumstances who could blame them.

We then marched around the gaping hole in the Sydney's flight deck to the big, double-bladed helicopter waiting to cart us inland. We tramped up the open back door — which resembled the back door of a Hercules C140 — and sat down in the red, webbed seats along the sides for the short flight over to Nui Dat. Before noon that day we landed on what was not much more than a rounded, grassy patch, about the size of a cricket oval. To one side of it stood a small, dark-green shed which proudly declared itself to be Eagle Farm in red lettering nearly a metre tall on its side.

This was the pad our choppers would be using to transport us out into the field from then on. On this occasion, however, the American Air Force Chinooks, which had brought us inland from the Sydney, would pick up still more of the people whom we were relieving and transport them back out to the ship.

The moment the Battalion set foot on Vietnamese soil at Nui Dat we immediately became the Fourth Royal Australian Regiment/New Zealand (ANZAC) Battalion. Instead of having just three Rifle Companies and Battalion HQ, we would now also have Victor Company from New Zealand as part of our make up. This was a great honour indeed. I for one was very proud to be known as an ANZAC. I mean, being an Australian Digger was huge enough in my book, but to add ANZAC to that was one hell of an accolade, one that nobody would ever be able to take away from us no matter what the future holds.

Nui Dat translated into Vietnamese means Red Hill. Twenty-six Yanks died taking it from the VC. Our SAS lived on it now in well constructed bunkers amidst thick, lush, growth when they were "in", thus its nick name SAS Hill. To the north, east and around to the south side of SAS Hill was a rubber plantation: 4 RAR were going to occupy the eastern portion of the rubber in the lines newly vacated by the departing 2 RAR;

3 RAR were already on the north side with Reo (Reinforcement Group); and HQ 1 Australian Task Force (1ATF) in among the rubber on the south side of the camp. Luscombe Air Field ran east/west to the north of SAS Hill, close alongside the 3 RAR lines. There was a smaller but wider strip south of SAS Hill. It was known as "Kangaroo". It ran alongside the rubber in which were concealed the lines of the Reo mob and 1 Australian Task Force. There was always one or two small aircraft on this strip: the bubble type Possum Helicopter, a new jet powered Kiowa and the light, fixed-winged French-built plane which resembled an Auster but was in fact a Porter. At the southern end of this strip was the Red Cross station. Between our lines and SAS Hill was a cleared piece of ground serving as a helipad from where the noisy giant "Skycrane" took away cargo such as newly repaired field pieces, jeeps or supplies in a jumble of light coloured wooden boxes, all being slung in big nets hanging from its undercarriage.

The whole complex of Nui Dat was surrounded by a three tiered fence constructed of nine rolls of barbed concertina wire: three along the bottom, two on top of these and one apex of the "pyramid". Outside this fence were the deadly ankle-high, boot-grabbing, barbed-wire entanglements which were partly obscured by the accumulated leaf litter from the rubber trees.

Arriving at Eagle Farm we were immediately taken by a very up-beat Blue McNiven to our allotted places in the Dat to be shown where we were to camp while ever we were "in". This was a time for reunion, a time to hear a story or two from Blue about what it was like to be out in the field for real. We were also introduced to Mick, our new Sig, who although he had been a Signal Operator in the now departed 2nd Battalion, had elected to stay on in Vietnam to finish his time as a Nasho ... I suppose he had his reasons; no-one really asked. Mick was around one hundred and seventy-five centimetres tall, of a dark complexion, slim built, gaunt and with a slow smile.

Our lines in the Dat were rudimentary. A five-metre square of slightly raised floorboards was surrounded by two-thirds of a metre thick blast walls made from full sand bags placed between sheets of corrugated roofing iron held in place with iron fence posts (Star pickets). A large, heavy, dark olive-green tent was suspended above this structure as its roof, which extended about sixty centimetres out over the wall and came down to around sixty centimetres above it — a very tropical style camp to say the least, shrouded under the rubber trees and painted in the customary, drab olive- green. The front and back exit were each protected by yet another small blast wall about one-point- two metres across and sixty centimetres out from the sixty-centimetre opening which constituted a doorway. Each room contained four thin, steel-framed beds, each with a thin mattress; two lines of these tented rooms formed the southern boundary of our compound.

Moving clockwise from my digs, I could see firstly a volley ball court, then to the back of this our shower room; a small building with a little water tank raised on four poles above it. To the right of this was the Mess, which looked like an old shed with a rough, concrete floor, heavy wooden tables and seating benches and a fair-sized opening in the end facing the road. This road ran from my front door to the gate.

A bit further on was the Boozer which was another, slightly

larger shed. The side facing us was mostly closed in except for the door about mid-way along. Once inside though you could see that the end facing Eagle Farm was open as well as half the side opposite our lines. Previous occupants had made curtains out of the pull-rings of hundreds of beer cans and lined the entire roof and most of the open walls with them — a tradition which we resolved to continue. The bar and storeroom was at the road end. Beyond the Boozer was the gate — not much to write home about, but it did boast a flat stick that raised to let in friendlies. Standing proudly beside the gate, of course, was the Office; small but nevertheless the Office.

The rest of the complex was obscured from our view by rubber trees. However, on the opposite side of the compound to our lines were: beside the Office a wooden room called the Store Room for want of a better description; then, in sequence, Boxall's office, the CSMs Office and the Officers and Sergeants Mess; and in front of this stood a concrete bunker which was the CP (Command Post). Heading back towards our lines from there was the Officers' and Sergeants' Quarters, an assortment of tents which resembled our own digs but to the best of my knowledge housed only one occupant each. In the middle of the compound nearer again to our lines was an underground ammo bunker. Fox holes had been dug in among the rubber trees just east of each of our digs. These were partly obscured by the shadow of the rubber trees and leaf litter.

After a day of getting to know our surroundings, we were loaded onto trucks and taken on a guided tour down to the fishing village of Long Hai. The coastal hamlet lay about thirty kilometres to the south-east of Nui Dat at the tail of a range of mountains called the Nui Long Hais. No Aussies went into these hills anymore as the Viet Cong had dug themselves in there and were now impossible to shift, regardless of the constant bombardment inflicted upon them by the American B52s. As we were driven along in our convoy on this hot, clear morning, we could see the craters that these bombs had made scattered all over the side of the range.

The people of Long Hai used the sun to cook their fish. In the front of almost every little house on the western side of the one-and-a-half-kilometre long main street were three or four fish cut in half and laid neatly side-by-side on the footpath. In the afternoon it would be the turn of the people on the eastern side of the street to do their cooking for their evening meal. The whole village therefore stunk of rotting fish.

We arrived back at the Dat just after mid-day. After lunch, Blue McNiven came through our new lines asking everyone what they did for a living back home. We had about four blokes who had been working for butchers. "Butchers Hooks" he called them, but quickly decided that he had too many of these to call one "hooks" so he left that one. When he fronted me, I told him, 'I've been worken forra drover.'

'We'll call you Dog,' he said immediately. It stuck.

Day three in country, we were given a demo of the fire power we would have at our disposal on a cleared area out the back of the Dat. I met a couple of blokes at this show who were in Eight Platoon with me at Kapooka.

'Ow yurs goen? When did youse get 'ere? Who yur with?' I asked them, beaming at them while enthusiastically pumping their hands in turn.

'We're in Reo,' they informed me, brightly. One of them was the good-looking, smooth-skinned little bloke with the jet-black hair from Katoomba on the Blue Mountains west of Sydney. They looked happy to have run into one of their old number from our Kapooka days.

'We been 'ere a couple a weeks,' they told me, 'but j'ear wot 'appened to your mate, Shoemaker? 'E got 'e's ear drums busted.'

'Nar; gees, I didn't know 'e was even over 'ere. 'Ow'd that 'appen?'

'E's with 3RAR. They got followed into camp one night an' then the Noggies bombed them after dark, an' a mortar went off in 'is tent, but he and the Louie were out of it by then. 'Es the Louie's batman, yer know? 'Es bleeden from both ears, but 'e donn wanna go 'ome in case 'e loses 'is War Service 'ome loan.'

'Es awright though?' I asked them.

'Yeah, apart from 'es ears bleeden, 'es awright,' they replied.

I've seen neither hide nor hair of those two blokes since saying my goodbyes to them that day.

At this do we saw for the first time the unbelievable fire power of the *Cobra* helicopter gunships. They could pepper a field as big as a Rugby League football ground with what looked like a shotgun blast, but was, in fact, two thousand 7.62 rounds being squirted out of a nose-mounted mini-gun in seconds. The attacking *Cobra* would emit a small puff of smoke followed by what sounded like an extended fart and then suddenly every square inch of that field copped a 7.62 round simultaneously. We saw white "phos" (phosphorous) rounds going off and, when asked, I had a go at walking into tear-gas to test it out. Man, that stuff catches you in the throat. Good demo all round boys, thanks.

Within a day or two of this we were taken out by chopper to the north of the Nui Dinhs for a little "in the field training" with tanks. On this particular occasion, all the proper protocols were put in place for the safe landing of troops from a flight of choppers. The chopper pilot in the lead chopper asks whoever awaits them on the ground to 'Throw Smoke'.

The pin is pulled from a smoke grenade by the people on the ground. When it hits the turf a thick cloud of one of many coloured smokes emanates from it with a hissing sound.

'Smoke thrown,' they advise the chopper.

In this case it was interesting to watch lighter green smoke billowing up from out of the dark green jungle below us as we neared the spot the choppers were going to drop us off at. It was a comfort to know that there were friendlies down there on the ground waiting for us even if we could not see them as yet. Then the chopper pilot called back, 'I see green smoke. I see green smoke.'

Now that every thing was verified, it was, 'Roger out', from those on the ground and in we went.

We were dropped in a disused paddy field and no sooner had the choppers left when Jim Pollard came over to where I lay behind a paddy bun. 'You'll do Dog,' he said, 'come wiff me.'

I followed him away to the edge of a light-green entanglement of growth which obscured our sight from five metres on. There he pulled up and pointed to a small track leading in our direction.

'Your job is to make sure no Nogs come down that track,' he said, then asked me, 'Yer got a round up the spout?'

I nodded and gave him a grunt that meant 'of course I have', and went to ground at the thin butt of a very nasty bush: Spiky Bamboo. All the vegetation that grew in front of me was this light green bamboo stuff.

'You know all thu rules; no stick books an' all that shit?' he asked again. Again I grunted.

'Well,' he ran on, 'if any Noggies come down that track shoot 'em, they're enemy. You'll be relieved in an 'our' ... Then he was gone.

I lay very still and quiet with my finger on the trigger and my thumb on the safety catch until my whole body ached from the tension. Left to my own devices, I got to thinking and for some inexplicable reason was a little proud that I'd been given the honour of being the very first one in our Section to be asked to go out on guard in an actual combat zone? I suppose that was because I didn't get to be first at much in my life. I was a little anxious too; not that I didn't know what was expected of me, but more that if anyone did come it would be my first real test in open warfare, while the enemy would most likely have the advantage of being an old soldier. Nevertheless, I was sure I could cope with them quite adequately.

Suddenly there was a rustle in the leaves a little way out in front of me. I stiffened even more, if that was at all possible. Silently, I checked to make sure the safety was off.

'Here goes,' I said to myself as the rustling sound came nearer. It stopped ... It came on ... It stopped again ... Then it was on me ...

A small, red squirrel scurried right up to within a foot of the wrong end of my gat and stopped. The furry creature stood and stared down my barrel for a second sniffing the air, then deciding that I was definitely an alien it scampered away to the right of my position. I almost laughed out loud at myself. Fancy letting a little red ball of fluff like that put the shits up me.

The tanks we'd come out here to play with were Australian owned *Centurions.* When we finally linked up with them the "Tankies" took great pleasure in showing us what firepower they had to help us with should we ever want to use them in the future. At one point we got to ride on one of these big, chunky machines. With some of us sitting on the parcel rack behind the turret, the Tankies demonstrated the effectiveness of a "canister round". When the shot was fired out of the muzzle of the *Centurion's* long barrel, the great beast rocked backwards from the recoil. The round itself smashed into the ground like a shotgun blast; however, the "canister" was actually a myriad of darts which pealed off as they came out of the barrel and covered the space in front of them as if a shotgun had hit it.

This deadly weapon was used in the tanks and another one like it called a "Splintex" was used in our field guns. We were told that when the Nogs had overrun the Fire Support Base Coral back in what was known as the 1968 "Tet Offensive", Splintex had been used to great effect all over the embattled Fire Support Base throughout the fight, enabling the Australians to take back their seized guns and their mortar positions. It was said that in the morning following that terrible night, Noggies were found pinned to trees, AK47s (Chinese supplied assault rifles) fastened to their corpses by the lethal darts.

After the three-day stint with the tanks, we made our way back to the Dat on foot. In doing so we encountered a fairly big creek called the Soui Neigh. Here Shortarse gave into our pleas for a tub in the lazily-flowing, brown water. We then trudged east-nor-east, stopping for dinner camp at a small clump of trees near a little banana plantation. From here we could see Nui Dat down across the flats on the other side of Route Two.

I very quickly discovered at this stop that I'd left my dog tags and the small black scorpion that was attached to them back at the Creek. There was nothing I could do about it. Under different circumstances I might have been able to go back and see if I could find them — I knew exactly where I'd left them — but we were on patrol in a foreign country in which the enemy could be anywhere at anytime. Besides, we were due back in the Dat tonight, so I decided not to make a fuss; I'd get some new dog tags whenever I got to Vung Tau. If anything happened to me in the meantime, surely one of the boys would be able to identify me; if not, too bad. The scorpion was my loss.

I'd made that scorpion out of a squashed-down old penny out at the farm using a pair of tin snips to cut the basic shape and a small file to finish it off before painting it black. I'd given it to the Police Sergeant's daughter as a gift, but just before I started training she'd returned it to me saying, 'When you get back, you can give it back to me and I'll know you got home safe.'

While we sat about eating our lunch, a small boy suddenly appeared in our encampment. He was most likely ten years of age, small of stature with a very full, rounded, smiling face. We knew straight away that he was pretty harmless; nevertheless Coggins interrogated him. 'Wot you doen 'ere? Why you not at school?'

'Cow, I chase cow,' he answered holding up two fingers to indicate that he was looking after two cows. They would be his families. Cows mean wealth in Vietnam; the more cows, the wealthier you are.

'Where you from?' Bob asked him.

'Dat Do,' he told us, smiling all the while.

'Shit, that's miles away over there,' someone chimed in. Bob quizzed again, 'Ow'd yuh get 'ere?'

'With cow,' he answered in a tone that said, 'how else do I do it, silly?' So this little bloke was the family drover, getting a feed for his cows wherever he had to go to get it.

'You got sister-san?' Coggins asked the little drover, smiling that wicked smile of his.

'Yeaah,' the drover answered straight away.

'How old is your sister-san?'

'Orr she err welve.'

'Your sister-san, she boom boom?' Coggins was tormenting now.

'Yeaah, she boom boom.'

'How you know she boom boom? You sleep with sister-san?'

'Yeaah, I sleep with sister-san.'

'Yeah,' we said, 'that'd be right, probably only got one room in his family's home.'

We gave him some of our rations to give to his family when he got home that night. He was tickled pink with his haul. At about two in the afternoon we said our goodbyes to our new found friend and headed off back to the Dat.

11
BLOODED

We were only in Camp for one night before it was time to go out for real. When we left the Dat next morning we were fully packed and ready for war. We wore greens, a green giggle hat and black GP boots. Around our waist we carried four full water bottles. Attached to the same belt and just in front of our hip bones we carried two full basic pouches. These neatly carried six, twenty-round magazines of new brass for each Rifleman in each section. There was two thousand rounds for the Gunner, some of them being sheared among the Riflemen in two-hundred round links which when thrown over a shoulder resembled a large, brass necklace. Then there was two hundred rounds each for the blokes carrying the Armalites; their brass carried in mags inside a bandolier and carried over the shoulder down to the opposite hip. In our Platoon, the Diggers carrying the Armalites were the Forward Scout of each Section, the Section Commander of each Section plus Shortarse and Boris. The gun had two hundred and fifty rounds attached to it at all times. Apart from the Gunner, each man had a full twenty-round magazine clipped into his respective weapon. A Field Dressing about the size of a full pouch of *Drum* tobacco was strapped to the butt of each weapon with black tape, while the Gunner had his attached to one leg of the gun's stand.

In the bottom portion of our packs we carried our hutchie, silk, groundsheet and oblong, one-man mosquito net. In the top part we carried five days worth of rations, a *Mills* grenade, a smoke grenade, a *Claymore* Anti-Personnel Mine and a rolled-up length of white det cord and a det to go with it. The Hexagon Stove closed in over a square of *Hex* tablets along with a spare accompanied our extra packets of smokes and any other personal effects one might need in the field. Things like shaving gear and toothpaste and such were carried in one of the two pouches on either side of the top of our pack. On the outside of the pack and secured in a place of our choosing was our blunt machete in its seethe; and of course that infernal entrenching tool hung from the middle of the back of the pack.

Mick the Sig, however, had the 25 Set (Army issue Wireless set) to carry along with his weapon and the set took up all the space in the top portion of his pack except the two little outside pouches. He was forced to rely on those in Platoon HQ to help him carry his rations and one of them would have to add the extra battery for the set to their packs. It was little wonder that Mick looked emaciated.

Our faces and the backs of our hands were streaked or splotched with brown and green camouflage cream and most of us had our crocheted sweat rags around our necks. Once we had assembled and we'd checked each other's gear for rattles or anything that might shine, we were right to go — well, we certainly look the part anyway.

The sun was shining brightly and bearing down on us as our convoy of open cattle trucks turned north into the traffic on Route Two that day. The road was teaming with commuters.

It appeared as if there was some sort of festival happening up ahead of us and all the people in this part of the Province were intent on getting there by whatever means of transport they had at their disposal.

My most enduring memory of that morning is the two very small girls, dark-tanned with jet-black bobbed hair cut to a fringe, riding atop a slow-moving, full-grown water buffalo. They looked like sisters; their family most likely owned the beast. They were smiling and happy, with the taller of the imps sitting in arrears and using a short, thin stick in her nimble hand to great affect in an effort to persuade the reluctant animal to career along at a touch more than a snail's pace.

Along came a bloke carrying no less than four passengers on board a small motor bike and there was a kid riding in front of him on the handle bars. Then there were the three other kids with their arms clasped around each other clinging to him from behind. The kids on the back all smiled up at us as they burned past our transport and literally disappeared behind a screen of blue smoke belching from the exhaust pipe of the hard working two-stroke machine.

Lambrettas inched their way past us loaded with anywhere up to eight persons. The tiny, three-wheeled utility vehicles were adorned with four or so large wicker baskets hanging loosely on the sides at the back of the curved, covered, passenger's compartment. Some of these passengers, mostly woman, peered out curiously at us as our trucks rumbled slowly along picking their way through the throng.

Fresh-faced girls with long, flowing, shiny-black hair and dressed in brightly coloured Ao dais (Traditional Vietnamese

Dress) sat side-saddle on motor bikes with obvious practised ease behind young riders who tore past the line of trucks weaving in and out of the traffic with gay abandon. Older motor bikes laboured under large and small loads of all kinds; one with a great stack of thin brambles of what I presumed to be firewood and others with baskets of live chickens loaded four or five high up behind the rider.

Then there were the animal-drawn vehicles; drays of all descriptions being pulled by a horse, cow or buffalo. There were some small wagons loaded right up and hauled along by pairs of cows or buffalos. On top of all that there were a heap of people of all ages walking this way and that and there was even an odd motor car chucked into the mix, although none of these were of a make or model I was familiar with.

Flying over the top of all this movement appeared a dark-green *Pilatus Porter.* This light, French-built, fixed-winged, propeller-driven aircraft had the ability to almost hover like a hawk over a field searching for prey. It was powered by a small, high revving motor in an elongated nose, enabling it to take-off and land on a relatively short runway.

On this day, the Porter was flying very slowly along quite low over the crowded road. Through a loudspeaker attached to its underside we could hear someone calling out instructions to the people below in Vietnamese. This was just another propaganda programme badgering the VC to chuck it all in and come over to our side and telling them that they would be treated well if they did so; or if someone below knew a VC and they pimped on him or her, they would be well rewarded in US Dollars for their courage (treachery). Sometimes this propaganda plane dropped tons of leaflets onto the populous below with much the same messages written on them.

This rush-hour traffic we were in only started to thin out as we got up along the road a bit. In the first tiny enclave we passed through we encountered a handful of scruffy kids of all sizes lined up along the side of the road. They stared up at us giving us peace signs, more in hope of us chucking them some of our rations than in fear of us busting them.

When we went through a village called Ngai Giao there was an even bigger line of kids lurking along the side of the road to the left side of our trucks. As we came to the first of them, we saw one of the bigger kids bending over and helping a three or four-year-old's two fingers up in order to give us a peace sign. However, as we passed, the last of them, a youth of about fifteen years of age slowly dropped one of his fingers to turn a peace sign into a one-fingered salute. In Vietnam this gesture was delivered with the palm facing out towards the intended.

There was a swift movement and a very audible click as up to twelve weapons on the left side of the truck swung to the ready and pointed menacingly at the insolent youth.

We were ready for anything. It may have looked like an overreaction; however, we all knew we could not trust these kids. We'd heard about how a three-year-old child had rolled a grenade under a Yank truck over at the Horseshoe Feature back when the Australian Task Force was using it as a safe haven for the surrounding peasants, and how in the aftermath of the explosion seven truckloads filled with the bodies of innocent people — who had fled out into an Australian-made minefield after the blast — had been taken away for mass burial. For all we knew, this kid was VC and might well be out in the field tonight trying to kill someone either by planting a mine or setting up a booby trap. If not, he most certainly would be able to tell his masters how many fully armed Diggers went north on trucks this day.

Further along the road we passed a rubber factory which seemed to be part of the enclave of Xa Bang. It had small, tanker-type trucks parked at it ready to unload their cargo of white, liquid, rubber sap. From here we went into an area where rubber trees grew on both sides of the road. There was a broad expanse of about one hundred metres from the side of the road to the edge of the mature rubber trees with a multitude of re-growth rubber about a metre and a half high filling the space between.

Sometime in the early afternoon on the day after my mother's forty-sixth birthday, we were dropped off by the side of Route Two just short of the big house which was owned by a family called Courtney. We were pointed towards the rubber which ran along the west side of the road and were told that that's where we were to go walk-a-bout out through the Courtney Rubber Plantation.

On the day we arrived in the country, a patrol of Kiwis from V Company had encountered some VC in this rubber. The Kiwi Diggers had been stopped from their task of eliminating the enemy by civilian workers who by all accounts had run between the two warring factions and had allowed the VC (of 274 Regiment) to escape. We were to presume that the workers we came across in the rubber were VC sympathisers, forced or otherwise. However, even though they seemed very wary of us, we got no trouble from them as we moved through them and on out to the west.

It was interesting to see how the rubber workers got the rubber sap out of the trees. A bloke with a very sharp, specially-designed knife with a curved end scraped around the tree in a downward spiral, starting at the top and ending up directly under the first part of the cut. A small piece of what looked like a slightly curved length of tin about seventy-five millimetres long extended out from the end of the cut. The sap ran down and around the scraped bit until it got to the end, then out along the tiny tin gutter where it dripped off the end and fell into a ceramic bowl tied to the tree just below the funnel. Other workers, mainly women from what I could make out, then came along when the bowls were full and emptied them into a two-gallon bucket (10-litre). These were carried to a waiting cart with a container on it that would probably carry around one hundred gallons. I thought that this cart was most likely hitched to a cow or buffalo and the sap was then hauled to a bigger tanker to be conveyed to the factory back down the road.

After patrolling in the "J" west of Courtney Rubber for five days, the whole of the Company were given seven days' rations instead of the usual five and was airlifted by no less than seventeen Yank Choppers in one swarm. I call it a swarm because that's what it felt like to me; that is, we were part of a large swarm of giant, flying creatures humming our way across the sky. Wherever I looked there seemed to be choppers all at or about the same level as ourselves spaced not too far apart and all flying in the same direction. I got this feeling in my gut of the awesome threat of strength in numbers we posed as we flew to the east over Route Two.

When the choppers lined up the Landing Zone (LZ) they

opened up with all the fire power they carried. Not being seasoned to the "GOOD OLD ALL-AMERICAN WAY", this fairly put the wind up us to a man. We thought we were going into our first "Hot Insertion".

Being the last to board the chopper, I was sitting crossed legged on the floor facing out — which became my place — and watched rockets hiss from the pods attached to the skids below me and streak away forward — fourteen to a chopper — then the chopper's gunners started firing wildly into the jungle from the M60s mounted on either side of each machine. Our pulse started racing as we got lower to the ground. Suddenly, there was no time to think. Remember the drill. Throw yourself out prone. Cock your weapon while still in mid-air. Fall like lead balloon. Crash land under extra full pack. Lie still ready to fire at whatever comes. Be ready to move instantly when called upon to do so.

In this case it was not a "Hot", just the Yanks with the jitters. However, none of us felt safe until all the choppers were gone and our respective Commanders called out to us to re-group, whereupon we leapt from the knee-high grass and made a dash to the safety of the scrub, only to find that the Nogs we were sent over this side of "the road" to get were still some four or five kilometres east-nor-east of our present position.

What we were now going to do was to sneak in from here forming up with the rest of 4RAR and some Yank APCs to establish a blocking force to the south-east of an enemy Bunker System which our Intelligence knew the location of. Then we were going to sit in wait while 3RAR came down on them from the north-west to bust them. It would be our job to block anything that came our way.

The jungle was thick here. It was what we called 'close country'. That afternoon someone made a blunder in sighting our harbour and, as a consequence, we were camped in a dry creek bed which according to standing orders (SOs) was just not on. When Jim indicated to Andy and I where we were supposed to camp that night — on a steep bank halfway between the gun on level ground about one-point-two metres above us and Jim himself again on level ground the same distance below us — Andy and I both snorted our disapproval like young, unbroken horses.

Andy started, 'Aw, fuck me! Look at this, will yuh?'

'Well, I'm fucked if I'm sleepen there,' I added, surveying the situation and noting the flat ground which Jim had picked out for himself.

'This'll do me right 'ere,' I said and dumped my pack on it. Andy followed suit.

Needless to say, when Jim returned from showing the others in our Section where they were to go down for the night, he was none too pleased to find the place he'd reserved for himself had been confiscated by Andy and me.

'Wot the fuck do you two think yur doen? I thought I jus' putyur down there,' he said angrily, and pointed at the slope.

'Youkin go an' get yerself well an' truly fucked, Jimmy boy, if you think youken make us sleep on the side of a 'ill all night.' Andy stated, starting to get steamed up.

I jumped in to assist him, 'Yeah, Jim, yur put everyone else on flat ground including yurself and yur expect us t' camp there, well, yerken get fucked f' mine too.'

'Youes two will do wot I fucken well tell yur to, that's an order and if your not careful, Andy, I'll have yur charged for disobeying a command,' Jim seemed to puff up when he issued this.

'Aw, so yur gunna pull that shit on me, are yuh?' Andy was getting real hot under the collar by this. He stared unblinking at Jim for a bit and was just about to turn on me when I told him in no uncertain terms that he could, 'go t' fucken 'ell, itsnot my fault.'

With this, he stalked off in search of our Sergeant Boris. Boris didn't help much.

'Itsnot my problem, go an' see yur Padre,' he told Andy, airily. Not to be outdone Andy went higher up the ranks. Having received no satisfaction whatsoever from Shortarse, Andy now confronted Toddy Smith who in turn referred him to the 2IC of the Company, Captain (Babs) Babington. After getting nothing from him, Andy turned on Major Boxall. He would have gone all the way to the very top, to the Commander in Chief of 4RAR himself, Lieutenant-Colonel J. C. Hughes, and abused him too if he'd been there, but he wasn't, so Andy had to stop at Boxall. All this time he was bellowing like a wounded scrub bull. I reckoned he could have been heard for a kilometre or so in all directions even within the confines of this thick jungle.

He apparently didn't do any good with the Big Boss either, but he was told to quieten down or he'd lose his stripe. Like a red rag to a bull that was.

'Yuh know wot yurken do with yur fucken stripe, don't yuh? Yurken stick it right up yur bloody great arse, is wot yurken do; 'ere takeut, I didn't ask fur the fucken thing in the first fucken place, did I?'

The stripe didn't matter to Andy. What mattered to Andy were Standing Orders, that's what mattered.

At any rate, by the time he got back to where I was, he'd calmed down somewhat. I grinned at him. 'That sure fucken told em, didn'et mate?'

He just glared at me in his usual way. Despite everything, Andy, Jim and I camped on the flat ground under the same hutchie that night.

Next day we were moved into our respective positions before the assault on the enemy bunker system began. To form the blocking force, each Platoon of the entire Battalion split into halves. Then these half-size Platoons were spaced out along a line and each group of fifteen or so men went down into small harbours about two hundred metres apart. The Company Headquarters groups of each of the four Companies were stationed just a little way in arrears of the main line, each behind their respective Company, forming a rear guard as it were ... don't know if they split into two or not.

When the offensive began, one of the scouts from the attacking 3RAR was the first to go down. He'd been using a rather large tree as cover when a whoosher exploded in its uppermost branches. The blast broke a limb off which fell down hitting the poor bastard killing him. The Nogs often used this method of blasting the treetops with RPGs in order to shower intruders with shrapnel. It was not by accident that all their bunker systems had certain trees lined up for this very purpose.

We'd been given orders to dig Shell Scrapes in our position. In doing so, Andy or I dug up an 'RTA Bug'. This RTA (Return to Australia) Bug very much resembled a sandy coloured spider about the size of our common garden spiders (Wolf Spider), but in the front where poisonous spiders normally have two fangs, this bloke had four. He was sort of quartered off, with a short, black, curled spike attached to each quarter near the middle of the circle formed by his biting bits. We'd been taught that this bloke also had a very bad temper and would attack at the drop of a hat if stirred up, so it was with some luck that this particular bug had some of its body damaged by whoever extracted him. Even if it would have been nice to have been RTAed this early in the proceedings, I didn't fancy spending the next six months of my life laid up somewhere paralysed down one side of my body, just because this little fellow was a bit mad at us for uprooting him out of house and home in order to protect as much as possible our own miserable hides, so I killed it.

As night fell, the constant rattle of gunfire that had raged since being triggered off earlier that day now started to quieten down a little with just spasmodic gunfire to be heard from that sector. Then suddenly the Yanks began pounding the enemy placement with big guns. Fifty-five pounders whistled quietly over our position from some fourteen or fifteen kilometres behind us and slammed home about three-quarters of a kilometre off. They would keep this up all night.

The Jungle seemed to me to be more alive that night; yet despite this, the rain and the constant barrage of exploding shells, I managed to snatch a little sleep before being called for gun duty at midnight. I found to my horror when I got to the gun that some useless bastard was firing parachute flares into the sky above us and that these were revealing me for all to see every time one of them went off with a pop, which lit up the night sky, to turn it into daylight — very disconcerting, to say the least.

Just after two a.m. at about the same time as I'd got back into my swag and was trying to get a little more restless sleep, one of the Yank shells changed its tune from a low whistle to what started out as a low scream, which got louder and louder until it was the highest pitched and eeriest spine-tingling scream you've ever heard. It ceased at full pitch like it had been cut off by death itself. There was a pause of the most unearthly silence ... than an almighty CRASH. The shell erupted almost on top of us, shattering the inky-black jungle night. It would be impossible for me to explain properly the terror that now gripped me as dead shrapnel began to rain down upon us in the dark.

With that shell exploding at what seemed to me to be a fair bit short of fifty metres distance from us and remembering clearly from our training that our camp was in the line of fire of at least one of the next volley of rounds, which I could hear being sent forth at this very instant from the Big Guns, I knew what was about to happen. At this range they sounded like distant thunder BOOM-BOOM-BOOM. That first one had just been their range finder.

My mind went wild. I could see myself alone. I was stark naked and lying unable to move on a vast expanse of flat desert. It went on forever on all sides of me. I lay there watching this shell coming down on me from a long way above me, but I was powerless to stop it from hitting me. If I moved this way or that it followed me. At the same time it physically pinned me to the one spot. Then, in almost the same instant, I got a picture — as clear as a glass full of rain water — of hunks of raw flesh being blasted out though gaping holes in small, green tents.

I don't know if I got up or not, but I do remember screaming out to the blackness at the top of my voice, 'TELL THEM CUNTS T'CEASE FIRE!'

By this time, Shortarse had gathered enough sense about him to call out to Mick the Sig. 'Sig, Sig, where are yah, Sig. Tell them to cease fire.'

Mick came back to him in a low, heavy-but-very-calm, drawl, 'I already 'ave.' Remember, I told you that Mick had been here with the other mob so he knew what to do in a situation like this. Thank Christ, too.

I waited with heart almost stopped, ready to fly into our shell scrape at the first shell burst in our position …

Fortunately for us, the remaining oncoming rounds fluttered through the night sky overhead and on to complete their mission at the sight of the enemy bunker.

You know, no one ever talked about it, so I don't know and can't tell you how any of the other blokes felt at the time. One thing I can tell you though is that there was no more thought of sleep for me for the rest of that night.

Just before midday the next day, shooting erupted to the east of us. There was a CRACK-CRACK-CRACK and suddenly our whole area was inundated with live lead. It cracked and whistled through the trees around us. We hit the deck. Chopped leaves drifted down on us like confetti. We waited with baited breath for the enemy to come. Soon the noise of the skirmish died down and we had to wait for a radio report to find out what had happened.

Some Nogs had slipped through our cordon and had come across a lone sentry lying beside a track. It was Boxall's Batman. They'd walked up behind him on the track and, suddenly spotting him, they let him have it with a quick short burst from an AK47 and bolted into the scrub.

Instinctively, Company Headquarters opened up with everything they had to protect their man and we just happened to be in their line of fire. 'Cease fire' was called for. Then when 'sentry's in' was called and the sentry didn't respond, CSM Toddy Smith got up and raced out to his position to find a wounded Digger. He pulled him onto his back in a fireman's lift and rushed him back into the safety of their campsite. The sentry had got two slugs in the leg, but had been bloody lucky not to get a full burst up his back, bloody lucky. 'Never walk again,' they told us, but we did hear a little while later on that he was up and walking about eleven days after being RTA-ed; having only got it through the fleshy part with no bones broken up.

After a search of the now inactive enemy Bunker System, it was found that 3 Battalion 33 North Vietnamese Army Regiment and members of D445 Local Force Battalion had been holed up in it.

Now that we'd done our job over on the east side of the road, we were picked up by the same swarm of Yank choppers and flown west again to where we were to patrol out around the north-west province border region.

For the first time, we "landed without smoke". Protocol was out the window, but at least this time the Yanks didn't blast piss and pick handles out of our LZ before they dropped us. One of the pilots though must have been high or drunk or something because he appeared to lose control of his craft as he was about to land. He came in with the tail right down below the level of the rest of his airframe, swaying wildly from side to side.

Watching it descend, I thanked Christ that I hadn't landed that one at the same time feeling sorry for the poor bastards who had; however, they somehow managed to be put down safely.

Soon we were to get our first kill. At this stage, Eight Platoon had split off from the rest of the Company and was separating into half-Platoon-size patrolling Sections. I was with the group who had been sent to investigate the immediate vicinity to the south of our Base Camp. We were poking around in bamboo country and, having gone far enough away, we had turned around and were on our way back when a sudden barrage of rifle and M60 fire burst the silence apart just ahead of us. Instinctively we scattered in all directions, hitting the deck and slithering to whatever cover we could find.

'Shit!' They seemed to be almost right on top of us. 'Fuck! The bamboo.

'Don't shoot til yur see the whites in their eyes,' Coggins warned me, as we lay side by side at the bottom of the same clump of bamboo.

'Get fucked,' I retorted. 'I've been in this war as long as you fucken 'ave.'

In silence we waited tensely in our sparse cover until it was confirmed through the Sig that we were not being attacked and that we could now come back to camp.

Apparently the other half of us back in camp had spotted a small band of VC heading west and had immediately opened up on them. When all the commotion died down, it was confirmed that the enemy had fired back at us and it was thought that at least one of them was seen to have been hit.

A Guy was told to take a couple of others out with him to

confirm the hit. He refused to move from his position inside the harbour. This is the same bloke who was getting quieter and quieter on the ship coming over. He'd told us during training that he had to leave SAS because he broken his ankle on his first parachute jump. Now it seemed more likely that the SAS could see the writing on the wall and had bushed him early in his training. He was demoted to Private immediately and bushed from the field when the next chopper came in. We never saw him again.

During a search of the area, only a little blood was found. A little while later the Kiwis found a partly buried and badly decomposed body — most likely rooted up by wild pigs — at this same place and claimed it as their kill, but we protested strongly; claiming the Kiwis had not been in this area at the time of the shooting. After stringent argument over the airways which lasted nearly all day, it was agreed by all that it was indeed our kill. Not being too greedy though, we gave half of it back to the Kiwis for having found the deaden; while we Eight Platoon Charlie Company went on our merry way claiming one half of the first kill for 4RAR/NZ on this tour. He was most likely from D445.

A few days on and Clarkey was treated to a surprise birthday cake on the day he turned twenty. We were encamped at the time. All of a sudden song burst forth from the boys on the eastern side of our harbour site and there were our two scouts, Coggans and Mullan, with a couple of other blokes following them as they made their way around the string-line towards Clarkey's position. On a make-shift platter they carried a small fruit cake which had come in a tin with the Yank ration packs. A couple of lighted matches stood out of the top of it and they were singing 'Happy Birthday' as they went. Jim was appalled by the racket. Clarkey just beamed with joy — they'd remembered his birthday.

A day or two after this, in or around the same area a couple of the boys came to me full of excitement.

'You'll know wot t'do, you'll know how t'catch 'im, you're from the bush.'

'Wot? — Wot do yur want me t'catch?' I asked, quietly.

'Quick come withus, we'll show yuh,' they said.

When I got around to where I'd been dragged off to, 'it' turned out to be the biggest scorpion I have ever laid eyes on. It was as long as a man's hand span and a deep emerald green in colour.

'Woddayur want me t'do with that?' I inquired calmly, while bending to take a closer look at it.

'We want yur t'catch it for us,' they chorused.

'OK, go getus a couplea empty cans, an' see if yurken find me abitta black tape,' I told them.

Within minutes they were back with the two cans and the tape. I placed one can on the ground just in front of the giant scorpion with the open end facing it and we waited and watched. It took just seconds for the big fellow to see this as a place of refuge and crawl right in. I quickly and quietly placed the other can end to end with the one that the scorpion was in, open end to open end so that he'd have a bit of room to move about in there, and held it up in front of them.

'Gee, is that all yur have t'do? We didn't know it was that easy!' one of the onlookers remarked, wide-eyed.

'Right, now put the tape around the middle. Wot are yur gunna do withut now?' I quizzed them.

Their excitement replaced the awe immediately. 'Awe we're gunna get two of em an' we're gunna put a ring a fire round 'em and we're gunna make 'em fight.'

'Yud better punch some 'oles inet for him t'breathe,' I told them, as I handed them the caged scorpion, 'poor bastard might be in there forra long time waiting f'you blokes t'get 'im a mate t'blew with.'

I wandered back to my area then. They never did tell me if they ever found an opponent for it, or how it got on.

When the mail came in on the Maintdem (Maintenance) chopper, I received a letter from Narelle telling me she had moved down to Sydney to live and work. It came as a bit of a shock really. I thought she was quite happy living at home and working in Townsville.

A couple of mornings after this we were patrolling west and when the smoke break came we were on the top of a small ridge. As usual, we sat and idly burnt the leeches that had attached themselves to us while we were travelling, with our cigarettes. There were always two to four of them sucking the blood from our ankles every time we pulled up. They'd attach themselves in the gap between the tops of our boots and the elastic bands which pulled in the bottoms of our dungarees. They were always the first to be disposed of; next the ones which ventured too close to us while we smoked had to go.

Anyway, with the smoke break over, we continued on along the ridge which curved a little to the south until Mullen came across some tracks that ran down the slope to the west.

He immediately followed them down. Then we stopped and Shortarse was signalled to go down and check it out. He too became a little confused when a whole series of tracks criss-crossed the bottom of the slope, so he came back to Mick to make a report of his findings to CHQ.

While this was going on, Sections Six and Four stood on the top of the ridge-line waiting to pass, but they never did get going, not that way at any rate. I'd heard what sounded to me like someone chopping wood just a little way to the south-east of our position. They'd told us during training that every time we heard a woodchopper we had to check it out straight away. As soon as Shortarse stopped gasbagging to Boxall, I informed him immediately of the presents of one near by.

'Nonsense Private, who'd be chopping wood out here?' He said curtly, then mocked me. 'You must be hearing things.'

If you knew me you would understand my retort to such an accusation; that I, a Bushman, would mistake what sounded like the blade of an axe being hammered into a tree. Well, Christ, I'd cut enough trees down myself on Beefwood Downs during the '65 drought to feed our sheep and cattle not to know what it sounds like, so I stood my ground.

'Well, if yur jus' stand 'ere long enough an' listen, you'll 'earut f'yerself, Sir.'

I'd heard the unmistakeable sound twice already and something in my voice must have convinced him to stay and listen. We waited together — much to his annoyance — for it to come again, and after a bit it did.

Shortarse sent a message to CHQ that we would investigate the woodchopper immediately and we were hustled back to the top of the ridge where we all went to ground and took up firing positions. Part of Five Section faced down the slope toward the woodchopper, while the other half faced back down the other side from where we'd just come, to protect our rear.

I lay facing the direction from which the noise had come, listening intently, not moving a muscle. I was trying to pick up the exact position of the woodchopper. Fortunately for me, I was lying behind a small, embedded rock and I had managed to score a good fire-lane as I went to ground. It went for about six metres or so. Everything was deathly quiet and time seemed to stand still while we waited for the next move.

Unbeknownst to me, Shortarse had dispatched Four Section and had sent them across the front of our waiting barrels. I don't know why, because at the time they were the furthermost Section from the woodchopper. They were now moving across our sights and no one had even bothered to give us the "friendlies moving your way" covering hand signal.

The first thing I noticed was the faint sound of a click which may have been made by a man breaking a twig, And then another ... I eased my rifle into my shoulder, thumbed the safety catch to check it was off and waited. Another click, then a dark shape the size of a man moved slowly into my fire-lane. Ever so slowly it moved, giving me ample time to quietly aim my rifle. My movement, however subtle, had not gone unnoticed by Clarkey. He raised the butt of the M60 and sighted her up.

Into my aperture sight appeared firstly the rifle barrel of my enemy. I noted that he had tied a piece of clear plastic around the muzzle of the weapon.

How peculiar, I thought, *We do that.* It was to stop the mud and dirt from going up the barrel of our gats.

I also noticed that the rifle being carried was an M16, the type some of us used, a weapon, nevertheless, that the Nogs didn't seen to have any trouble getting their hands on.

I now moved my line of sight up the body noting the greens he was wearing as I came slowly to his head. At this distance I could not possibly miss. A head shot is always a kill. He was dead the second I squeezed the trigger. I applied a little more pressure. I checked again with my thumb to make sure the safety catch was indeed off. I noted the green giggle hat. Again, our enemy had no trouble acquiring these. I moved the front sight to the temple of the Nog, breathed in slightly and held my breath.

As I started to squeeze off the shot that was a sure death to its receiver, I suddenly became conscious of a thick, black moustache which curled up at the ends. With that a realisation swept over me. There was only one person that I knew in this whole world who could be wearing that handlebar moustache ... Charlie Hill!

I froze with shock. I'd come ever so close to shooting my mate, Charlie. He most certainly would not have moved again had I gone through with that shot. Then I suddenly remembered Clarkey and the M60 and I knew I had to move fast. He most likely would not see what I'd seen down my sights because I'd had an uninterrupted view from where I was, but Clarkey may not have and might only see the moving shadow. That M60 could spit out a lot of lead in a quick burst and if Clarkey squeezed the trigger, it would be goodbye Charlie Hill and there'd also be a few others that would go in the fire-fight that undoubtedly would ensue.

I somehow caught Clarkey's attention, giving him the

thumbs-up sign, and pointed towards the slow-moving Hilly. He immediately dropped the butt of the M60 to dear Mother Earth, then using common sense he signalled the same sign to the Riflemen on his right who had reacted the same way as Clarkey had done when he saw him raise the gun in the first place.

The ever-chattering birds had fallen silent. No other sound could be heard save the occasional quiet click of the secateurs Charlie used to cut a clearer path through to the enemy as he went about his business completely unaware that he himself had come so close to his own demise at my hands.

On the other hand, I was seething. Someone was going to get a piece of my mind, but not right now, as Charlie would soon be onto the enemy and he had to get as near as possible without attracting attention.

Time dragged as the Section sent to deal with the woodchopper passed through my fire-lane. Then the axeman started to chop again, but he never got to cut down his tree that day. Yet, despite the hail of lead that was showered upon him and his two mates, they made for the scrub and got clean away apparently unscathed. They even had the audacity, we were told, to shoot back at their assailants as they scampered away up a slight incline and over a small ridge and so to cover, taking all their belongings with them.

From the ridge top where we lay in wait, the noise of the ambush was dynamic. The whole world seemed to be torn apart by the sudden harsh rattle of automatic weapons all striving to outdo one another. With the crackle of the enemy's AK47s added in, there came also a couple of dull crashes from the M79's ogive.

As quickly as it started, it stopped. All was quiet and still again. Half a minute of absolute peace prevailed before the sound of human voices brought life back to this place.

We converged onto the spot to find that we had not come across a woodchopper as I'd first thought, but, in fact, we had attacked a transfer station. The chopping on the tree was indeed one of the men in the station sending out a signal of their whereabouts to the couriers who'd pass through them.

We found, by what they'd left lying around the place, that they had been eating only bananas, small fish and chicken. How long they had been set up here was to remain a mystery. Instead of following up the quarry or getting back onto those original tracks, Shortarse now decided to go east.

Just a little way on, we came across a small unused banana plantation which ran north-south. We halted in this while Shortarse went walkabout with a scout to find out what lay to the north of the bananas. While we were waiting for his return, some of us tried the little green bananas, which tasted like flour. The trees offered us a little shade from the sun, which was fierce to say the least, once we were out from under the cover of the "J".

Eventually, we set up camp just east of the northern end of the banana plantation. The scrub here was a little sparser than what we were used to. It was decided we'd use this position as an ambush site. We sat there for two days before anything happened.

Andy and I were out on sentry duty just to the north of our camp and sitting on a large mound of red dirt, when suddenly the whole place erupted into a multitude of gunfire. We scurried for cover and flattened out behind the mound of dirt.

We lay there at the ready, quite and still, not knowing where the enemy were or how many we were up against for that matter.

Then we could hear Pollard yelling over the din. 'Sentries in, Sentries in.'

'Fuck 'im, I'm right 'ere,' I called across to Andy. After all, that great lump of dirt was affording us better cover than the blokes in the Platoon area were getting as there was nothing but flat ground, small trees and bamboo where they were.

'I gotta go,' he said, simply, 'gotta 'elp wid thu gun.'

Then he was gone. For less than a minute I lay alone behind my great lump of dirt, but only for less than that minute. I looked back over my right shoulder to see Andy's back as he disappeared behind the bamboo towards our Platoon harbour.

'Fuck this, I'm not stoppen 'ere on me own,' I said aloud, and then I too was running; running with head down, arse up and running like mad for fear of being hit by stray lead or of being cut off by the unseen enemy. The next thing I know I'm throwing myself on the ground beside Andy. As I flattened out, I'd seen that all our weapons were pointing east. The place reeked of burnt cordite. The noise of the barrage was a dull roar somewhere in the background.

Andy was squatting with one knee on the ground, his other leg tucked under his bum and with one elbow resting on his raised knee. 'Shoot lower, shoot lower,' he was yelling, as his M16 bucked in his hands and spat a shower of lead in the direction of the elusive enemy. I felt like I was moving in slow motion as I raised myself to join him in the sit position and shoulder to shoulder we let rip. Someone yelled, 'Cease fire, cease fire.' The racket stopped.

There was some quick discussion. Andy, being our Army trained tracker, and a couple of others were sent out to see if we got anything. The rest of us waited tensely at our posts. The moments ticked away then there came a call from Andy. 'Ere's one. E's over 'ere.'

'Is he dead yet?' Shortarse yelled back.

'Yep, 'e's dead,' Andy answered, dryly.

Two men then dragged the dead Nog back into camp with a leg each over one of their shoulders. His head wobbled from side to side; reminding me of back home when Ned and Claudie dragged dead roos back to their vehicles to cut the legs and tail off them for their dogs. Another two men were employed to carry all the stuff he'd been carrying when he went down and, seeing as Four Section was first to see the small band of Nogs, he was dragged into their area. Apparently, the Nogs had heard someone bang something against a metal mug and, upon seeing us encamped, had turned away to avoid tangling with us.

While all this was going on, Smithy was getting more and more excited.

'They shot back attus. They shot back attus. I seen the flashes,' he kept repeating over and over. I looked around at him to find him shaking like a leaf.

'Awe, f'fuck sake, Smitty, come an' sit over 'ere wif me an' 'ave a smoke, will yuh. Yur'll 'ave me as bad as you in a minute,' I said to him, and coached him over to sit at the base of a small tree.

I rolled him a smoke and handed it down to him, then struck a match and, bending towards him, I cupped my hands around the flame and lit him up. I was standing looking down at him while dragging on my own fresh-lit rollie when I noticed that something had cut into the bamboo just behind him. I stepped around him and with the point of my bayonet I extracted a couple of pieces of twisted brass from the bamboo about thirty centimetres above the ground. Bringing them back around to Smithy in the palm of my hand, I held them out to show him and put it to him with a grin, 'Ere, Smitty, get a load of this, willyuh. Just imagine that tearen inta yur gut, ay?'

His reaction was immediate. 'I told yuh they shot back attus,'he cried, 'I told yuh,' and the shaking started all over again.

Andy arrived back at our position about then. He showed me a flat-faced wrist watch he'd lifted from our downed Nog.

'Didja get anything else? Did 'e 'ave any money on 'im?' I quizzed him.

'Nar, only got this. No money. He was a doctor or somethin' goen by the little bags a' drugs 'e was carryen. All tied up in little plastic bags they were, rubber bands aroun' everythin'. Wot do yur think a'this though, hey?' he asked of the watch.

'Not bad,' I said to him, 'What are yer gunna do wivet?'

'I'm gunna takeut 'ome for a souvenir,' he was telling me, when someone called out to him, 'Hey, Andy, you didn't find anything on that Nog, did yah? He didn't have a watch on 'im or anything, did 'e?'

His answer was predicable as he shot a sidelong glance at me to make sure I wouldn't dob him in.

'Nar, never got nuffen.' He had his back to them, so they didn't see him quickly shove it inside his shirt.

I left him then and went to see "the deaden". His head was

flattened to half its normal size and both his eyes had been blown out of their sockets. There was very little blood, but I supposed most of that was left where Andy had found him as well as on the track where they had dragged him back into our camp. I stood there for a second and a pang of sadness overcame me. This poor bastard has a mother somewhere who will never see him again; he might even have a wife and kids too and we've just put a stop to him. Just as quickly I snapped back to reality and chastised myself. We both knew the rules of war before we got to this point. He'd have bopped any one of us given half the chance; it's first in, best dressed, here. We get them before they get us.

I was still around in that area talking to one of Andy's mates when the M60 in Six Section burst into action again quickly joined with a wing of the semi-automatic rifles from the west side of the camp. I hit the deck and stayed with the blokes from Four Section. 'Cease fire,' was called for and it was found that the boys were a bit jumpy and were shooting at nothing really.

Then Pollard was yelling out for me, 'Over 'ere Jim, waddayur want?'

'Where the fuck aveyur been? Waddayur think yur doen over there? I thought yur were out there getten shot at,' Pollard showed his concern for my safety as he angrily strode over to where I was stationed.

'Donn be fucken stupid Jim, yur donn think I'd be dumb enough to get out there in fronta these trigger 'appy bastards, do yuh?'

I went back over to my part of the camp and began to kick up a stink about getting the Nog's Ho Chi Ming sandals. I wanted to take them home with me and put them in an RSL as an exhibit. After an Oscar winning performance that lasted for half an hour or more, Pollard gave in and begrudgingly brought them over and chucked them to me.

It was getting on a bit in the day by this and the dead Nog's body was starting to bloat and pong a bit. They went and got some banana leaves to cover him up with until the chopper came to take away his belongings to be analysed by Intelligence. They eventually came in around dinner. By this time he was real ripe.

Now it was time to put him down. A shell scrape had already been dug beside the body. They told Obie to do the honours.

'I'm not touching him. Youse killed him,' was Obie's reply.

He was then "ordered" to do the honours. All he really had to do was to roll the dead Nog over and he would literally fall right into his hole.

'I'm not touching him. Youse killed him. Youse murdered him,' Obie cried out, getting louder as he went. In the end, they were telling Obie that they were going to charge him for disobeying a lawful command and Obie was wailing at the top of his voice.

'Youse murdered him, yer murderers, yer murderers'

Andy's mate ended up pushing him into the hole just to stop the noise Obie was making.

We left this place next morning feeling pretty cocky. We had ourselves another kill. That afternoon around three, after patrolling south-east for most of the day, I got my chance to vent off some steam over nearly busting Hilly because of no covering signal three days back. We'd come upon a small, round, very foul-smelling swamp about a hectare in size with dark-green, thick-stem grass growing all through it. Five Section must have been the tailing Section at the time. Suddenly, there were people moving across on the other side of the swamp and, for a second, Muzzy, Smithy, myself and a couple of others who'd spotted them at about the same time had our gats to our shoulders. We were about to let go before we recognised who they were. I yelled to Andy from my place as Tail End Charlie.

'Andy, tell them useless bastards over there t'giveus the covering signal or some prick's gunna get it.'

Pollard got stuck into Andy about me making too much noise and told him to put me on a charge, but Andy ripped it right back into him, pointing towards the blokes at the other side of the swamp.

'Yer can't blame us. Them cunts over there didn't give us a signal that they were goen that way. If this sorta shit keeps up someone's gunna get shot.'

No more was said and in reality no more had to be said. That was the last time the 'Thumbs-up, goodies" sign didn't get through to all participants.

Nothing much happened for our Platoon for the next week or so. We did a lot of patrolling, harbouring up and then more patrolling. The other Platoons were getting a little action though.

We were told at one of our nightly 'O' groups about an APC that had been attacked and was blown wide open and that its sides had been buckled in the blast. According to the report, it was suspected that a VC had somehow dropped or slung a satchel charge into the open hatch on top of the Carrier and it went off inside killing six Reo Diggers and the Carrier's Crewman with them and wounding the driver and Carrier Commander.

* * *

12

SUGAR AND SPICE

Finally, after six weeks in country, we were picked up by chopper and transported out and back down to the Dat. Soon after arriving there we were bundled into trucks and taken out round the back of the barbed wire-enclosed Base to the Weapons Range. Here we were allowed to expend — or, if you like, waste — all the lead that each man carried with him in the scrub. Even Officers like Shortarse could do it! We emptied our mags into make-shift targets in the direction of the Long Tan Rubber Plantation, which was the site of one of Australia's most notorious battles with the Viet Cong during our years of involvement in this here bloody war. We'd be given a full supply of new brass when next we ventured out.

Even though our minds were now focusing on our first R&R (Rest and Recreation) in Vung Tau, Nui Dat had a few home comforts of her own to offer. We treated ourselves to our first shower in six weeks, washing our bodies clean of the sweat, mud and grime. We had the chance to sit on real beds, swing our legs over the side or while away the afternoon yarning to mates from the other Platoons, blokes like Stretch and Robo and others who were shacked up in the tent next to us. Although we were all in the same Company, we hadn't seen one another since going out as our individual Platoons were kept pretty much to themselves and only stayed in contact through the radio. It was also a time to strap on a pistol obtained from the "Orderly Room" (Office) located up at the gate into our area. Our personal weapons and other things like grenades had been taken from us and locked away in the Ammo Bay due to the fact that our bosses didn't want to give any of us the chance to "frag" them when we got a bit of piss in us, which was quite on the cards. It had happened over here already, before we got in country.

Anyway, with pistol on hip, one could go walkabout over to the PX store or down across the flat to the Nog store, which was about halfway between us and the Reo mob, a little under half a kilometre away south-east of our lines. This store was really a number of adjoining building all facing into a large, square quadrangle. They were well constructed of wooden planks and here we could get our hands on varïous knick-knacks for ourselves or to send home to the folks. We could get a haircut if we fancied — or if we were ordered to — as I often was.

Then came time to open the Boozer — grog and lots of it for our thirsty hides. Each homeland State sent cartons of cans of their particular brew over to us and as time went by whilst we were out in the "J", our daily ration of two cans per man per day grew into a mountain in a room beside the bar. The barmen filled a battered, old bathtub with ice and emptied whatever carton came to hand into it, then when we breasted the bar, they asked, 'Wot can we get yah?'

'A beer.'

'Wot colour would yur like?'

We didn't ask for a *Fosters*, *XXXX* or *VB*, we asked for a blue, yellow, green or white, according to whatever was bobbing around in the ice at the time. No one complained, but then, who would, with cans at 15c a piece and Whiskey 15c a shot. It was cold, it was piss and it was going down real well after so long in a dry camp in the tropics.

Then suddenly, to our profound horror, they closed the Boozer down only two hours after opening. We hadn't even got settled right in. We protested most vigorously, but to no avail. Instead, we were told. 'Ittle be awright, youse'ill be able t'come back, but now yur gotta go an 'ave somthun t'eat.'

Looking mournfully back towards the Boozer, we slowly drifted off in the direction of the Mess hut. We were confronted with what can only be described as a feast. Tables from the Mess had been brought outside and joined together to form one big, long one. This table was loaded with every kind of tucker that you could imagine. We ate stand up buffet style out under the stars on a warm, tropical evening.

At one such banquet, I recall the cooks had somehow got hold of a rather large fish, which was something like sixty centimetres long, two hundred and fifty millimetres or so high and its body complete, eyes and all. Cooked to the colour of lobster, it sat on a big, round plate taking pride of place right in the centre of mobs of tropical fruits and meats and things on the table. It was, to my knowledge, still sitting there in all its glory long after we had eaten our fill and were standing around licking our fingers and watching for the Boozer to reopen.

However, our second assault on the pisser was always a slightly more subdued affair involving slower, more moderate, drinking. Not that we didn't try, but with our tummies bloated from the first crack at it, and then being followed by the big feed, we were forced to slow down some.

This whole idea was worked out so that we didn't get too far under the weather and start taking to each other on our first night in. After all, we were lean, mean, fighting machines, conditioned to do nothing but kill and with too much piss in us something could go wrong. Most of us usually managed to potter off to find our huts before closing time. Here, unlike in the bush, we could crash on the steel- frame beds, up off the dirt and in just our undies and without boots on our feet. Those mates who couldn't walk were carried back, of course.

Next morning we were up early rearing to go. In our Compound, we were loaded aboard a convoy of trucks and with each of us carrying our civvies in our carry-all bag, we were transported south down Route Two, through the large township of Baria and out onto the highway which ran from Saigon, around the big, sweeping bend and down to Vung Tau, which was a big island cut off from the mainland by mangrove swamps. It jutted out into the South China Sea.

Vung Tau at last. Now I would find out first hand all about oriental ladies. I was determined to go to these girls with a very open mind, having heard so many assorted stories of what one could expect of them from the blokes who'd been over here before — most of whom had also spent time in Singapore — and only half believing them.

'Yurkan get anything yur want,' they'd say about the massage girls, 'They'll even walk on yur back.' Then they'd stand there with glazed eyes staring away towards the north, lost in memories of past forbidden pleasures.

So here we sat in the middle of the huge complex that was the Australian Army Camp in Vung Tau dressed like real people again and busting our guts to get out there amongst the action. We were sitting on chairs beside an Olympic-sized swimming pool like a mob of schoolkids at an outdoor lecture while a Captain laid down the rules and regulations of what was expected of us while we were in town on leave. Someone had kindly handed each of us a can of beer just before this joker started spruiking. The beer went down real well.

We eventually tumbled out of the trucks in the heart of town at a structure known as "The Flags". From here we dispersed in all directions to explore the bars. I just happened to team up with Pig Pratt and together we made our way south hurrying past the bars which had three or four girls crowding the narrow doorways, all waving and calling for us to come in and join them. Bright lights welcomed us from inside narrow, low doors and loud American rock music blasted out of the establishments which were joined side by side along the street, but we kept moving, looking for something that would take our fancy.

On the opposite side of the broad avenue which ran sort of south from The Flags, I noticed one of the bars had been closed up. The Australian authorities had a policy in Vietnam that if anyone of our blokes got the "Jack" from a girl in a certain bar — he didn't have to say what girl it was who had infected him — all he had to do was name or point out the bar she worked in and our MPs would put an OUT OF BOUNDS sign on its window. This action usually closed the bar down because it wasn't long before everyone who came to visit Vung Tau for their pleasure began to heed the signs. It actually had a two-fold effect; ensuring that none of our blokes got it from that place in the future and forcing the managers of the girls in the other bars to keep their girls clean.

At the bottom end of the Boulevard — or whatever you'd call it — where it split into two roads going in two different directions, Pig and I spotted a massage parlour, 'The Blue Pacific'. We decided we'd try it and made our way into it off the hot street.

We first encountered a barber shop on the bottom floor; not your everyday barber shop as you know it, though. Here you could not only get your hair cut, but your neck and forehead massaged, finger nails cut and cleaned, fingers cracked or clicked and what have you. I was told that what the list on the wall didn't mention was that while you were in the chair getting all these things done to you, if you paid the right amount of money, a spunky little thing would go in under the sheet that covered you from the neck to the floor and do a superb blow job on you. Never did get to try that one though. After looking up the list, Pig and I decided on a sauna bath followed by a massage. We were soon being ushered up a thin flight of stairs by four very attentive and smiling young ladies, one clinging to each of our arms. We must have really stuck out to them as new boys in town.

Pig seemed to have been in a sauna before, but I had not. I'll try just about anything once, though, so I followed him in. When the door closed behind us we were in a large, wood-lined box with a bench along the back wall on which we sat on while the girls added more steam. It was hot, stuffy and stunk like hell in there. I had a job to see Pig through the fog, but he looked like he was enjoying himself. I, however, wasn't so keen on being locked up in this confined space in a foreign country with no means of escape. It didn't take me too long to persuade him that this was not for me. Upon his reluctant agreement, I went to the door and waved through the little window in an effort to make contact with one or all of the girls who sat along a bench on the wall opposite the door, a few of whom had already looked inquisitively in through the little fogged-up window at us. Five or six of them sat there looking as if they were waiting in anticipation for us to come out. As soon as they saw me at the window, they all jumped to their feet and rushed the door. Once freed by the smiling and fussing beauties, it was time for our massage. We were each led along a narrow passage and shown into a small room off to the right. Everything was clean. Piped music and the voices of Vietnamese girls softly singing in their own haunting tongues filled the entire area.

I was told by the girl who claimed me — a sweet little thing of about eighteen years of age — to lie face down on the flat, hard bed at the far wall, whereupon she proceeded to chop me with swift little Karate chops, slowly moving all over me to the beat of the music until I felt like I was floating. All the time she was working on me I was trying to feel her up.

'Me no do,' she kept insisting as she went about her task, but by the time she smacked me on my bare bum and proudly announced, 'Finish,' I was sure she'd come around. I felt so good I reckoned I could take on a tribe of these pretty little things. I asked her straight out, 'You want boom-boom?'

She looked pained. 'No,' she said, 'me no boom-boom.'

Disappointed, but not discouraged, I changed tack. 'OK, go find me someone who can boom-boom then.'

'Ockay,' she answered with a grin, and departed, saying, 'You wait.'

A little time later she returned, but she bought with her a real scrag who I didn't fancy pegging at all. Very quickly, I asked her, 'You suckfuck?'

'No,' she said, 'Me no suckfuck.'

'OK,' I told her, 'You go find me someone who can suckfuck.'

Away they both went, reappearing at the door soon afterwards with another young lady of about the same age — a hard-looking bit with short, close-cropped hair. Producing a rubber from nowhere, she smartly covered my old boy and immediately started bobbing up and down, much to the delight of the other two girls who were still standing in the doorway.

All the time I'd been waiting, Pig was doing his own thing in the booth next to me. Through the paper-thin walls that failed to reach the ceiling by at least sixty centimetres I couldn't help but hear everything that was going on in there.

He asked the girl who'd been given him his massage, 'Are you a Catholic?'

'Yarhh, I Catholic,' she answered, quite matter-of-factly.

'Yur notta bad fuck furra Catholic,' Pig told her, then stated, 'I've never fucked a Catholic!'

I lay there trying to figure out why Catholics should or should not be any different to Buddhists or girls of any other religion, for that matter. After all, females are females the world over. Once they've got their clothes off and are in bed with a horny male, religion pulls the pin and natural instincts take over, thank Christ.

But now just as my girl bobber was beginning to make

headway with me, I heard Pig yell in a voice which drowned out the piped singing. 'Hey! Look at this willyuh, Dog's getten a suckfuck.'

He had climbed onto the bed in his booth and was now looking down on me from the top of the partition with a broad grin. All I could do was laugh as I looked up at him. Consequently, my previously willing old fellow curled up and died in the girl-bobber's hands.

We paid for "services rendered (or not)" and, with smiles all round, left the Blue Pacific and headed back towards the bars. After losing Pig in the Blue Angel, I met up with some more of my mates. Together, a team of us checked out all the bars that were on the lower side of the street which ran south-east from The Flags. At the end of a line of bars known as the US Sky Bars, was the Chikito Bar. We promised the girls here that we'd be back and moved on until we'd past the Kingdom Bar. Finding no more bars from there on, we turned about. One of the girls from the Chikito was in the process of mounting a motor scooter as we arrived back there, but, upon seeing us, she immediately discarded the machine and, all smiles, made a bee-line for me and grabbed me by the arm, thus I was lead towards her bar with her telling me that she was just about to come looking for us.

The Chikito Bar was much the same as most of the rest. Darker and cooler inside than the hot, sunlit street, it was much like an old-style Greek café back home. The lights were low and the latest Yank hits were being blasted throughout the place. A bar ran almost the full length of one wall and bench seats facing each other ran along the other wall.

We were shown to padded bench seats at the rear of the room

by a bunch of excited girls who began trying to find out who among us were the "Cherry Boys". It was quite significant to be a Cherry Boy in Vung Tau and all honour to the girls who actually found one. The lucky finder would then delightfully take off with her prize, whereupon she'd have the pleasure of taking his virginity. She could be first to teach him the art of actually making love the Asian way. On top of all that, that first one was free. I believe a couple were found on this first trip. We certainly had fun trying to convince these girls that we were all Cherry Boys, but, alas, somehow they seemed to know.

It didn't take too long for us to discover why Australian troops were known as "Cheap Charlies" in the sin cities of South Vietnam. After a taste test of what was known as "Saigon Tea" and "Vung Tau Tea", we realised that we were paying about twice the price of a *Five Star* — a can of Yank piss — for no more than a small, four-ounce glass of Sarsaparilla or Lime, respectively. The girls had developed a great capacity to sit on their drinks as we wouldn't keep paying such high prices for what amounted to nothing more than lolly water. Still, they loved us just the same even if we were Cheap Charlies.

Within ten minutes of being in the bar, we also found out first-hand what Captain Spruiker was warning us about back at Camp that morning with regard to watching out for our personal possessions. One of the girls in our little group, her arm lovingly placed around the bloke from Wagga, was very slowly and very carefully sliding his watch off his wrist. It had a steel, expandable band and she had no trouble getting it halfway over his hand before being sprung. The other girls immediately chastised her most vehemently in Vietnamese.

With all the fervent female attention that I was getting, I soon wanted to sample more than just cuddles, so I put it on my admirer for a bang.

Now I'd better tell you the set-up as far as the girls and the bars were concerned: Each bar had nine or ten girls working in it. They were sort of owned by a "Muma-san" or "Popa-san". There were around one thousand nine hundred bars in Vung Tau. Some had more girls in them than others. There were about nine thousand girls for us to pick from, but only seven thousand or so of these were considered to be safe and to a greater extent clean of VD. However, as we had no way of knowing which one of these girls presented a risk, we were given "No Sweat Pills" before we left Camp to help protect us. These were large, green capsules with no writing on them. They were full of yellow powder. Two with milk before you got started was the way to use them. Rubbers were also available if that's the way you wanted to go.

To get one of these girls out of the bar, you had to pay the Muma-san or Popa-san who sometimes turned out to be the bar owner as well. The going rate for a quickie was about two dollars "MPC". MPC money was military money, which had the same value as the Yank *Greenback*, worth nothing outside war-torn Vietnam. Twelve dollars would get you an all-nighter for which the girls received five pieces of pink paper, about two inches square, which she would cash in later in order to collect her cut. One yellow for every "Tea" she could manage squeeze out of us.

Once you got her out of the bar, she was yours to do whatever you both wanted to for as long as it took, but every time she went back into the bar she once again became its property. To get her out again, you had to pay again unless you had something worked out with all parties, which usually involved more dough.

At any rate, having paid the bloke behind the counter of the Chitiko, I went with my admirer, Lyn, to a hotel just down the street. Lyn seemed to know this piece at the hotel and, after some chatter between them, we were shown to a room on the ground floor which opened in off the verandah. I handed this other woman something like two hundred *Piastre* — about eighty cents MPC — and, giving me a warm, knowing smile, she let us in.

As I closed the door behind us, Lyn walked to the middle of the room and simply stepped out of her clothing. She then turned towards me and indicated that I do the same. She seemed so much at ease that I did so. First on her agenda was a shower. I followed her in; it was cold but refreshing. As soon as Lyn was happy that we were clean enough, we dried each other with clean, fresh towels and got down on the bed to made love. She seemed to know more about me than I'd anticipated; at this stage in my life I had only ever had three girls and none of them in a bed.

This was different. Lyn, quietly, slowly and deliberately taking her time, showed me how it was done. Even though I could see the shadows of people through the slatted door and could hear the soles of their flat shoes clicking on the stonework of the verandah floor as they passed by right outside, she made it that way that it all seemed so natural that we be in here making love in broad daylight. A lazy hour or so later, she was satisfied. Then, after another cold shower, we wandered off happily chatting back to the bar where I spent the rest of the day with her drinking *Five Star* — An American beer which had as much affect on Australian Diggers as lemonade.

About seven o'clock that night, Lyn asked me if I wanted to go dancing with her.

'Yeah, OK, where at?' I answered.

'I show you, you come,' she said happily, and taking me out of her bar led me to a door two doors away that led up a flight of stairs and into a bar known as the Sky Bar, which had a small dancefloor at one end. Behind this, a band of Vietnamese youth were playing electric guitars and carrying on just like the Yank bands of the day — indeed they were singing the latest Yank songs. We'd had one dance and were just sitting down to order our first drink when suddenly the heavens opened. Without making a sound the whole roof slowly slid away above us, leaving all of us looking up at the stars. Next thing a young Nog kid was asking for our orders. When the drinks came — a beer for me and a Whiskey and Coke for Lyn — we were expected to pay three times what it cost at the Chitiko. I protested to Lyn and we got out of there as fast as we could.

Lyn's flat was extremely clean and tidy when we entered it that night. She lived on the top floor of a two-storey building off a small street that we would call a lane. She had bought some mangetts and another fruit 'for our tea', she told me. The Mangetts were small, about as big as an apricot and the colour of a mango. The flesh inside the thin skin was clear, like Vaseline, and extremely sweet to taste. The other fruit — the name I have since forgotten — was almost the same to eat, but just a little larger in size.

After a cold shower, she and I sat on the bed naked while she explained the story line of the Nog show we were watching on her small black and white TV. We ate the sweet tasting fruits and best of all drank Whiskey from one of two bottles she came up with. A good, long, relaxed session of love making to finish off the day and we fell to sleep in each others arms — my first time ever to camp all night with a woman — and very pleasurable indeed.

Next day, after starting off with a good morning bang, we went back to the bar. At about ten I noticed one of the girls get a visitor who went with her to a booth at the back of the bar and gave her a shot from a needle. She immediately went to sleep right there in the corner for about an hour. When she suddenly awoke she seemed to be full of beans and bouncing all over the place. Just before midday I went walkabout to see who I could find and what they might be up to. Around past The Flags at the Blue Angle, I found Perkins having a good time with a stunning girl called Sandy. I didn't find any of the others though — still shacked up somewhere I supposed. I spent the rest of that day in the Chitiko and went home with Lyn to her place for tea that night for more Whiskey, TV, then boom-boom and sleep, all without any fuss whatsoever.

Around two in the morning I woke with a start and sat bolt upright in bed. A small dog was barking madly at the bottom of the stairs. All my instincts were fully alive and my mind went wild with questions. Did someone know where I was camped for the night? Did Lyn know the VC? Had she set me up? Was it the Vung Tau Cowboys and they knew they had someone isolated? The Cowboys were dangerous little hoods who rode around on small motor bikes. They would cut your throat as quick as look at you. Lyn woke slowly from a deep sleep and asked me. 'What is matter? Why you no sleep?'

'It's that bloody dog down there barken,' I told her, in a worried voice.

'No worry,' she said, completely unperturbed about the din outside. When I wouldn't settle down though, she took me in her arms and made love to me again. Then she said 'shower' and tried to push me out of bed towards the shower room, but there was no way I was going to have a cold bloody shower at this ungodly hour of the morning. Lyn did ...

The following morning after our wake-up boom-boom, while I was having the cold shower, she sat on the toilet having a piss. She pulled the chain and with her hand scooped water up out of the bowl and washed her fanny with it.

Christ, and I've bin rooten that all fucken night, I thought, *but at least she made an attempt to clean herself, so why worry.*

She carefully cleaned the flat. Then she came to me and handed me a small, gold cross on a thin, gold chain.

'You wear this all the time you are here and He will protect you,' she said, sincerely. It was real gold. I bit into it with my teeth to make sure. When we were about to leave the flat, she took up the small broom made of some sort of dark straw and, bending over, swept everything towards her as she shuffled backwards towards the door, then with a flick she swept what was in front of her little broom outside the door and threw the broom back inside the flat quickly closing the door behind it.

Later that day, I said good-bye to this gentle, part-Japanese, part-Chinese result of a World War II liaison and to Vung Tau for the time being and by twelve o'clock we were heading back up the road in trucks to Nui Dat and thence to the jungle.

13
CONSOLIDATION

For the next month we cemented even more into that great anti-Gorilla fighting force they were trying so hard to train us to be back home. We really were becoming the Uc-Dai-Loi: the proud, fierce "Warrior from the South" ... leastways we did a hell of a lot of patrolling.

One thing, however, was noticeable: our animal instincts were becoming quite considerably sharpened. Gradually, we became as one with the creatures of the jungle whose only ambition is to stay alive at all cost. To that end we would kill.

Like the jungle inhabitants, we were the hunters as well as the hunted; creatures with greenish-brown skins which moved silently around on the jungle floor in lines, but nevertheless hunting as a pack. We began to sense danger when it lurked near and feel things much more acutely than ordinary man. Like the animals, we were acquiring the skill of using the foliage to conceal ourselves. By the end of five days our outer skins would have turned almost to the very colour of the ground we slept and ate upon.

On Maintdem days we'd find a place for the choppers to get into us. When they did, we'd be given our clean greens in exchange for our dirty ones and a pair of new socks as well as enough rations for a five day period — and for my part two packets of *Drum* tobacco, special order. When the choppers left, we once again became the sinister creatures of the scrub who roamed quietly about searching for a particular prey. If we found our prey, we'd be expected to devour it immediately, then go right on hunting as if our hunger for their blood could never be satisfied.

Every once in a while we would venture out onto open ground. This would be a paddy field or just open grassland where the broad-leaf Elephant Grass grew as high as our shoulders. Shortarse was virtually invisible in the long grass, his giggle hat being the only thing that could be seen of him or his as it moved along at the same level as the tops of the leaves. The heat was always intense out in the open, but worse than that we were far too exposed to our enemy out there, so we soon faded back into the friendly cover of the greenery again.

Days became a blur except for Saturday: Race day. Every single Saturday Muzzy would get a loan of my pocket wireless with its ear plug and give me his "tip" for the day.

'Put two bucks on so an' so,' he'd tell me, earnestly. 'Youcud win a few bucks, he's gunna win t'day.'

As I've said before, I'm not a gambler. Any money I earn I'd rather piss up against a wall than give it away to a shonky dealer or a crocked jockey in a rigged race, especially at a Metropolitan Meet so, naturally, I declined his offer time and time again and every Saturday afternoon Muzzy would come back to me and tell me, 'If you'da put yur money on that horse like I told yur, you'da made eight bucks t'day,' or whatever the win was.

That never bothered me. What really gave me the shits was how the rest of the Platoon behaved on these days. Poking along minding my own business I'd be called upon to relay messages up and down the line all day.

'Hey, Dog, tell Boris that Bogged Down just won at Randwick,' or 'Hey, Dog, tell Muzzy that Slowcoach just got up at Flemington.' All they ever got from me week in, week out, was 'Tell 'im yur fucken self.'

Sometimes they would tell whoever was ahead of me or behind me at the time to relay the message on. A lot of the time they just yelled up the line, 'Ay, Boris, Bogged Down just won at Randwick.'

Maintdem days on Saturdays was the pits. Trying to get some sense out of the people handling the distribution was almost impossible if they were the ones who were also into the "ponies". Most times it would be a matter of helping oneself. However, the job always got done in the end.

While all this was going on, we were also getting to know some of our other friends with whom we shared the jungle floor. Firstly there was the Chomper Ants: a ginger-coloured ant not quite the size of our Meat Ants back home. Their large head and extra long, curly, black pincers, which joined in the middle in front of them, were bigger than the rest of their bodies, giving them a tendency to fall nose- first onto their pincers as they moved about. At night you could actually hear their pincers clicking together. Then there were the ones we called Soldier Ants mainly because of how they used to get about in groups of ten, which reminded us of a Section of our Infantry. They were smaller than the Chomper Ants, about the size of our home-grown Green Ants.

At times the Soldier Ants could be observed standing out from a line of Chomper Ants and when the Chomper Ant guards — who were patrolling each side of the column at two hundred-millimetre intervals — were exactly one hundred millimetres apart, they would dive in and grab one of the smaller Chomper Ant workers and cart them off undetected.

On one occasion, Andy and I were sitting in a camp when a patrol of Soldier Ants came through the space between us at an angle. We didn't take too much notice of this at first, but when one of them — the Scout — suddenly appeared, coming back, we took notice. It wasn't until the first one was practically all the way across the clearing that the Second Scout came running out and followed the leader. When it too was almost to the opposite side, their Section Commander came out and headed across, but it was only halfway there when the Gunner started over. When the Gunner was halfway, the second Gunner came out but before it got halfway the 2IC of the Section made its dash for it. I leant down and before the 2IC got halfway across the cleared ground I drew a line from one side to the other across its path with my finger. The 2IC stopped at the line and, after a quick turnabout to get its bearings, it went straight along the line until he got to the end and came back along it until it found the original track that they had been using thus far and proceeded along it. Meanwhile, the first of the Riflemen appeared on the edge of the clearing followed closely by his mates moving in a spaced group of four. Instead of going down to the line I'd pulled across the track they turned and went straight to where the 2IC had gone around the end of my line and straight across at precisely the same angle until they picked up their original track out near the end of the cleared area whereupon they disappeared out of sight in the undergrowth.

There were also huge pythons, bamboo snakes and the little

snakes to contend with. One day while we were at lunch, a small dark-green snake wriggled at great speed through our camp space passing between Andy and myself. It was being pursued by a line of Soldier Ants about fifty millimetres wide. As the snake passed me, I gave it Karate chop across its back and stopped it in its tracks. It was immediately set upon by the ants, the lead of the column swarming all over it. I didn't particularly want to share our space with a mob of angry ants, so I picked up the slightly crippled snake by its tail and flicked it out of our position. The ant column stopped dead in its tracks. Andy observed. 'You watch, they'll send a scout out till they find that.'

We watched and they did indeed send a scout out to track down their intended kill. When the first one reported back having only done a small circle around, another one went out in a bigger circle. After he got back to his start point, yet another one went forth to find their elusive dinner. As soon as this ant located the still writhing snake, the whole column moved as one, lined up the victim and proceeded to run as a thick line directly to it where they once again swarmed all over it.

Enough of ants ... Because the nights in the jungle are so black we had to follow a string line tied from tree to tree to get to the gun for our shifts. I was going down to the gun one night when all of a sudden there was this tug on my silk that I had wrapped around my shoulders. It came from low down, about shin high. At the same time a huge bamboo bush next to me burst into life. For seven or more metres in all directions the whole bloody place shook and rattled. My heart jumped, but not just into my mouth as one might expect; it felt like my whole heart jumped right out of my mouth. I could feel it hanging thirty centimetres down from my mouth and thirty centimetres out from my chest. I thought every Nog in Vietnam had jumped me at once. I knew I was going to die. Time stood still and the black of the night became even blacker. I think I died a thousand deaths in the split second. An eternity passed — well, it felt like it anyway.

I somehow managed to regain my composure to find that the loose bottom part of my silk had caught on a spike of the bamboo. When I'd pulled, it had set the enormous bush off. Breathing heavily, I gingerly made my way to the safety of the gun site.

A day or two after this we'd just left a small creek and had been brought to a holt for a smoke break and Loc-stat (Location status) when our two clowns started acting up once again entertaining us with something or other. They had all of us close enough to hear them giggling like school kids. Pollard wasn't too impressed with the level of noise being created.

'Shsss, you're making too much noise down there,' he insisted for the umpteenth time.

Suddenly, Andy jumped up and strolled meaningfully up to where Jim was sitting in the line one back from Mullen and Coggins.

Standing over Jim, he let fly. 'Listen, if these 'ere bastards donn start laughen soon they'll start t'cry and isnot too good seein big men cryen,'

Pollard was unimpressed. 'Go and sit down,' he ordered Andy.

Real laughter rippled out along the line of sitting men. Andy steamed as he made his way back to just behind me, but before he got to his place Boris had to have his niggle at him. 'Wot's up, Andy, they given yuh a 'ard time up there?'

Andy was not amused, although the Sarge seemed to be. He just sat there and smiled sweetly as Andy again went off and put him right on the state of affairs as they now stood in Andy's eyes.

When it was time to move, we stayed on the same well-used track we'd followed up out of the creek. We were making good time when I started to get this overwhelming feeling of insecurity. It wasn't "close country". The trees on the left-hand side of the track were old, gnarly-looking things. The shadows close by the track seemed darker, the jungle quieter than usual and the trees themselves seemed more sinister than normal. I tried to put this rot out of my mind. Mullen was a good scout — he'd not let us down yet, but, somehow, I just had this feeling that something was wrong.

When the enemy sign came back along the line a few minutes later, I was not the least bit surprised. However, when the next signal reached me, I was stunned. I passed it on and was left to ponder. Mullen stayed where he was with Jim while the rest of the Section spread out and went to ground. Shortarse made a call to Boxall, only to be told. 'Don't be ridiculous. What would a hut be doing away out here in this AO?'

Looking about to ascertain what lay around us, I noticed another small track going off to our right.

'Shoulden sumone be coveren that pad?' I whispered.

When no one moved to do so, I presumed it was my job. I'd also noticed a very large tree just behind where I'd first went to ground and that the spot where I lay was very exposed. Fearing the storm of shrapnel that would undoubtedly rain down on us if the Noggies decided to get a little rough and started shooting their whooshers up into its top branches, I whispered to a couple of blokes near me, 'Jus' watch out for whooshers inta that tree there behind yuh, hey.' I pointed towards the tree as I moved away to secure the pad. They grunted acknowledgement, Bob Denholm turning to glance at it before giving me the thumbs-up.

In a low crouch, I crossed over the path we'd come in on and moved off a little way along the pad where I went to ground. Now I could ward off any flank attack if trouble started.

From behind the wall of bamboo we could hear the low jibber of the enemy. Then one of the Nogs came out to within about three metres of where Mullen was squatted on one knee. He stood there casually relieving himself, quite unaware that he was standing so close to death at that very moment. Mullen, with this Nog firmly in his sights, whispered to Pollard. 'Can I take 'im now?'

'No, let 'im get a little bit closer,' Jim whispered back, 'We donn wanna miss 'im.'

So Mullen just squatted there and waited for the foe to move that little bit closer. There was a shout from in behind the bamboo. The pissing Nog turned and in a flash was lost from sight. All went deathly quiet. Even the birds stopped whatever they were doing.

It was precisely then that Shortarse took a call on the radio. He was told, 'Get out of there, you'er holding up the operation. Go two hundred south, two hundred west, two hundred north and get back on your original bearing.'

When we heard the order, we protested most vehemently.

We knew that there were at least two of them in there. We had no idea what else lay in store for us behind that bamboo wall, nevertheless we protested.

'But Sir, can't we 'ave a go at 'em? Awe c'mon Sir, give us a go at 'em, we can bust 'em Sir, c'mon Sir.'

'You heard my orders, now move out,' he said harshly, and away we went.

As we moved quietly back along the track we'd just come in on, someone pointed out a hole in the ground just off the track that could have been used as a sentry post. It was covered over with a freshly downed tree branch. Someone also said that they thought they'd heard the click of a rifle safety catch coming from that same place while we were all going to ground up ahead of them. We were not allowed to "check it out" though because Shortarse was trying to make up for lost time now. It was getting late in the day and we had a good way to travel to get back onto our original bearing.

The hole in the ground might very well explain why everything went quiet when it did: the Nogs would have known we were there and they'd gone to ground. The element of surprise would surely have been lost if a sentry from their side had scampered back along a tunnel to tell his mates of our presence. It would have taken him a little time to move unheard around sixty metres along a tunnel.

After going the two hundred metres south, we started west. We got held up with a thicket of spindly bamboo. This stuff was different to what we were used to. It was about fifty millimetres in diameter and so thickly grown that it was extremely hard to penetrate and seemed to grow all the way up to the sky. When we got out the other side, it was way past our usual harbour-up time. By the time they got us all in the harbour and down it had become quite dark.

Due to Shortarse's attempt to appease his masters, we were now not in a conventional night harbour situation — far from it. Instead, we were in a very tight ring all jammed in on top of each other, this though wasn't worrying us as much as not having eaten. However, this state of affairs was soon put to right when a light suddenly flickered to life on the other side of our small harbour site.

'Corporal, Corporal, tell that man t'put that light out!' Shortarse cried out in utter horror, but an angry rebuttal came to him from the pitch-black darkness.

'Tell that useless cunt t'get fucked.'

This was a signal that was heeded by one and all. Little groups of four to five men huddled in the night around a Hexagon Stove waiting for their brew. We shared the one cup. Eventually there was only one light going in the area, and no points for guessing whose it was.

'Hey,' someone called into the night, 'who's the useless bastard with a light goen now?'

He'd set out the full regalia and was heartily hooking into his normal evening meal.

'Corporal, Corporal, find out who that man is,' Shortarse demanded, but the message just went all the way around the harbour site with the odd giggle thrown in until it got back to him. By the time he finished his meal, most of us were already laying down to sleep beside each other on the damp ground minus a hutchie.

The next day we got going early, making our way north to pick up on our original bearing. Having gone about two hundred metres or so, we came across a well-used track heading west to east. We followed this track west at a hectic rate, all the time being scolded by the big Boss for not being in position. We were going in to make a great assault on a transfer station that members of Nine Platoon had found and were now just observing. As we converged we could hear the rumble of our Tanks moving down from the north towards us.

Suddenly, there was a fluttering above us as the first of six artillery rounds passed close over our heads. We stood and watched and in the early morning light we could see the sun flashing off them as they passed us rotating in flight. They landed with an awful CRASH right in front of us. Apparently we were in position? Before the last of this salvo had hit its intended mark dead shrapnel began to rain down on us. Shortarse raced to the head of Five Section and started throwing orders.

'Pull back, pull back,' he cried, as he run around in a small circle. 'Gun, you go down here,' he ordered pointing to the ground at his feet. There was nothing we could do but go to ground close to the Gun. We lay there looking up in an endeavour to dodge the white-hot dead shrap as it rained down through the leaves onto our position. The metal downpour increased as the artillery barrage continued.

As soon as Arty had finished showering the place with their shot, we were ordered to "close in". Following the track we'd been on, we proceeded west until we came across the place where the tanks had descended upon the three Noggies from the north.

We followed their tracks down to the south-west through the broken, twisted "J" until we suddenly got a call to abandon the pursuit of our elusive foe — undoubtedly miles away by now — and to locate an LZ for a quick extraction. The Kiwis had come across a VC bunker system to our north and it was thought that they might need a bit of a hand from us to clean it out.

Now, before I go any further I had better explain the reason for having three full Companies of the Fourth Battalion, plus tanks, to take on three little VC in a Transfer Station. Well, it just so happened that there were three or four high-ranking Officers from the C.M.F. (Citizens Military Forces) in Vietnam to see first-hand how Australian troops worked on the ground in combat situations. So while the boys were huddled in behind the tanks and following them in to finish off "the Enemy", these big Nobs were flying overhead in Choppers making notes to pass on to the Cut Lunch Cowboys back in Australia.

To get back to the business in hand: We were landed on a big open field of Elephant Grass and we literally disappeared into it. The choppers left and we found to our astonishment that the Kiwis were by this time ready to leave the area as well.

They were laughing and waving goodbye to us as they melted back into the cover of the "J". They had done the job on a six-bunker complex and its occupants before we'd even turned up. Apparently, the enemy were just beginning to construct this system when the Kiwis found them. There was nothing left for us to do but lay about completely hidden in the long grass and await our next orders. We made this our dinner camp, which wasn't too bad seeing as we'd not eaten the previous night and had gone without breakfast that morning.

With that out of the way, I penned the last words of a poem I'd been working on into my small notebook. It's a poem about taking a smoke break out in the scrub. I called it "The Past and the Present". I put the last full stop in place and grinned. It was finished. I'd written a poem. I was so pleased with myself that I stood up to take it to show Pollard. Some time back he'd seen me writing in the little, yellow notebook that had the wire wound like a spring down its spine and asked me what I was doing.

'Hey Jim, where are yur, Jim?' I was standing in a field of green. It was like standing alone in a big unripened wheat crop. I looked about me, nothing, no one. I called out again, 'Jim, where areyur, Jim?'

'Over 'ere, woddaya want?' he answered from north-west of where I stood.

'Wave yur 'and about so I can see yur,' I called.

A dirty giggle hat appeared waving above the grass-tops. I headed across towards it and stumbled over a couple of bemused mates whose positions were now revealed to me. Jim was horrified as I strode into his camp area of flattened long grass.

'Git down fur fuck sake, will yuh, woddayur think yurdoen?' he yelled.

'I finished that poem!' I told him, excitedly.

'Git down, you'll get yur 'ead shot off,' Jim ordered.

I stood and looked around. There was nothing but the field of grass to the south, east and north and the jungle to the west, into which the Kiwis had not so long ago disappeared.

'Fuck off Jim. If them little bastards ken 'it my little 'ed from ear they'd be fucken good shots.'

'Get down,' Jim growled at me, seriously.

I handed him the notebook and sat down with him as he read my first ever poem. This is that poem.

Up through the leaves of the Vietnam Jungle,
There rises a small column of smoke
And there with his back to a tree,
Sits a young, Australian bloke.
He has long become accustomed
To the constant rain and the heat
And its obvious by the look of his face,
He hasn't shaved all this week.

With my rifle resting on my knees,
One hand near the butt,
A hand that is scratched and scarred,
Where the spikes of the bamboo cut.
But I see not the hand,
Nor where the skin has been torn,
For I've drifted right back
To the land where I was born.

I see myself again as a Drover,
So young, so wild, so free,
Riding across the plains
That stretch like a big, golden sea.
Oh, I wish I had a dog and a horse
And could be shepherding still,
Where life was smooth and quiet,
Like the breeze that turns the old mill.

Suddenly my head shoots up
At the sound of a breaking twig
From in behind the dense foliage,
Where Enemy could so easily be hid.
I search the leaves for the movement,
Or shadow that will betray,
Eyes moving like a big jungle cat's,
In search of her prey.

As I relax a little and settle down,
I fail to see the blood-sucking leach,
Instead in my mind there is a girl
Standing alone on a moonlit beach.
As she looks out over the dark moving water,
So deep and so wide,
It being night, the tears in her eyes
Are now easy to hide.

And again with the morning sun
Playing tricks with her hair,
I see her skipping through life
Without, it would seem, ever a care.
With a smile on her lips and a twinkle
Like a star in her eye,
Then I sadly remember, I never
Even kissed her good-bye.

I shift a cramped leg a little
And ask a mate of the time.
Receiving a whispered reply,
It's only half past nine.
Again I go back, this time to a room
In which I had once been.
I see again the floor carpet
That was a very dark green.

And the bronze plaque of a peacock,
That hung on the far wall,
And from somewhere in the my head
I can hear that big bird's mating call.
I remember the neat finish,
Of this little family home
And wonder if I can build one
The same, with my war service loan.

My thoughts are abruptly broken,
By the movement of a hand,
The signal is for us to move,
Clearly understood by the jungle-fighting man
And a fearless young Digger,
Cursing the weight of his pack,
Moves off silently — down
the shadows of a deep, jungle track.

* * *

We patrolled south from here with Nine Platoon coming along with us to keep us company. We came across a couple of nasty creeks which we had to cross wading up to our armpits in muddy water and eight days later we suddenly emerged from the "J" onto a clearing. Not a natural clearing, though, as this one had been created by two B52 bombs. About a hundred metres away in the centre of a barren lunar landscape were two huge craters adjoining each other. It was obvious that the scrap metal scavengers had not found this lot yet for, sticking out of the ploughed up earth, we found great hunks of brass fifty millimetres thick and up to two hundred millimetres wide and some up to a metre in length. Their jagged and splintered edges were razer sharp. About half a kilometre from the centre of the cleared ground was a complete ring of smashed trees. We made camp in a very small rubber plantation immediately to the south of the scarred landscape. We were not too far to the east of where nine days earlier we'd been told to abandon any attack on whatever or whoever was behind the wall of bamboo.

Andy and I took the first watch. We were sitting with our legs dangling over the edge of the closest bomb crater to our camp when it started to rain heavily. I looked back towards our campsite in the hope of seeing that someone had dragged our packs in under cover and out of the deluge, but nobody had. When I angrily pointed this out to Andy, he just sat there unmoved, saying nothing.

Then I looked down at my rifle and suddenly became very annoyed at the sight of the rain washing the oil off the outside of its barrel. I went off — not only was our packs getting soaked right through, but now every drop of bloody rain that fell was slowly washing away the protective coating from my gat, so I let go a string of foul oaths. To my utter astonishment Andy suddenly started to laugh quite heartily.

'Wot's so fucken funny?' I scolded in amazement.

'We are,' he said, 'jus' look attus, we look like a pair a ducks jus' sitten 'ere on the bank of this pond waiten forut t'fill up so wekin go forra swim.'

It took a second or so for it to sink in, but, yes, that's exactly what we did look like.

After twenty more minutes went by and the status quo remained, except that the pool at the bottom of the crater was indeed growing, Andy remarked, 'Yur know, I donno wot we're doen 'ere, there'snot one single fucken Noggie in the whole of Vietnam who'd be stupid enough ta be out in rain like this. They'd be all snuggled up, high an' dry someplace.'

I agreed with him. A vision came to me of this little Noggie sitting in a tree just up off the ground. He was completely covered in a clear plastic poncho affair with not a skerrick of him getting wet.

At midnight that night it rained again. No, I shouldn't say it rained; it poured. From the edge of the cleared ground I'd been watching the tops of a big storm brewing up all afternoon out to the west towards Saigon. Feeling that we'd most likely get a bit more rain later on, I set to and scraped a small levee bank up along my side of our hutchie. Within minutes of the cloudburst, the small bank gave way and the water rushed right through our camp. The ground between the rubber trees where we'd harboured up was bare and it sloped sightly away to the south-west, so it wasn't long before I was flooded out. With the cool water surrounding my prostrate body, I abandoned my ground sheet to sit up on my pack. I bent down and tested the place where I'd just been lying with my index finger. Seventy-five millimetres of water covered my campsite. Andy was out cold and completely unaware of the happenings. He was snoring as loud as I'd ever heard him when I tested his side of our camp and found the water there to be one hundred millimetres deep. I shook my head and talked to the night, 'Ow the 'ell canyah sleep through that, Andy?'

Seconds later the snoring stopped abruptly and Andy called out, 'Christ Almighty, its wet in 'ere,' as he sat up.

'Yeah,' I said, an' yur've bin sleepen in et. Sit up on yur pack an' 'ave a smoke withus.'

And so, in the dead of the night, with the rain tumbling down, we sat on our packs enjoying a smoke. Suddenly Andy said to me, 'Get a loada this, will yah?'

'Wot?' I asked in surprise.

'Ave a look under the side of the hutchie.'

The tiny red glow from lit smokes could be seen all over the harbour site; it was like looking at the lights of a small town from a distance. There was no danger of us being sprung for the deluge curtained us all from the outside world.

We found out in the morning that there wasn't a single bloke in either of the two Platoons who'd missed out on getting flooded out that night, Officers included.

We were also informed that sometime through the night, a band of Nogs had moved to the south along our side of the creek which was about half a kilometre to our west.

'Owdoyer know?' I asked Johnny McKinley in surprise, when he told us.

'We could see their lights,' he said. When the enemy moved in big numbers at night they employed a Torch Bearer or Lantern Carrier to lead the way and sometimes more at odd placements along the length of the column.

'Why didn't we git uppum then?' I asked, in dismay.

'Because they were too far away for us to get attem properly, an' Aussie troops never move at night, so we coulden go down to the creek t'engage 'em.'

Around eight o'clock in the morning the Engineers were choppered in. They were going to blow up whatever we found at the other end of that track we'd been on ten days back. The choppers also bought with them a full supply of tucker for us and some more ammo, but not the M72s that Andy had asked for. He'd said earlier when he'd requested them, 'At least we'll be able t'match the whooshers the Nogs are sure t'ave in there with 'em.'

Andy was not very impressed that these had been left out of the re-supply. I was in total agreement. 'Yeah, we coulda give 'em a little bitta their own medicine.'

We approached the target with deliberate caution as we were pretty sure the Nogs had been aware of our presence the first time we were here and it wasn't unlikely that they'd set up a booby-trap somewhere along the track as an early warning device. All we found, however, was a fresh footprint coming in our direction. Maybe this track was left by the Caretaker leaving his post, or maybe the Caretaker was still there.

We inched into our assignment unopposed and came across eleven unoccupied bunkers. Along with these were an assortment of tables and small beds made from bamboo. The beds were more like small platforms thirty centimetres or so off the ground. They were made from strips of bamboo about thirteen millimetres across and tied together with flat vine. Some had a slanted roof about sixty centimetres above the bed, made in the same manner. The tables were well constructed from larger pieces of bamboo and bench-type seats had been attached to each side. Six Diggers, three to a side, could dine at these tables quite comfortably. We also found a piece of bamboo shaped into a mug and tied to a tree with a pair of chopsticks in it and it was half full of water — a great way to get nature to help with the washing up.

Ever mindful of booby-traps, we spent a little time looking around for caches of rice or anything else the enemy may have left behind and by dinner camp the bunkered complex was completely searched. After we dined on the site, the Engineers started to wire the place up with det cord wrapped around PE and attached to everything in sight. They connected double the normal amount of PE in the ground above each bunker while we were moved a little way to the west where we waited for them to do their job. When all was set they joined us and the count down began after instructions were relayed to us to open our mouths to counter the shockwaves sent out by the blast. After the huge bang, Shortarse went back with the Engineers to inspect the damage.

'A great gaping hole in the jungle,' he said and, judging by the amount of PE the boys had bought with them, it was no surprise to any of us to hear this.

It was found in the subsequent search that this system was a camp of the Chau Duc District Forces Headquarters Group — forty men in all. I would give anything to know what they thought at the time of the Uc Dai Loi pissing off and leaving them to it ten days prior. Incidentally, the Australian and New Zealand troops had been trying to catch up with this mob for quite some time, but had never managed to lay eyes on them. Now they could start afresh somewhere else. So close yet so far away ... God alone knows what the outcome would have been had we attacked them on that first day we'd been here, especially with so many friendly troops close at hand.

* * *

14
CANDY

After wandering about in the sticks for another week or so, we were picked up by chopper and transported back to the Dat. When we got into Vung Tau, some of us were allocated the place where the Officers usually camped while they were in town. This was a three-storey joint of French design which stood on the main drag about three blocks north-west of The Flags. Inside there was a courtyard and all the rooms opened onto it. From balconies on the upper levels you could look over white, wrought-iron banisters down to the light-blue mosaic in the middle of the floor below.

In my room I found the zipper in my dacks was rusted up and try as I may I could not make it move. A cleaning lady, who I took to be in her thirties, came by and upon seeing me she stopped outside the door. 'Your friends, they go,' she told me, earnestly.

Then she noticed that I was having trouble and immediately offered a hand. 'I help you,' she said, all smiles, as she strode boldly into the room.

I thought for a bit that she was about to race me off, but, no, she was only there to help. She giggled and I laughed as we struggled in vain with this stubborn, bloody zip. In the end we gave up and as she went on about her duties, I decided that I'd just have to buy some new dacks.

Foregoing a massage, I went straight down to the Chikito Bar to find Lyn. She wasn't there so I asked around. Eventually, another girl from that bar called Lee told me that she knew where I could find Lyn and that she'd take me to her. Lee was quite young and a good bit bigger in height and weight than the average girl working in Vung Tau. She was moon-faced with a messy fringe and straight, black hair which came to just below her shoulders.

First, though, I had to go and get myself a pair of new dacks. She offered to escort me down the street to find a menswear shop. We headed off nor-west back towards The Flags, but she would not walk beside me, instead keeping about two paces behind me and to one side. Suddenly, a whole heap of kids surrounded me. One stood in front of me whacking a folded-up length of printed paper at my face, all the while yelling, 'You read, you read,' while at the same time I could feel a heap of small hands trying to go through my pockets. I clenched both my fists and struck wildly outwards leaving five urchins sprawling on the footpath on either side of me. We moved away, but the little bludgers followed us along at a safe distance yelling abuse at me in Vietnamese. We rounded the corner at The Flags and by this time Lee was getting really pissed off by the brats. Even though she was yelling at them, they ignored her, and as we entered an Indian menswear shop that was just past the Blue Angel, they crowded the doorway still shouting.

The Indian storekeeper asked Lee what was going on and she angrily told him in Vietnamese. He rushed past us to the door and went right off at them. I don't know what he said, but whatever it was it worked because they disappeared up the street never to be seen again.

When the Indian said five dollars for a neat pair of black dacks made of a light but tough Indian cotton, I said 'OK' and immediately paid him for them. On the street outside I could feel I was in trouble with Lee, but I didn't know why. She kept her distance all the way back to the bar and once inside I asked her what was wrong.

'You stupid,' is all she said at first.

'Why am I stupid? Wot 'ave I done to make me stupid?' I kept asking, until she came out with it.

'You stupid, you no bargain. You stupid, you pay five dollar. You bargain, you pay three dollar.'

'But that was a bargain,' I told her, 'Back where I come from I'd pay around thirty dollars for a pair of good pants like that.'

But still she scolded me. 'You no bargain, you stupid.'

Later on she took me to a place in some back street and pointed out to me a block of flats. 'Lyn there. Lyn live with Yankee. He buy her everything. He love Lyn very much. Lyn not go work in bar anymore.'

Whether this was true or not I could only take her word for it. Needless to say, I ended up at her place for the night. Strangely enough, it was very close to where she'd said Lyn was living with the Yank.

Lee's place was small, but who was looking, all I wanted was a boom-boom. When she got her gear off, I saw a multitude of bruises that were perfect circles about three inches across and they were all over her torso, back and front and covering the soft parts of her legs and her upper arms.

'What's this?' I asked in astonishment, pointing at them.

'Budda Nuns do it,' was all I could get out of her at first.

She eventually told me she'd been feeling a bit crook and went to the Nuns to be cured. They apparently put a spirit-like substance, much like Metho, in a glass, tipped it out and lit the fumes that were left in the glass and quickly placed the open end on the patient, thus extinguishing the flame and causing a sucking action to take place inside the glass, thereby sucking all the bad out of the patient.

She wasn't much of a bang, mostly lying there like a bag of shit and pretending to be interested, but I was too tired to be concerned about that. What got on my goat more was the large, cylinder-shape pillow which she insisted on keeping between me and her, wrapping her legs around it as she slept. At first it didn't matter as I went off into a quick sleep, but it was still between us when I made advances towards her somewhere around two in the morning looking for another boom-boom.

'Get rid of this fucken thing, wilyah. Wot the fuck iset anyway?' I scolded her as I pulled it from her and threw it over the back of her where it came to rest against the wall. She looked very pained and turned her back to me. I found out later that her dead husband's ashes were in a little jar in the centre of that pillow thing.

The red light that continually shone on the wall above the bedhead didn't help much either. When I told her to turn it off, she again looked pained and said a definite 'no' to my suggestion. Can't tell you if the light was of any significance or not.

Back at the bar in the morning, she said she would look after all my money and that way she would be mine for the rest of my stay in town. No sooner had I handed it over and she was gone.

She came back in a couple of hours and when I quizzed her as to her whereabouts, she said that she'd been to see the Doctor. This, of course, had taken up all the money I'd given her earlier.

'And wot thu fucken 'ell am I s'posta do forra fucken drink now, ay?' I admonished her.

'You go Camp get some more,' she told me.

I wandered about and found Donks and a couple of other blokes who were in the same boat as I was: broke, but I suspect not for the same reason. Four of us piled into the back of a *Lambretta*. The little three-wheeled, covered-in vehicle was fully laden now. For one dollar MPC we could go anywhere in Vung Tau in one of these taxis.

'Uc Dai Loi Camp,' we told the driver.

As we approached the big intersection along the wide road heading north from the large Catholic Church, Donks and I stood up on the back of the little vehicle. When the ever-smiling driver went to turn east towards the Camp, we leaned back and the single front wheel of the *Lambretta* reared up off the road. The driver was franticly turning the handle bars this way and that and was shouting 'No, no, no, no, no, no,' as we careered out of control right on through the intersection.

Out at Camp, I was told by the Paymaster that I was fully drawn and could have no more. Bugger. I had decided upon getting "in-country" and that I'd only draw half my wages each time we came in. That way I'd have a bit in my paybook to buy a car with when we got back home.

Walking back to the front gates to get a lift back into town, I crossed paths with the pink *Citron* which the nurses used to drive around the Camp. It still had bullet holes in it. It was quite a sight. It was found by some 4RAR Diggers of the first tour up near the top of the Province where a local politician had been shot up in it by the VC.

Back in town stony broke and walking, I came across the beautiful Sandy in the doorway of the bar next to the Chikito.

'Where your friend?' she asked me.

'I dunno.' I told her, truthfully.

I knew she meant Perkins. Remember, I told you I'd seen them together around at the Blue Angle on our first trip in. I presumed he must have made a good impression on her at the time until she announced, 'You tell him I have his baby. Him no come, I kill baby.'

'Ow yer gunna do that?' I asked her in astonishment.

'Knitting needle,' she said with conviction, at the same time demonstrating with one hand just how she intended to do it. I was convinced, so I went off to find him, feeling that he'd be around at the Blue Angle again, but, alas, he was not there. I spent the rest of the morning with Sandy. She was a very striking, twenty-one-year-old Chinese girl from Taipei. Slender, and just a little taller than most of the other girls here, she wore her silky black hair bobbed and had the most beautiful soft, coppery- coloured skin. Always smiling, she was a girl with an abundance of energy who just couldn't sit still. I sat on a stool at the bar while she bought me drinks in between darting in and out of the bar.

Around eleven o'clock, I felt a tug on the sleeve of my shirt. I looked around to find a small girl in dirty clothes grinning up at me through a row of rotting teeth. She shyly handed me a small square of thin, white cardboard on which was written:

Please Help Me.

I am an Orphan.

Thank You.

God Bless You.

Sandy indicated to me that I should ignore her and proceeded to distract me with something or other. However, when I stole a glance over my shoulder, the little girl who was still standing there looking lost, with her tiny hands clasping the sides of her grubby dress as she swung from side to side. My heart bled for her, but what could I do? I had nothing that I could give her. Suddenly, Sandy was gone again leaving a half-empty can of Coke sitting on the counter. I gathered up the little one, plonked her on the seat beside me and handed her the Coke. You should have seen her beam. Then Sandy was there again, but she didn't take the slightest bit of notice of the waif.

'You want candy?' she asked me, excitedly.

'Yeah, I suppose so,' I answered cautiously, not really knowing what she was on about. She disappeared out the front door again and within minutes she was back handing me a wafer cup containing what looked like an ice-cream swirled to a stiff point at the top. I licked at it; it was the most overly sweet thing I'd ever tasted in my life, sweeter even than Fairy Floss. It was far too sweet for my liking, but with Sandy looking on what could I do but lick at it tentatively. I didn't want to offend her as she had gone out and bought it especially for me.

'You like?' she asked, her eyes all lit up.

'Yeah, yeah,' I lied to her.

Then she was gone again and in doing so left me the opportunity to give this candy shit to the little girl, who began to hoe into it with gay abandon. Suddenly Sandy was back and, on seeing the little brat chomping on the gift she'd just given me a couple of minutes before, she blew up. She snatched the candy away, shoved it into my mitt and angrily dragged the child from the stool. She then proceeded to give her a long dressing down in a very hostile tone in Vietnamese. The grubby little thing just stood there with head bowed but she did not cry.

As soon as Sandy had said what she had to say, she was off out the door again leaving the little girl still standing there. I handed her the candy and with outstretched finger pointing to the outside world, I told her, 'Go, quick, before she comes back.'

She beamed up at me and, holding her candy up like it was an Olympic torch, she ran like mad out of the bar and onto the sun-drenched footpath.

I saw a wrinkled man later that afternoon, who I think could have been her father, waving her away from the cart he appeared to be pulling and telling her, 'Go, go sell flowers.'

She had half a dozen rings of what looked like white frangipani flowers draped around her tiny neck and looked pained that she was being hunted from him.

Around Dinner Camp, I suddenly became aware of another Bar Girl standing a little way behind us and pointing at me, so I asked Sandy to ask her what she wanted. They exchanged a couple of sentences in Vietnamese.

'She say she love you,' came the reply.

'OK, tell 'er if she loves me she'll have t'buy me a drink,' I told Sandy.

She relayed my message, whereupon the girl feigned a pained

look, pouting the most gorgeous pout and departed the bar. I didn't think any more of it until a few minutes later she was perching herself up on a stool beside me, all smiles.

Her name was Thao Ly. She was nineteen and always seemed to be happy. She also wore her hair cut up above her shoulders and was about average height for a Vietnamese woman. Best of all, though, was what you saw is what you got as she wore no make-up at all.

Though Sandy kept ducking in and out of the bar to check on us, between them they kept the Four Star up to me for the rest of the day and into the night. At precisely ten-to-eleven the two girls bustled me outside as everybody left the bar.

'You go now, be safe,' they told me and we quickly exchanged goodbyes. The whole street from building to opposite building and as far as the eye could see was a walking mass of happy people, who all seemed to be heading in the same direction. Some silly bastard was trying to drive a car up against the moving throng. Every time he blew the horn on the car he was greeted with loud, ironic jeers and much joyful laughter.

At The Flags, the crowd started to disperse and by the time I got to the next block there was only a few people on the darkened street with me. Two young ladies talked happily to each other as I caught up with them.

'You girls want boom-boom t'night?' I asked them, thinking that I might be able to score a more cosy place to camp for the night.

'You pay,' they giggled.

'Nar, I got no money,' I told them, and then I said optimistically, 'I'll get some for yuh in thu morning.'

'No,' one of them said very seriously, 'No money, NO boom-boom.'

Oh, well, it was worth a try. We said our goodnights and they went their way as I went mine.

* * *

15
IRON FOX

Before mid-day the next day Charlie Company was all safely back inside Nui Dat. On the way over on the Sydney, I'd contracted a fungal infection down around my genitalia which would not go away. I'd been given some sort of ointment to fix it. This, however, was having no effect on the condition and just before we'd come back in the last time I'd noticed that it was spreading. This was most likely because we were in the Tropics, so I decided that now was the time to do something about it.

I went down to the RAP where the Captain who was on duty at the time tried to fob me off with another small bottle of the same stuff our Platoon Medic had given me earlier. He didn't bother having a look at me; didn't seem the least bit interested in my problem at all. In fact, he seemed rather bored with what he was doing, but I wasn't going to be palmed off again and insisted that I wanted more of him.

'This is all we've got to fix that up,' he told me, dismissively.

'Well, thatsnow good, I've already tried that shit an' it donn work,' I insisted.

He must have known that I was not going away, so he said, 'What do you want me to do about it then?'

'Givus a chit t'say I can't go out this time an' I'll get rid of the fucken stuff meself.'

He wrote me out something that I could take to Pollard. He'd given me two weeks.

'If you fix it, come back an' show me, an' tell me how you've done it, won't you?' he told me as I was about to leave.

'Yeah, righto,' I said, as I went out the door, but that's not what I was thinking.

'Yeah, that'd be right. You're the bloody doctor here, the educated one getten three times as much as I am an' yur want me t'tell yur 'ow to get ridda tinea, so you can go an' say yur found the cure foret. Yeah, likely.'

Fungal infections thrive in damp, dark places. To fix it all one need do is deprive it of the environment it likes best. My intention was to sit with my genitalia exposed to the sun at every opportunity I could find until I could see an improvement in my condition. When I got the time I'd sit on a chair at the back of our tent and pull my shorts up to expose the tinea to the sun. It stung a bit to start with but then so did that shit they'd given me before and it had done no good at all. At the end of the first week the condition was already showing signs of drying up. Of course that bitch, Lee, would be feeling the itch in her crotch region by now. Most likely have to fork out to see another doctor for treatment for that. Rip me off, would she?

The ones who stayed "in" had to do a thing or two around the place. I spent some time manning the Company Command Post (CAP) which was the nerve centre of our compound. It was a heavily fortified underground bunker into which Command were supposed to retreat if we got attacked in our area of Nui Dat. It had an old-fashioned telephone exchange all hooked up in it. I had to learn how to take incoming calls and transfer them to whoever they were for. It was pretty quiet while the boys were out, but I did manage to glean a bit of information from it just the same.

I also did a heap of mowing all around the place. During one session a blade flew off one of the mowers and cut a slit in my boot about half way up the front. Good thing they were made of tough leather or I might have had more than just a bad bruise on my lower shin.

We had to do a little guard duty on the wire as well and one night we were sent over to a very well-made gun site in the Delta Company area which looked new. About closing time at their Boozer we suddenly heard shots being fired away to the north-west. At first I thought the next gun position along from us must have had movement on the wire.

I was actually down in the bunkered part of our position below the gun emplacement when it all started, about to take a break so that I'd be all right to take my stint later on in the night. After a couple of shots were fired, I went up top. The bloke who was on the gun at the time was a little jumpy and I couldn't blame him, really; he'd had his hat shot clean off his head by his own men not long after getting over here. He'd been out on picket and spotted a couple of enemy coming his way. He dropped one of them and was trying to get the other one when he heard his Section Commander yelling 'Sentries in'. He got on the toe and was bolting back to the safety of his lines when a stray bullet from the intense fire that was suppose to be covering his retreat went through his giggle hat. This bloke was always so neatly dressed while we were in Corps training that I thought for sure he'd have at least one stripe by now, especially by the way he used to suck up to the NCOs back then. Mind you, he may well just have been a Bank Johnny or some such in his other life.

At any rate, the occasional shot from beside us kept up until we suddenly received a ring on the phone which was sitting beside us on the top part of the structure. Old mate got such a start he nearly fell off the top of the bunker. The caller informed us that one of the Delta Company boys had gone off a bit and was shooting up foot-powder tins in his tent. I tried to convince my companion that we were pretty safe where we were, especially if we went down into the bunker, but he was all for hooking it back to somewhere safer.

'I'll sit on the gun if it makes yuh feel better, 'esnot shooting at us so much, 'es jus' poppen away.' I told him.

He went down, but soon came back up to join me — one in all in I suppose — maybe he was a staunch Union man, I don't know? Soon we got another phone call.

'You people might be safer if yur were to come up to the Boozer,' we were told.

'Nar, we'll be awright 'ere, nuffens comen this way,' I assured the unidentified caller.

'The CSM says yur'd better come up 'ere to the Boozer an' wait till this is sorted out.'

This pleased old mate no end when I told him. He'd been all for hooking it to the safety of the lights from the start even if I couldn't see the need. We had a bunker right here for protection; and besides we were unfamiliar with the layout of Delta Company's lines, so I didn't think it was such a good idea for us to go wandering off into the dark exposing ourselves to any stray lead that just might happen to come our way.

Suddenly, some blokes turned up from another gun position. They too were a little excited. 'Wot are you blokes doen, we jus' got told t'go to thu Boozer, woddyuer reckon?

'I donno, I reckon we're safe enough 'ere, but we bin told t'go too,' I told them.

'I'm for going to the Boozer now. What about you blokes?' old mate spoke up.

'Well, yeah, I spose we should do wot they wantus t'do, might be safer.' agreed one of the newcomers who was talking for his mate as well. That was three to one we move to the Boozer. We crouched down and made our way towards the lights at a very quick pace and, once there, we were met by someone who told us what was going on.

By his account, while Delta were "out" this last time, an older Digger called Tassie contracted Malaria and as a result perished in the field. Now his best mate down in the tent wanted to get Delta's OC for it. However, as soon as they got back "in" the OC was diagnosed with bleeding ulcers in his stomach and was RTAed immediately.

A Major Jerry Taylor was then appointed OC of Delta Company. His first big job as their boss was to go down to the tent and to see what he could do to put a stop to what was going on there. Delta's CSM had already tried, but after a slug was buried in the floorboards at his feet and he was told in no uncertain terms to 'ooket or coppet', he'd retreated in tack.

Major Taylor got in and sat down on the bed with the disgruntled Digger and, after talking to him for a bit, he eventually talked him into giving up his weapon. The worse thing was the unhappy Digger would now have to spend time in the stockade while the former OC was home free.

Then there was a little Nog who turned up at our Boozer a fair bit. He could play a Guitar extremely well — played *A Bridge over Troubled Waters,* the best I've ever heard it played. He was in fact a Chu Hoi who'd surrendered to us and was now supposed to be helping us out by showing us where "their" booby-traps were and that kind of stuff — what we called a Bushman Scout. I don't think he could have been doing too much of that while he was spending so much of his time getting on the piss at our Boozer. He was most likely a bit windy about going out, seeing as his old mates would now consider him a traitor; and who could blame him or them for that matter?

We'd heard via the airwaves that the Battalion was involved in some action on a bunker system up the top of the Province. By now, sick of being behind the wire, I asked our ever-smiling, thick-set, black-haired Staff Sergeant, Peter Webber, if I could go back to my mob on the next Maintdem chopper. Although Webber was a little reluctant to let me go at first, he gave in after I hassled him continually all morning while we worked to put the re-supply together.

It came to pass that APCs were going to deliver this re-supply. I rode on top of one of them as we rolled along in convoy up the road. We followed Route Two right on past Courtney Hill which was situated a smidgen over the Phuoc Tuy/Long Khanh provincial boarder. Presently, we came across Black Horse, the massive American Army Base near the bottom of Long Khanh Province. We turned left here onto a fair road just shy of the Base itself from where we could see into the sprawling compound. I have never seen so many vehicles lined up before in my life, let alone Army vehicles. There were lines and lines of Jeeps, trucks, APCs and light tanks near as far as the eye could see. I found myself thinking, *'Gees just imagine the damage we could do if only we could get our hands on all that stuff — we'd tear this place apart.'*

We finally found our blokes about two in the afternoon, but only after one of the APCs had gone a little off course and became entangled in some old wire. Shortarse didn't look too happy to see me, but who cared? The rest of the boys were and it was they who gave me a bit of a run-down of what went on in their raid on the bunker system which the Nogs had built only a few clicks west of Black Horse and a couple north of the Phouc Tuy Boarder, but you will have to ask one of my mates who was actually there at the time for all the details — things like them following the tanks in and VC being squashed in their holes as the tanks over-ran the position.

Among the papers found by our men in the busted bunker complex, Australian Army Intelligence discovered that the VC had figured out a way of stopping a tank by firing a series of RPGs at the same spot on its hot barrel from close quarters. This could only be achieved in a bunker raid like the one recently conduced and, as none of the tanks had been stopped by this method this time, it could only be presumed that the Vietcong had not told their men what to do or they were not confident that it would work so they did not deploy the edit in this battle. Maybe they tried it and it just did not work.

Now that I was back with my mates, I can tell you we deployed back down over the Province Border from here and continued to carry on as before either patrolling or ambushing as was our mandate.

At one stage, we were sitting around when there came a hiss from Bob Denholm who was camped close to Andy and me. We turned to see him giving us the thumbs-down sign as he and the others were quickly and quietly going to ground. After a very short wait, Six Section's side of the harbour burst into sustained gunfire. I let a couple go just for the hell of it and the next thing I know Andy is up me. 'Gees, wot the fuckayuhdoen? Yur nearly blew me eardrums out. Why the fuck didn't yur tell me you were gunna shoot?'

I was about to answer when the ceasefire was called and someone called out, 'Andy, you wanna go out an' see if we got somethen?'

He left our position and was out in the scrub for a bit. When he got back, he said to me, 'You ever see an' emu runnen at full stretch?'

'Yeah, why?' I said to him with a grin, remembering the one that had hit a new Ring-lock fence beside me one day on Beefwood Downs with its head stretched out flat and it at full tilt and the explosion of feathers which followed.

'That little prick would outdo an emu any time! There was one step 'ere and one step way up there,' he told me, indicating with his hand how far apart the Noggie's footfall had been as he fled. Incidentally, it appeared that our fleet-of-foot enemy had not been hit in this encounter.

Apparently, someone was outside the Platoon area doing a goonnah (bowel movement) when he spotted a person coming wandering along in the bamboo. He came back into camp and asked if any of us were out there wearing black pyjamas. Six Section went to ground and lined the unidentified up and as he lifted a length of fallen bamboo to walk under it, they used this as a signal and let rip. How that Nog got away from that much fire-power unscathed, God only knows.

When the next Maintdem chopper came in Andy picked up his backpack and strode away towards it. He didn't have his giggle hat on and was carrying his pack in his spare hand.

'Where yur goen?' I asked him in surprise.

'ome.'

'Wot. Is your time up?' I called after him, but he didn't answer. The chopper went and Andy went with it and I never saw him again

* * *

16
EARS AND EYES

A couple of days later I was ordered to take a "Promotion in the Field".

'As of tomorrow onwards you'll be up front as Scout,' I was informed at our nightly O Group.

'Wot! Why? Wot's 'appened t'Mullens?' I growled, angrily. After all, Mullen was a good scout –one of the best in my books, even if he was a city slicker.

'He's gone inta thu Medics.' I was told by Pollard, 'so you're it Dog, you're it.'

'Like fucken 'ell I am.' I shot back at him, 'Get sumudda useless bastard t'go up there an' get shot at. Get one of them new blokes from Reo t'go up there. I'm right here.'

'Here', of course was my accustomed position as Tail End Charlie. Forward Scout was a totally different kettle of fish to being Tail End Charlie, I can tell you. As Tail End Charlie, I was just one of the mob. Pollard, however, would not be dissuaded.

'You're the only one in the Section who is trained as a Scout,' he insisted, calmly, and he knew that to be true because, remember, it was he who'd trained me for the position during Corps training back in Townsville.

'So what?' I protested, 'that's live fucken lead they're chucken at us up 'ere, not fucken blanks.'

'Look Dog, I know it is, but you're the only bloke 'ere who can do et, besides you'll get more dough too, as yer know,' Pollard went on.

'Fuck the money! Itsnow fucken good to a bloke who's dead, is it? Get someone else,' I threw back at him.

'Look, we could make it 'ard on yuh, yur know, now yur gunna go up front or not?' He was putting on his serious face now.

'Sure, sure yur could makeut 'ard on me, pull rank and all that shit. Well, the answer's still fucken no, now piss off, fuck yuh,' I was getting a bit short by this time.

'Yur know what disobeying a lawful command in the face of the enemy means, don't yuh?' he asked.

'Yeah, yeah, Court Martial or gaol,' I answered, unperturbed.

'Or they could shoot you on sight more like,' he said.

'Bullshit,' is what he got from me.

'They've done it in the past, so wot's t'stop'em from doen et now.'

This put the clinchers on it. When we moved out next morning, I was up the front as Five Section's Scout. I was now what they called the "Ears and Eyes of the Section". My life would never be the same again from that day on. The standing joke among the Diggers at the time was that 'if you can get through the first week as a Scout, you just might make it back home.'

I'm here to tell you it was one the loneliest places on earth being up front as a Scout in Vietnam. There was nothing out in front of me but the jungle and, of course, the enemy trying to kill me by whatever means possible. I was the only thing between the enemy and my mates. Yes, they were there — but they were all behind me.

I had to keep myself alive for as long as possible — that was a given — but now, for the forty minutes while I was up front as their Scout, I had twenty-odd of my best mates depending on me alone not to lead them into something too big for us to handle; depending on me not to trip a wire which would set off a booby-trap which would take some of them out behind me, especially Shortarse and those close around him; depending on me not to miss any sign that the enemy may have left to indicate that they may have set a trap; depending on me not to miss the three matchstick-size prongs sticking up a centimetre out of the ground of a Jumping Jack Mine — that's if they were not hidden by leaf litter — if I set one of these off, I'd be sure to take out at least two mates even if I managed to hit the deck in time to save my own hide.

I now also had the wives, girlfriends, fathers, mothers, brothers, sisters and, for some, children of everyone back there behind me depending on me not to make any mistakes; to see and hear every thing that was a danger to us so that their loved ones could come home to them safe and sound at the end of all this. It was no wonder we moved at a snail's pace between smoke-breaks.

That first morning as Scout, Jim handed me the accepted symbol of the Scout: an M16 Armalite, and told me solemnly, 'Ere, yud better take this.'

'Bullshit! Stick et up yur arse, I'll stick to wot I know,' I growled at him.

'But this'ud be so much lighter,' he told me, frowning.

'I donn give a shit,' I shot back at him, 'if you want me t'be Scout, then this is wot I'll use, at least I know when I start shooten wiff this thing I'm gunna penetrate the "J" an' it somethen,' I told him, holding up my battered SLR.

'OK,'he said, 'but you'll be sorry.'

'Yeah, yeah, piss off Jim, an' take that fucken thing wiff yuh.'

'Well, you WILL need this,' he told me, as he handed me the other essential tool of the Scout: a pair of secateurs. I took them grudgingly from him and squeezed the handles together to reassure myself that they did indeed work.

The only bonus of this Scout lark was that I now had a legitimate reason to ride on top of the APCs. For the past three months, I'd been fighting with Jim about riding on top of them instead of in them, but now I could push the issue when it come up, with "but I'm the Scout, I havta know where I'm goen at all times".

I got a card in the next mail from Cheryl Neale, Darby's teenage daughter. On the front was a picture of the head of a beautiful, thoroughbred horse and on the back her words, 'Don't you forget horses.' It must have been around the Horse's Birthday which falls on the first of August each year.

Not long after my "promotion", we came out of the thick stuff from the west late one afternoon and made our way east into a fair-size clump of trees with a good clearing under them. Here, Six Section found a twenty-five-pound bomb with its fuse removed that had then been rewired and rigged up as a booby-trap. We deactivated it and camped on the site overnight.

Before we left camp next morning, we were told that someone had found the tracks of a dog and a man wearing sandshoes on a pad to the south of us. Straightaway Bill Keenan said that it was the CSM and his pet dog Spotty going for their early morning jog. Everybody laughed and mysteriously we,

Eight Platoon, immediately adopted the imaginary Spotty as our mascot.

By just after eight we were moving south in some pretty open country. The morning was very bright and fresh and we'd only been going ten minutes or so when suddenly Hillie yelled from up front, 'Dung loi!'

'UC-DAI-LOI!' Crack, crack, crack, from an AK47 was the immediate response.

Charlie let go with a full mag from the Armalite into the bamboo behind which the Nogs had a night camp. Next, Pig emptied thirty rounds from his SLR which he'd had doctored up by the Armourer to make it fully automatic, aiming at a Nog who was running almost parallel to our twenty- eight-man column and brandishing a Chinese-made AK50. Our practised drills slipped into action and immediately we were running straight for the firing up ahead of us as fast as our loads would allow us. Billy Keenan was running ahead of me and yelling at us, 'Don't bunch up, don't bunch up.'

He was craning his neck to get a better look at what was going on. Suddenly, he stopped on the spot and I run smack-bang into the back of him hitting my forehead on the handle his infernal entrenching tool. So much for not bunching up! It was as if the sounds of the shots were like a giant magnet drawing us with immense power towards the action. They were our mates up there in front of us and they needed our help NOW.

The shooting stopped and we were down to a brisk walk as we got to the site of the initial contact. As we swept through their camp, I just had time to see the black, silk hammock still swinging and a pair of sheila's knickers lying on the ground directly below it as I hurried past. We followed up the tracks in the dew on ankle-high, lush grass which had been left by those that got away.

Then someone called out from just west of the position, 'Ere's one over 'ere.'

Someone else asked, 'As 'e got any money on 'im?'

'Nah.' It was Pig. 'e tor'et all up in front of 'imself. Must of donnet just before 'e popped 'is pill.'

We did a thorough sweep of the area, but only found a platform up a tree just north-east of the campsite. It looked out over the vast expanse of Elephant Grass which stretched to the east from here to Route Two. We presumed this was being used as their lookout. On finding no more Nogs for about five hundred metres in all directions around their camp, we regrouped and organised ourselves into different work details. I was at first assigned to help in making a helipad out in the long grass to our east, then when it was done I was sent off along the APC track that ran north between the long grass on its east side and the timber line on the west, to act as Sentry.

That now made two-and-a-half kills for Eight Platoon and we were, in fact, about a kilometre east of our last kill site. This lot were most likely using the same track to bring the stuff they'd hooked west from the villages on Route Two.

We camped a little to the south of the buried Nog that night. Just on Stand-To, I was sitting crossed-legged beneath my hutchie having a leisurely last smoke for the day when suddenly a pair of grubby GPs came to attention in front of me.

'Put that smoke out, you're on a charge,' I was told by an angry Pollard.

'Wot? Wot areyuh bungen on? S'not "Stan' To" yet.'

But my protest fell on deaf ears.

'It is and you're being charged for having a light on after dark,' was Jim's curt reply.

'But no one's told me it was Stan'To! You always tell me when it's Stan'To, Jim, you know I never carry a watch.'

'You've been 'ere long enough t'know when it's "Stan' To". Now, quieten down or you'll be upfuhmaken too much noise as well.'

I couldn't believe what I was hearing from Jim, but as I looked out from under the side of my hutchie I saw what was really going on. Jim was looking nervously back towards where Shortarse was holed up in the middle of our harbour. It was obvious to me right away that it was at Shortarse's insistence that Jim charged me. As soon as I became aware of the situation, I calmed down. It wasn't Jim's fault, he was just following orders and, besides, Shortarse still hadn't got me back for pulling out of being his Batman when we were coming over here.

Then, having travelled south for a day or two, we came into a disused rubber plantation. The re-growth rubber was very thick here and grew as high as a man's head between the mature trees. Some way into the plantation Shortarse decided to set up a night ambush on the road which ran along its eastern side. We were to set our hutches as low as possible to the ground and to cover them with green leaves broken from the re-growth rubber so as to hide any shine from the stretched fabric which might give away our position and the all-important element of surprise.

We started setting up in a triangle-shaped ambush with

Four Section spaced out along the road that was to be our Killing Zone, Five and Six Section meeting at Six's gun at the apex, Four Section's gun was at the south end and Five's was at the northern end.

I was totally absorbed in spreading the leaves on the carefully-constructed, low-slung tent which Jim and I would be sharing for the night when WACK-WACK-WACK-WACK-WACK-WACK, the M60 from Six Section blasted into action, splitting the quite afternoon air apart.

The next recollection I have is crawling as fast as I could on my belly through undergrowth, searching desperately for somewhere to hide; searching for anything that would afford me the slightest bit of cover. I was flattened out like a big Goanna; the smallest depression in the ground would have been enough for me to slide into. All the time the M60 was whacking away in the background, followed shortly by M16s and SLRs cracking and bopping into earshot. Suddenly, I stopped wriggling northwards. Some instinct told me to take stock; that I might well be in danger. To my horror, I found myself completely alone in the re-growth and by the sound of the weapons behind me I'd travelled a fair distance away from where I'd started. I was cradling my trusty SLR in my arms, but I couldn't for the life of me remember how I managed to pick it up or where it was in our position, or even how far I'd run before I hit the deck to start crawling, or if I'd even run at all. To this very day, as at the actual time, there is a big, black hole in my memory bank that I cannot come to grips with.

I started yelling out to Pollard. 'Wot thu fucks goen on? Where thu fuck are they?'

By now I was still, but it wasn't before I heard Jim that I could ascertain how far away from our Camp I was.

'Owthu fuck woodi know?' Jim yelled back to me, and he seemed a long way away or at least further than I thought he should have been.

'F'crysake, find out, willyuh?' I called back to him.

Pollard started yelling again, directing his shouts towards the Six Section gun. 'Wots goen on over there?'

At last someone from that area called back, 'It's aright, they're gone.'

Quickly making my way back to our position, I found that I'd travelled some thirty odd metres or so and that Pollard had gone nearly the same distance towards the middle of the harbour.

It turned out that the blokes on the Six Section gun were completely engaged in making their night's camp, just as we had been, and had left the gun unattended at the base of a rubber tree. Suddenly, out of the corner of his eye, their gunner noticed a small band of fully-armed enemy standing on tip-toes watching our endeavours, only two rows of rubber trees back from the Six Section gun position. He had dived towards the gun to take to the observers, but went down on the wrong side of the tree at first and had to scramble around it to get the thing going. He wasn't going to muck about warning anyone; he was going to save us all. Most likely, by the time he'd pulled off the first burst, the enemy were already on the toe and in little fear of their lives. Needless to say, nobody wandered through our carefully prepared "killing ground" that night.

Now it was time to return to the Dat. We were picked up by

APCs and spirited away towards the south along a well-used bush track. At one point the APCs had to "swim" a creek. It was a fascinating feeling to be up on one of these heavy beasts as they surged through the small, fast-flowing stream.

From up on top of the machine, a low branch of bamboo snatched my giggle hat from my head as we rolled along and for me there was absolutely no way of retrieving it. We turned east and came out onto Route Two at a little settlement just north of the Base.

When we got back to our Company compound, Andy was still there getting processed for his RTA. The first morning we were in, he was on the loudspeaker system in the Office bright and early.

'Wakey wakey, hands off snakey, everybody. Com'on all you men, and that includes Officers. Get outta bed before the sun boils yur piss an' the crows pick yur eyes out, it's two and awakey and they're all days, an' I'm gunna be 'ome fucken round eyes. Suffer, you cunts, suffer.'

He would have gone on, but I think someone took the mic off him for the morale of the remaining troops. To say that Andy was happy about going home at this point in time would have been the understatement of a lifetime.

The next morning, it was on again, 'Wakey, wakey,' and all that stuff, only it was 'one 'an wakey' this time. Good luck, old mate. See yah.

* * *

17
AFTER ANDY

I needed to acquire a new hat as soon as possible after we got in, so I went down to the Q Store at the first opportunity.

'Wanna L n D a hat,' I told the burly Sergeant at the desk.

'Why? Wot 'appened to thu larss one?' he questioned me.

'Lostet on me way in off the APCs.'

This seemed to satisfy him. He came back to the counter and threw me a brand-new hat, only this one was the "lamp-shade" type. It would have been labelled, 'Hat — bush, olive-green, for the use of'. I hated them.

'Nar mate, I wanted one of them ones wifthu gauze in thu holes in thu side an' thu flat brim.'

'I gave yur a 'at, now get out,' the grumpy, old bastard told me.

I sat on the bed in my tent and looked contemptuously at this horrible thing that was supposed to constitute a hat. What was I to do? Then, struck by inspiration, I got my bayonet out and cut a gash along the crown. Using a cigarette lighter, I scorched the edges of the cut on both sides, then I took it outside the front of our tent and rubbed it vigorously in a puddle of dirty water with my boot.

One of the mates came along and seeing me so engaged enquired, 'Wotta yur doen?'

'LnD'en a 'at,' I told him.

Back at the Q Store a short time later, I ran into a different bloke at the counter. 'Gotta L n D a 'at,' I stated, before adding, 'I want one a them ones wiffa flat brim.'

'Yeah mate,' he said, 'You go down the back there and get wotever one yur want.' He pointed the way.

I was like a sheila in a dress shop as I fussed about until I got the exact hat I wanted and, pleased as punch with my prize, I high-tailed it out of there. Just as I got to the door however, the original Sergeant of Supply called out to me.

'Hey, wait a minute, weren't you jist in 'ere?'

'Nar mate, wasn't me, musta bin sumone else,' I assured him and I bolted back to our lines with my new hat.

That night I saw what I would have to say was the cruellest thing I'd ever seen in my life. While we were pissing it up in the Boozer, Clarkey was walking around the outside of it in full fighting regalia, bar his gat. He was picking up cigarette butts that we'd thrown out through the openings. Apparently, he was on KPs.

KPs are when you have to wear a full pack around all day and every hour it is inspected by your Commanding Officer. The pack's contents have to be displayed out on your bed for the inspection, then immediately re-packed so that the offender can go walk-a-bout for another hour. Clarkey's clean- up around the Boozer was just some extra shit on top of that. The boys were adding to his misery by calling out to him as he passed, 'Hey Clarkey, come an 'ave a beer wivus.'

Poor bastard just grinned at them and went on picking up butts.

I asked Bob Denholm who was setting beside me at a table in the Boozer, 'Wot's 'e done t'd'serve that?'

'Oh, 'e fucked up big time,' Bob told me, with a wickedly, knowing grin, but I never found out what.

Charlie Company was put on "Ready Reaction Force" duties. We had about five days sitting around in the Dat all brass up and packed, ready to go at a moment's notice, should we be needed to spring into action and help any of the other three Companies that were out in the field.

Boris came through the tent one day saying, 'Who wants a game a football?'

'Woddyah call football?' I asked him, as he stood in the opening to our tented area.

'League, of course.'

'Yeah, I'll be in that,' I replied.

It turned out that the Company were going to play the Reo boys over at a ground near their lines. However, League is a professional sport and the Army in its wisdom did not allow its personnel to play professional sports, so we were supposed to play Union instead.

All decked out in green jerseys and ready to go, we started to run out onto the field, but as we were about to line up, someone piped up with, 'Why donn we play League? There's no Officers round here, is there?'

The players looked around at each other and the quick decision was made to bush two of the players on each side, me being one of them to go. As I walked dejectedly away, someone called to me to come back. 'Youken be ref.'

'Where's me whistle?'

'There's no whistle, you'll jest havta sing out.'

'Roger that,' was my answer and we were on.

The only way I could pull the game up for anything like a scrum for a knock-on or the sixth tackle was to scream out at the top of my voice,-'HOOOLLD URTTTT'.

The contest became a bit of a whitewash. When the Charlie Company men were about thirty-something in front and we were walking back to the centre line for yet another Reo kick-off, one of them started calling out to me, 'Sir, sir?'

I ignored him.The bloke beside him asked, 'How'd know e's a Sir?'

'Es gotta be to 'ave control of this game.'

If only they knew! I was, in fact, the only Private on the entire team. Every one else had ranks from Lance Corporals right up to the Charlie Company 2IC Captain C. H. Babington.

The final score was about 50 to 0. At one point I had to caution my own Sergeant, Boris O'Brian, for unnecessary rough play when he went charging into the opposition and deliberately punched the first jaw he could connect with for no apparent reason other than it was there to hit. It made an awful sound when he connected, but I didn't send him off though, as I put it down to him letting off pent-up steam.

A day later, Toddy Smith lined us all up and, walking along behind each rank of three, he said in a loud, concise voice, 'Some of you need haircuts. Whoever I tap on the shoulder will proceed down to the barber's and get yourselves cleaned up at once.'

When he got to me, he gave me a particular hard dig in the back. 'Haven't I told you before, Digger?'

I visited the barber down at the Nogshop and got my hair cut to the regulation — short back and sides — just to please old Smithy. When I asked the Noggie barber, 'ow much'es that, mate?' he acted real dumb and pointed toward the other skinny little Nog sitting near the door on the way out. He was nodding and all smiles, so I paid him instead.

During this time, I got seconded to help a Cook out over at the Officers' and Sergeants' Mess. Piece a piss really; all I had to do was go in and ask each one of them individually what they would prefer for lunch then go out the back and tell the Cook what they wanted. Mind you, the tucker was exactly the same stuff the men were eating over at the ORs' Mess, just dished up by a Cook and served to them by a Cook's assistant.

When our time as the Ready Reaction Force ended, we were choppered as a Company out to a big clearing opposite Ngai Giao and about three kilometres west of Route Two. We set off in a south-westerly direction, but almost as soon as we got going, the "five fingers hanging down" signal indicating booby trap came back along the line. We halted and waited until someone told us it was right and we could move on. However, we'd only just got going when the sign came our way again. After the third time, Boxall got the shits with us and told us to cut it out and get going. We were in fact on the site of an extinct Fire Support Base. There was wire coming up out of the ground all around us, but none of it posed any real threat.

We pushed on. An hour or so later the same sign came back along the line and again we halted. Whoever was up front at the time had come across a metre-deep hole in the ground with what looked like a solid lump of steel in it. This turned out to be an unexploded twenty-five-pound bomb. They called for some Engineers to be choppered in to fix it and so we moved on, bringing the "Gingerbeers" with us.

Just before going into our Night Harbour, the five-fingers-up, like your holding a piece of invisible fruit in your hand, which was the "mine sign", came back along the long line of Diggers following each other in single file. On closer inspection, it was found that we'd entered an area which had a Cluster Bomb dropped on it. Cluster Bombs are what you get when a large bomb is dropped from an aircraft and it explodes a little way above the ground and disperses a heap of smaller bombs, scattering them about on the ground. This particular cluster looked like one of the latest version of these weapons. The first ones the Yanks sent down were about as round as a baseball; yellow, with dimples on them, like golf balls. These failed to detonate and the ever-resourceful enemy used them as booby-traps, so the Yanks made another type that looked like an olive-green jam tin; these had wings which would open out from the sides, causing the small bomb to spin. Thus, wound up, they were supposed to detonate on impact; however, these too proved inadequate and again the Nogs used them against us, so they now came up with a model which looked like the first one, but which could be set off by the vibrations of a man moving past them — or even by the change of temperature — caused by a man standing over them for too long.

Not being too sure what to do, therefore, we suspended all walking and stood quietly about, waiting for the Gingerbeers to make an assessment of the menacing giant golf balls. When one of these blokes picked up a device near where we were standing and it didn't immediately go off, we crowded around him to get a better look at it.

He slowly rolled it over in his hands and, when he was satisfied that he had it the right way up, he proceeded to screw a one-third portion of it off the top. All the while Jim was scolding us while keeping a safe distance himself. 'Get away from him, you lot. That thing might go off at any minute an' blow yur fucken 'eds off.'

We ignored him as we watched with keen interest the work the Gingerbeer was doing. On top of the device, we saw a clean, silver, steel plate. He pulled out a small screw driver and very carefully lifted one edge of this plate a little, so we craned our heads in closer to see if we could get a better look at what was under it.

'C'mon, you blokes, get away from him.' Jim pleaded incessantly, to no avail.

The Gingerbeer fiddled a bit more under the plate and there was a slight click. He produced a huge sigh of relief, to which I asked him, 'Wot was that for?'

'Well,' he explained, 'if that didn't go "click" it woulda went "boom" an' weeda all went up.'

'Yeah, right, thanks for tellen us that now!' I said to him, and we both laughed a relived laugh.

We harboured up early that afternoon in what turned out to be a prick of a campsite. There were Chomper Ants everywhere and we had to make our camps around them as they didn't want to give up their positions lightly. Don't blame them really; they had picked this spot carefully for themselves, after all, and we were the intruders.

With time on my hands, I stripped my gat right down and was giving her a real, good clean when the new 2IC of our Section, acting Lance Corporal Bob Coggins, came past me and announced, 'You're on thu gun at three-thirty,' then he looked at his watch and went off at me, all the while looking nervously over at Boxall, who was sitting up in his hammock just behind my position.

'Fuck me, you should have been down there ten minutes ago, get down to the gun NOW.'

'Go an' get yurself wellen truly fucked, Bob. I gotta put me gat back t'gether an' I'm not goen anywhere 'til I doet,' I told him, angrily. As he stormed off, I hurriedly reassembled my gat before going down to the gun.

Bob Denholm was sitting there and greeted me with a broad grin. 'You'll be in big shit now, Dog,' he told me, as I sat down beside him to take up my position behind the gun.

'Why? Wot 'ave I done this time?' I asked him in surprise.

'Boxall was sitten there with his big ears flappen all the time you were goen off at Coggins.'

'Arr, I donn give a shit. Coulden really come down 'ere with me gat in bits, could I?' Boxall must have seen it that way too as nothing ever came of my outburst at Coggins.

That night when I went to find the gun for my stint on gun duty, I suddenly found myself at the end of the string line with no gun crew at my feet. I called out in a whisper to the blackness. 'Gun, where are yuh gun?'

There was no answer immediately, so I called again, this time a couple of decibels higher. 'Gun, where the fuckareyuh?'

'Woddayur doen wonderen about out there, yur wanna get yurselve fucken shot up?' Bob Denholm growled at me from out of the darkness. He was behind me and slightly to my left and there was a hint of mirth in his voice.

'Wot the fuck are youes doen back there?' I shot back at him. It turned out that the Chomper Ants had invaded the gun position not long after dark and in doing so had forced Clarkey and Smithy who were on the gun at the time to shift camp.

We patrolled south-west the next day with nil results. Again, we made an early camp so I took advantage of the time to go see my mate, Ralf Bodsworth (my Second Scout in Corps Training) who was now Sergeant Upton's Sig. Sergeant Upton was the Ordinance Co-ordinator for Charlie Company; that is, he calculated and brought in the big guns for us. On my way into the centre of the harbour, I came across this skinny, little bloke swinging a weight attached to a string line around and around before letting it go so that it flew high up into the trees. I was fascinated as I watched him for a bit, then I told him seriously. 'Wot yer doen there, mate? Yer not gunna catch any fish up there.'

He didn't see the joke. I just grinned at him as he explained to me angrily that he was trying to set up an aerial to get a bigger range for his radio set.

I found Bobby not too far away. 'Hey, 'owset goen mate?'

'Good mate,' he greeted me, all smiles.

As we sat and talked, the leaves of a small book flicked over in the limited breeze that found its way down onto the jungle floor and suddenly they stopped and there on the page was my name and it was the only thing written there.

'Wot's this?' I asked Bobby, while pointing at it.

'It's your name in a book,' he told me with grin.

'Yeah, Iken see that. 'Awe, I know wottet is, that's the charge they put me on, I thought they'd forgotten about et be this, it's been so long.'

'Donn look like ut. Bloke orter tear that bloody page out,' he offered.

'Geeze mate, donn do that, donn want yur getten inta trouble over me, nar, she'll be right,' I told him. I left him after a bit, saying as I departed. 'I'll see yur later mate, hey?'

'Yeah mate.'

Next day we went on travelling in a south-west direction. At one point, the column was at a standstill when four or five half-grown pigs of all colours trotted in our direction at an angle from the west-sou-west. Boxall was standing in a dream-like state two back from me as the pigs headed straight for him and they were at his feet before they realised he was blocking their path. They let out a series of squeals and distressed grunts and split up in all directions, at which point Boxall suddenly sprung to life. First, he kicked out at the nearest pig which had nearly run under him, then he took "the stance" and, wide-eyed, he waved his M16 this way and that, aiming at one pig, then another, to protect himself.

I killed myself laughing; I couldn't help myself; however, Boxall's Batman didn't see the funny side of it and got right up me. Oh, so protective of his great leader was he.

Next day we were pulled up in a small disused Rubber plantation waiting for the Maintdem chopper to come in when a most extraordinary event took place. More than one half of a Platoon — I think they were from Nine — were stood down and marched in to be charged. Imagine what it looked like from our perspective seeing all these blokes rifleless out in the "J" standing around waiting for their turn to be brought up and Boxall sitting — yes, sitting on a small chair behind a small table on which a pile of papers fluttered in a slight breeze — as

Toddy Smith marched each and every one of them up one by one in turn to cop their shit.

After moving on from here we camped in a spot where extremely thick regrowth grew only just above a man's head. While I was on gun duty that night I searched for the Southern Cross in the sky to the south, but no, I could not find it. I became depressed at not to be able to glimpse just the tiniest bit of it and I fretted over it for an hour wondering if I'd have the pleasure of seeing that familiar comforting constellation hovering in my night sky ever again.

The morning after this we were given a reprieve and Eight Platoon was once again sent away from CHQ and out on our own. We went north and about mid-morning I happened to see a piece of wire poking up out of the ground just off the track we were on, so I sent a signal up ahead of me to call Shortarse back to check it out.

'Well, c'mon,' he said, 'you saw it first,' as he made his way off the track towards it.

He looked at it for a second before pulling out his bayonet and prodding at it. I stepped in behind him so that his whole body covered me if he struck anything that had an anti-lifting device attached to it, fully expecting it to explode. Nothing happened. Then, he brushed his hand around in the leaf-litter that surrounded the wire. Still nothing happened. He stood up, turned around and headed back towards the others saying as he brushed past me, 'There's nothing there.'

However, as he was departing, I noticed a leaf move slightly in the depression which he'd just finished excavating. I removed my bayonet from its scabbard and, using the point carefully, flipped back the leaf. With supersonic speed the tail of one of those huge, emerald-green Scorpions popped up out of the loose brown and yellow leaves and then went stock-still ready to strike. I skewered the insect through its shell-like back and hauled it up out of its place of ambush. I quickly caught up to Shortarse and tapped him on left shoulder. As he began to turn to face me, I extended my arm and shoved the bayonet with the squirming Scorpion attached under his nose and said to him, 'Look wot yur nearly put yur 'and on, Sir.'

He waved at it as he shrunk back from me. 'Take that away from me,' he cried, his eyes wide.

'E can't 'urt yur now, Sir, I got 'im,' I told him, with a cheeky grin. He glared daggers at me for a second, then quickly turned around to re-join the patrol.

A day or two later we were told we had to join back up with CHQ to be lifted out. It was a humid morning with low cloud cover almost blocking out the sun. Clarkey wanted to have a go at scouting, so they let the big bloke have a crack at it. Before long he got the shits with it all and, instead of secateurs, he took to the scrub with his machete. He sounded like a bull elephant busting his way through up front and would never have heard anything else until he tripped over it. Clarkey was no Scout.

At the smoke-break after Clarkey's stint, the NCOs and Shortarse got into a discussion as to where our present Loc-stat was. There were five compasses, maps and protractors in our Platoon and each holder had a different place on the map where he thought we were. Even though the sun was a small, white glow in the slow-moving cloud, I'd been watching it over my shoulder as we moved. I'd noticed that Clarkey had slewed a little off course in his endeavour to lead us and I tried to inform Jim of this fact.

'Bullshit, owdyur know that?' he asked.

'Just goen by thu sun.' I told him yet again.

'Yur can't go by the sun,' Jim insisted, very annoyed as always.

'Look, Jim, jus' show us where yer think we are now an' where yer think we're gunna end up an' I'll show yur wot I mean.'

Jim showed me the map and pointed out our objective. It was a big clearing and we were supposed to come out near the eastern end of it.

'Right! Going on the way we've been goen, we'll end up down 'ere an' we'll avta go all the way along that clearen t'get to where we're goen.' I told him.

'Bullshit,' is all I got from him.

When we moved off we again travelled in the same direction as Clarkey had led us; and yes, when we emerged onto the edge of the clearing, we then had to patrol nearly two kilometres along the northern side of it before getting to CHQ who were waiting for us in the "J" at the eastern end.

As we moved into their position, thick-set, short-cut, blonde-haired M'goo went down. He was sitting hunched up shivering uncontrollably unable to look up, but still clinging to his gat as I passed him. Boxall stood over him and if any of us attempted to go to his aid or even step out of line a bit to ask him, 'You awright mate?,' he told us, 'Move on, I'll look after him.'

Bit rough when you can't even comfort your own mate. M'goo had contracted Malaria.

* * *

18
AND ALL THINGS NICE

When this stint was over, it was our turn in Vungers again. I left the boys at The Flags and went straight down the wide street to the Blue Pacific. The woman who claimed me to give me a massage this time was most probably in her early thirties. She was more matronly than your average massage girl. I was so relaxed by the time she had finished the chop-chop stuff along my back that I didn't notice she'd climbed up onto the bench until I felt her bare foot on my back. She gently manoeuvred the ball of her foot along a vertebra or two at a time and then gave a small, sharp push-down. I absorbed it all as she moved along the length of my spine. I didn't believe the NCOs when they told us on the ship coming over that 'the girls will walk on yur back', but here I was being walked on and it was heavenly. After that wonderful massage I headed off towards the bars feeling so uplifted that I felt I could take on the world.

I found Sandy at the same place I'd last seen her in the bar beside the Chikito. She was happy to see me again.

'Is Thao Ly 'ere?' I asked her, when we met at the door to the dimly-lit establishment.

'No, she go Minh Bar,' she answered, pointing back in the direction I'd just come from. I was a little disappointed that I'd now have to go and find her in another bar, but very quickly and happily discovered that the Minh Bar was only three doors down at the other end of the US Sky Bar building. As I entered the darkened bar, Thao Ly spotted me at once. She let out a stifled squeal of delight, ran towards me and she flung her arms around me. I was a little bit embarrassed, to tell you the truth, as no girl had ever done this to me before. It was huge for me that she'd show so much delight upon seeing me.

'Yes, hello to you too,' I got out. Then, when she let me go, she told me, 'Last time you go, I cry.'

'Nar, bullshit,' I said. '*Working girls don't cry for anyone.*'

Then a friend of hers standing near by chimed in. 'Yes,' she said, seriously, 'she cried two days for you before.'

I didn't know whether to believe them or not, but, gee, it was good to be in the company of this happy little soul again. Now all I wanted to do was to make love to her. In no time at all we had procured a room overlooking the street just east of the US SKY Bars. After our first torrid session of passionate love making, Thao Ly went back to her bar leaving me to sleep it off.

Around midday, she came back to check up on me bringing a couple of her colleagues with her. They stood in the door and giggled at first as sheilas are wont to do. Then suddenly, for no apparent reason, one of her mates let out a yell of joy and rushed the bed. She literally threw herself upon my prone, naked body and began dry-humping me while laughing her pretty little head off. I saw Thao Ly give her a vile look from where she stood at the door. A few rapid words in Vietnamese to each other and then all three of the girls were gone.

Thao Ly came back to me around two in the afternoon. This time I took my time. I was in the process of kissing her silky, light-tan skin all over and was down about her belly button when she suddenly grabbed the top of my head and literally shoved me down onto her honey pot.

I was instantly transported to a place beyond my wildest dreams as I devoured her essence of life. I've no idea how long I was there, but I was delirious with the joy of it and when I finally came up for air and made tender love to her, she slept for an hour in my arms. Later, looking down on her lovely, naked body, I noticed small stretch-marks on her tight tummy and I ran my fingers across the slight mauve indentations on her soft skin.

'You got a baby?' I asked her.

'Yeah,' she said and I could see the justifiable pride in her eyes.

'Where's your baby-san?'

'He Saigon,' she told me quietly, and this time I detected an edge of sadness in her voice.

'Ow old is 'e?' I wanted to know.

She immediately brightened and smiled back at me. 'He two year now.'

'Where baby's popa-san?' It was a legitimate question, given that she was working here and the boy lived in Saigon with someone else.

'He die,' she told me, her near-black eyes not showing the slightest sign of emotion.

'The war?' I asked her.

She looked down towards the bed. 'Yes, war,' she answered, softly.

I'd worn a black, silk shirt to town that morning, one of two that I'd had made by the clothes merchant who traded from the little cubby-hole he called a shop in the Peter Babcoe Club out at the Australian Camp. The girls in the bars just loved it, greeting me with 'VC number wonn' and lots of laughter when they saw me in it. As I was climbing aboard the truck to come into town, I tore a small hole under the sleeve along the stitching and one of the girls in the Minh Bar thought it was a right laugh to make the hole bigger, so she grabbed it and ripped it open even further. I asked Thao Ly if she knew where I could get it fixed.

'You wait,' she told me eagerly, and took off. I waited and waited. I eventually convinced myself that she'd done a runner back to the bar and was working again while I languished here in our room alone. I tossed up whether or not to go back down to the bar myself, but decided, 'Nar, I need the rest, why not stay put.'

Eventually, when I'd given up all hope of seeing her again that day and was considering the real prospect of spending the night alone, Thao Ly came through the door all smiles.

'You do come back?' I scolded her.

She held up a reel of black cotton and a small needle in triumph. 'I get,' she beamed.

'I see, an' where did yur get'em?'

'Muma-san,' she told me brightly, and I knew who she meant instantly.

'Muma-san! Your mother lives here in Vung Tau?'

'Yeah, she live out that way, she make me work,' Thao Ly told me nonchalantly, waving her arm in the direction of the turn-off where Donks and I gave the Lambretta driver a heart-attack last time we were in.

Gees, how wrong can you get? Here I am thinking she's dumped me in preference to work and all the while she's out visiting with her mother.

She sat crossed-legged in an old, cane chair in the room and went to work on mending the shirt. Her face serious, she concentrated on the job in hand, her tiny, nimble fingers working expertly with the material, gathering it along the needle before pulling it through in a blanket stitch. While she worked she talked to me about her afternoon's visit with her Mum and I even got a mention, apparently, with her mother being quite pleased that her daughter had a new boyfriend. As I watched her work and listened to her idle chatter, I felt the tentacles of my heart begin to reach out towards her. How could I not fall for this gorgeous, entrancing young woman?

In the morning as we were about to leave our room, I jokingly said to a very bright and cheerful Thao Ly, 'Make this bed before we go, woman, look at the state of it.'

She pouted that most beautiful pout of hers, then giggling she leaped up onto the bed and tore about on it like a naughty, three-year-old child. Suddenly, the toe end of the double bed collapsed under her and hit the floor with a thud. Thao Ly gasped and then stood there with her arms held up, elbows bent, her mouth open and her eyes wide with astonishment for a few seconds before jumping off. It was a real 'ooowah' moment. We laughed aloud as both of us bent down facing each other and put the bed back together, albeit temporarily.

We went down to hang out at the Minh Bar and I sucked on that Yank Four-Star piss for a bit while Thao Ly just hung about keeping a close eye on me. At one point I was sitting on a bricked garden bed out the front of the bar minding my own business when an elderly woman started getting stuck into a kid on the street right in front of me. In Vietnam, at this time, until a boy was of age — that is, around twelve — the oldest woman of his household had the job of disciplining him. After he turns of age, he was expected to go outside to be with the men. Well, the old lady had this kid by the ear and she was belting him with a flat hand up the other one. A small crowd of excited women had gathered to bear witness to his chastisement. All seemed to be going according to the rules until the kid caught me nonchalantly watching the proceedings. His face all screwed up in pain and twisting away from the whacking hand, he started pointing at me and shouting.

Suddenly, all the women in attendance turned towards me and began shouting what appeared to be some sort of abuse in Vietnamese. Next thing Thao Ly is at my side grabbing me by the arm and dragging me urgently back into the bar saying, 'Taboo, taboo.'

I was flabbergasted. 'Why, wot's wrong?'

'Number ten you no watch.'

Apparently it is forbidden for an of-age male to watch a boy cop it from a woman. I was supposed to turn my back on the proceedings and act as if nothing was happening. Gees, you could get into so much trouble over there when you don't know all their customs.

In the early afternoon Thao Ly asked me if we could 'go swim', but I had a better idea. Right then I wanted her body again and although she scowled at me at first she relented and we made our way back up to the room. As soon as we got onto the bed, however, it collapsed again. She went off to find management to acquire another bed and when she returned she was accompanied by a slightly older, stern-looking woman of slim physique.

They got into a heated discussion in Vietnamese. I let Thao Ly go — she looked very capable of winning these negotiations — but when management produced a form for me to sign, I burred up.

'No, no, no, I'm not signing nufen, you sign et,' I told Thao Ly. I had absolutely no idea what it was that they were trying to get me to sign.

Reluctantly Thao Ly signed the document and we were led around to another room at the back of the building, the original part of it by the looks. The room was drab with cream, three-metre high, flat, timber ceiling and small, high windows on the south side to let in limited light.

Nevertheless, we got into what we'd come up here to do. After a very relaxed and lengthy love-making session, I rose and got myself dressed to go, but Thao Ly remained on the bed lying very still and staring up at the high ceiling.

'Hey, you awright? You c'men?' I asked her.

With a gleeful smile slowly gathering on her upturned face and with her fists clenching into knots just above her chest, her knees gave a series of little jerks, 'Make love number wonn,' she cooed.

That night I quibbled about paying another twelve dollars MPC to get her out of the bar, after all I'd already paid that morning. She took me up to the Muma-san's quarters above the bar where I was ordered by Thao Ly to ditch my R.M. Williams

Santa Fee boots at the door before we padded into a very clean and tidy apartment, she in her tiny bare feet and me in black socks.

The Muma-san that Thao Ly worked for proved to be a huge, Indian woman who this night wore a predominately light-purple, flowing, floral-print sari and looked somewhat peeved by our intrusion. At first, she didn't want to go along with Thao Ly's proposal, but Thao Ly persisted and, of course, I understood nothing of what they were saying in Vietnamese so I just stood back mute. Besides, I'd already seen that Thao Ly was quite capable of holding her own in negotiations anyway. Then I heard the word 'love' and every thing changed at once as the big woman beamed at us — it would appear that the word "love" is universal. Muma-san relented and we departed with her blessings to spend the night wrapped up in each others arms.

* * *

19

THE NUI DINHS

In Nui Dat we were told. 'We are goen up into the Nui Dinhs this trip. They want us up there for ten days around the time of some elections that are going on in Baria and the old Chief thinks the VC might come down from camps in the Dinhs and stuff things up for him by harassing the locals and we're to stop them.'

We waited that morning at Eagle Farm while a duo of Cobra Gunships did a shoot-up on our proposed LZ. While we were sitting around waiting, we were told, 'A TAOR patrol shot up the barber larss night in an ambush just outside the wire.' This was the same bloke who was pretending he couldn't understand me down at the barber's shop before and now they'd found that he had information on his person at the time — he was presumed to have been a member of Chau Duc Local Force Gorilla Unit.

Eventually, just after dinner camp we were lifted and carried away to the south-west of the Dat. We landed without smoke on a small clearing that straddled a razor-back ridge and which served quite well as the LZ.

Of course, old, faithful Eight Platoon being first in again, had the job of securing a harbour spot, which unbeknownst to us at the time, was meant for Company Headquarters once they arrived.

From the clearing of rocky ground and sparse, short, dry grass, we poked off northward into jungle and up a bit of a rise. There wouldn't be a Nog within coo-ee of this place that was plain to see as the gunships had done their job well and every square inch of the LZ and the big rocks on the small hill we now climbed were scarred with evidence of their shoot-up.

When CHQ finally got up to the small hill, they immediately took over our positions as head of this castle. We, the peasants, were told, 'You will need to go down and fill up your water bottles and you've got to take extra ones for CHQ as well.'

Going down to a tiny, fast-running gutter at the bottom of a steep slope which had a good covering of lush, green grass wasn't too bad, but coming back up to our now-occupied positions was no Sunday stroll, I'm here to tell you, with full pack and gat, full water bottles, another man's full water bottles tied together with toggle rope and all the while being told by the big Boss to hurry up. Christ knows why we did that trip anyway, as we'd only just left Base Camp so CHQ's water bottles should have been full and, besides, it rained that night. I suppose we were just looking about a bit.

Next day we wandered about the ranges in close proximity to CHQ wearily making our way back to camp late that afternoon. In the morning we were told that we'd been ordered to go over to the highest peak of the Nui Dinhs to occupy Nui Dinh itself. We were pleased again to be splitting camp with CHQ from where they sat on the little hill giving orders and to go our own way again; however, it turned out we really had no cause to feel so good about it.

All day we dragged our way up over one ridge, down the

other side through a small brook which raced away towards the lowlands and thence to the sea then up to the next ridge. The only thing of interest I found all day was a gigantic, black spider about the size of a man's hand. The bloke in front of me dislodged a small rock as he slid down over a sixty-centimetre high rock ledge. When I slid over it, I sat back against the wall to rest and happened to look down at where I'd just placed my hand to see two shining eyes of the monstrous animal crouching in wait in a dark crevice. I sucked in a quick breath and pulled my hand away quickly. Then I cautiously moved a little closer and tried to get a better look at the enormous specimen and when I had to move on, I warned the bloke behind me, 'Watch out fur that big bloke there beside yur.'

He got such a start when he looked down that he nearly fell over. We also came across what appeared to be a ruined temple on some level ground high up on a ridge about three in the afternoon

By "Harbour-Up" time we were on the last ridge between us and the top of Nui Dinh. Below us lay a deep, dark valley, thick with growth and the view was way-out, if you like great views. It was raining now, not heavily, but certainly enough to get us wet. The Scouts had found an old, distinctively-Australian-style harbour site here, which I felt was rather odd this high up, overlooking the Dinhs. Odd or not, it would certainly do us as a camp for the night and we could easily get to the top of the mountain tomorrow because right now I felt buggered as I dropped my pack and grunted my relief ...

Short-lived relief, though, because I overheard Shortarse give CHQ our loc-stat and go on to inform them of our find and as Boxall's voice came back over the set I stood and listened disbelievingly at what I heard.

'3/2 this is 3, now I know that your men are wet and miserable, but you have not reached your objective. I would like you to push on and secure that position by nightfall, over.'

'3 this is 3/2, Roger, out,' Shortarse answered, meekly.

He then turned to us and said, 'Righto, you lot, we're moving out. Scouts, out.'

I found myself thinking, *'It's all right for that big cunt over there. He's sitting on his arse all high and dry, the useless bastard.'* I looked over at our objective. Gees, you could nearly touch it from where we stood, but there was a lot of dirt between us and there and a lot of very thick scrub as well. Small wonder that it took us quite a long time to get across that steep ravine through growth so thick that we lost sight of all our mates and went only by the small pad being made by those in front of us.

Then came the last twenty-five metres or so, starting with a thirty-to sixty-centimetre drop and gradually getting steeper until we were climbing straight up a cliff face about seven metres high. We clung to the vines and struggled towards the rim. As I swung to and fro, I remember saying to those closest to me, 'I know man was sposed ta come from monkeys an 'ere we are, us silly bastards acten jus' like'm.'

Finally, we all made it to the top of the Nui Dinhs. Everyone was elated; it wasn't exactly Mount Everest, but we were on the highest point in Phuoc Tuy Province. To our surprise, we found some more camp sites up here and again, distinctively Australian, but before we could find out too much about our new home Shortarse wanted to go walkabout. As far as we were concerned, he could go on his own for as far as he liked, but, no, he had to drag us along with him, but the silly bastard hadn't gone far when he turned us around and we went back to those old harbour sites to set up our Night Camp.

The view from our new home for the next six days was tremendous — if I'm allowed to use such a word in war — but it really was. We could see all the way down to Vung Tau, Baria, Dat Do, Long Hi and a few small places in between and north to the horizon. After dark we could see the lights of Than Son Nhut airport and part of Saigon, which were at least eighty kilometres to our west. The part we couldn't see was obscured from us by a portion of the range.

The top of Nui Dinh was a gigantic, flat rock. From the eastern side around to the northern side a shear cliff dropped two hundred feet or more. The west side I've described. To the south there was a small ridge which ran for about three-quarters of a kilometre before giving away to a steep one-to-one drop down to the grassy, flat country which ran about three kilometres out to the Mangrove swamps on the edge of the South China Sea.

Our job up here was only to observe and report any movement that we might see in the jungle-clad valleys below us. For the most part, we did nothing. Occasionally, we stood on the flat rock and watched the scrub below being blasted by a Yank ship which was harboured out in the bay to the immediate west of Vung Tau. We'd watch the ship until it would disappear in a cloud of black smoke from a full broadside, wait for the sound of the shot, then watch the valley below us for the great rushing noise of the shells screaming along and then the crash when they hit their allotted targets.

Late one afternoon, we watched a small cloud break out over the sea and dump some of its contents on the waters of the bay and the Yank ship and then sweep into the Nui Dinhs. The result was spectacular. We were above the level of the cloud as it raced towards us and we stood and watched it race up the valleys like a great, ghostly hand, splitting up and multiplying like a silky, white flame devouring everything it came to. It was awesome to say the least. If you have ever seen the classic movie picture *The Ten Commandments*, you'll remember the green mist which came to claim all the first born sons in Egypt. Well, what we were watching was the same, only in the purest of white. All too soon the mist engulfed us and it became quite dark, but it didn't rain for we were in the cloud itself and we only got damp as one does in a heavy fog.

I can't speak for the others, but for me there was one major drawback about being up here, especially at night. We could see the lights of Vung Tau away in the distance and, watching them, I'd think of Thao Ly; her dark, smiling eyes, her warm, silky skin and what I would tell her next time I was down there, if ever. I often wondered who she might be shacked up with on a certain night, Yank or Australian, black or white, curled up on those fresh, white sheets. I'd even made a pair of small bamboo chopsticks to eat my dry rations with, practising all that Lynn had taught me, hoping to impress Thao Ly with my effort on my next R and I.

We didn't get any Maintdems while we were here. Only one Kiowa came in to bring our weekly mail to us, so we were living on "Dehydrated Rations" known to military personnel as "Dry Rations". If you were to take a meal of boiled meat, spuds, pumpkin, beans and peas, freeze them, then take one-fifth of your usual portion, add water and mix into a goulash and heat, then you might have some idea of what Dry Rations are like. They came in an olive-green packet, lined with silver foil and opening out on one side to form a crude cooking utensil which we then placed over our Hexie stoves. It's good for you, though, with all the right stuff in it, or so we'd been told?

Eventually, our stay on "the rock" came to its end and on the appointed date we headed south-east along a spur, then down towards clear ground which was covered with grass between the main road to Saigon from Vung Tau at the bottom of the mountain. Our intent was to be choppered out from down there. We passed by another ruined temple as we went.

Bombardier Kevin Scrimshaw was crook that morning, so we moved at a brisk pace. Scrimshaw, a big bloke with a crop of short, thick, black hair always had a very pleasant smile for whoever he talked to. It was he who called in the Artillery when the Platoon needed it

'You'll be awright mate,' blokes could be heard saying from the file, 'We'll have yur outta 'ere in no time. Yur'll be on thu first flight out f'sure.'

It came to pass that he was on the only flight out that day because when we were only two hundred metres from our objective — our proposed lift off place on the level grassed area — Shortarse got the word from CHQ that the Province Chief was happy with his re-election, that all had gone well for him and we were of no further use to him. We were to vacate this AO (Area of Operation) and return to Base Camp immediately. So we did.

Scrimshaw was bloody crook by this time and, as we started off in a northerly direction up a steep ridge, someone took his pack and rifle from him to lighten his load. We kept telling Shortarse to stop and go back to the flat ground and call a "Dust-Off" (Medical Evacuation Helicopter) for him, but no, Shortarse had his orders. About halfway up the ridge, Scrimshaw fell to the ground exhausted, calling out to us to leave him there to die as by this time the poor bastard was delirious. A couple of mates managed to drag him to a big, flat rock where he lay murmuring over and over, 'You blokes go on without me, I've ad et,' and this is one bloke who wasn't trying to play the hero, I can assure you.

The Dust-Off was called then and he was winched off the side of the ridge in the strap that you sit in. He had blood-poisoning caused from eating off the ground, so the Doctors said later. We heard also that he'd nearly died; his balls were up like two footballs and he couldn't walk for a week. I know it took him a long time to re-join us.

Life goes on though and so did we. Over that ridge down through a gully and halfway up the side of the next ridge we came across an ancient road similar to that which the Ancient Romans constructed in their time. The hard dirt roadway was about six metres across. The stone wall on the south side dropped away at a slight angle for some four-to four-and-a-half metres down into the jungle and caught up with the slope of the mountain. The other side of the road ended or started — which ever you may prefer — with the mountain. The road ran along the side of the mountain at about a ten-degree angle down and we started to follow it as it wound its way sort of east towards Baria.

After a smoke break, I was up front and we moved at a good pace for some time, occasionally passing some weird-looking bunkers which stood almost in the centre of the road. They were constructed of baked mud about one hundred millimetres thick, forming the half cylinder curved roof. The roof was over what could only be described as a shallow shell-scrape. Someone said that they were used by the South Vietnamese to stop the Japanese from getting into the Nui Dinhs during the World War II.

When it was my turn as Scout again, a couple of kilometres further down the road we came across the first real evidence of Noggie movement in the Dinhs. Here, a small creek ran under the road through a neatly constructed pipe and on the right side of the creek — more a drain than anything — ran a well-used track heading north into thick jungle. There were footprints on the track so I called Shortarse up to check it out and he investigated the pad and the surroundings. To the west was a mountain of a 45-degree climb. To the east was the same and both slopes were covered with very thick scrub. Behind us was the road. Shortarse asked me, 'What are those marks coming down there?' as he pointed up the eastern slope.

'They're pig tracks Sir,' I informed him at once.

'We'll follow them,' he said, looking pleased with himself.

'But Sir, if you want Nogs, they're up that track,' I said, pointing to the track disappearing into the dark and forbidding undergrowth ahead of us.

'You heard me Scout,' he growled, adding, 'we'll follow those tracks going up there,' as he indicated the pig tracks up the steep slope.

'But Sir ...' That was all I got out as he strutted back to

his place in the line. I could only shrug my shoulders, shake my head and lean back to appraise the slope I was about to negotiate.

Halfway up the slope we were stopped for a smoke-break and I had to sit with both feet planted firmly against a small tree to stop myself from losing ground and sliding down on Jim who was perched just as precariously below me. I aimed a remark towards him. 'Not even mountain goats would be foolish enough t'climb along the side'a this ridge, but here we are an' we're s'posed t'be sensible creatures.'

At last we made it to the top of the razorback. Here I made a beeline to the north, not wanting to go down the drop on the other side, it being as steep as the one we'd just climbed. Besides, it would be dangerous to have half the Platoon on one side of the ridge and half on the other; that was to be my excuse anyway. I must have been on the right track though because nobody stopped me until I got the next smoke-break signal.

There was an enormous log lying across my intended path so I went to it and, turning to face the others, I crashed with the back of my pack against it. I was buggered. I'd made a smoke, lit it and was dragging on it gratefully by the time Shortarse got to where I sat propped up by the log, which was big enough to completely hide me from all up front.

'Look for a harbour spot,' Shortarse addressed me — this was another one of the Scout's jobs.

'Right 'ereill do me Sir,' I answered, 'put one gun down 'ere,' indicating where I sat, 'an' make yuh circle from 'ere back,' I went on, pointing with my finger and making a circle in the air to indicate the complete harbour.

But he wasn't happy with that. 'No, no,' he said, 'this is no good; we'll have to do better than this.'

I was beyond arguing by this time, so I said stiffly, 'Well, yur did ask Sir, 'an I reckon this'es as good as anywhere.'

He glared at me for a minute or so and, grunting his disapproval, left me to my smoke as he moved off around the end of the giant log and along through the large trees which grew on the razorback. I sat there and watched him go knowing full well that as the Scout I should be accompanying him, but 'Stuff 'im, I said this place'ill do, so why can't 'e accept et?'

Boris joined me then, all smiles as usual. 'Where's thu Boss?' he asked me, looking around.

'Gone up there looken f'a'arbour spot,' I said, squinting up at him.

'Who's with 'im?' he asked.

'No one,' I informed him, indifferently.

The smile was immediately replaced by an extremely stern look. 'No one? Wodda yur mean "no one"? You know it's your job t'go wif 'im at all times when 'e leaves the Platoon. Now git up there an' find 'im.'

I burred up at once. 'Fuck 'im. I said this 'ere would do as a harbour spot but 'e donn like it an if 'e wants t'go an' get 'imself shot up poking around up there on 'is fucking own, well good luck to 'im, but I'm fucking sure I'm not gunna copet jus f'issake, I said this'ill do me for a 'arbour spot an' that's it.'

Boris glared at me, but must have seen the resignation on my face, so lifting his gat high across his substantial chest, his moon face set, he took off around the end of the log to find Shortarse without another word. We made camp another two hundred metres along the ridge in an identical setting minus the log, of course; but it was Shortarse's choice, not mine.

In the morning when we came onto the little clearing on the razorback where we'd first been dropped in, I was up front again. I followed the path up the rise towards where CHQ sat when suddenly, to my utter dismay, I was challenged by a Sentry. This had never happened before to our Platoon.

'Halt! Who goes there?' a timid voice called to me from a rocky ledge about five metres away and three or so metres above me.

'Who in fuck's name do yur think is fuckenwell goen 'ere, yuh fuckin, useless cunt?' I yelled back.

Well, stuff him. I didn't know any code signs off-hand, but they'd said back home in training, 'If you are challenged and you can't remember the code sign, swear, because there is no one in the world who can swear like an Australian.' In this case, a tired and cranky one.

Another voice came from the place of the concealed challenger. It was the stern voice of Toddy Smith. 'Righto Private, that'll be enough a that,' he said, and stepping one pace to his right he appeared as if from nowhere on the big flat rock just above and ahead of me.

He ushered us into camp, but I wasn't finished yet not by a long shot. I still had a thing or two to spit out and I did just that as I got level with the sentry. He was lying behind an M60, in a "sighting up" position with the CSM standing beside him. As I stepped around behind them, I looked at the bloke on the ground and growled, 'How's the blisters on yer arse, Boy?'

Smithy, in his usual regimental style, again told me to

watch myself and move on, but I wasn't the only one in the Platoon who was going off about CHQ sitting on their arses on their safe little hill while we tramped around the Nui Dinhs at their behest, and the Bombardier's Medivac was still fresh in our minds. We were ordered to do another water run that afternoon and, as before, fill CHQ's bottles as well.

The next day, Eight Platoon secured the helipad and, after "throwing smoke", we made our way to where the incoming choppers would land. Spotty started playing up and doing his thing, so he got a kick in the ribs from all of us in turn while being told, 'Get up there f'fuck sake, Spotty, you'll miss yur flight if yur donn stop fucken roun'.'

On the edge of the clearing were two Yank Officers. They were Bombardiers from the Yank ship out in Vung Tau Harbour. They had been with CHQ during our stay in the Dinhs helping to coordinate the firepower sent forth from their ship. They now stood with looks of disbelief on their faces, holding their caps back off their foreheads and scratching at their hair while we gave Spotty the works. Boxall stood between them with a grin as wide as the Pacific Ocean on his face, making no attempt to try and explain to them what it was we were doing. The Yanks must have thought that we'd all gone well and truly troppo from too much service, going by the looks of them — and they were probably not too far wrong.

When we left the Dinhs, Eight Platoon was flown north to the top of the Province where we "landed without smoke" west of Route Two. We very soon took up an ambush site on the far western side of Courtney Rubber Plantation. For a couple of days we took turns to sit in the ditch which ran alongside the road on the edge of the rubber near our camp, which was set up a little way back off the road in the "J".

In the afternoon of the second day, Pollard and I were manning the site when two weasel-type creatures came along the road on our side of the carriageway. When they got to right square in front of us, they stopped and, standing on their hind legs, peered in through the leaves at us with small, beady, black eyes. They were no more than thirty centimetres from the business ends of our gats, but it took them a minute of sniffing the air to realise we might not be friendly, whereupon one of them dropped down to all fours and made to bolt in the same direction from whence they'd come. When its mate hadn't moved to follow, it was forced to come back and tug at its arm. After a couple of good tugs, it convinced its mate it was time to go and they scampered away. For a second or two I sat in silence before asking Jim, 'Didja see that?'

'Yeah,' he said, reverently.

We left the ambush site the next morning and patrolled uneventfully for the next few days, going this way and that all over the place. At one point we came up out of a small creek bed into bamboo and turned south along what appeared to be an old roadway. We had to stop so Shortarse could give CHQ our loc-stat. It was around three-thirty and it was starting to sprinkle, so we put it to Shortarse, 'Can we make camp here, Sir?'

But, oh no, as the drops got bigger, it was 'Saddle up, Scouts out,' and we were off again. It started pouring and, after going about two hundred metres south, he decided to turn us around and soaked to the skin we backtracked. I lost it. I walked along kicking at the puddles of water on the ground sending great splashes over the bloke in front of me while singing aloud, 'Just awalken in the rainnnn, getten soaken wetttt.'

The hapless bloke in front of me got a little pissed off at the excess water being blasted at him from behind from my boots. Almost at the exact place where we'd asked to make camp earlier, Shortarse pulled us up and announced, 'We'll harbour up here.'

Next morning, I led out going north and all too soon got into yet another argument with Jim. These disputes had become a daily occurrence since they'd given me the job of Scout. We'd gone past the place where we'd turned south the afternoon before and suddenly Jim is hissing at me and, when I glanced back, he was indicating that I'd once again strayed a fraction off-course.

'Well, of course I'm not goen exactly on thu compass line yur set f'me Jim, I 'ave t'go roun' this thick shit, but I'll get back onto et as soon as we get roundet,' I told him, when he caught up to me. 'Look, jus' show'us where yur want'us t'endup on that fucken mappa yours an' I'll get yur there.'

'We gotta come out right 'ere at this bend in the creek,' he told me, bending in close to show me the place on his map.

'Goodo,' I said, and off I went deliberately ignoring the occasional hissing from behind me. When the ground started to fall away a little to the right and the bamboo gave away to trees, I veered that way and came out right at the bend.

'How do yer do that?' Jim asked, in reverence yet again.

'I go by thu sun,' I told him for the umpteenth time.

'Yur can't go by thu sun,' he growled again for the umpteenth time.

'I jus' show'd yuh, yur can.'

'But the sun moves.' Jim's argument was always the same.

'Yeah, but yur move withet Jim,' I assured him one more time. Jim, though, would never accept my theory.

We were heading slightly east of a northerly direction a day or two later and, by my estimation, were just over the Phouc Tuy Province border in Long Khanh Province, southwest of the US Black Horse Army Base, when I came across a well-used pad on the edge of a very old, disused rubber plantation. The gnarled tree trunks were near as round as a two hundred-litre drum and still showed the signs of having been sliced around and down way back when they were young and serviceable. I called Shortarse up to check it out and he informed CHQ of our find. After moving off and having travelled only six metres or so into the rubber, I found another track running parallel with the first, but, unlike that track, this one was new and show signs of being used only the day before.

'There's been ten or so men on this pad, I'd say, sumtime yesty goen that way Sir, goen be the mud on them leaves,' I told Shortarse when he was once again beside me at the head of the line, 'and they are going east.' Again the Boss made a call to CHQ with the information and they told us to continue on the way we were going. I soon found that for every six metres or thereabouts we covered, we crossed a track similar to the one I've just described. We must have crossed twenty of them before they petered out. At the next smoke break, I told Pollard what I made of these tracks.

'Yud better tell them blokes on Courtney Hill they're gunna be in big shit if they donn watch out, going by the amount'a men who've jus' past through 'ere an' are 'eded in their d'rection.'

Jim quietly told me, 'It's not our job to think, jus' to observe and report. The rest is up to the higher authorities; Intelligence and the like.'

'Yeah, that'd be right,' I found myself thinking. *'Ours is not to reason why, but to just do and die.'*

For the next day or two, we circled around until we were heading slightly south of east. On one particular occasion during this time as we went to ground for a well-earned blow and a smoke after we'd been given the smoke-break signal, everyone automatically sat with our weapons pointing outwards on full alert. No one glanced nervously at each other or said anything. We all just know. We could feel ourselves being watched and had been able to feel it for some time now as we moved along. Most times we'd simply plonk ourselves down in the best place, rest our weapons across our crossed legs and casually burn the leeches, in between puffs on our cigarettes.

This was different. To sit there and feel unseen eyes watching you can give you a very uneasy feeling, to say the least. We sat still and silent waiting for something to happen. We were ready; ready for anything.

Suddenly, someone cried out, 'Gees look up 'ere, will yah?' We all looked up at once and there in the branches only three metres or so above us were these big, black monkeys. Well, they were Baboons or Orangs or something — monkeys without the long tails and with big, bare bums.

Apparently, they had been following us along from high up in the treetops, but because we'd stopped, they'd come down for a closer look. When no one on the ground had taken any notice of them, the biggest one started dropping small pieces of stick down on the motionless creatures below. One of these purposely and precisely-dropped twigs landed on a Digger, causing him to look up and yell, which startled all of us. We moved as one to cover the trees in his direction. As soon as the apes realised that they had been sprung and that we were reactive — maybe even hostile to them — they literally high-tailed it from their vulnerable positions, moving as a family unit high up into the canopy and out of our sights. They would most likely have come back after we'd moved on to check out what if anything we had left behind for them.

At an O Group around the same time, we were told that the Tracker Platoon had got two high-up members of Chau Duc District Forces HQ Group in an ambush to the south-east of us. They were found to be Bay Giang and Nam Trang. Was one of these blokes the bloke that was having a piss in front of Mullen and Pollard a month back or was one of them the bloke who warned that bloke that he was in imminent danger? Might one of them have been the bloke in the tunnel who'd warned the whole group of our presence? It may well have been, but we'll never know.

Next day we also heard, via Mick the Sig, about a Scout from another Company copping it and a Louie and Sergeant getting wounded in the same incident. They said the Scout came across a well-used track and called his Louie up to check it out. His Sergeant followed him. They were standing there looking at the situation when a whoosher was set off from down along the track. The rocket went right through the Scout then exploded in the trunk of a tree too close to the Louie and the Sergeant and they copped a shower of shrapnel.

* * *

20
SIDELINED

At our next nightly O Group, we were told about an incident in which two Australian Platoons had clashed. Apparently, they'd come together at the junction of a track. The Scout from one Platoon saw the Tail End Charlie from the other one walking about just ahead of him and let fly, dropping him instantly. A fire fight ensued and another Digger was wounded before they realised it was two Aussie Platoons at each other's throats.

On the morning that we were due to go back to the Dat, we were told that the villages of Ngai Giao and Cam My were hit with mortar rounds through the night. Later that day we emerged from the "J" onto a former Fire Support Base which we intended to use as our lift-off point. A Troop of APCs had already secured the clearing, so all we had to do was sit and wait for our choppers to come. However, a small storm was raging about halfway between us and the Dat and it was in the direct route of the choppers and ourselves, so we were told we'd have to wait for the scud to go before they'd come and get us.

'Why can't we go on the APCs, Sarge?' we wanted to know. There was another small storm brewing in the otherwise clear sky just to the west of us and it was heading in our direction, but, oh no, not on your dear sweet Nelly were we to go by APC.

'They're jus 'ere t'secure thu LZ f'us, that's all,' was Boris' reply.

A couple of minutes passed, then the storm from the west broke over us and we stood about in the pouring rain. It didn't last long, but we got soaked and no sooner than it was over we were ordered aboard the APCs and away we went to the east across to Route Two and on down to Nui Dat. Christ alone knows why we had to get drenched first; perhaps they thought we needed to clean up a bit before they'd allow us back into the Dat.

On the range at the back of the Dat, we expended our unused brass as per usual. However, this time, we were given a few extra boxes to get rid of, so when Shortarse said, 'There's more rounds here if anyone wants t'ave another go,' I was first at the stores to get a crack at it.

I reloaded all my seven mags and proceeded to empty them at the make-shift targets out across the open expanse which faced towards the Long Tan Rubber Plantation. Not everyone had taken up Shortarse's offer, so that by the time I'd finished with this lot there was still a bit of live brass left in the abandoned wooden boxes, so I filled up again and let fly.

The barrel on my gat got so hot that the wood where it connected near the front site started to smoke. This prevented me from seeing the targets, so I dropped her down to my hip, placed my left hand flat over my left ear and started plugging away from there. I became aware of someone yelling at me over the din I was making, so I looked across to see what the fuss was about.

'You can't do that,' one of my mates was saying aloud.

'You fucken watch me,' I told him earnestly, and proceeded to cut the targets out front of us up into splinters. I'd run a couple of shots out to line them up, sending plumes of dust into the air, then, once connected, I'd drive it into them. It was a real thrill watching them smash to bits.

'Ha, ha, ha, stand in front of me now, yur slanty-eyed little bastards, now that I know how to use this bloody thing,' I laughed aloud to myself remembering that big bloke on the twenty-five-metre range down the back of Kapooka.

When I'd expended all the ammo there was to expend and the smell of cordite was dissipating on the lightest of breezes, I slowly came down off my high. By then there was only three of us left at the range: Shortarse, Mick the Sig, and myself. A *Land Rover* would be sent to pick us up soon, so with nothing else left to do, we crouched down in a three-man circle and listened with interest to the radio set. There appeared to be something big going on up in the north of the Province.

Over the airways a Yank pilot's voice came through telling someone he was in the area. When he was asked, 'Wot ave yur got on board there mate?' he replied in a Southern Yankee drawl, 'I got forty pounders, I got twenty-five pounders, I got napalm. Where do yah want 'em dropped, buddy?'

'Dropum where yuh fucken well like mate,' came the laconic Australian reply.

There was a short break, then, 'Bombs away,' from the Yank fly-boy.

'Wot canyer see down there?' asked an Aussie voice.

The Yank came back on with excitement edged in his voice this time. 'I see burnt up bodies everywhere — they're like ANTS!'

Then the *Rover* was there to take us back inside the wire and

I heard nothing more of what was going on that night at our Open Air Dinner or in the Boozer.

The next morning Charlie Company went back down to Vung Tau for our scheduled R and I. South of the Baria turn-off and out in the middle of the mangrove swamps which were prominent on either side of this part of the Saigon to Vung Tau highway, we spotted a Noggie fishing with rod and line, up to his tits in water. This in itself was not that unusual; however, this particular fisherman — or what we could see of him — was standing beside a large sign on which was painted a bright red skull and crossbones with the words DANGER — MINE written beneath them.

At the Blue Pacific Massage Parlour, I waited in the barber shop on the bottom floor of the building for a particular masseuse to become available. As I sat there, two burly pistol-wielding Yank MPs pushed their way in and immediately sat in the two vacant barber chairs. As the barber went to town on their scant hair, another little Nog massaged their necks, while yet another cleaned their fingernails and generally fussed about them. What happened next dumbfounded me and makes me ashamed that we Australians had anything to do with the Yanks while we were over there. The mongrel pair of bastards got up and, with sickly-sweet smiles on their faces, just walked out the door without paying a cent for services rendered.

As they left, my special masseuse came down the stairs. How she knew me I don't know, but her smile said it all. She must have worked on more than a hundred soldiers of all nationalities in the month since I was here last, but the moment she saw me she recognised me at once. Even before she had got to the bottom step she was beaming and waving that now familiar and unique wave these people give –which looks like they are trying to splash water into their faces from just above their heads — to indicate that I should come to her. After leading me back upstairs, she again gave me that once-in-a-lifetime massage as only she could.

Feeling like a new pin, I happily made my way to the Minh Bar to once again be in the arms of my Thao Ly. However, before I got to the Bar I came across a couple of my mates in a very agitated state.

'J'ear wot 'appened t'D Company? They got busted, five killed, an' twenty-eight wounded in justa couple a 'ours,' they reported.

'Wot? Wen'd this 'appen?' was my predictable response.

'Yesty, there's a big mob of 'em in the hospital, they brought the last of 'em in this mornen, I'm goen out there now,' one of them told me.

'We shouldn't be here! We should be up there elpen 'em!' we cried out in anguish. I went along the street with them, running into more of our blokes and telling them about it. We were also looking for someone in authority who might be able to help get us out of there and back up into the blue.

Suddenly Major Boxall appeared in front of us on the street — which was strange because we'd never seen him in this part of town on previous visits. We bailed him up right outside the bar in which I'd first met Thao Ly.

'Sir, we gotta go an' 'elp our mates in Delta, Sir. C'mon Sir, gettus back out there, we gotta 'elp 'em.'

Boxall looked rushed, but he stopped long enough to say, 'You blokes are on leave, make the best of it, you don't know if you'll ever be back in here again.'

Then to our utter astonishment, he produced a great wad of Piastre from his pocket and said to us, 'Go an' have a good time. Here, d'yuh need some money? Here, take some of this.'

He started to peal off bills to hand out to us, but we declined. 'Nar Sir, you keep yuh money.'

This is not the way it was supposed to be: Our mates being busted by the VC up in the top of the Province, while we were down here living it up. We're Australian Diggers! We help our mates out when they're in trouble and the last thing we needed right now was rest. We needed to be helping our mates, so why the hell won't they let us go and do that?

I felt like that little puppy desperately scratching at the laundry door trying to get out while my masters who were just outside it were ignoring me. I felt so small and utterly helpless. Apparently, Delta had run into a bunker system full of 33 North Vietnamese Army Regiment troops. Bravo Company had dead and casualties as well from separate incidents with the same mob in the same area. This battle became known as the Battle of Nui Le. It was the last time Australian Soldiers tangled with a mob of VC from the North. Exactly what happened up there on that fateful day you will have to ask someone from D or B Company who was there; what I could tell you would only be hearsay.

Feeling numb and disillusioned by what had just occurred, I made my way slowly into the Minh Bar where I found my ever-smiling Thao Ly. The joy she displayed in seeing me again was comforting, but I was not good company for her that morning.

After a cool reception from me, she decided to try and cheer me up by telling me, 'You go home at …' She couldn't find a way to say the word she was looking for, so as if from nowhere she produced a small booklet, opened it and pointed to a word on a page, 'You go home now,' she told me again.

I looked at the word indicated by her thin index finger. It read "Christmas, the time when the birth of the Christ child is celebrated."

'No,' I told to her, then added, 'who told yur that shit?' After all, I'd not heard anything official about us going home as yet.

'Your big man, you know, top man, he say on wireless,' she assured me, her dark eyes flashing.

I thought to myself, *'Shit, how the hell would she know something like that if I've not even heard about it yet?'*

The rest of the morning was a drag. The only highlight coming at one point when I'd gone outside and was sitting on the raised flower bed and a pair of pre-teen boys accosted me.

'Shoe shine, shoe shine, shoe shine,' they hassled me excitedly, their eyes bright, their teeth white in their smiles. My Williams boots must have presented a great mark for them. When I looked down, I saw that each of them carried his own gear to do the job.

'Ockay, youkendo one shoe each,' I told them, holding up one finger. They beamed, then proceeded to get stuck into it. One bloke finished enthusiastically buffing my right boot before his mate had finished, and tugged at my trouser leg just below my knee.

'Finish,' he told me. I looked down and, yes, the boot shone.

His mate got into the act. 'Finish.'

I looked to see how he went but found that his boot did not resemble the right one.

'Nar.' I said, tormentingly pointing at the right boot, 'Not same same, you do same like this one, same same.'

His mate, who was a little bigger, scowled at him and snatching his buffing rag from him he proceeded to buff the living daylights out of the offending boot. He looked up with big, dark, enquiring eyes when he thought it was right.

'Yeah, yeah,' I told him, fishing into my pockets and pulling out two twenty Dong pieces. I handed them a twenty Dong piece each and told them laughingly, 'ere, donn spendet all at once, hey.'

To my great delight, they quickly gathered up their belongings and, with the broadest of grins, tore off down the footpath dodging in and out among bemused pedestrians, each holding the silver Dong high above his heads like he was running with the Olympic Torch.

Just after one that afternoon I mentioned to Thao Ly that I'd like some rice for lunch. What I really wanted to do was to show her my prowess with the chopsticks which I'd spent so much time practising for up in the Dinhs.

Thao Ly lit up like a spotlight. She was so delighted to be doing something for me and disappeared at once to obtain my dinner from one of the street vendors on the footpath outside. Suddenly, she was back, asking excitedly, 'You want fish, you want fish?'

'No, no, no fish,' I assured her most emphatically.

She took off again and soon returned with a small, white bowl piled high with very small-grained rice. It looked alright except for the fact that they'd used the same utensil to put the rice into the bowl as they used to scoop the fish out of something else with. I've already told you about how they sun dried their fish in Long Hai and, going by the smell of the fishy sauce on top of this lot, they did the same here in Vung Tau. It was high to say the very least.

I couldn't bring myself to even attempt to taste it. Thao Ly mistook my lack of enthusiasm in taking on the rice as an indication that I could not use the chopsticks, so with me sitting there staring at the mess in the bowl, she raced away to reappear with a fork in hand.

Sitting up on a bar stool in front of me and laughing with her friends, she attempted to feed me fork full by fork full as one does a child. They thought it was hilarious, but for the life of me I could not take a single bite of what was being offered for fear of bringing it right back up and over her. Feeling nauseated, I kept waving Thao Ly's attempts away. Eventually, with a sad look, she gave up on trying to feed me and with the help of a couple of her close friends got stuck into the mess herself. Waste not, want not?

A short time after this, I was again sitting outside the front of the Minh Bar when a small girl sidled up and sat down very quietly beside me. She was the same small girl I'd seen hanging around outside this area at different times before. The bar girls seemed to have a special affection for her and were always looking out for her and, as usual, she was impeccably dressed in the best of clothes. I was told she was the love child of an Australian Digger. I stole a glance at her. 'Where's your muma-san?' I asked of her.

She took my hand in her tiny little one and led me into the bar next to the Minh Bar. She only stopped leading me when we got to the back of the bar. There, she forcefully sat me down in a booth and indicated that I should wait there. She then disappeared behind a curtain, which was just behind where I sat. I looked under it and could see a pair of GP boots, so I knew from this that her mother was entertaining a Yank back there. The little bugger was pimping for her mum. Thirty seconds later, the little girl crept out from behind the curtain and stealthily made her way past me towards the front door of the bar. So determined was she that her rouse should work that she failed to see me exit the bar right on her hammer.

The second day in town was as bad as the first. There was really only one thought going on in our heads and that was to get back out into the scrub and give it to the bastards who had got our mates. When I informed Thao Ly that I was going out to see some of my mates, she scowled at me.

'Shiit!' she said to me once again, 'you butterfly me.'

This time I had to ask, 'Wot's this butterfly stuff you're always on about?'

'Butterfly, you know? Flit flit from flower to flower,' she said, demonstrating with her hands how a butterfly goes from flower to flower collecting pollen.

'Nar, me no butterfly you, I'm jus' goen looken for me mates.'

'Shiit, you butterfly me, I butterfly you,' she told me, all serious now.

'Ockay, go get one of them Yanks over there,' I told her, pointing out some Yanks in their greens over on the other side of the street. I wasn't in the mood to argue with her right then and left her standing there with a very black look on her face.

We were back in the Dat about nine the next morning and by ten we had congregated outside our Office fully armed, dressed in greens and ready for war. We sat on the ground, crossed-legged, facing the Office in Section lines waiting for the trucks to take us north. We presented a sombre group.

Boxall wandered out of his office and slowly approached us with his hands behind his back. He placed the stuffed, rearing two-metre Cobra from out of his office quietly on the ground beside the first line of blokes he came to and stood back with a big grin on his face to see what the reaction would be when someone spotted it.

Next thing there was a loud shout, 'LOOK OUT!'

Everyone threw themselves flat onto the ground in lighting speed with the exception of the bloke who'd yelled. He swung his gat around in a flash intending to blow the frightening snake away. Christ alone knows what stopped him letting go a burst and Boxall, finding himself instantly staring down the wrong end of a gat in the hands of an extremely tense Digger, turned white. Had the bloke let go from his place on the ground, he would have filled Boxall's chest with lead. Why Boxall did what he did, only he knows. He may have been trying to ease the tension that prevailed in the ranks that morning before we set off.

When our transport came for us at eleven or thereabouts, it was the APCs. By two, we were sitting at the bottom of the narrow roadway which led to the top of Courtney Hill. After a while a Kiowa chopper flew in and tried to land on the road which had been carved into the side of the hill and ran at a fairly steep angle up the eastern side except for a four-metre level section mid-way up. The pilot was trying to land on this strip of roadway; however, every time he was about to settle, he'd hesitate, throw the machine sideways off the side of the hill and swoop away to his right, dropping below the height of the level bit of road before smoothly rising up again. It was like watching a giant wasp trying to land on its nest, but not managing to do so, and flying off to try again. I can't remember how many times this bloke in the chopper tried, but he eventually gave it up as a bad joke and flew away to land somewhere else.

After an hour of sitting in the hot afternoon sun atop the APCs, someone eventually told us where to go. Eight Platoon were taken straight east into Courtney Rubber on the east side of the Road. The rest of the Company went back down the road and started to patrol east from their drop-off point. Some way into the rubber, we turned south, then south-west to eventually come out on the south-west corner of this part of the plantation. There, in the sparse jungle beside the plantation, we camped for the night.

The next morning Hilly led out and we patrolled east in the "J" at the edge of the rubber. Just before Dinner Camp, we were pulled up for a smoke-break when an explosion went off a little way to our north and up in the rubber. We waited for Mick to tell us what had happened.

'An APC just hit a mine,' he relayed to us. Suddenly there was another explosion and we all looked at Mick again. 'Yeah, that was another one going to help the first one,' he verified. They were the same APCs that had dropped us off last evening. Sobering!

A short time after this, we came across a well-used track coming up a slight incline out of the jungle to our right before heading off to the north through the level ground in the rubber. We stopped here for Dinner Camp and learned via Mick that the rest of Charlie Company was struggling through swamps to our south. They were up to their tits in water, though they had destroyed a cache of rice which they'd found on a platform in a tree, despite the murk.

After we finished eating, we moved south along the track we'd found. I think the intention was for us to meet up with CHQ who were still in the swamps. The track, however, presented me as the Scout with some problems. There having been so much enemy activity here recently, I had to make a decision about the safety of myself and the others. I decided to follow the track on a parallel line about two or three metres to the west of it. This way, if I spotted any Nogs coming along the track towards us, I could set an immediate ambush with less chance of our Platoon being spotted first. Also, by keeping off the track, there was less likelihood of my setting off a mine or booby trap.

We had not patrolled far when I was stopped by a steep creek bank. After a quick assessment of the situation, I decided that I'd be better off following the Nogs' track through the creek as they had used a good place a few metres to my left. I sent the signal back along the line that we had a creek-crossing ahead and that I was moving left onto the Noggie track. I followed up my instructions and moved across onto the track and from there out into the bed of the dried-up creek. It was mostly course white sand underfoot, while the opposite bank was just a wall of jungle about fifty metres away.

I was halfway across before it struck me as to what a predicament I was in. In front of me was a wall of dark green and I was standing alone in the middle of an empty creek bed. I stood out like dog's balls. There was nowhere for me to hide and I realised now that no one had followed me out of the jungle, the normal practice being the Scouts would ford the creeks one after the other and secure the opposite bank together. As I didn't have a Second Scout, it was Pollard's job to follow me across to help out, but he had not done so.

Christ alone knows what they were doing behind me, but here I was, a sitting duck for any Noggie hiding on the other side bank. There was no question of turning back. I had no choice but to go on and even though my body moved at a snail's pace, my mind was absolutely alive.

'Shit, wot a place for an ambush. Good cover for them and me standing in the middle of a perfect fucken killen groun'. Fucket! If they start shooten now, I'm a goner f'sure, yur stupid bastard. Wot in the bloody 'ell were yuh thinking of? It won't hurt if I cop it in the head, though; it'll be just "lights out", sort of.'

As I walked steadily on, I began to feel small, rounded river stones beneath my boots, but dared not look down at them. My own personal mantra, which had stood me in such good stead many a time when I was trying bluff my way out of some big shit in my College days, now came to me. *"Boldness, be my friend,"* resonated in my brain.

I watched the jungle wall immediately in front of me intensely, waiting for the first shot. I wondered what it would feel like to get a slug in the chest. Be like getting whacked with a big lump of four by two, I imagined. Then I started cursing again, all the time inching forward.

'Where in fucken Christ's name are them udder bastards? Fuckem, leten a bloke go in alone. Fuckem!'

Finally, after what seemed like an eternity to me, I made it to that wall of shrubby and, I expect to the watchers on their side of the creek, simply disappeared into the abyss unopposed. To my relief, there were no Nogs there, so I cleared a short way to the west, then to the east along the top part of the bank, before dropping back down out of the "J" to the edge of the creek to signal that all was well and that they could now cross safely over to my side.

When at last they were across, I was given the signal to lead out again. I followed the same track. It had turned towards the south-west. I was about one hundred metres along when I suddenly picked up what appeared to be a bunker immediately in front of me. One quick sideways movement and I was standing stock still behind a big tree waiting ... nothing happened. I glanced back at Pollard. He was frozen to the spot, his colour drained from his very being. He had been caught out in the open and could not see for the life of him why I'd moved so fast to secure good cover, but he had guessed why.

I carefully poked my head around the tree and checked the "bunker". The pile of red dirt at the base of a tree forty metres ahead showed no sign of being hostile, so I relaxed and went to move on. Next thing, Pollard was beside me and breathing fast and heavy, he scolded me most vehemently, 'Donn yur ever do that t'me agen, yur frightened the fucken shit outta me.'

'Serves yurself fucken right, yuh cunt, f'leaving me out there in thu middle of that creek back there on me fucken own,' I growled at him, then added, 'Anyway, I thought we 'ad ourselves a bunker.'

After we passed the pile of red dirt, the track veered back towards the south and a little further along it crossed what looked like a well-used logging track which ran from east to west. I sent the signal back to call Shortarse up to check it out. There was a slight rise towards the east and it looked and felt sinister to me.

'If you want Noggies Sir, they're up that way,' I told him, when it looked like he was unsure of what to do.

'We'll go that way,' he said immediately, pointing along the track we'd been following.

'But Sir!' I protested. He turned away. I followed the track. I had not gone far when I noticed freshly-cut tree stumps about seventy-five to one hundred millimetres across and about a metre off the ground covered with mud in an attempt the conceal them from the air. Again, I called Shortarse up. He contacted CHQ and reported our find. While he was jabbering, I saw that the leaves along the side of the track were covered with dry, red mud. I pointed this out to him.

'How long ago?' he asked.

'Two days back, I'd say,' I told him. More jibber to CHQ on the set, then we moved on again until the smoke-break signal came my way.

About an hour later, we emerged from the west out of the "J" onto a large, oval-shaped clearing. We were quickly detailed to spread out and secure the whole area as D and B Companies would be coming into here later today for re-supply. V Company was already settled in the rubber at the top end of the clearing awaiting theirs.

There was a line of small, thick bushes growing three or four metres back from the bamboo on the cleared ground and I slipped into one of these and, sitting down, I made myself as comfortable as was possible in its shade.

Presently, I detected movement to the south-west of my position. I tightened up. Then I saw them: first one, then two fully-armed men in drab, brownie-green clothing came slowly out of the bamboo in front of my hide.

'Is this thu place? Urt looks rite,' one of the two said to his mate. They were the Scouts at the head of Bravo Company.

'Yeah mate,' I called to them, 'you're right, come on in.'

'Yeah thanks mate,' the lead bloke called back and then indicated to his mates to follow him in. He came over to where I sat tucked up in my hide and stared into it. 'Where the fuck are yah? I can't see yur in there!'

It must have seemed to him that the bush had spoken to him. I had to move myself about a bit before he was convinced that there was actually anyone in it. The rest of Bravo filed slowly past my position and when they were nearly all in, I heard that Delta Company was coming in from over on the eastern side. Delta had copped it the hardest in the recent barney. I left my post and made my way across the clearing in shin-high grass to where the first of them were slowly arriving and hung about watching them come in, hoping to say 'G'day' to Kapooka mate, Mincho. I wanted to confirm to myself that he was alright.

When I saw him, he looked terrible. He was pale and gaunt. 'You OK?' I asked him as he came alongside me, but he just looked at me through dull, unseeing eyes. I doubt he even know I was there and he never said a word as he dragged himself on by me. He was not a shadow of the man I once knew.

When the Maintdem choppers arrived, the Kiwis went off at their end of the harbour. They could be heard all over the clearing laughing and coo-eeing out, but I suppose they had it right. If the Nogs didn't know where we were before, they would certainly know when the choppers dropped in. Half their luck; we would never have been able to get away with that much noise, no matter what.

Next day Eight Platoon was sent east out of the clearing and soon crossed an area that had been excessively logged, where very few trees remained standing, over a huge expanse to the south of where we traversed it. Standing beside one big remaining hardwood tree, I watched the largest centipede I have ever seen in my life — easily twenty-three centimetres long — making its way up out of harm's way.

We patrolled into some pretty thick scrub from there and at Dinner Camp we dined near a junction of an old, barely-defined track. When it came time for my turn as Sentry, I went down where I was told to be, but for some unknown reason, I was a little jittery with the position. It may have had something to do with our first casualty in C Company when the batman copped it up the back of his leg. From where I lay, I couldn't see who was coming up behind me; consequently, I lay so still and on guard that I actually cramped up like I had during my very first posting as sentry way back on our first day "out". I was sure glad to be relieved from this post.

Next day we were even further east and in more thick jungle, so much so that we couldn't find a LZ for our Maintdem choppers, but we did find a B52 bomb crater in the side of a small hill. It was decided that we'd clear away some of the vegetation from the edge of this crater and use the space created as the drop-in point for our routine re-supply. So, with that ever-present warning of, 'Shsss, you're making too much noise there,' ringing in our ears, it was out with our machetes. However, it was soon discovered that these had little or no effect on the particular type of hardwood trees that grew in this part of the jungle as, in fact, each time a machete blade struck one of these trees it did little more than vibrate in our hands.

To overcome this little problem, it was decided to get a couple of Engineers with chain saws dropped into the position. 'Shsss, you're making too much noise there?"

When the chopper dropped them off, they got stuck into it with some of us being "asked" to throw what they cut down into the bomb crater. One of these Engineers looked to me like he really knew what he was on about with a saw.

'Where you from? Where'd yer learn ta use a saw like that?' I asked him, when I got the chance.

'Yeoval,' he told me, with a smile, 'been attet f'years up in the hills b'hind town.'

'Yeah, it shows,' I assured him.

Yeoval is a small town seventy-one kilometres south of the large regional town of Dubbo which is on the Macquarie River in the middle of New South Wales. I knew I'd be able to work with this bloke, so I stuck close and at one point when he called 'TIMBER' I looked up to see a fair-sized tree falling towards me. I dived towards a dark spot in the branches that lay in front of me and descended into a hole big enough to swallow me whole. The

Yeoval man helped me up out of the subsequent entanglement of branches, some of which I'd used to escape the falling tree — some the top part of the fair size tree he'd just downed.

'You awright?' he asked, with a grin.

'Yeah mate. Nar, I'm awright,' I said, dusting myself down and grinning back.

It was now found that some of the tallest trees were not coming down because the vines attached to their top most branches would not break free to let them go. When the trees were cut, they would simply drop off the stump and stay upright. What to do? Bring in some more Engineers with explosives and blow them away. What else? "Shsss, you're making too much noise there."

In came a new crew by chopper and these four set to with their det cord and PE and tied up everything in sight while the rest of us were told to go a little way to the west. On the way out of the position, I noticed that they'd used det cord to tie a couple of paver sized pieces of PE to either side of the trees they intended to bring down.

When we were in place about one hundred metres away in a clump of thick, gloomy jungle they told us, 'Now on thu count of three, open yur mouths so that thu percussion of the blast doesn't bust yur eardrums. OK, wait for the signal. Now here we go, one, two, three ...' We sat there with mouths open like the clowns at the show. BOOMMMMMMMM.

"Shsss, your making too much noise there.," ... That's the Army for you.

After the blast, we were instructed to make our way back to the newly created LZ. The trunks of the trees that the machetes would not scratch were now splinted stumps — great stuff that

PE when tied right. Now we could get our Maintdem choppers in to re-supply us and the "Gingerbeers" out. Thanks, boys. After that, Eight Platoon got lost again drifting west in the "J" for a few more days until suddenly being told to find a LZ quick as some Nogs had been spotted west of Route Two near Courtney Hill. They were supposed to be carrying what appeared to be two mortars and our job would be to get in front of them, block their way any further to the west and take them out.

Our Choppers landed us "without smoke" late that afternoon at a spot not too far west of Courtney. From the drop point, we made our way to where we found signs of an old harbour site, but as we moved into the camp, Pollard and I had words. I couldn't remember ever being in this place. However, he insisted that we had, in fact, made the camp site ourselves some time before.

'It isn't like me ta forget a thing like that,' I was thinking as I dropped my gear. *'This clapped out, fucken war must be geten t'me a bit, I think.'*

'You and Andy made that bed site together,' Jim told me, then to rub it in he said, 'Youken camp there again.'

As I sat there trying to remember, it slowly came back to me, the only thing missing being the exact time. *'It must have been months ago.'*

Just before "stand to" that night, Pollard, Muzzy, Denholm, Smithy, Coggins, Clarkey and myself were in a small bunch having a conflab about nothing really. We lay on our bellies propped up on our elbows and each with a smoke all facing each other in a small circle with our legs pointing out like the spokes of a wagon wheel. Suddenly, out of the blue there came a series of explosions which sounded like big guns or mortars being fired.

We froze, our eyes fixed on the bloke opposite. I felt the hairs on my back stand on end. From the very end of my tailbone a cold shiver clambered up the entire length of my spine and when it reached the top of the back of my head it spread both ways circling my crown to meet at the front. My skin crawled. I got this awful sick feeling deep in my guts as we listened tensely to the fluttering sound of the incoming shells. We'd been caught.

I remember thinking, *'Well, this is it, boys, this is the last time we'll be see'n each other like this. Been nice known yurs. There can't be any better way t'go out than this, in this circle, with youes blokes, and we all go out t'gether ...*

They missed us. The fluttering shells passed harmlessly overhead and continued on to the west of us to crash into the jungle some distance away.

'Gees, I thought we'd addet that time,' one said for all. We grinned at each other as we collectively caught our breath, but there was no time for complacency for those shots might be the first of many pointed in our direction and meant for us.

We got onto Courtney Hill to see if they knew what was going on and they told us, 'A Pink Team (two *Cobra* gunships and a Kiowa used as their spotter) had seen smoke from a campfire about a kilometre west of your present position and we are going to shoot up the Grid Square where it was seen throughout the night. We didn't know you were even in the area, so that's why we didn't informed youse in advance.'

'Didn't know? Why didn't they know? They're supposed to be the ones giving us our orders, aren't they? So why the hell don't they know we're here?'

According to Mick, the Gunners did say, 'We're sorry that

we've upset yurs, but we have our orders too, yuh know.' They were probably shooting up the party of Nogs we'd been sent after anyway, so good luck to them.

I got another letter from Narelle on the next Maintdem chopper. In it were tiny photos of her walking along a deserted beach south of Sydney and her footprints were the sole marks on the otherwise undisturbed sand along the entire length of the beach as they trailed away behind her.

We also got a couple of Reo blokes in on the same chopper that the mail had arrived. Better late than never, I suppose — we could have done with at least one of them ages ago.

When one of the new blokes came to get me for my turn on the gun on his first night with us, I was awake as usual before he even got to my position. I felt him coming and when he was about two metres from the end of my hutchie, I stage-whispered, 'I'm right mate,' before he could even ask me if I was.

'Right mate,' he said and went, leaving me to put my boots on and follow. I felt my way out along the string line which took me from my camp out to the main line which ran around to our gun. Then, right at the junction of the lines, I caught the slightest glimpse of what looked like a man's face silhouetted against the night sky. It was one of those all too rare moments when I could actually see sky through a small break in the foliage. My heart jumped a beat as I froze on the spot. I instantly swung my SLR to the ready, pointing it directly at my would-be attacker. I watched intently for a few seconds and, yes, it was a man's face. I realised that he could not see me at all. I gingerly inched forward as every sinew in me pulled as tight as a drawn bowstring until I had the muzzle of my gat a mere two-point-five centimetres from his temple. Still he had no idea that I was even there. Friend or foe? I had to know one way or the other before I squeezed off the round that could only have one result. I asked in a quiet, steady voice, 'Ay mate?'

'Yeah mate,' he answered, as casual as you like. I flew at him. 'F'fuck sake mate, donn you ever, EVER do that again. Yur nearly got yuh fucken 'ed blown off. You go straight backta thu gun when yuh call someone, straight backta thu gun, yuh 'ear.' I growled sternly. If I could have yelled at him, I would have.

'But I was just making sure you were right, I ...'

'Yuh donn gotta make sure with any of these blokes mate. Your job is t'wake 'em up an' get straight back to thu gun as soon as yur can, till we get there; hanging around the string line, some cunt'll plug yuh f'sure,' I cut him off mid-sentence. In this circumstance, there was no room for argument.

When we got settled at the gun, he started on and on about how he did this and how he did that at Singleton and when I could take no more of it, I growled at him, 'This isnot fucken Singleton mate, they're live fucken lead they're shooten at us 'ere.' I never got a sound out of him for the rest of his one-hour shift.

For some unknown reason, I copped both the Reo boys that same night. They only did half our normal shift each and when the next new bloke came down along the string line, he had a bit of trouble finding me sitting at the gun. He was calling just above a whisper as he stood, but inches from my back. 'Gun, gun, where are yah, gun?'

'Right 'ere mate,' I piped up, a little louder than usual.

He must have nearly died in the arse when he heard me. I got him settled in beside me and after a little while I whispered, 'Might 'ave a smoke, I think.'

He was horrified. 'Yuh can't smoke 'ere!'

'Why's that?' I asked, innocently

'They'll see yer,' he told me, most seriously.

'Tell yur wot,' I said to him, 'I've always wanted t'know, you tell me if yur see anything?'

With that, I proceeded to roll myself a smoke following our usual procedure and got down under the ground sheet and my silk, covered everything with my giggle hat and lit up, then carefully brought my smoke up so that I could sit back and drag away on it tucked up inside my shirt and cupped by my hand.

After a bit, it must have got the better of him. 'Gawd, I could do with a smoke,' he announced.

'Ave one then,' I told him.

'Did you have yours?' he enquired eagerly.

'Yep.'

'But I diden see yuh, owja do that?' he asked, a surprised tone in his timid voice.

'If you're stuck out 'ere long enuff an' yur busten furra smoke, you'll work et out,' I assured him. We sat in gloomy silence for a spell then.

That night a cicada began making a hell of lot of noise up in the tree just out from our position. It got so that every time it started to carry on, the piercing noise felt to me like it was going right up through me, along my arms and actually extending out through my fingers for a metre out into the blackness. I got sick of it so I scooped up a handful of dirt from the ground in front of me and threw it up into the bushes in front of us. It made a rustling sound as it cascaded down over the large leaves of the jungles trees. It stopped the infernal noise, but didn't go down too well with the mate because in the blackness he had not seen my movements.

'Wotsat?' he cried, in a whisper.

'Wot's wot?' I teased him.

'I heard sumthun out there,' he insisted.

'Nar, yur jus' 'earing things mate,' I told him, as the Cicada started up again. Scooping up more dirt, I put a stop to it once more.

The mate then grabbed me by the arm and I could feel his fingers digging in. 'There et tis agen,' he said, his voice shaky.

Just when I thought he was about to up and leave me, I gave in and told him, 'Nar, ets jus' me mate. I can't stand that noise that thing is maken out there, so I'm frowen dirt at et t'shut et up.'

Worked wonders, it did. He calmed down right away and was soon throwing dirt at the insect himself when it got started, then from out of nowhere he pipes up with, 'Wot are we guarden 'ere?'

'There's a track cumen down from thu north-west, an one cumen in from thu west goen east an' they meet at a junction right 'ere in front of thu gun, an' when Charlie comes along we'll jus' squeeze on the trigger an' cut 'im off at the knees, 'ay?'

He reflected for a moment, before stating in a slightly alarmed voice, 'But I live down there, what if 'e gets t'me before 'e gets to the gun?'

'It's awright mate, yur won't feel a thing,' I assured him.

* * *

21
SHIFTING CAMP

Next evening Johnny McKindly came around to give us our O group. 'I got good news and I got bad news, do yur want the good news or the bad news first?'

'Givus the good news,' we chorused.

'You'll all be home before Christmas,' he told us with a grin.

'Yeah! Yeah! We know! Now wot's the bad news?' Not one of us believed him. If this was true however, Thao Ly may well have been on the money last time I saw her.

'The bad news is that we have a big walk ahead of us t'morra t'link up with CHQ t'get extracted out.'

'Yeah, that would be right.' This we did believe.

Late next day we linked up with CHQ and were taken out by chopper the following morning. No sooner were we back in the Dat and we'd done our shoot-up, I copped another duty helping the Cook out in the "Pigs' Pen" (Officers' and Sergeants' Mess). I knew I had to put a stop to this immediately. When I went in and stood beside Toddy Smith and asked him what he would like, he answered, 'Wot 'ave yur got on the menu t'day?'

'Broad beans, sausages and gravy, Sir.'

'I'll have the lot, thanks Private.'

There was a partition with a half-metre gap between the top of it and the ceiling separating the end of the Mess and the service area where the Cook dished up the slops.

'Yippiddy beans fer one,' I called out in a particularly loud voice, turning to aim it at the gap above the partition just like they used to do in the Fish'n'Chips shop in Forbes, where we used to go to get some proper tucker into us before going back out to the College following an afternoon in town. I then walked out to collect the Officer's nosh.

The Cook was horrified. 'Yuh can't do that,' he informed me, a little apprehensively.

'You fucken watch me,' I told him, seriously.

I took Smithy's dinner back into him and went around to Boxall. 'Sir.' We went through the procedure as before.

'Yippiddy beans fer one,' I called again over the partition.

No one stopped me as I went through the entire upper echelon of C Company personnel in the same manner — well, six Officers: one Sergeant Major and five Sergeants anyway.

'This is no good,' I told myself when they'd all dispersed and no one had a go at me. With the Mess empty, I went in and opened their fridge and in there I found a couple of different bottles of sprits, so I pulled out the Bacardi Rum bottle and poured myself a full glass of the opaque liquid. When I took this out to the Cook's enclave to start doing the washing up, he spotted the full glass sitting up beside the wash-up dish and put it to me accusingly, 'Wottve you got in there?'

'Water!'

'Donn look like water t'me,' he said.

'Yeah, well, that's wot I'm gunna tell anyone who asks,' I told him.

I helped myself to a couple more before I left and arrived

back at my lines in great spirits — pardon the pun — before the afternoon was out. I didn't get that duty again.

Around ten the next morning Jim and I were sitting on the blast wall outside the front of our digs having a bit of a yarn when Shortarse came strutting down the road from the Office towards us.

'I want you t'find me some men t'do a job up the road,' he addressed Jim.

'I'll go Sir,' I cheerfully volunteered at once — yes, yes, I know the rules "never volunteer for anything", but I hated being cooped up behind the wire of the Dat and I was desperate to get "out" again.

'You're goen anyway,' Shortarse spat at me, giving me a black look.

'Why? Wottov I done this time?' I asked, a little surprised at the venom in his retort.

'You missed out on that charge,' he growled at me. I knew immediately that he was referring to the "light after dark" charge that Jim, under his instruction, had put me on ages ago back out in the scrub.

'Aw, thanks Sir,' I cooed brightly. Shortarse turned crimson as he glared at me. Then he dismissed me out of hand as he went on to explain to Jim the gist of the upcoming excursion outside the wire. I stood listening in as if invisible less than half a metre from them.

Within half an hour, one third of Eight Platoon were riding shot-gun on empty, drab, olive-green cattle trucks heading north up Route Two. When the truck driver proved to be the uncommunicative type, I got jack of sitting in the cab with him and climbed up through the round hole in the roof of the passenger's side and out onto the back of the moving vehicle.

On the back, standing reflective and alone and staring out to one side, was the Padre. He was a beanstalk of a man over two metres tall, greying at his temples, with a long, thin, weathered face. I noted with some interest that he carried a pistol in a holster on his hip, which was held in place by a dull, sickly-green web belt around his waist.

'Hey, Padre!' I said to him, 'I thought you were a man a God?'

He looked inquisitively at me. 'I am,' he told me and I immediately discerned his heavy New Zealand accent, 'Why?'

'You got a pistol on yur 'ip. Wodda are yuh gunna do with that?' I asked, cheekily.

'Fuckum boy, ef they start shooten I'm shooten back,' he assured me, bluntly.

'Well,' I said to myself, *'you'll do me furra Padre, that's f'sure.'* There'd be no bullshit with this bloke, "man of the cloth" or not.

When the convoy got up past Ngai Giao, we started seeing APCs parked at intervals along both sides of the road and these were parked in their traditional manner: three Carriers in a three-pointed star with their noses out and their rear ends facing each other.

Then almost at the same time short-wheeled based *Land Rovers* with mid-mounted M60 guns raised above the driver's head appeared and showering the convoy with dust, they raced up and down between us and the rubber trees on either side of Route Two. Wow! Such security we Infantry had never seen the like of before and all for a handful of trucks poking along up the road?

Our destination was Courtney Hill. The Engineers were up there to dismantle the infrastructure (sandbag-roofed bunkers) at its summit. Until very recently, this had been the HQ of One Australian Task Force as well as the Advanced Command Post of 4 RAR/NZ (Anzac) Battalion.

Upon arrival, we were welcomed with open arms. 'Oh, good, now if you jus' go down there, they'll show yuh wot they want yur t'put on trucks an' wot they're gunna leave 'ere,' a young, unidentified Officer ordered us.

'Wot? We're only up 'ere as security,' we assured the still-wet-behind-the-ears whipper-snipper addressing us.

'No, well, now that you're 'ere, yuken do some work,' he told us, and then took off to organise another work party.

'Wot are we gunna do?' someone asked the most obvious question.

'Come with me, I'll show youes wot we're gunna do,' said Hilly, taking command, and with that he led us in the opposite direction to the work details going hard at it up on the top of the Hill. We strolled casually back down the road we'd just come up on. Before we were halfway down to the place where the Kiowa was trying to land when we were here eleven days back on the 24th of September, we turned off and made our way around a very steep hill along the eastern side until we came to an almost level portion on which we could recline. Here we went to ground, laying back on the warm, lush, green grass unseen by those up on top. Union rules, you see, there'd be no crossing demarcation lines here. We were Infantry and as Infantry our job description was to seek and destroy the enemy. We shoot people; we don't load trucks; that's an Engineer's job.

Next day in the Dat we got all our gear ready to shift Camp for now we were going to take over the lines of the soon-to-depart Third Battalion. They were going home, which would leave only one Battalion of Australian Infantry in all of South Vietnam: 4 RAR/NZ (Anzac). This had not happened since Australia first got into this war six years back when 1 RAR was here on its own at the very beginning of The Royal Australian Regiment's involvement.

Our Boozer ran out of grog that night, so a team of us went looking for another Boozer. We found one down the road a bit at the Engineers' Camp and they too were a bit short on piss, so we had a go at some rice wine which they'd procured from someplace. It was the pits; best described as rice water and metho. To prove the point, one of the men splashed a small amount of the offending brew onto the back of an empty beer can and lit it up with a cigarette lighter. A light-blue flame danced about on the can.

A thin, pale, very young-looking "Gingerbeer" then asked me if I thought he might be able to sell a small movie camera that he had in his possession. It was about 150 by 100 and 25 millimetres thick. 'Yeah, can't see why not. Yur best bet might be t'put her up f'auction,' I advised him.

'Ow do I do that?' he asked.

'Givet 'ere! I'll show yuh!' I took it from him and yelled over the noise in the oblong, sparsely-decorated tin shed.

'Righto you blokes, we've got this great little pocket-sized movie camera 'ere, guaranteed one owner only, a real goer, yurken take 'er anywhere. Who'll start me off with thu bidden, com'on boys, seven dollars. Eight, do I 'ear eight?' No one was taking the slightest bit of notice of me. 'Do'I 'ear ten? I'll take ten, an' I'll take 'er 'ome wif me f'ten. Sold, to the bloke whose doen the auctioneering, f'ten dollars.'

I gave him ten dollars for it and he seemed happy with that even if he did look a little bewildered at the proceedings. Gees, that rice wine must have been stronger than we thought. We drank on, mixing it with beer — it sure stuffed a good beer up though.

Next day we shifted all our stuff over by truck to the now vacated 3 RAR lines . 3 RAR had been flown out to the waiting HMAS Sydney that morning. The lines were not exactly the same as our old ones, but I didn't care much — they were only temporary accommodation anyway. They ran alongside the Luscombe Airfield, which was a short runway inside the wire of Nui Dat where RAAF Caribou and Wallaby aircraft landed. The Wallabies were shaped like half-size *Hercules* with twin engines and were usually painted in dark camouflage colours. Both the Wallaby and the Caribou were small enough to land on this airstrip, but even so the Caribou did have to employ extreme reverse thrust to avoid running off the end into the rubber trees. When it was time for them to leave, they would stand at the end of the strip and rev up to full pitch before letting the breaks off and cutting the blades in, making one hell of a lot of noise before hurtling down past our lines then lifting off out near the end of it. We'd never heard such a commotion over at our old lines.

My digs were down a small slope in the middle of the complex not too far south-east of the Boozer and the Mess. What more could a man want: a place to eat, a place to get pissed at, and a place to lay down his head, and who gave a shit where we were in the complex just as long as we could find them at the appropriate time.

About nine o'clock on the first morning there Jim was explaining to me that I had to go do a demo on the "Under and Over" (Composite M79 under Armalite which he carried) for some high-up Army types later on in the day.

'But Jim, I donn know thu first thing about thu bloody thing, yur know I've never used one.'

'You'll be right, just bullshit to 'em,' he told me, with a grin.

'Nar, but why donn you do et, you carry the fucken thing all the time.'

'I'm going on a garbage run.'

He had just finished telling me this when Boxall suddenly appeared in our tent. He walked to my bed and picked up my gat from where it lay in the middle of it and examined the weapon before exploding. 'Who owns this rifle?' he commanded, angrily.

'It's mine Sir.'

'Clean this rifle at once, it's a disgrace, an' report to Mr O'Brian at twelve o'clock'n show it to him clean, d'you hear?'

'Sir.'

I got to and cleaned it right away and I must say it did look a mess down the barrel.

Just on Dinner Camp Jim swapped his gat for mine and went off to do his Garbage Run. He was in his element; I'd not seen him so up for some time. Jim was a Truck Driver in Four for quite some time before this trip over here. He was an original of the 4RAR Unit from when they had formed at Woodside in South Australia in 1964. He'd done a tour of duty during the Malaysian Emergency and the 1968/9 tour in Vietnam as a Driver.

At any rate, I'd not long got back to my tent when I heard Shortarse hollowing out for me. 'Bishop, Private Bishop.'

'Arr, wot thu fuck does 'e want this time?' I said to no one in the tent in particular. He came barrelling down the slope like a pissed-off bull as I went out to meet him.

'Wot?'

'Where's your rifle? You were s'posed t'show me your rifle.'

'I donno where etis, Jim's gotet.'

'Where's Jim?' he growled, a black look on his face.

'Gone on a Garbage Run in the truck,' I informed him.

'I'll find it,' he declared, and spun around to head back up towards the Mess.

'Arf yur luck,' I told the back of him as he went, fully expecting Jim to be long gone by this time, but as Murphy's Law would have it, Shortarse was back at my digs in a matter of minutes with my gat in his hot little hands.

'You're on a charge,' he gloated with glee.

'Wot thu fuck for? I cleaned thu fucken thing,' I retorted.

'There's dust on the trigger guard, here, look,' he told me, as he handed the rifle to me to check and, sure enough, there was a speck of dust the size of half a pin head on the inside of the trigger guard which almost needed a magnifying glass to find. He left me standing there holding my offending gat as he bustled away to find Boxall to formally charge me. All I had to do was brush a smear of oil over the speck of objectionable dust to make it right, after which I went to find Jim to give him my gat again so that he could take it with him on the Garbage Run while I went off to do the demo with his.

Colonel Hughes was at the demo site when I got there and

I didn't want to let him down so I ad-libbed as best I could, not being all that familiar with the operating of the "Under and Over". I finished off by telling my captive audience, 'We use nice, shiny little ball bearings in our weapons, to kill our enemy, not rusty nails like they do.' While I was wrapping up my presentation, I stole a glance in Hughesy's direction and saw he looked pretty pleased with my effort.

The day after this I was on Guard Duty at the Gun Post on the edge of the airstrip from where we could see out across open ground to the west and along the side of the bottom half of the strip. For most of the afternoon I spent my time looking at an old bloke and a young woman through field glasses. They worked up and down rows of small plants with hoes, fussing about in what looked like a vegie patch, right across the road from where any vehicle coming out of the front gate of Nui Dat would turn right or left to go either north up the road or south towards Vung Tau. It seemed quite obvious to me that these two were VC spies and I found myself wondering why no one had shifted them from there as yet, but of course there would be no actual proof of this and as they were on the other side of Route Two and for all intents and purposes were merely Vietnamese peasants, what could we really do but watch them while they watched us. The thin woman wore black pyjamas and they both worked under white coolie hats all day long in the blazing sun.

Every afternoon late the seven RAAF choppers we had access to would fly back down to Vung Tau to camp for the night like giant birds of prey going back to their nest. Most times they would fly down the airstrip just above the tar and when they got beyond the confines of the Dat or at least past SAS Hill they'd split up — some going high, some low — and in staggered formation would disappear out of sight towards Vungers.

On this particular afternoon, however, the last one of them went burning past my post and out to the end of the airstrip, whereupon it went straight up. Up and up it went, then high up out over the road it stalled. It hung for a second nose up, then its energy died and the main rotor stopped spinning. It went from nose up to nose down and then it fell like a stone from the sky while the others flew on seemingly unaware of their mate's peril. I sat and watch, unmoved.

'Well, that's the last we'll see of that lot,' I said to myself, fully expecting all those on board to die in front of me as they headed towards the ground nose-first on their way to their inevitable untimely end in a fireball less than a kilometre away. About two hundred metres up, the aircraft's engine gave a couple of choking coughs, then with puffs of black smoke coming from its exhaust pipes amidships, the great machine come back to life as suddenly as it had died. As that familiar whop whop whop filled the air, she levelled out and was away again flying low and hard to hook onto the tail of her mates going home.

Mid-morning the following day I was summoned to appear at the Mess to answer the charge Shortarse had bunged on me two days back. When I got to the double door leading into the Mess, Charlie Hill and Pig Pratt were there as well. Before I could find out what they were doing there, Boris — who was acting as the CSM on this occasion — sorted us out.

'You two are up first,' he told Charlie and Pratty, then

addressed me, 'You'll be their escort. You two,' once more referring to the others, 'leave your rifles by the door.'

We proceeded indoors and I marched behind Charlie and Pratty carrying my clean rifle at the "shoulder arm" position where we found Boxall sitting by himself at a table about halfway down the long eating hall.

'Escort and accused! Halt! Escort and accused! Righhhht turn!' Boris put us through the drill once we'd reached Boxall and this put me beside my mates. 'Escort! One pace step back! March!' put me behind them once more.

Boxall read out the charges that were being levelled against them: Failing to adhere to a directive from the Australian Military Police; Entering a private home; Attempting to escape whilst in the protective custody of the Australian Military Police, and, of course, that old Army favourite, Neglect of the Prejudice.' I couldn't believe my ears. Neither Charlie nor Pig had said a word about this in the Boozer?

Boxall then called an MP into the Mess through a door which was halfway down the side of the building. He was a huge, red-headed bloke who looked about twenty-eight or thirty years of age. He was asked to explain the circumstances surrounding these charges.

He stood erect and as still as a post and looking straight ahead he told his story. What transpired was that he and a colleague had been called to a disturbance in Vung Tau on a date which just happened to coincide with our last visit there. They had occasion to caution our two blokes on at least two separate occasions and they'd told them to behave themselves while they were in town otherwise they might find themselves in the slammer. They left;

however, they were called again later that night and found it was the same two offenders, only this time they were found to be in a residence above a bar and refusing to leave. They were taken into custody and taken by vehicle out to the Guard House at the front gates of the Australian Main Camp where they were incarcerated in the gaol there. One offender then attempted to escape whereupon he was re-captured.

Boxall, who had been listening carefully to him, looked up at the Sergeant with a deadpan expression. I thought that Hilly and Pratty were goners for sure given the relationships Officers form with Sergeants as opposed to with their men. 'Thank you, Sergeant, you may go, we will take it from here.'

The big bloke didn't look too pleased to be sent away by Boxall without further input; however, he snapped to attention saying, 'Sir' very loudly and marched stiffly out of the Mess by the side door.

'Now that he's gone, would one of you blokes like t'tell me your side of thu story?' Boxall asked, looking expectantly up at his men.

Charlie started in his distinctive voice and his unique style. 'We didn't do anything wrong, Sir! We were jus' siten roun' in a bar an' these bar girls were tryen t'get us t'buy them drinks. When we didn't, they got thu shits with us an' thu muma-san told us t'go. When we wouldn't, they got the MPs on us, but when we went into another bar we saw these bikes just siten there so we started t'ride them round in thu bar an' thu MPs was called agen. They told us t'move on so we went to another bar an' the girls were trying t'get us t'buy teas. One of them come over to our table an' told Pig, "Er Private Pratt, Sir, 'e'd bought her a tea, You pay now," an' Pig just picked it up an' poured it out on thu floor at her feet. Well, all the girls in thu bar went off, so we left, but thu girls from thu bar were yelling attus from thu doorway of thu bar, an' next thing we know there are these big knives flying through the air past us. When we looked around there were these Rangers chasing us down thu street, an' one of them was picking banana knives off his mate's arms as he held them out for him an' chucken them attus. We ran into a bar, but when they came in too, we thought they might kill us so we ran upstairs an' found ourselves in some people's 'ome, an' we 'id there till they got the MPs an' they took us out to thu camp an' chucked us into gaol. Pig went straight t'sleep, but I kicked thu back wall out of thu lock-up an' made a run for the lights a town, but when someone shouted "Stop or I'll shoot" I sat down, an' they came an' got me an' put me in thu Guard House for thu night, Sir.'

Boxall shifted his impassive gaze from Hilly to Pratty. 'Do you have anything to ad to his story, Private Pratt?'

'No Sir,' Pratty replied.

'Is this how it all happened then?'

'Yes Sir.'

'Well, as this all took place in Vung Tau,' Boxall drawled, making Vung Tau sound like it was a million miles away, 'and it would seem that nobody really got hurt, and as it does not adversely impact on the successful functioning of this unit, I think we can dismiss all charges, but let this be a warning to you boys, don't go playing up when you're on leave in town. That will be all. Thank you, Sergeant O'Brian.'

You could have knocked me over with a feather. Boris responded, bringing us back from the shock.

'Sir! Escort! one pace step forward! March.'

I obliged.

'Squad! Right turn. Squad! Quick march! Left- right- left- right ...'

No sooner were we outside the entrance door of the Mess than we were re-orged and I became the accused. Pratty or Hilly — I'm not sure which, but I think it was Hilly — was my escort and we were marched back in again.

Boxall read out the charges. 'Disobeying a Lawful Command and Neglect of the Prejudice.'

Shortarse was then called in through the same side door which the MP had retired a short time before. He refused to look directly at me as he stood to attention in front of his immediate boss who asked. 'What sort of soldier would you say Private Bishop is, Mr O'Brien?'

Well, according to Shortarse, I was the very worst kind of soldier there could ever be. I was 'undisciplined, ill mannered, sloppy, untidy, and irresponsible, a total disgrace to the uniform' ... There was more, but I didn't hear it.

I saw red. While he was verbally crucifying me, I stared out through the opened louvres behind Boxall not knowing what showed on my face, but I'd say my eyes would have narrowed somewhat. I was thinking, *'You fucken little prick. I've been busten my gut for months tryen t'keep us all from geten killed, especially you, yur little bastard, an' this is how yur repay me. Don't ever let me catch you out on civvie street. I'll kill yur with me own bare hands if I see yuh.'*

I heard Boxall dismiss Shortarse. 'Yes, thank you, Mr O'Brian, you may go now.'

As soon as Shortarse had smartly extricated himself from the premises, Boxall turned his attention back to me.

'So, you've heard what Mr O'Brian has had to say, do you have anything you want to say for yourself in your defence, Private?'

I was still at boiling point. 'No Sir,' I told him in a low growl, my eyes still burning into the rubber trees out through louvres.

'Come on, you must have something to say.'

'I don't think you want to hear wot I have t'say Sir,' I assured him.

'Come on then, spit it out,' Boxall said, sternly.

At this point I'd gone beyond reasoning, for as far as I was concerned it was "in for a penny, in for a pound". I was in the shit anyway so why not make it worth my while. I looked directly at Boxall and hissed through clenched teeth, 'You don't think I'd go crawlen on my gut up to that mongrel little bastard just t'show 'im my fucken rifle, doyuh?'

'CRAWLING!' Boxall exploded, his face contorting and turning redder than I'd ever saw it before. 'I was the one who was crawling. You should have been up against the Big Boss. It should have been two hundred dollars and two months in gaol for you. Ten dollars, march him outta here.'

For the second time that day, I was bowled over. Boris quickly bought us back to reality as he put us through the drill once more with, 'Escort! One pace step forward. March! Squad! Right turn! Squad! Quick march! Left- right- left,-right' ... About half way along the hall, Boxall's clear voice reached us, 'Send that man back into me when you're finished with him, Sergeant.'

When we got outside the Mess doors, instead of Boris

bellowing out at the top of his voice so that all and sundry could hear that I'd been busted and had done some dough, as was the practice of some CSMs, he simply said to me quietly, 'Yur got ten bucks, yur better go back in there. 'E wants t' see yuh.'

I fronted up again for the second time that morning, only this time I was alone.

'At ease,' Boxall offered.

'Sir,' I accepted.

'What's going on between you and Lieutenant O'Brian?'

'Nothing Sir, 'e hates my guts, I hate 'is.'

He looked a little shocked at this, but said to me in a fatherly manner, 'look, you've only got a short time left in this Army. If you just keep away from him and don't get yourself into any more trouble from now till we go home, you'll be awright.'

'Sir,' I answered him.

'OK, you can go now.'

'Sir,' I said again, as I stood to attention and nodded in his direction. He held his clenched hands firmly on the table top and acknowledged me with a curt nod. I performed a perfect right turn and marched myself out.

A day or two after this we were outside the wire again with the extremely uncomfortable knowledge that we were now the only Australian troops in the whole of Phouc Tuy. The tanks were no longer in-country and the Third Battalion were gone as well. The only conciliation for us was that to make up for the loss of the tanks, the Army adapted a short, four-inch gun to an APC. They called this adaptation "The Beast" and the VC hated it because it could manoeuvre around in the scrub a lot quicker than the tanks and could get at them a lot easier. Despite this attempt at protecting us, I actually felt quiet naked and raw as we patrolled out over the road towards the west of Nui Dat.

We spent a long time crossing the expanse of the paddy fields that morning because of the way each paddy was set out as we could not proceed in a direct line from one side to the other and thence to the jungle beyond. We followed the tops of the paddy bunds in a zigzag fashion which made us look like a lot more men than the Platoon size we were.

I was surprised to see small, round crabs in the clear water at the edge of the fields and it was of some interest to me to see how the farmers would flood one field with water then break open a bund and let the water go into the adjoining one to fill it up, always with the water moving in a southerly direction. Mind you, we didn't actually see any farmers out here, but with it being so hot during the day in this exposed landscape, maybe they broke the banks at night or very early in the mornings.

I must say it was a real relief to be back in the jungle and off the paddy bunds once we got there, for apart from anything else, we were not so vulnerable now as we melted away into more accustomed surroundings.

When the next Maintdem Chopper came in, Muzzy was on it. He'd been home to Australia on his R 'n' R leave and we were all pretty pleased to have him back. However, almost from the onset, I noticed that something was amiss with him. He was uncharacteristically subdued. I thought at first that this was completely understandable, given that he'd just returned to this shithole from the bosom of his family and assumed he'd come around in a day or two.

After a few days, with no visible signs of improvement

though, I started to get really worried about him. He had not said anything to anyone. He was far too quiet. Someone in this state of mind in a war zone was a danger to himself as well as his mates and I thought I'd better get to the bottom of it quick. I feared the worst as I thought he'd gone home and had found his missus with someone else or some such thing. I waited until I got him alone on a gun duty one day before I put it to him, 'What's wrong mate?'

'Nuffen,' he told me, sullenly.

'Fucken bullshit mate! There's something wrong awright, I ken seeut. Wotever ut is, yurken tell me mate, yur know yur ken.'

He sat quiet for a bit then said, 'It's me little girl, she donn know me as 'er dad, she cried every time I picked 'er up when I was 'ome.'

Relief flooded through me. 'Or f'fucks sake mate, is that all uttis? Donn worry about that. Chrise mate, yur can't really expect 'er t'know yuh when she's never seen yuh, you wait til yur get 'ome, an' yur with 'er all thu time, she'll know yur then. She's only bin sayen daddy cause mum's been sayen it all thu time t' 'er, but donn you worry mate, it'll be right once yuh get 'ome an' yur with 'er all thu time.'

'Jur reckon?' he asked, seriously.

'Yeah mate, it'll be awright, you'll see, once yuh get 'ome outta this fucken place.'

He gave me a hint of a smile. I hoped against hope that we had our old Muzzy back with us and it turned out that by the time we got back to the Dat after a few more uneventful days of patrolling, Muzzy was his usual smiling self again and none could be more pleased than I was to see this.

Soon we were back in Vungers. When I got to the Minh Bar after my monthly massage, the girls informed me that Thao Ly was not there. When I asked them why, I was told, 'She go Saigon.'

'Most likely over there to see her boy,' I thought, but it was a bit of a let-down just the same. Most of the first day I hung around the bar drinking. Early on I got into a conversation with the most gorgeous girl in the Minh bar. She was petite with fine features and the most beautiful head of lustrous, wavy, long, black hair. She was heavily made-up with light-green between her large false eyelashes and her thin black eyebrows and she wore pink lipstick. All the time we sat facing each other on bar stools and talked, she held onto my genitalia. I tried to get fresh with her after a bit, but she scolded me. 'No. No can do. You Thao Ly's man.' Apparently, she could play with me all day long, but I couldn't touch her because I belonged to another bar girl in that bar. However, if I'd have encountered her in another bar that would have been all right.

At one point we got onto where I lived. She was of the opinion that Australia was in close proximity to America. I took great pleasure in educating her as to where we stand on the world map. She had a bit of trouble grasping the concept that Australia was so far away from the U.S. and in the other direction. Again when I drew a mud map for her with her pink lipstick on a scrap of paper she secured from behind the bar and showed her how far inland I lived in Australia. I watched her staring away into the distance trying to picture it all in her mind.

By mid-afternoon I went looking for a nookie. I ran into a girl called Suzie around at the Kingdom Bar, but that turned out to be no more than you'd get up at the Cross; a telephone call — "Three minutes, are you extending?"

When I told her to 'Fuck off, I'm not finished yet,' she came back with, 'I friends with cowboys, I get cowboys.'

This time I growled at her, 'Shuddup 'n' let me finish.' So she just lay there like a bag of shit.

When I was leaving, I noticed an impeccably-looked-after HD *Holden* Sedan in the paved, enclosed yard at the side of the bar. At the time, people outside of Australia in places like Singapore and, by the looks of it, Vietnam, could buy a new *Holden* for one third of the price we Australians paid for them.

By now I had the shits. Thao Ly was not in town and the root I'd just had was a rip-off. I went back to the Minh Bar and got stuck into some Yank Whiskey. An hour or so later I was following one of the girls as she headed out of the bar, when she encountered two Yanks coming in the opposite direction. They were both nearly two metres tall, and each weighing about twelve stone or a bit more. Instead of standing aside and letting her go, they just walked on, forcing her to jump aside for them. I blew up. I hit the first of them in the chest with both palms of my hands, elbows locked in place.

'Git out of 'ere yuh pair a bastards, where's yuh manners, yuh donn walk over women like that, git outside 'n' I'll 'ave thu both of yuh.'

To my utter astonishment, they turned around and walked out the door without a word being spoken. I followed them up. I wanted them bad, but to my further astonishment, they walked away once out on the street. I called after them, 'Come back 'ere an' fight, yuh bastards.'

They hurried off without even looking back. I went back into the bar but the big Indian Muma-san collared me, 'You number ten,' she scolded me.

'Why, wot'ove I done?'

'You number ten, you chase my customers away,' she told me.

'But they got no manners, in Australia girls go first.'

'You not in Australia now. You in Vietnam. In Vietnam, man go first, girl go second,' she informed me most seriously. What could I say?

Next day I was sitting outside the Minh Bar watching the world go by when an extremely thin bloke with an Afro hairdo asked me for a smoke. He was sitting with his knees up on the pavement on the other side of the entrance to the bar and had just seen me make a rollie from my packet of Drum.

'Sure mate.' I threw him the packet. He laboriously rolled himself a thin smoke and handed me back my tobacco packet. When I threw my butt out across the wide footpath in front of me, I caught sight of two burly Australian MPs as they stepped out of their *Land Rover,* which was parked on the other side of the street. Fixing me with their gaze, they crossed the street and strode meaningfully towards me. The thinner, younger one of the two bent down and picked up the discarded remains of my smoke, breaking it apart. He sniffed at the weed, and in turn his fingers. I couldn't believe what I was seeing.

The heavier bloke stood menacingly over me. 'Can I 'ave a looked wot your smoken?' he asked, stiffly.

'Yeah, it's Drum,' I told him, fishing the near-full packet back out of my trousers pocket and handing it up to him, whereupon he opened it as if to start making a smoke, but then he brought it up to his nose and sniffed inside the opened pack instead.

'What's goen on?' I had to ask.

'We jus' thought yur might be onet like yur mate 'ere,' he informed me, while pointing at the skinny bloke sitting silently by the other side of the door.

'E'snot my mate! Donn know 'im from a bar a soap. Never laid eyes on 'im before,' I retorted.

'Yeah, well jus' watch 'im awright,' the big fellow told me sternly and they walked away, got in their *Rover* and drove off.

I took another look at the Afro bloke. His face was extremely drawn and he was dressed in civies. The Yank troops dressed in their greens while on leave in Vung Tau and this bloke might have been just an ordinary Yank dopehead or he might have been one of them blokes that they left behind because he'd got the "Black Jack" (a particular virulent, venereal disease which turns one's genitalia black and rots it away).

Late that afternoon, I was looking out onto the street from a second-storey room I'd secured earlier, when I spotted old mate Ralth Bodsworth poking along the footpath below me.

'Hey Bobby, wotyuhupto?'

'Nothing much, wot are yur doen up there?'

'I'm camping up here. Wanna come up?'

'OK.'

Within minutes he was up in my digs, but not being content with just being in the room, he climbed out through the window facing the street, saying, 'Wot canyur see from up 'ere?' I joined him and we squatted at the edge of the awning from where we started giving cheek to anyone we knew as they came along the street.

Presently, he asked, 'Hey, why donn we do a bar crawl. D'you wanna do a bar crawl withus?'

'Nar, I got no money mate.'

'That's awright, I ain't got none neither, but we can try an' get a bit somewhere, yur never know.'

'Yeah, righto.'

So we started down towards The Flags on the north side of the street. Three or four doors up the side street heading north-east from The Flags, in a bar called the Gina Bar, I came across the mother of that Australian-fathered kid who was usually around at the US Sky Bars. She recognised me the moment I walked into the dimly-lit bar. She was on for a talk, but we didn't stay here long as they found out pretty quick smart that neither of us had any dosh. Back down the street, we crossed over and headed east on the south side of the main street back towards the Sky Bars. Just inside of the ornate archway leading into the Bonglai Bar there were some girls sitting about talking and waiting for some action, by the look of them. Among them was a blonde, an extremely rare attraction in Vietnam — but then blondes have more fun, don't they say? I stopped when I saw her and went in through the archway to put it to her, 'Ow much you boom-boom?'

'Eight thousand piasta,' she said, with no expression on her face.

'Fuck off,' I retorted. We paid way less then half that for a quickie any other time.

'OK, you fuck off too then,' she came back to me in no uncertain terms and in perfect Australian. I found out later that these girls used to come over from the Saigon University and spend the weekend out the front of this bar picking up a little extra cash to help with their learning.

Bodsworth and I popped in and out of bars all the way along the south side of the street until we came across what looked more like a dance hall than a bar way down past the Kingdom Bar. However, there were working girls here too. Ralf disappeared into the crowd of dancers while I sat at the bar. An elegant older lady closed in on me and said, 'Hoi, my girls not have you tonight, I take you home my place.'

'Nar, mate,' I told her, 'I got no money.'

'Shiit, stand up.'

I extracted myself from the bar stool and stood in front of her. She was most likely no more than one-point-three metres tall, slim and had obviously been a real looker in her late teens.

Smiling brightly, she frisked me all over, then she unexpectedly shoved her hand down the inside of the front of my dacks feeling to see if I had a pouch of money hidden there, as the Vietnamese were wont to do. While she was feeling around in there, she took advantage of the situation and felt up my old fellow.

'Ooh, number wonn,' she cooed.

When she finished feeling me up, I sat down. 'See, I told yer I got no dough,' I assured her once again.

'Take off shoe,' she ordered, while looking nervously around at the dance floor.

'Wot?'

'Take off shoe,' she told me, more seriously.

I complied, taking off one of my Santa Fee riding boots, which I'd always worn for work or play since leaving school.

She held it up and tried to screw the near-two-inch heel off the back of the boot. I laughed. 'Wot areyuh doen?'

'You hide,' she told me, but the heel did not move, so she ordered again, 'That one,' while pointing at the other boot.

Once more she tried in vain to screw the heel off the boot. 'No,' she said, 'you number ten,' and with that she turned abruptly and was walking away before I could even put my boots back on.

'Well, I did tell yuh?' I called out to her fast disappearing back, but she just waved me away without a second glance. Needless to say I slept alone that night.

* * *

22
THE CUP

When we arrived back in the Dat we were told that we'd be doing one more trip outside the wire just to let the VC in the Province know that we Uc Dai Loi had not yet gone away. Boris would be leading Eight Platoon as Acting Platoon Commander this time out because our illustrious leader was away on his R 'n' R in another country. In the morning we packed all our personal belongings in our travel bags and anxiously left them sitting ready on our beds before making our way out onto Luscombe Airfield beside our lines, fully brassed-up and ready to go by ten o'clock.

Well, almost all of us were fully brassed-up. I had decided that as this was to be the last trip out, I'd take my newly-acquired, pocket-sized movie camera with me. To carry it where I could easily have access to it, I bushed one of my twenty-round magazines from my right side basic pouch and substituted it with the camera. It was a great fit.

The choppers came slowly along the airstrip at about ten-thirty, flying a metre or so above the tarmac. Then, spinning around, they set down to absorb us in the usual orderly manner. We flew high out over the paddy fields west of the Dat and north of the Dinhs and, for supposedly the last time, Eight Platoon "landed without smoke" on the western side of a disused paddy not too far north of where we'd done that "in the field training" with the Centurion Tanks in what seemed like a lifetime ago, but was, in fact, just six months back.

We quickly trudged through ankle-deep water for thirty-five metres to our west until we gained the now familiar sanctuary of the jungle, which turned out to be a lot of bamboo at first.

As we ventured further to the west the "J" closed in on us. At one point we had to partly use the steep side of an old B52 bomb crater to get by. It was a golden opportunity to get some good footage of my mates, so I raced around the rim of the giant hole to the opposite side and, using one hand to hold the camera and the other to hold my gat, I captured the scene as members of the Platoon passed me by. When Jim emerged from the thick bush and spotted what I was up to however, he let fly at me, 'Wot thu fuck do yur think yur doen? You'll get yuhself killed doen that!'

'I'm the newsreel photographer, didn't yer know,' I told him, brightly.

'Get back in line an' donn be so fucken stupid,' he scolded, but I didn't care as I'd got the shots and that's all I wanted.

Two days later we came across a small, deep, gently-flowing creek shrouded in thick, lush jungle. We were now on the western boundary of our present AO on the banks of the Suoi Neigh and we were going to spend the night harboured up here listening to the faint tinkling of the brook in the background.

About eight o'clock on the morning of the 1971 Melbourne Cup, we heard a loud explosion just a short distance to the north-west of our position. When we'd steadied, we once again looked to Mick the Sig for the answer. He reported that a Vietnamese youth of about fifteen years of age had just been leaving his village of Ap Suoi Neigh to go to work and had stepped on a mine, which killed him instantly. We now knew that Ap Suoi Neigh was only a kilometre-and-a-half from us, but I'll bet they didn't know we were here so close to them.

After a little gentle persuasion, Boris reluctantly relented and sanctioned a tub in the creek for those of us who deemed it necessary. I, for one, gladly took up the offer as this was only the second time in all the time we'd been "in country" that we'd been allowed to take a tub outside Nui Dat. Yes, we'd been wet right through plenty of times in between from the incessant rain or from fording a creek up to our tits in water and/or our own sweat, but a tub in the bush? Well, that meant we could get our gear off to go skinny-dipping and clean up properly. Incidentally, this was the very creek that we'd been afforded the same privilege in six months back, all be it a little further down the stream.

With two of our mates sitting as lookouts in the shadows on the top of the far bank, I took the plunge. The clear, running water of the creek was freezing when I entered it, but I soon got used of it and I eventually used my sweat rag as a washer and enjoyed a good bogie (tub/bath) while Muzzy captured the event on my borrowed camera for posterity, hoping all the time to get a full frontal. No such luck, Muzzy.

So that he would not miss hearing the Cup, Clarkey carried a big, brown wireless set out with him this time and at least fifty millimetres of it could be seen sticking out each end of the flap on the top of his pack which he'd pulled down real tight for fear of losing it while we travelled. As the time for the race grew nearer, the men started getting anxious about start time and arguments could be heard throughout the Platoon.

'No, but its always at three in Melbourne an' we're on Wes'trailin time up 'ere, but Melbourne's doen that daylight saven time now, isn't et, an' that putsem three ours aheada us'...

And so it went for at least half an hour, until right on eleven o'clock Vietnam time someone yelled, 'She's on!'

Everyone who had them pulled out the earplugs from their radio sets and turned them up. A free-for- all ensued as we bolted to the nearest set and squatted around it in small circles of five or six persons to listen in.

Seeing as I had no money on the race, I was done once Silver Knight went past the post in first place. I had no interest whatsoever in the odds and placings and all that shit, so I turned around to go back to my camp. What I saw will be stamped into my mind for all time. There were rifles lying willy-nilly on the ground everywhere in the little clearing we were on.

My first thoughts were, *'Gees, wot the hell would a Nog be thinking if he were sitting up in a tree somewhere near by and seeing this?'* Then it was, *'How stupid are we, myself included, that we'd abandon our weapons just for a bloody race seven thousand miles away?'* But this race was the annual Melbourne Cup and we were Australians after all and, fuck this war, it didn't need our fullest attention just then. I was the first one of us to pounce on my gat though.

Next day we left this place and headed east back towards the Dat and the following day Shortarse flew back in to assume power in a *Kiowa* which he said was being flown by none other than our own Major Boxall himself. We must have been making too good a time in our endeavour to get home as Shortarse immediately turned us south so that we could go the long way around.

The day after this we were patrolling across a well established path in some tall grass when Bob Denholm quite unexpectedly come face-to-face with a youth and immediately bailed him up. 'Wottayuh got in yer bag, cunt,' Bob demanded, while pointing the M60 directly at the Noggie kid.

'Uc Dai Loi number one, Uc Dai Loi number one,' is all Bob could get out of the frightened kid as he bowed time and again in front of the unaffected gunner.

'Wottayuh got in yer bag? C'mon, giv'es a look. Tipet out.'

Bob got him to up-end his load out on the ground in front of him and after a search found nothing but a bagful of bamboo shoots.

'Yeah, righto, pick etup,' Bob told him, and we moved on, but almost immediately the whole area suddenly resonated with the shrill voices of unseen women.

'Uc Dai Loi number wonnn,' they yelled from all points of the compass. We'd patrolled into a large grove of bamboo where the women were collecting bamboo shoots. To do this they used a long piece of bamboo to dig down to the tender shoots which strike out from the roots up to half a metre or more below the ground.

'Uc Dai Loi number wonnn,' they yelled. It was a bit unnerving at first as we could not see the majority of them, but they sounded as apprehensive as we felt.

Someone spotted a sheila in black pyjamas and Jim went with him to investigate her. Even though they knew she was VC — most likely Chau Duc given the area — they could do nothing about her.

'Why the fuck didn't we plug 'er?' one surprised Digger asked Jim, when he'd joined us after letting her go unscathed.

'She 'ad an ID an' she was inside the civilian access area,' Jim told us, 'She could have dumped a gat anywhere round 'ere as soon as she heard these women calling out Uc Dai Loi, but she was VC f'sure probably carting information out t'er mates further west.'

Then he said to the bloke who'd gone to investagate with him, 'D'ja see 'ow old that other piece was? It only said thirty-one on 'er card but she looked at least fifty t'me.'

'Yeah,' he said, 'she was pretty wrinkled up awright.'

We melted away from their work area with the calls of 'Uc Dai Loi number wonnn,' fading away behind us as we struck out south-east from here.

Later on that day we came across a well-worn track through the scrub that some would call a road. It most certainly carried two-wheeled vehicles of a sort. We went east-nor-east for a bit on this bush road, which was the same track that we'd used to go back to the Dat the first time we'd been outside the wire doing that "orientation" with the tanks.

If no one had found them by now, my original Australian Army-issued, copper dog-tags and the black scorpion that I'd made out of a beaten penny would still be lying in the grass on the southern bank of the Suoi Neigh just a short distance in arrears from where we'd come onto the track. Even thinking of going back to find it never enter my head as we moved away, the Police Sergeant's daughter had not written to me all the time I'd been over here "in country", so she most definitely will never know if I got home or not, and the dog-tags I'd replaced with a new set of silver, oblong Yank type way back.

A lot of the bush around here was thick and low, with some of it being only as high as our heads. Shortarse decided to ambush the track in these low-set bushes overnight with nil result. However, in the morning, before we left the site, a diminutive, old peasant with a long, pointed, wispy, silver beard came slowly by driving a cart which had two solid wooden wheels and it looked like he was still half asleep on the job. The cart was being pulled by a very slow-moving, black water buffalo with enormous horns which looked like it had been in a good paddock and was wishing it was still there.

Right when they were beside the first gun along the track, the old man looked down to see the two Diggers manning the M60 with a belt of brass across it glinting in the morning sun. His eyes grew large and he was immediately on his feet as he gave the reluctant animal a series of rapid, successive strokes with an old, long-handled whip as he screamed out something in Vietnamese, which was no doubt a call to his charge to take wings and get them out of there pronto. The beast never altered its stride one bit as the two of them careered through our carefully-prepared killing ground at a snail's pace, with the old man looking straight ahead and whaling into the tough hide of the buffalo while giving it as much encouragement as he could muster. The gunners were sure he thought he was doing a much better pace than he actually was.

We packed up and continued on in an east-nor-easterly direction out towards Route Two. At Dinner Camp we pulled in off the side of the road into a small clump of jungle just shy of a banana plantation. Before we'd even settled in, a couple of two-wheeled wagons drawn by pinto-coloured cows pulled up between us and the bananas. The carts were loaded with lengths of dry, natural timber, as long as the tray and a metre high above it and held inside hungry boards constructed of two lengths of sawn timber.

We kept a very wary eye on the peasants in charge of these carts, even though they were mostly women, for fear that at any moment they might produce some type of weaponry from its concealment within the wood and start boring it up us. They, in turn, watched us, but appeared to be just as wary of us as we were of them.

Just as they were starting to move away, our little mate, the cow herder, suddenly materialized in our encampment. 'Where Bob, where Bob?' he began asking straightaway.

We all knew he meant Coggins, of course. 'Hey, Coggins, yur little mate from b'fore is 'ere looken for yuh,' we told him with some amusement, and Bob beamed an almighty smile revelling in the fact that the little bloke had remembered him alone out of all of us.

It wasn't long before we were once again giving him our excess cigarettes which he'd placed on top of his ears before putting his hand out and asking for more. With his pockets full of chocolate bars from our ration packs and smokes neatly balanced on both his ears and chock a block in his top pockets, he sneaked away, only to reappear in a couple of minutes looking for more handouts.

Then, from out of nowhere, came another two Noggie kids. The oldest was about thirteen and was quite smartly dressed, while the other one, his brother, was slightly smaller and younger than our little mate. It appeared that the three of them might have known each other, but the two new arrivals were of a higher cast than the drover, so they bullied him a bit as the upper crust are wont to do.

Because it was obvious from the start that this older bloke was educated, Coggins got him to explain the correct pronunciation of certion place names around this portion of the Province.

'How you say this?' he asked him, pointing at a place on the map written as Xuyen Moc.

The youth seemed pleased to be of some help. 'Xuyen Moc,' he told us, but his inflections made it sound a lot like "S'warn Mock" instead of "Swan Mock" as we'd been saying it.

The handouts kept coming as the early afternoon wore on, only now there were three recipients. The big fellow took charge of the distribution and it became a one-sided affair. We watched in amazement as he doled things out.

'One for you.' That was for our little mate. 'One for you,' he said, putting one aside for his little brother who beamed with joy, 'and two for me.'

'Gees, that's a bit rough,' someone observed, but we did not intervene. This might very well have been their way of doing things in Vietnam and the little mate seemed happy enough to go along with the procedure.

Then Smithy came over to me and said with a laugh, 'Yur ortta see wot the little bloke is up to down 'ere, 'es got a stash a mile high down be'ind a tree over there.'

I went with Smithy to investagate and there behind a tree all stacked up nice and neat was little mate's haul; treasure he'd collected before the other two had turned up to crash his party as well as the stuff he'd most recently obtained. 'He'll do alright when he grows up, this bloke; a regular bower bird is he.' After giving the kids almost everything that could be eaten and near on all our smokes to be divvied up between them, we said our good-byes and at about three in the afternoon we wandered off towards Nui Dat once more.

As we came out onto the "road" we passed close by the girl in the black pyjamas and the old man in the vegie patch, but neither of them looked up from their continual hoeing. However, you can be sure they knew we were there.

We crossed Route Two and were within arm's length of the Front Gate of the Dat when Shortarse directed us to change course. We went north-west parallel with the "road" along the bottom side of the airstrip. There was none of the obviously expected complaints or arguments, however, as Eight Platoon were well used to this sort of crap by now.

Once we got past the wire at the bottom end of Luscombe Airfield, we headed straight towards a very large tree, which stood like a sentinel on the cleared ground north-west of the Nui Dat Wire. So much for our last evening meal in the Dat. Good thing some of us had saved a coffee satchel or two and that most of the men had at least half a pack of smokes left for the top portion of our packs were really hollow looking.

We slept out under the stars that night as there was nothing to tie our hutchies to around the huge tree. Everyone was up early and eager to get on the toe. The thought was that once we were inside the wire we would be home free. However, we were given one last "O Group" whilst out in the field, during which we were informed, 'Eight Platoon are going to be the very last Platoon of Australian Infantary to ever go back in through the wire into Nui Dat. We are going to wait around out here until eight o'clock before we go in.'

At eight we moved off, making our way to a hole in the wire just west of our lines, which was a designated gate through which Australian troops had been secretly coming and going from the time the Dat was established. As we patrolled along the short lane in the wire that would lead us through that last gate, some of the boys started pushing and shoving each other, vying for the opportunity to be the very last person in history to "come in". I can't be sure, but I think the honour ended up going to Clarkey.

The place was deserted, no friendly cooks to give us a hearty brekkie;, no one anywhere. We were instructed to pull the pin on all of our smoke grenades and throw them into the one pile. The result was a large cloud of green, red, blue, purple and yellow smoke all rolling into one as it billowed up from the ground and some of the mates took photos of the spectacle for posterity.

Then we were off again. We went down the slope from the Mess into our lines, picked up our carry- all bags off our beds and wandered straight out onto Luscombe Airfield. There waiting for us was a RAAF Caribou aircraft and, without any of the usual "hurry up and wait" shit so synonymous with Army manoeuvres, we virtually walked straight across to the plane's narrow loading ramp and up into its belly.

The inside of this aircraft is basic to say the least. There were those webbed seats again lined up along the unlined walls. We could see up front to where the two pilots sat and their instrumentation was thredbare, but we could see the twin throttle bars cradled together on the cowling in the middle of the cockpit and everything inside the plane was dark, shiny-green.

When the plane was full, they closed the rear loading ramp and the pilots rolled her back up to the top of the airfield. Turning around, they reved her motors up to such a pitch that the airframe rattled from the virbrations, then they let the brakes off, twisted the blades to get pull and gunned her down the strip.

The noise of the engines and the vibrations increased as we moved and once again there was that exhilaration I always experience when a craft of this size powers its way towards take-off. When we were airborn and pointing towards Vung Tau, I couldn't help comparing the *Caribou* with a *Douglas* DC3. They sounded the same, were as draughty as each other and seemed to fly in that same sluggish, yet reliable, manner. After a ten-minute flight we arrived safely at Vung Tau Airport.

23
ONE AND AWAKEY

We were in for a disappointment that morning as our new lines in Vungers became a real shock to the system, because instead of being taken straight to the sprawling Australian Logistics Main Camp on the east side of town, C Company were transported across town to the north-west side of the CBD.

This camp resembled a POW camp more than anything with an oblong yard of wire completely surrounding us. The fence was near new of two-and-a-half-metre high netting and three barbed wires running along the top of it. A broad street came right up to our double front gates from the south and it was here that a bus could turn around, but there was no other way in or out of the compound. We were surrounded by young Noggies in training and most of them would have been fresh ARVN (Army of the Republic of Vietnam) troops. They looked no more than extremely skinny, teenaged kids in tight, predominantly-green, camouflaged uniforms. It was a bit strange to watch them walking around hand-in-hand like a mob of girls, but we were reliably informed that that was quite the norm and an acceptable custom in this country.

Inside our compound were long, low, wooden buildings sectioned off into separate spaces and each one of these rooms accommodated up to thirty beds; fifteen a side, with a corridor down the middle dormitory style with a door at each end. The Officers' and Sergeants' Quarters were at the western end of the complex, while the ORs' Mess and our Boozer were located about a quarter of the way along and the rest of C Company's personnel were shacked up in the remainder. The shower block and bog were at the eastern end facing the last rooms there, which turned out to be storerooms. A water tank, which was raised on stilts for gravity feed, ran the water to our showers and was the last piece of infrastructure on the east end. Between that and the back fence was a space of about forty square metres onto which we never had cause to venture.

Apart from the fact that our temporary home was crap, Vung Tau was going to be alright for the next month until "awakie" (away from here). We had been warned not to get too complacent, though, as according to our bosses, we could be called upon at a moment's notice to go out and help the ARVN if they got into too much trouble, but we didn't care as we knew we'd be able to handle that if the need arose.

Meanwhile, we'd be reverting back to the standard Australian Army practice that we'd been accustomed to in Townsville and of which the Pogos (non-combatants) here in Vung Tau had been afforded for the duration of their time in Vietnam: four o'clock stand down — our time would be our own until the First Parade at eight o'clock in the morning unless we were on Guard Duty. There was just one hitch, however. At eleven o'clock the Guards for the night would close and lock the gates into our compound, which happened to coincide with a night curfew, which was rigorously imposed upon the entire Vung Tau inhabitants and woebetide any one seen outdoors by the “White Mice” (South Vietnamese Police) after curfew. These blokes wore grey cap and trousers, a simple white shirt and had a justifiable reputation for shooting first and asking questions later. The gates did not open again until exactly eight o’clock next morning, by which time we’d be on parade. If by chance we got caught out and had to stay the night holed up in town, we could never make it back in time for First Parade and, by definition, we’d be AWOL and charged as such.

Of course, the first night I was in town, Thao Ly was excited to see me. ‘Now you see my place,’ she told me, busting with joy.

‘Your place?’ I questioned, hesitantly. I thought she was talking about taking me to see her mother at her home and I don’t think I was quite prepared for this one right then and there.

‘Yes, my flat. Since I see you last time I get place of my own. You come now I show you,’ she told me, her eyes shining brightly with enthusiasm. How could I resist?

The Lambretta puttered north-west out along the same street our new camp was on. One or two streets past the French-style building where the Officers used to hang out while they were in town on R ‘n’ Is we turned off to the north-east. A hundred metres on the little taxi slowed down, turned around and pulled up. Thao Ly quickly paid the driver and hustled me out. She was as eager as anything to show me her new camp.

The entrance to her tiny, one-room flat was by an external staircase, which put it on the second floor, and it was cosy, but, as I said, it was just the one room. Directly in front of me as I walked in was a cupboard with double doors, there was a single bed against the opposite wall and the whole place was extremely neat and tidy almost to the point of being sterile. Thao Ly was so upbeat about it as she showed it off to me. On the top shelf of the cupboard she had packets of laundry power and bottles of Whisky, which were no doubt gifts from satisfied Yank clients, stacked neatly from the largest to the smallest. It was only just after dark when we arrived and as I had until a-quarter-to-eleven before the bus left its station on the street corner just north of The Flags to take the night revellers home, I made the best of the time allotted.

The Army didn't want us getting soft while we sat around awaiting our RTA, so a day or two after we'd been ensconced in the compound in Vungers, the Inter-Company football games got under way. Only this time they insisted that we play Union. Oh, man, did I have some trouble getting used to this form of the game.

I'd cut my teeth on Rugby League in the dust, rusty nails, broken bits of glass and small pieces of old tin on the back flat at the Convent in Brewarrina. Over the ensuing years I'd became a devil at pouncing on every loose ball and claiming it as mine by lying all over it until the Referee blew the whistle and decided whose it was and therefore which team would have the loosehead in the resulting scrum; if no knock-on was found the play-the-ball was always mine. Also, in League when you're tackled with the ball you wait until the tacklers get off you, whereby you jump up, face the marker and play the ball back to your dummy-half.

However, there is none of that in this Union game. You've got to get rid of the ball at all costs the moment you're tackled, otherwise you'll be squashed, trampled on, or have the shit raked out of you by opposition boots if you don't. I'd be under the stack desperately hanging onto the ball with blokes crashing down on me and encaging me with their legs and all I'd be able to hear was, 'Get ridda the ball; throw the ball out; they'll stomp on yuh; get ridda the ball, f'crysake.'

And all the time I was getting pounded, I'd be thinking, *It's my ball, it's my ball.* Only pure League players would understand that sentiment.

We played B Company first and, although I cannot recall the score, I did have a thousand bruises on me. A good game was had by all, though, going by the broad grins on everyone's faces as we lined up and shook each others hands with the teams walking past each other in the opposite direction before coming off the field.

A couple of days later when we were due to play D Company, some of us in C Company got "volunteered" to go do a security run out to Baria, and here I was thinking we were finished with all that shit.

We were trucked across town to the Main Base and were aboard our chopper before half-past-eight in the morning. We flew low up along the extensive beach towards Long Hai and a bit over halfway there we passed over a wide stretch of water which joined the sea from out of the mangrove swamps; this was the water which separated Vung Tau from the mainland of Vietnam. From here we lifted higher and turned towards Baria.

We landed on an area of open ground on the eastern side of Baria's CBD. As we alighted, we were met by an Officer. "Oh, good you're here, your job will be to blend in with the Pioneers you see over there, but be ready to act if called upon,' he told us, while pointing to some Aussies in uniform who looked like they were engaged in some sort of construction work on nearby buildings. This we did as "blending in" was by now a piece of cake for us.

It wasn't really obvious to us at first as to why we were up there until another RAAF chopper landed on the same open area at around ten-thirty and disgorged our CO, Colonel Hughes, and a couple more higher-ups. They were there to participate in a Farewell Parade that was bunged on by the Province Chief.

It was an elaborate "do" conducted out on the open field. We observed from the shadows of the construction site as ten young maidens, looking resplendent in white Ao Dais and light-yellow pants, placed leis of white frangipani flowers delicately over the heads of the Aussies and Kiwis lined up to receive them. Hughesy looked quite chuffed with it all.

They were choppered away about twelve, but we had to stick around until later, so I went walkabout and at length came across an old bloke sewing white shirts together on a verandah of one of the buildings, so I watched him for a while, but he was so focused on his task that, after a cursory nod in my direction, he gave me no more heed. No giant sweatshop here, just one wrinkled, little bloke going hell for leather on his own in the warm, afternoon sun. We returned to Vungers by chopper late that day.

Our next game of footy was against Victor Company and it turned out to be a torrid affair mainly because I still hadn't mastered this "chucking away the ball when tackled" thingy, but I was learning. At one point, however, mid-way through the second half, I got an almighty break down the right wing and went scooting towards the open line from over halfway back with no one in front of me. I had the head back and was at full tilt when I saw them descending upon me. One of them was coming at me from the north-east with a very determined look on his face and I glimpsed another one coming at my side from the north out of the corner of my eye. I felt more than saw the one hooking in from the north-west. They collided with me as one and at once I was literally lifted off the ground and carried well out over the sideline. Three twelve-stone-and-thereabouts Kiwis crashed down on my nine-and-a half-stone frame.

They got off me and ran back onto the field to gain their positions as I struggled ungainly to my feet and slowly made my way back onto the field of play. I ached from head to toe. I've never been hit by anything that hard before or since and it took me at least one whole minute to get back into the game.

The broad grins on the faces of our Kiwi opponents was justified as we all lined up and shook hands at the end of the match. They had flogged us. The best part of the event was when we reached the sideline after the game. I was met by Corporal McGurk, our Battalion interpreter, who spoke fluent Vietnamese among six other Asian languages. He was surrounded by a noisy mob of happy Vietnamese kids, all of whom looked no more that ten years of age, and he pulled me to one side and told me, 'These kids say you number one runner.'

'Oh, yeah?' I answered. They all cheered in acknowledgment and wanted to reach out and touch me and I thought, *'Even if I failed to impress the Maoris with my turn of speed out there, I did manage to impress these young fellows.'* I had me a fan club, albeit short-lived.

On First Parade the next morning, we were told by Toddy Smith, 'As of this morning and for each morning from now on you will all be brushing up on your parade ground drills with Sergeant Filewood until you look and behave like soldiers again. You will be participating in a couple of very important parades in the near future and you'll have to be at your best as you are representing the Australian people, the Australian Army and, of course, most especially the Fourth Battalion, in front of these people and we don't want to let them down, do we?'

The drill started in earnest at the end of that parade out on the open ground between the front gates and our lines. However, the impassive Filewood didn't bellow near as much as that mob down at Kapooka did, but what he did do was to introduce a numbers game into proceedings.

Our mornings became, 'Whar two three, one' to everything we did.

Upon hearing 'Company, company shoulderrrrrrr arms', we'd all act as one, bringing our rifles up, clutching the pistol grip and resting the weapon neatly in the "shoulder arms" position while yelling, 'Whar, two, three, one.'

Then 'Company, company orderrrrrrr arms' and off we'd go again, 'whar two three, one', dropping our gats back down again until there was but one very discernible click as the butts of over one hundred SLRs hit the ground simultaneously. When it was right we'd move on and I can tell you with this numbers thing, we got pretty darn good at it, even if I do say so myself.

We'd drill until morning smoko, after which a few of us would catch a bus and journey across town to the Australian Main Camp and thence to Back Beach for a spot of surfing.

Yes, the Australian Pogos had a surf club on our fenced-off portion of Back Beach and we could obtain a board from their surf shed down on the sand. As I'd never surfed before coming to Vietnam, I started out with a long board, but this was of very little help to me. The waves coming off the South China Sea were choppy little buggers and all I seemed to be able to do with them was to drive the front end of the board into the bottom of the wave every time I tried to stand up, thereby getting busted.

Donks attempted to talk me into giving one of the newer, smaller boards — which he had no trouble riding — a go. 'Yer wanna try one of these; yer might do better on one.' I found I couldn't even sit on the bloody things while we waited out the back for a wave, so I reverted back to the battleship of a thing I started on. It was alright for Donks; he could surf, and he'd give me the shits when he'd laugh and say, 'See yuh in there,' as he'd paddle away from me to pick up a wave, stand up and ride the wretched thing all the way in. I never rode a single wave, but I had one hell of a time trying.

The first of those big parades that we were supposed to attend was for some dumb-arsed Four-Star Yank General. The Battalion was absolutely spick as we marched out onto that tarred square, halted and turned to face the podium. Our new greens were freshly pressed and everyone's black GP boots shone and the brass on our blackened web belts fairly glinted in the mid-morning sun, while the silver Australia bars on our epaulettes flashed. Our scarlet lanyards were hard to miss and, of course, our Skippy badges gleamed brighter than ever on the left hand side of the turned-up brim of our slouch hats. When the Parade Commander's shrill voice rang out in the still air over the arena and called us to attention with 'PERADE, PERADE ARTENNNNNNN HUN', all that could be heard was one almighty crunch as over one thousand boots hit the hot tar at exactly the same time. When the order rang out 'PARADE, PARADE SHOULDERRRRRRR ARMS', there was the slightest sound as we performed the drill to perfection: a click as the rifle was smartly lifted to the shoulder and the pistol grip engaged, then the slap sound as the left hand was snapped back to the side while 'whar two three, one' echoed in our heads.

Similarly, when called upon to "Order Arms" all that could be heard across that parade ground was the solid click as the rifle butts of an entire Battalion hit the tar as one. Australia, you would have been so very proud of your fierce-blooded Uc Dai Loi if you could have seen us that morning.

The Yank drawled at us for a bit telling us we were a well-turned-out outfit before giving us the sloppiest, most tired-looking salute imaginable. I found myself thinking, *'You miserable bastard, we've been out there fighting your bloody war for you and you can't even afford us the respect of a decent salute.'* To top it all off, he got into one of our *Land Rovers* and was driven around to inspect the troops. He seemed to not really know who we were or what he was doing there in the first place.

The night after that parade I got into town at around seven just in time to see Thao Ly push a tall, skinny Negro GI out through the back door of the bar, saying, 'No!' as she spotted me coming in the front door. I don't think I was supposed to see that, but what the heck, she was a working girl after all.

By this time I knew the rules. No girls from the same bar, so I went down to the Gina Bar to see if I could crack onto the girl who had the Australian kid. The bar was its usual darkened place with low lights and quiet Vietnamese music being played as I entered, but there didn't seem to be anyone around so I propped myself up on a bar stool at the far end of the bar and ordered a Five-Star. I was about halfway through the first can when this cute little thing popped herself up on the bar stool beside me. 'You buy me tea, honey?' she cooed in a light, pleading voice.

'Piss off, I'm drinken beer,' I growled at her.

'Ockay, I drink beer too then,' she persisted, unfazed by my snarl.

'Givus another one of them,' I asked the thin Vietnamese barman. I handed the can to the girl and said to her, 'ere, getet inta yuh an' sleep on bags.' She beamed a great, big smile and proceeded to get stuck into the poor excuse for beer which gave me time to take a closer look at her. She was a real "China Doll". She would have been no more than one-metre-thirty-five tall with black, shoulder length hair which she wore with a fringe that came down to her eyes which were made to look rounder by the use of heavy, black, false eyelashes and thick, black eyeliner top and bottom. Her eyebrows were perfectly arched, thin, dark lines.She had a button nose and wore pale pink lipstick on small, sweet lips and she looked so young, small and breakable.

'Wots yur name?' I asked her.

What she said sounded like 'Hung.'

'Hung! Owjuh spell that?' I asked again.

'H,u,o,n,g,' she told me.

'Right. Ow old aryuh?'

'Eighteen,' she answered brightly. However, she didn't look it.

'Ow long ave you bin worken?' I pried even further.

'One week.'

'Yeah, well,' I thought to myself, *'that don't mean too much. That's a standard answer around here even if they have been working for years. It's always the same; one week'*

'You speak pretty good English, yur know! Wherejah learn t'speak English like that?'

'Yankee teach me,' she said. I asked myself, *'How would a Noggie girl so young have that much contact with the Americans to be able to learn to speak English so well?'*

'Where at?' I quizzed her.

'Saigon, I work in laundry there, wash GIs' shirts,' she informed me, while demonstrating with her tiny hands the back and forth movements she would have used to wash clothes on the old-fashioned washing boards. I don't know, but her delicate, little arms didn't look to me like she'd done a lot of this type of washing.

We had another beer, then I put it on her, 'ow much t'take you 'ome?'

'You take me your place?' she exclaimed excitedly, her heavily mascaraed eyes open wide.

'Nar, bullshit, you take me your place. 'Ow much?' I both told her and asked her in the same sentence.

'One thousand piastre,' she cooed.

'Fuckoff, yer donn wanta go 'ome wiff me then?' I came back to her.

'Ockay, how much you say then?' she challenged me.

'Seven 'undred,' I countered.

'Ockay, no sweat, you pay, we go,' was her immediate and

unreserved response, as she picked up her purse and jumped down off the bar stool and made ready to go.

I was a little taken aback. The barkeep who'd been listening to our exchange approached along the bar quickly and taking the seven hundred piastre from me beamed me a full smile while giving me a friendly nod.

We got a *Lambretta* not too far away and went in a nor-easterly direction for a couple of streets before turning to the north-west. Another street on and over to the left there was a large, open area lit up by bright lights and the whole area was taken up with what looked like one thousand men and boys engaged in Martial Arts practice. They were all dressed in white Gee (Martial Arts attire) simultaneously throwing punches and stepping forward en masse.

The *Lambretta* stopped on a lit street which appeared to go no further. We hopped out and Huong paid the driver, and then led me into a badly-lit, narrow alleyway that ran between two dark walls. I got a bit toey at this point thinking that she had friends among the Vung Tau Cowboys and that she had set me up for a mugging or worse death, so I steeled myself ready to spring into action, prepared to kill with my bare hands if needs be to save my miserable hide.

Suddenly, we emerged from the dark into a small, well-lit square surrounded by a wing of homes with red-tiled roofs and low, narrow verandahs. She led me quickly across the square to the front of a house opposite to where we'd emerged from the dark alley and we entered. After passing through what looked like a lounge room, we entered another room within the home where we startled a tall, thin, young Vietnamese woman with bobbed hair. Huong spoke to her quickly, in what I presumed was Vietnamese, which caused them to laugh together then bobbed hair lowered her eyes and quickly retired leaving us alone.

The room was spacious. In the middle against the west wall was a good sized double bed made of ornately carved polished wood and on the bed were two plump pillows emblazoned with a bold coloured embroidery of a male peacock strutting his stuff?

'You sleepen with 'er?' I teased, with a grin.

'Yeah,' she laughed back. I didn't know if she was pulling my leg or not, but whatever. Each to his own, I say.

It was the worst love-making session I've ever had. Huong was so small inside that I was half hanging out of her all the way through it, so afterwards when she went to have the obligatory shower, I rummaged through her purse and pulled out her ID card.

'Hey, yur lien little slut, yur told me you were eighteen, yur've only jus' turned seventeen,' I called to her through the sounds of the shower.

'Yeah, no sweat honey,' she called merrily back to me.

'No sweat, my arse; yur'll get me fucken shot, yur will.'

Huong looked particularly smug and pleased with herself as we journeyed back to the Gina Bar in the back of the *Lambretta* and when we were back inside she told me, 'You wait.'

Presently, she was back at my side all smiles, whereupon she handed me a black and white photograph of herself, on the back of which read, "Please don't forget me. I give you picture. I think I love you. Love always, Huong."

The second one of those very important parades that we

had to bung on was a farewell shindig for none other than the President of South Vietnam. Once again the Fourth Battalion presented resplendently in our best regalia and, as before, it was hot on that parade ground in the still, late morning air and when President Thieu addressed us from the stand out in the front of us, he did so in that time-honoured tradition of all politicians the world over. He blustered on and on for yonks, pissing in our pockets. Well, he might have been pissing in our pockets, but who on that parade would have known other than himself and Mac McGurk because he entire speech was given in Vietnamese and the only words that we understood were "Uc Dai Loi", delivered once about a quarter of the way through it. The parade was perfect and it's an absolute disgrace that just one piss-in-the-pocket President of a foreign country and a goddamned disinterested Yank General were the only people to ever see all the members of the Fourth Royal Australian Regiment and New Zealand Army Corps, Second Tour on parade. No Australians or New Zealanders other than those of us on parade that day ever got that privilege.

24
GAME OVER

I come across Obie O'Brian after this "do" and while we were talking he informed me out of the blue, 'I owe you twenty two bucks.'

'OK, so where iset then?' I asked, putting my hand out. I couldn't for the life of me remember even giving it to him, so I must have been pretty bloody drunk at the time.

'No, well I haven't gotet 'ere, Phew's gotet.'

Phew was the ugliest Asian sheila you could ever wish to lay your eyes on. She was from Cambodia and worked out of the Chikito Bar. We met her there on our first trip to town.

'Phew's gotet? Wodjyuh mean Phew's gotet?' I asked him, astonished.

'We're married, she gets all my money an' 'ands out wot I want when I needet,' he confided in me.

'Wot! 'Owed that 'appen?'

'I was drunk one night, woke up in the mornen an' she said "We married", then shows me the signed certificate an' everything.'

'Yeah, well, when do I see me dough?' I put it to him.

'I'll get it for yur off Phew next payday,' he promised, and we left it at that for the time being.

That night when I went home with Thao Ly to her flat I failed to perform — failed even to get a horn. All I could see in my mind's eye was the skinny GI in the Yank uniform disappearing out through that back door with her and an image, real or otherwise, of his huge dick penetrating her. I saw red. Even though it was the irrational unconscious part of my brain that was causing my current impotency, Thao Ly suffered the brunt of my internal turmoil. She did not understand, but tried to console me, which led to me flinging her away from me where she hit the back of her head against the wall behind her bed as she landed on it. Her eyes closed on impact, her hair flying everywhere. I stormed out of the flat with my Williams boots in my hand. I was still sitting on the top of the stairs just outside her doorway pulling them on when she emerged behind me and locked the door after her.

We walked in silence the short distance down to the main drag together where I let her hail the *Lambretta* that was heading back towards the bars, but then once we were seated in the tiny taxi and were moving, she asked me, 'You have two dollar, you give me?'

Even though I knew it was only a dollar to go anywhere in Vung Tau in one of these taxis, I begrudgingly fished into my pockets and gave her the two dollars MPC as I was in no mood to argue. Immediately after she had secured the money, Thao Ly spoke to the driver in their tongue and suddenly he turned left off the main road we'd been on and putted along a street that grew increasingly dark.

I began to think that I was going to be in some sort of trouble now as for all I knew she might have Cowboy friends that she was taking me to and I'd already witnessed how persuasive she could be. Suddenly, she told the driver to pull up outside a well-lit, fair-sized place with clean, modern lines and large front windows which made it look like it may have been a pharmacy or the like.

'You wait,' she told me, as she bounced out of the back of the *Lambretta* and hot-footed it into the building.

Before long she was coming back out all smiles and as she climbed into the back of the three-wheeled machine she held up a small package which was wrapped neatly in brown paper for me to see. 'You buy,' she explained.

'Yeah, well I spose I did, it was my two dollars, 'ow much you got left?' I growled at her.

'One dollar,' she told me brightly, obviously pleased with herself.

'Good, you ken pay for the ride back to thu bar then.'

'No sweat,' she happily agreed.

When we pulled up outside the US Sky Bars, Thao Ly paid the driver, ran across the extended footpath and into the Minh Bar well ahead of me. I still had the scours and was not in the mood for anything, so I ambled slowly in behind her. As I came in through the door I was met by all Thao Ly's friends from the bar who, I thought, if she'd had told them what had happened, would be pretty hostile towards me, but to my utter surprise they weren't.

'You number wonn, you love Thao Ly very much, you buy Thao Ly present,' they told me, beaming the most genuine smiles and gently touching me on the arms.

'You buy Thao Ly cassette, her song; she like very much,' her closest friend relayed to me. I was flabbergasted. One minute I thought we are at loggerheads with each other, the next we're madly in love and I had nothing to do with the make-up gift other than unsuspectingly supplying the doolah to fork out for it. Once again, I felt the tentacles of my heart reach out towards the beaming Thao Ly. Even though I knew I'd never properly understand this amazing woman, I just wanted to hug the living daylights out of her there and then.

At the next morning parade we were warned by Toddy Smith, 'It has come to my attention that certain parties are leaving this Camp at night and going under the wire over to the ARVN Camp next door. If you are caught doing this you will be charged with being AWOL. This sort of thing will not be tolerated. See to it that this does not occur again.'

'Wot? Wot hole in thu fence? Why didn't I know about this?' I whispered to those closest to me.

'Shsss, we'll tell yuh later.' Bob Denholm whispered back, out of the side of his mouth.

It just so happened that I scored a Guard Duty that night and around about ten o'clock I was strolling along the wire at the back of our compound when I came across two blokes down on their hands and knees preparing to crawl through a hole in the netting wire, which was only just big enough to allow one man at a time through on his belly.

'Allo allo allo, wot do we 'ave 'ere, then,' I mimicked a London Bobby coming onto some mischief, as I approached them.

'Awe fuck, yur wonnputes in willyuh?' one of them pleaded.

'Nar mate, didn't see a thing, might wanna go in there meself sometime soon.' I assured them, as I stepped around them and patrolled on as if nothing untoward was happening behind me.

Then, about eleven o'clock a commotion erupted around the back of the shower block and I bustled around there to see what was going on thinking that I might have to break up a fight or something. There, a handful of men were surrounding a little bloke from Seven Platoon who'd somehow burnt both his hands really badly in, or on, the boiler that supplied the hot water for our showers. He was pretty drunk and it was quickly decided by the Company Medic that he should go across to the Main Camp Hospital for immediate and expert treatment. A Long Wheel Base *Land Rover* was called for, which arrived on site in no time.

'You're on guard, you'd better go with them as escort,' I was "volunteered". I was prepared to do anything to help him, so that was a given, so without any more ado we hustled aboard the *Rover* and with these word ringing in my ears we were off. 'If anyone tries t'stopes or starts shooten, shoot back, we're not stoppen f'anyone, yuhear?'I knew he was referring mainly to the White Mice.

'Yep, you're right,' I assured the driver as I settled down in the back with my gat pointing out at the ready. Of necessity the four of us — the driver, the medic, the patient and I — sped along a darkened back street straight across a residential part of town towards our Main Camp. Its got me beat how the driver knew where he was going, but we managed to arrive at the Hospital unscathed and in reasonably good time. Once our man was taken off our hands and into care, it became another hair- raising ride back along that dark street to our Camp.

A few nights later when I'd run out of money and couldn't hit the town, I too went through the wallaby-hole in the fence to watch TV in the Nogs' Camp next door. They had a large, open room that may have been a lecture theatre where a black and white TV was set up on the small stage out the front of the auditorium. The programme that was on was one of those love stories where the players are dressed up in elaborate head-dresses and ornate clothing and appear as puppets and follow the predictable lines of bad man takes girl, good man goes after bad man, fights him and kills him and takes girl back to grateful father with long, silver beard who gives girl to victor as wife.

Because Lyn had explained the essence of these stories on that first time I was in town at her place, I could follow this story quite well and I was able to laugh at the appropriate moments, which must have tickled the Noggie boys no end. As the show went on, one by one they came down and sat beside me until I had anywhere up to twenty of them sitting around me laughing along with me and slapping me on the back. They really seemed to appreciate that I got the story. One of our blokes, who was also AWOL, asked me, 'Ken you understand wot they're sayen?'

'Nar mate, its theatre, I ken jus' see wot's comen next,' I told him' with a grin. He returned me a most peculiar look.

The next day one of the mates was showing a few of us some photos he'd taken of this big Buddha statue somewhere in town and, as things were getting rather quiet around the compound since the big parades, I went and found Jim.

'Jim, d'yur reckon youkud organise a bus trip f'us so we ken all go an' see that big Budda statue, it's pretty boren jus' sitten round 'ere, an' idded be good f'us t'get out an' about forrabit.'

'OK, you organise it, see'n as you thought of it, an' if youken get enough blokes interested enough innet, we'll getyuh a bus,' he obliged me.

Within no time at all and without the slightest bit of

pushing on my part, I had a busload of men all rearing to go on a photographic excursion out of the compound. Armed with cameras — mine being my super eight movie camera — and dressed in greens because we were officially still at work in the Army until "stand down" after the four o'clock parade that afternoon, we boarded the drab olive-green Army bus outside the front gates of our compound and away we went.

First, it was over to Back Beach, then south along the front of the South Korean Camp which was located next to ours, past the Yanks' Camp and down around the mountain which rises up at the southern-most tip of Vung Tau Island where we encountered a group of women wearing white Coolie hats excavating rocks from a quarry. This was not all that unusual in this part of the world at this point in history; I had noted with interest that all the road maintenance work being done on the streets of Vung Tau was being carried out by women. Once around the southern most tip of the mountain, the road followed the water in a north-westerly direction and in a small, picturesque bay along this way we saw a fair sized, rusty freighter sitting upright stuck fast in the sand. There were kids in bright clothing running happily among the rocks and on the beach in front of it while mothers watched on from under colourful beach umbrellas.

As the road swung around we passed the infamous Palace Hotel on our right. I'd not been down there yet but it proved to be a modern multi-story building with views out over the South China Sea. I'd heard from someone who had witnessed it first hand the first time we were in town — that this was the place where Yogi Upton had kicked some strippers off the stage and performed the 'Dance of the Flaming Arseholes' to rapturous applause and calls for encores from a very appreciative audience some of which included the strippers.

On our left a flotilla of multi-coloured fishing boats lay up on their sides in the mud awaiting the next high tide and on the right the Vung Tau Post Office and as usual the area reeked of dead fish. From here we went straight north along a street for some time before turning off to the north-west. After another good stretch, we came upon the giant white statue of "Sitting Down Buddha". He was gazing out to the north. As we ascended the stairs towards him, it soon became apparent that there was more to see than just the one big statue. In the ornate and manicured grounds of the complex we discovered to our delight an intriguing setting where a monkey was sitting up and an elephant lay on its belly, both giving offerings to a ring of small Sitting Down Buddhas who were in under a pagoda. The elephant had spikes sticking up out of its back.

'That's t'stop Aussie Diggers from sitten on 'im an' getten their photos taken on is back,' someone informed us.

Not far away we found an enormous Reclining Buddha. The white stature was over a metre-and-a-half high and from head to toe it was close enough to five metres long. We spent more then an hour here reverently observing and photographing the various depictions of the many states of Buddha. From this vantage point we could see all the way over the mangrove swamps to the Nui Dinhs and as I looked out towards the line of pale blue hills I found myself reflecting sadly, *'There's still a bloody war going on out there.'*

Leaving Buddha to his solitary meditations, we returned

to the heart of town where we were driven past The Flags and straight along the street of bars until we got just past the Kingdom Bar whereupon we turned around and went slowly back past the bars again, with some of the girls standing around in front of their bars giving us the finger as we went. From here we went north again, then onto a road that led us out to the Main Camp where our tour terminated.

Back over in our compound, we found that the Army had given us steel trunks to put all our stuff in to go home. They were eighty-six centimetres long, half a metre wide and about thirty centimetres high, with a handle attached to each end to grab, and two lockable latches on the front of them. They were painted drab olive-green, of course, and to our question we were told, 'Yes, they're yours to keep. Yur have to paint yur name and yur home address on them with that yellow paint they've provided for yuh.' It was a bit of a shock. 'Like, wow, the Army has given us something for nothing!'

Next morning, I took my time painting my name and my parents' address at Hoskin Street, Temora, on my trunk and after I'd finished I took the bus back over to the Main Camp to catch up with Obie intending to get the twenty-two dollars that he had foolishly told me he owed me. His digs were a lot like our own at the compound and at the far end of the slightly larger bunkroom I found a trunk with Obie's name and home address in Melbourne neatly printed on it in yellow paint. There was a four-point-eight-litre tin of the paint with a brush lying across it sitting on the floor beside the trunk, but there was no Obie, so I took up the brush, dipped it into the paint and wrote BISHOP'S GUNNA GET YOU in big letters all over the top of the trunk covering his recent attempt at sign-writing. Satisfied, I left.

About five days before RTA we were all given a separate piece of paper to look at individually. It was, in fact, a questionnaire asking if we wanted to stay on in the Army once we got home and if so did we want to sign on for three, six or nine years. When Coggins handed me my slip of paper, it had a very definite N/A written across it in big, bold pen strokes, so by the look of it this man's Army didn't want the likes of me contaminating its ranks now or in the future, it would seem. They'd got what they wanted out of me so now it was time to be rid of me? I felt that it could have only been Shortarse who would have written it, given his sentiment towards me.

Nevertheless, this incident quickly brought home to me the realisation that I'd better hurry up and do something about getting Thao Ly home to Australia with me. I had a real dilemma on my hands about this. First, in my mind's eye, I could see the look on my old man's face if I walked in with her and said, 'Look who I've brought home.' I knew my mum would be happy for me, no matter what, but my old man was a different matter as he fairly hated Asians and who could blame him? He was in Milne Bay when the head of the red-headed Sergeant turned up in a box. Sent in to the Australians there, as a warning from the hated Japanese to give up or die like this at their Imperial hands. He was also privy, as was all the Diggers in New Guinea at the time, to the tales of cannibalism and such atrocities the starving Japanese soldiers were committing on dead Australian Diggers as they were being doggedly driven back over the Kokoda Track. To my Dad, all Asians were the same.

Then there was the question of Thao Ly's two-year-old son. If I take her home, I'd have to take her son as well — that was a given — but then what about her mum? Would I have to take her mum too? Could she live in Australia so far away from her homeland? Could I expect any of them to leave all they hold dear and come away with me to live in a foreign land for the rest of their lives? And, of course, I had not spoken to Thao Ly about any of this when we were together at her flat on the nights I could afford to be out as we usually had other things on our minds and so I had no way of knowing what she thought about all this. It would be a momentous move on her part if she were to contemplate such an undertaking. I was completely at a loss as what I should do.

With these thoughts swirling around in my mind, I found Jim and put it on him, 'Who do I 'aveta see t'sign over to Delta Company so that I'd 'ave time t'see about getten my woman 'ome wiff me?' Actually, I really wanted more time to talk to her about it and it was Delta Company who would be staying on in Vung Tau as a Rear Guard unit until February 1972.

'They donn need you, they got all the men they need over there right now,' he told me, impassively.

'But Jim, I need more time t'sort out wot I'm gunna do bout getten 'er 'ome,' I pleaded.

'Not my problem, go an' see yur padre,' Jim responded, totally unmoved by my plight. My spirits sank. Inwardly, I think I realised I'd once again procrastinated for far too long and had left it too late to affect the preferred outcome for myself.

However, next morning I went over to the Main Camp to find a Padre; realistically, though, I don't think the Pope himself could have helped me over this hurdle, and when I failed to find a Padre in Camp and as I was already there, I went to visit Obie again in search of my elusive twenty-two dollars.

As I walked in the door I found two blokes sitting just inside it where they acknowledged me with grins. 'Obie?' I asked them. They pointed towards the other end of the bunkhouse, so I wandered down and there laid out on his gut on the top bunk of a double bunk bed was Obie out cold, his mouth open catching flies.

I padded up to him and shoved the pointy end of my gat into his ribs. He come slowly out of his daze and found himself looking directly down the business end of the SLR.

'Where's my money, cunt?' I feigned a loud, nasty growl at him.

'I haven't gotet,' his answer came swiftly.

I cocked the weapon and even though it didn't have a magazine on it at the time, it sounded for all the world like a slug had slid in place up the chamber. 'I'm gunna shoot you, 'I growled as before.

The colour drained from his face. His eyes opened wide and he held his hands up in surrender. 'No Bishie, donn shoot, donn shoot,' he wailed.

The two blokes at the other end of the hut became petrified to the spot. They too lost their colour.

'Nar mate, you're awright, I'm not gunna plug yuh, I jus' come t'get me money,' I reassured poor old Obie.

'I'm sorry mate, but I haven't gotet, but I'll tell yur wot, which way yuh goen 'ome?'

'By Sydney,' I told him.

'Well look, I'm going 'ome by Adelaide, an' if yur give me yur parents' address, I'll send you yur money as soon as we land in Adelaide.' He got my address and I went on my way.

By this time the blokes at the door had regained their composure, as I passed them I could hear them telling some of their mates all about how I was going to shoot Obie.

Back at Camp I found that one of the mates had left a red-dyed, four-plait, greenhide bullwhip lying on his bed, so I picked it up and flicked it about in the confined space of the bunkhouse a couple of times. It had great balance and a beautiful fall. 'Who's owns this?' I asked.

'I do,' its owner answered.

'Nice,' I said, still flicking it about.

'D'you know how t'crack et?' he enquired, his voice lifting slightly as he questioned me.

I raised my eyebrows a little at his rhetorical question. He must have been one of the new blokes because he certainly had no idea of who I was or where I'd come from. 'Yeah,'I told him, laughingly.

'Take et outside an' showes,' he challenged, enthusiastically. Out we went through the door at the back facing the Noggie compound. I swung the whip up over my head and flicked it away from me, dropping its end close to the ground. The cracker exploded millimetres above it. CRAAACK.

'Go on,' he encouraged me, excitedly. I let her rip.

Crack- crack- crack ... Done right, it sounded just like an Armalite going off or the crack of an AK47 round zipping overhead. Suddenly, heads appeared from every doorway on that side of the bunkhouse all the way back down to the Boozer. They had startled looks on their faces. 'Gees, wot was that?' I heard them cry.

When they saw what was going on, someone said for all of them, 'Awe its jus' you. We thought someone was shooten.'

'Nar mate, jus' me muckenroun wiffa whip.' I grinned at them. Relived that it was only the Bushie playing silly buggers with a whip, they melted back into their respective rooms to continue whatever they were doing before I'd rudely interrupted them. Rolling the whip up, I gave it back to its owner and everything went back to normal.

Just before lunch the same morning, one of the men from next door came into our room and said excitedly, 'Yur should 'ear this!'

I followed him next door and we huddled around a fair sized radio set that was lying on a bed. We could hear people talking to each other over coms (communication systems). 'Wot's goen on?' I asked him.

'I've gotet on FM. I've bin listening to the Air Traffic Controllers talking to jets out at the Vung Tau Airport on et and et sounds like some bloke's 'aven a bitta trouble landen out there,' he told me, 'Listen.'

A Yank with a Texan type drawl came on the air, slowly requesting once again for permission to bring down his bird. The bloke in the control tower, also a Yank by the sound of his voice, then answered the bloke in the plane. I don't remember the exact call sign, but he told the pilot. 'We gonna have to get yah to do one more circuit, we've still got an obstruction on the end of the runway.'

After two more goes at this, the flyboy got so fed up with it he burst out with, 'Vung Tau, Vung Tau, this is Phantom two one one, Isa runnen low on gas. If'n you don't let me come in soon, Isa gunna ditch this thing.'

They relented right away. 'Er, Phantom two one one, runway two is clear, you are go to land.'

'Roger that Vung Tau.'

Early that afternoon I watched with interest as a bloke manufactured a bullet pendent. Holding a 7.62 round over a Hexi fire with a small pair of long nose pliers, he waited until the lead in the brass jacket turned silver and then he inserted the tail of the cut-off ring of a safety pin into the molten liquid and let it cool.

I was so intrigued by the process I had to have a crack at it for myself, but I went all out. Going first to Jim who carried an Armalite, I secured four rounds from him and busted them out of their shells, then using those four rounds and three of my own SLR rounds — which I gained by putting the lead into the end of my gat and pressing down gently until it was loose in the shell, thus separating the two — I sat down on the concrete floor of the bunkhouse and made a seven-bullet necklace as a memorial for the seven members of 4RAR who we'd lost on this trip.

Later that same afternoon, a parcel was given to each man in the Company. Apparently, one of these packages had been sent to all the troops currently serving in Vietnam as a Christmas present from the CWA ladies back home. After the Boozer closed that night, someone raided the Office and took back his forty-ounce bottle of Bacardi Rum, which had already been signed out as tomorrow's mail, and turned up back at our rooms with it. 'Anybody wanna charge?' he called, as he rushed in.

'Yeah! Wotjuh got?' The cry went up from the few men around at the time.

'Bacardi,' he said, 'but wotta we got t'mix withet?'

'I know!' someone said, 'we've got some tutti fruiti the CWA ladies sent us, we ken try summa that, I'll go an' get mine.' He slipped next door and returned with a small bottle of lemon tutti fruiti and we shared out the rum into our aluminium drinking mugs, which usually lived under one of the water bottles in a pouch attached to our web belts. It came to about a quarter of a mug each so we then added a goodly splash of the lemon tutti fruiti. It immediately started to swirl about in the mug looking quite sinister, but this didn't stop us though as we got stuck right into it. It didn't do a lot for the taste of the rum, but it seemed to get stronger the closer we got to the bottom of our mugs.

The day before we were due to fly home we all had to face the Medics for a bunch of needles. There were four Medics lined up behind two small tables on which the syringes were laid out and we were ordered to get our shirts off and walk between them, stand still and get two jabs in each arm at the same time and walk away picking up as we went a sugar cube laced with that much flu serum in it that we could actually see the pink interior of the thing. As we moved slowly forward chatting to one another, Hilly was showing me on his medical papers where it said "Suffers from Claustrophobia, had to spend night in Guard house" and laughing about it when someone twigged that Shortarse had not stripped down and quickly pointed it out to the rest of us. He'd been slyly shuffling men ahead of himself while holding back at the back of the line. 'Hey, C'mon Sir, yuh can't get outta this. If we gotta doet, yuh gotta doet, c'mon, git up 'ere an' take yur medsun like a man. Carn Sir, yur should be showen us 'ow it's done.'

At this, Shortarse turned quite pale, but eventually, with the help of our merciless ribbing and with smiles all round, we got him through it. A bit ironic, though, when you think about it; our fearless leader for the six months we were out in the scrub being scared of a little needle.

After the jabs, we had to front a Doctor for an examination. He was a Dutchman. 'N when whas you whis ze girls lars time?' he asked each of us in turn and of course my answer was the same as quite a few of the others. 'Larss night.'

'Oh, you stupid, stupid, stupid man, now you take 'ome to Australia thees terrible deseese from thees women 'ere and give them to your women at 'ome. You mus' no' 'ave sex for one month when you go 'ome, an' zen you see doctor, you see if you clean an' check you haff no worms' yarr. Now, piss off,' he yelled at me. It was the same message to all of us who had partaken of the flesh the night before.

Ignoring the good Doctor's advice I hit the town again that night which, for all intents and purposes was, to be our last night ever in Vung Tau, so who could resist? I spent over an hour with Thao Ly at her place before we ventured back to the bar and it was really hard for me. Everybody knows that "loose lips sink ships" so I could not even hint to Thao Ly that this was to be our last night together; I had to act as if we had weeks before we left. It wasn't that I didn't trust her; it was more that if I told her and she told a friend and if some unsavoury identity inadvertently heard that a group of Diggers were leaving in the morning, that would leave us vulnerably to enemy attack anywhere on the route to the airport.

With our impending departure getting closer by the minute, I thought I'd ask a couple of the locals what they would do once we Uc Dai Loi and the Yanks went away. One of the girls in the Minh Bar where Thao Ly worked shrugged her shoulders, waved her hand and said in the most off-handed way, 'Oh, they come anyway!'

When I put it to Thao Ly, she told me seriously, 'I get good job, I sell flowers.'

My friend Sandy, on the other hand, when I went down to her bar and put the same question to her, answered, 'I go school.'

'Nar, you're too ol' f'school,' I pointed out to her, with a grin, knowing that she was around twenty-two years of age at this point in time.

'No, big school,' she said happily, pointing upwards.

'Big school? You mean university?'

'Yeah, university.'

'There's no uni's round 'ere, is there?' I asked her.

'I save, I go back home,' she told me, seriously. Home for the beautiful Sandy was Taiwan, just as long as she didn't leave it too late to get out of Vung Tau.

I went the other way and found Huong in the Gina Bar sitting up beside a Yank in uniform about halfway down the counter. I didn't say anything as I walked past them, just touching Huong on the elbow, and the moment I sat on a stool at the far end of the counter she was beside me. The Yank sat there bewildered and looking like a shag on a rock.

'Wot are yer gunna do when the Uc Dai Loi and Yankee go 'ome soon,' I asked her.

'I wash cloths in Saigon,' she told me, looking up at me with sorrowful eyes.

She wandered slowly back to sit with the Yank as I made to leave, but when I was about to exit the bar, I stopped, half turned and called to her, 'Huong.' She was at my side in a flash with the bemused Yank once again cutting a lonely figure sitting by himself at the counter in the middle of the bar.

'You want me?' she cried, excitedly, clutching my arm tightly as she spoke.

'Nar love, 'ow do I get hold of you when I'm gone. Wot's your address?'

Houng was beside herself. 'You write me?' she said, her eyes big and bright. She raced in behind the counter and came back with a piece of paper with her name and address printed on it, but once she handed it to me sadly she had to once again avail herself to the Yank as I disappeared into the night.

* * *

25
RTA

By nine-thirty a.m. on the third day of December 1971, all the men from 4RAR who were going home to New South Wales or Queensland that day were waiting out by the shipping containers at Vung Tau Airport. Our RTA Transport was due in at ten o'clock and we were ready. We were dressed in new greens, black web belt and slouch hat and at each man's feet lay a full carry all bag with his rifle loitering on it.

All eyes were scanning the southern sky that bright Thursday morning when at precisely ten o'clock the silver *Hercules* appeared; only it wasn't just one of them. There were two planes coming in one after the other. These unpainted RAAF *Hercules* were known to most people who travelled on them — usually as RTAed casualties — as Silver Angels.

A palpable undercurrent of excitement could be felt as a hush befell the crowd of watchers and we craned our necks to watch the *Hercs* land. When the second plane touched down gently on the tarmac, however, it tilted over until its right wing tip was but mere centimetres from being ripped off on the tar. An audible gasp of shocked awe emanated from the midst of the spectators and then we collectively caught our breaths as the stricken aircraft partly righted itself, continuing down the strip on a slight lean until it came to a halt at the other end.

'Shit, 'e musta done a tire or sunthun,' someone observed aloud, reflecting what a lot of us were thinking.

'Or e's as pissed as a fart,' was another offering. The plane didn't taxi over to pick us up as expected, but proceeded to a different part of the Airport.

Sergeant Filewood, who'd been standing there with us with a list of all the men who were about to get on that plane to go home, told us, 'Youse'll have t'wait for a bit til we see wot's goen on.'

They could take all day as far as we were concerned; we were used to waiting around and we didn't give a shit; our plane was here and we were going home today.

After about an hour of us standing about in the heat, a couple of blokes drove out to where we were in a *Land Rover.* An Officer jibbered to Filewood for a minute or so, got back into the *Rover* and left in a hurry. As Filewood turned to address us, one of the men asked, 'So wots the go, Sarge?'

'Yur'll all have t'go back t'Barracks, yur transport developed a crack in one of its fuel tanks com'en over, an' that's why ut nearly tipped over whenut was landen. They're gunna taket down t'Saigon t'getet fixed today, an' they'll be back over 'ere tomorra mornen t'get youse.'

'Aw, wot? C'mon, Sarge,' the cry of anguish went up, but there was little we could do but comply and there were some pretty subdued men on that bus back into Camp that morning, I'm here to tell you. So near, yet so far away; we had glimpsed our freedom, yet we were still here, but even before the bus was loaded with disgruntled Diggers, the crippled *Hercules* was in the air and winging its way the short distance over to Tan Son Nhut Airport for running repairs to its busted fuel tank. I consoled myself with the thought that it was a good thing for us that they found that fault when and how they did or we might have been in some real shit later on.

I didn't go back into town that night. The night before had been hard enough, besides someone had told me there was going to be strip show over at the Main Camp that night, so I decided to go there and check it out.

'Two girls up on the stage at once!' they'd told me.

Strip tease shows were nothing new to me; I mean I'd seen my first one when I was fifteen at the Walgett Show, but what these two were supposed to be going to get up to with each other on stage that night ... well, that I hadn't seen before, so how could I resist?

The opening act at the Camp hall was a troop of Maoris in their traditional light-tan, beaded skirts doing the Haka and a couple of other equally impressive dances. I'd never seen Maoris dance before and was most intrigued with the blokes with the spiral-pattern tattoos covering most of both sides of their faces, doing it all in an elaborate Karate Horse Stance while slapping their thighs in time to the beat, sticking their pink tongues in and out extravagantly and making their eyes large and bulging exposing more white than usual. In doing so they reminded me of the elaborate heads on Chinese Dragon-Dancers or the masterly carved heads on the totem poles of the Indians of Western Canada. It was an awesome display done with passion by actual Warriors. Now for the sheilas!

Before they appeared, however, an official walked out to the side of the stage and announced, 'All the C Company personnel in the hall must leave immediately and return to your Barracks forthwith.'

'Wot? Why, wots goen on? We 'aven't seen the girls yet!' No further information was furnished and no further negotiations were entered into; it was just go, and go now, so away we went.

Back at the compound and in a foul mood, I found that they had taken our light, steel-frame beds away and we'd been left with nothing but a three-inch, foam rubber mattress covered in a dark-green covering which lay mockingly on the floor where the bed once stood.

'Yeah, that would be right,' I said aloud, when I was presented with this dismal sight and then, to top off an already crook day, when I got down to our Boozer I found that there was now an allocation of just two cans per man left there. I was one pissed-off Digger by the time I left that Boozer at no later than eight-thirty that dark night.

Two doors along from the Boozer, I ran into a couple of my close colleagues in the act of leaving a hut and they both started giggling like schoolkids when I went off about the state of things as they stood at the moment.

I knew immediately what they had been doing while I'd been trying unsuccessfully to make two cans of beer stretch beyond what was possible. 'Givus one of them,' I demanded.

'Yuh won't smoke et,' I was told accusingly, but I was in a real black mood right then.

'Like fucken 'ell I won't,' I assured them. I knew I'd never have enough money when I got home to get hooked on this shit, but right now two cans of beer had done no more than make me crankier than I already was before I went to the Boozer.

'Come around the back,' they invited me with another giggle. Out in the dark yard between the shower block and the front fence, one of the mates handed me a home-made smoke. It was fatter than the ones I made for myself and only three-quarters the length. Devious soldiers — and there were Australians in this as well — would sell cartons of cigarettes to unscrupulous Nogs in town, who would break the tailor-made smokes up and re-roll the tobacco with a good sprinkling of a white powder on it to produce this small fag at a dollar a pop, ten to a small plastic bag.

I sucked away on this thing, not quite sure what to expect, but expecting something nevertheless. Nothing happened?

'Ahh, you cunts are all bullshit, youes've been ripped off.' I growled at them, dispensing with the last of the tiny smoke.

'Ave another one,' they told me, 'draw onut more slowly, take it slow, like this.' With that they proceeded to instruct me on the right and proper way to smoke dope to get the desired effect and I got stuck into a second one not expecting anything to happen.

Not until I was halfway through my second durry did it begin to affect me and by the time I finished it, I was well and truly away. I was walking like I was pulling my feet high up out of mud and slowly stepping down into it again. It was like walking on cloud. Everything we did we did in slow motion. Everything we said was funny and I giggled along with my colleagues until at some point we began making our way back around to our lines still in "high" spirits, but stopped at the bottom of the water-tank tower. Here an "OUT OF BOUNDS" sign had been nailed up when it was discovered some time earlier that some of the men were hooking their booze back out of the "Out Mail" box in the Office at night after it had been signed out for home on next day's mail and getting pissed as newts on it up the water-tank stand.

For some inexplicable reason, I suddenly took exceptional offence to this sign on this night, so I leaped at it and, managing to grab it with both hands, ripped the offending sign down and immediately began jumping up and down on it where it lay defenceless on the ground. I had to kill it.

Others had turned up by this time and were asking what was going on, but my mates must have thought my antics hilarious, going by the way they were laughing. Having done my good deed for the day, I made my way to my bed where I stood at the foot end of the thin mattress which lay on the cold, concrete floor and let myself drop like a felled tree. It felt like I slowly descended into a cloud and when I flattened out I floated back and forth in a see-sawing motion until I settled. Once I did, I was out like a light in seconds.

When I awoke in the morning my head was crystal clear. I felt as bright as the cloudless new day that was just beginning, like I'd had the best sleep I'd been afforded in a hell of a long time. I fully expected that I should have had a splitting headache or at least a hangover of sorts, given where I'd been the night before. Of the greater surprise to me was the fact that I was not hurt and not the least bit sore from literally crashing onto the thin mattress on the solid floor. I began to suspect that I had not done any of the things I remembered doing the previous night at all and that perhaps I had merely imagined it due to the drug-induced state I was in. I had to find out before I saw anyone else, so the first thing I did was to go around to the tank to check the OUT OF BOUNDS sign, but no; there it was covered with dirt and exactly how I'd left it after stomping the living daylights out of it last evening.

We were on the tarmac at nine-thirty dressed as before and by nine forty-five the big silver bird could be seen turning to line up the strip before dropping in. We held out collective breaths as she touched down and, with no extra drama, we were boarding her by ten and disconcertedly we had to relinquish our trusty weapons to ground staff as we were about to step onto the lowered back door of the aircraft. They would be shipped home in a shipping container after us.

'But don't forget,' they told us, 'though its not all that likely to happen, you could be turned around and brought right back here if we get into trouble and we need your help between now and when you get to Australia. Once you're on Australian soil we can't bring you back and someone else will have t'do it, but should you have to come back your weapons will be right here waiting for you.'

I'd only just got to the top of the wide, dropped-down door when I heard an unfamiliar voice hail me from behind. 'Bisho!'

I spun around to see who called me and standing there in front of me with the broadest grin on his face was none other than George Pissani. I hadn't seen him since I left Kapooka. He'd trimmed down a bit and looked quite solid. We shook hands vigorously.

'Pisser!' I exclaimed above the scream of the plane's engines which never seemed to turn off or even throttle back while we were boarding them. 'Ow long 'ave you bin over 'ere? Yur looken good. Who you been runnen wiff?'

'I'm wiff One O Four,' he told me. By One O Four I knew he meant 104 Field Battery, of course. So, he'd been in country as long as I had been, having trained with us as our Gunners in Townsville before we came over and having been an integral part of our make-up all the time we were here.

The central internal partition had been removed to make more space in this *Herc* so we could just plonk ourselves down wherever we liked on the floor. I settled myself down with my bag about a quarter of the way in from the back door and, no sooner was the ramp closed shut, we were off. As we taxied out to line up the strip for that most exhilarating take-off, one of the aircrew in the light-green jumpsuit started stacking cans of beer up in pockets at either side of the tail gate. 'Ay! Wotjur doen? Givus one of them,' we called, but the crewman just smiled at us knowingly and said, 'Nar, they're f'later on, they gotta cool down first. Awe, yeah, an' while I got yurs, there's no smoking in this area of the aircraft. We'd likut if you could come up an 'ave your smoke, up on the flight deck behind the pilots.'

As soon as the *Herc* was airborne, I was on my feet and looking out of the nearest one of the small, round portside windows I could get to. We looped around and climbed at a rapid rate until we were flying high above Vung Tau. Looking down on the fast-disappearing buildings gleaming white beneath their red-tiled roofs, I suddenly became quite morbid. It was alright for the likes of Hilly, McKindly, Boxall and some of the others; they were going home to their wives and children; Jim Pollard and Ray Graham to their future wives, but my woman was down there and this infernal machine was quickly carrying me away from her forever. A prang of great sadness and guilt overtook me. I knew deep down I'd never see her again, no matter what, nor would I ever see all those other happy people down there again, but, worse than that, we were running out and leaving them to their fate at the hands of a brutal regime, leaving them to fend for themselves against our enemy, the VC, a regime which has no concept of the sanctity of human life, male or female. What would become of our friends? I felt that we had failed them miserably by abandoning them and I felt like my heart was shattering into bits, some of it falling back to those we were leaving as this silver, airborne prison stole me away.

I was so torn. I desperately wanted to be in two places at once. I wanted to be down there with my Thao Ly and at the same time I wanted to be back home in the bosom of my family. When I could no longer see Vung Tau and we were flying smoothly over the blue expanse of the South China Sea, I sat down glumly to brood with my fellow passengers. The light-green-clad airman handed out a can each to us now, which was greatly accepted with thanks and smiles all round and now that we were relatively safe so far up and off Vietnamese territory, I found myself reflecting.

Even though we'd only been in-country for a tad over seven months, it felt like it had been ages since we'd left home. How are we going to be received upon arrival back on our own soil? Here we'd been totally loved as "Uc Dai Loi number one". Back in Australia, we were still considered no more than "baby killers" in the eyes of lots of Australian people, but, come to think of it, I did not see a single baby all the time we were here. Not a single child under three years of age and perhaps they too believed that the big, bad Australians were only here to take their babies out and nothing else, so they kept them hidden away; or maybe it was just another of their quaint traditions to keep babies indoors until they can actually get about unaided? Musing thus, I lay comfortably back against my bag, hid a durry in the inside of an empty beer can until I smoked it, after which I drifted off into a sleep of the dead.

I woke with a start at three or thereabouts and was instantly ready to go; but where was anyone going to go stuck up here in this drowning machine? I took a look out the starboard porthole to find we were travelling high above land and it didn't take much to deduce that we were in fact flying over the middle of Borneo given the time of day and the course we were on.

I could see huge, sun-kissed, yellow sandstone cliffs towering hundreds of metres up out of jungle- clad valleys culminating at the top into a vast, dark-green, thickly-forested plateau. The scale and beauty of this landscape reminded me so much of the Blue Mountains west of Sydney in New South Wales. *'Only halfway there, so we're not out of the woods yet,'* I told myself.

It was pitch dark when we eventually arrived in Darwin, not that anyone would have known we had in fact landed in Australia because it was hot, humid and it was raining. We might well have been in any one of a number of airports in the tropical parts of South East Asia for all we knew — Singapore came to mind immediately. The raindrops themselves were extremely large and they glistened in the lights coming from the airport lounge as they thudded down upon us so hard that they actually hurt when they hit us while we were wandering through them across the wet tar towards the building.

It wasn't until we'd entered the big plate-glass sliding doors of the Darwin Terminal building in a gaggle and had sniffed out the bar that a huge wave of relief swept over me. The young blokes behind the bar were "round eyes" and greeted us in a brogue of our birthplace. 'G'day, wot ken we get yurs?'

We were in for a real treat as they placed a glass of frothy, draught beer pulled from a silver tap from behind the bar up onto it. That was my first beer in a glass in two hundred and five days. Glorious, simply glorious.

While we were enjoying this luxury, a young couple walked in and sat together at the end of the counter. The bloke was tall, lean and dressed in civvies, while the girl, a blonde, was thin as well and dressed in a light, floral frock, white high-heeled shoes and was most definitely a round-eye. She was the first white lady we'd seen for month's, a real sight for sore eyes. They were very quiet and kept to themselves at their end of the bar while eyeing us off with stolen, suspicious, sideways glances. Perhaps they were friends with Dr Jim Cairns and members of the Australian Labor Party and were looking to see if they could actually see the babies' blood on us.

After two or three coldies, we got called away from the bar to the Arrivals Lounge, which was empty apart from ourselves at this time of night, and here we found our steel trunks strewn about in the middle of the large floor space in a higgledy-piggledy manner.

'Open yuh trunks an' stand by them so that the customs blokes can 'ave a look in them when they come around,' we were ordered by airport staff.

We chattered among ourselves and moved steadily about between the trunks for what felt like two hours until some of the men started to get a little toey and began voicing their concerns. 'Hey! Wenna these pricks gunna get 'ere? We're been waiten 'ere f'ages.'

'They were waiten round 'ere f'ours f'youse larss night an' they didn't know when you'd be 'ere t'nite, we 'ad t'call em out,' the airport staff informed us, like we should have been interested.

'Yeah, well they're sure taken their own sweet fucken time about ut, s'pose they were all pissed when they went 'ome t'nite after work,' one man was heard to retort, while another went on, 'Yeah, wot, so jus' because our plane got busted, they're gunna make us stan' aroun' 'ere f'owers. Snot our fucken fault, yuh know?'

Eventually, four middle-aged blokes turned up, coming in through a side door. They were dressed in exceptionally white uniforms of short-sleeved shirts, shorts and long, white socks in shining black shoes, but there was no Bronx cheer on their arrival; it was more a case of, 'Oh, you shouldn't 'ave boys, we wouldn't 'ave give a shit if yurdda turned up in yuh birth'd suits, jus' as long as we didn't avta 'ang about 'ere waiten — yur've been cutten inta our drinken time, yuh know.'

Now that they were here, they wasted no time inspecting our opened trunks for contraband, but in actual fact they just walked about giving the contents of each trunk a cursory glance and asking each owner, 'Do you have anything to declare?'

'No,' was always going to be the predictable answer to that, no matter what was up in the steel- capped toe of my boots.

'OK, close 'er up,' each man was told in turn.

Almost immediately after the "thorough search" of our trunks by the conscientious inspectors, we were told our plane was ready for us. 'You will make yuh way out to it now, so yurken get on yuh way.'

It had stopped raining by this time, but it was still repressively hot and dark when we flew out of Darwin that night.

The thrill of knowing that no matter what, they could not turn us around and take us back from this point on was most exhilarating for me; however, my fellow travellers on board were very quiet, with each most probably lost in their own individual expectations of what they perceived might occur in the coming day.

About three in the morning I was hanging out for another smoke and decided on spec not to use the beer can to hide my activities, but to go, as instructed the day prior, up to the flight deck to have it. I made my way slowly, picking my way cautiously around the prone bodies of my sleeping mates to get to the five or six solid, aluminium steps which rose up onto the flight deck. Standing alone at the back of the deck, I was immediately granted the most magnificent sight that could be bestowed upon any real Dinky-di, patriotic Australian.

Expertly framed in the front windscreen of the aircraft were all the stars of an extremely bright Southern Cross. I was home. From deep inside me welded an overwhelming sense of joy, which slowly expanded until it got so enormous that it threatened to bust me apart. It was the same feeling I used to get each time we turned the last kink in the Brewarrina/Goodooga Road before the turn-off to the Cumborah Road which took us south-east to the Narran River and home, all through my boarding school days.

It was always that bend that I associated with being home and now the first sight of the Cross for the seven months we'd been away invoked that exact same reaction in me. I would hasten to say that almost everyone who has ever been sent away from home to attend a boarding school will have had a particular place on the road home that brought to life that special feeling each and every time they came to it. I sat there gazing at the Cross for a long time after I'd finished my smoke, then as I stood up to leave I looked out over a great expanse of inland Australia. With no moon this night, it was hard to appreciate the vista from so high up, so I moved forward and asked one of the pilots, 'Werra we at?'

'Jus' past Mount Isa,' he volunteered. I looked towards the east, remembering how Old Claudie and I used to navigate our way around the paddocks down there using only the Cross on dark nights like this when we were up this way roo shooting. We were flying not all that far west of Richmond.

The relief and excitement could be felt when we landed in Brisbane close to eight in the morning. We said our goodbyes to the mob who were getting off here, most of whom were going on back up to Townsville and, within ten minutes of landing, we were off again on our last leg. To make it even better, the RAAF crewman started handing out the last of the coldies which had been stashed in the back door, some of which I'm sure was meant for the Queensland mob and, as a result, by the time we landed in Sydney around eleven o'clock we were all a bit on the merry side.

From the back of the *Herc* we scrambled aboard a small, pug-nosed, airport bus, which was devoid of seating, and it proceeded across the tar passing gas-powered tractors pulling lines of connected trailers full of luggage to a back entrance to the airport building. Instead of us being able to exit the crowded little bus, however, the driver who was of northern Mediterranean appearance, kept the door firmly shut.

The merriness started to wear thin as we stood waiting for over half an hour not more that ten metres from a glass door at the back of the terminal, expecting it to open at any moment and not knowing exactly why we should be made to wait out here in the stifling heat of December's late-morning sun.

Eventually, with each of us sweating profusely and getting a bit loud and toey, they opened the doors and the driver let us rip. To our surprise there were no protestors in the Arrivals Lounge of the International Terminal to applaud our triumphant return. There was always someone who could find out when we were due in, but this time they must have thought we weren't worth the effort.

While we were standing around together at the carousel awaiting the arrival of our steel trunks, Pisser asked me, 'Where are yuh stayen t'nite?'

'Donno, I thought I might book into the Peoples Palace near Central,' I answered.

'No way matey, yur can't do that, yuh comen 'ome with me. Youken stay with us til yuh ken go 'ome,' he insisted.

'No, but wot about yur Mum an' Dad? They won't want a stranger 'angen roun' on yuh first nite back.'

'Fucken bullshit mate, they'll love t'ave yah. Nar mate, your comen 'ome wiff me,' he assured me, very seriously.

'Yeah, righto, thanks mate,' I said lamely, giving into him as we collected our trunks off the carousel. He was so insistent I didn't have the heart to disappoint him.

We put one trunk on top of the other and, grabbing a handle each of the lower trunk, we walked out. However, right outside the main doors we were confronted by a couple of teenage girls. One was one-metre-fifty-something and blonde with a wide, flat face, milky-blue eyes and a sharp nose. The other was gangly with her brown hair cut short and framing a face full of freckles. Both were attired in short, inexpensive, floral dresses made of light cotton that hung from their bodies rather then fitted them.

'Did any Americans come in with you on the plane from Saigon?' Freckle Face asked timidly.

Being taken completely by surprise, I didn't get a chance to react before Pisser beat me to it and, in truth, I don't believe I could write down on these pages exactly what he said to them, as he went off in a tirade of abuse that would have made the devil himself blush, ending with '... and no, there wasn't any fucken Yank pogo cunts on that plane with us. We're fucken Australians, an' we came in from Vung Tau, yur fucken slags, so fuck off.' I stood completely dumbfounded for I had never heard anyone berate a woman like that in my entire life and I certainly had nothing to add, so we simply turned our backs on them and walked away.

Within half an hour, we arrived at the Pisani's home in Kogarah, a seaside suburb ten kilometres south of the Sydney CBD on the western shores of Botany Bay. His folks were over the moon to have him back in their midst, giving him an enormous hug as Mediterranean people are wont to do and which they extended to me when he explained to them who I was and what I was doing there. They didn't mind at all — they had their boy back and safe from the war.

Next morning one of Pisser's brothers drove us into Central Station in his *Falcon*. With the windows down and speeding along, I was struck by how big and clear and fresh Sydney was compared to Vung Tau. From Central we caught a train out to Parramatta in the mid-west of Sydney using our free Army-issue Travel Warrant and from there a taxi to the Dundas Migrant Hostel just north of the Parramatta CBD.

The Hostel was a fenced compound of low, connected, wooden huts which had forgone their use as dormitories for incoming European immigrants to become a series of offices. We were sent from one office to another, getting things signed off and everything was going fine until I was asked by a Doctor if I had any problems to report with regards to my overall health. When I told him I had a re-occurring gut burning problem, he said to me, 'You'll come back tomorrow and we'll do a BM on yur then.'

At two, they told us we could go, so I went back out to the Pisani's with Pisser and later that afternoon his brother again took me back into town to get a bus up to North Bridge, a suburb on the north side of Sydney Harbour on the road over to Manly, to spend the night with Narelle Watson and her three flat-mates. There was no hanky-panky though, firstly because of what the good Doctor had said a few days back in Vung Tau and secondly, I seemed to have lost any feelings I may have once had for her. I was dead inside. That night we got pissed together, her on beer and me on straight Bacardi Rum.

On the second morning of RTA, I fronted the Discharge Centre at ten as ordered, but had to wait around until one-thirty before they gave me a glassful of brown gunk to down, which near made me spew. Then they took an X-ray of my innards to see if they could see what was causing my gut problems, after which they let me go, so I rang home to see if the old man could come down from Temora the next day to collect me.

Day three, I left my carry-all bag in one of the lockers at Central and arrived at the Centre at ten or thereabouts and around eleven a lean, young Officer with caramel-coloured hair and apprehensive hazel eyes sought me out and said, 'Look, I'm the Safety Officer here an' we've gotta do a fire drill, 'ow d'yur reckon I should go aboutet?'

I couldn't believe what I was hearing — a bloody Officer actually asking me how he should proceed with a missive from above. What a turn-up for the books. Maybe he was of the opinion that because I'd just come back from over there I'd be capable of anything; or maybe it was his private way of saying he respected me for having been away, I don't know. I told him, with a grin, 'see that rubbish tin there in thu corner, stick some papers in et, putet in thu centre of one of them store rooms down there, an' light 'er up an' start callen fire.'

'Yes,' he said, 'but we can't do it inside, we might accidentally burn the whole place down; we'll have t'take it outside.'

'Yeah, right, out sidledo,' I laughed.

We covertly slipped out and around to the side of the building where, using a plastic, see-through cigarette lighter, he bent down and ignited a fire in the little rubbish tin. Then he and I stepped back and he called in a good clear voice, 'FIRE, FIRE.' In no time flat a mob of personnel in Army uniforms had congregated around us, where one of them who arrived carrying a fire extinguisher used it to douse the flames; mind you, he could have turned the tin upside down and stood on it, thus saving the foam in the extinguisher for a real fire if needs be. It was all a bit ho-hum really.

After lunch, I was told to report to someone down in a room at the very end of the building and I was fairly taken aback when I walked in to find none other than the big, blonde Fox sitting behind a large desk. The very same bloke who'd graduated out of Kapooka fifteen-and-a-half months ago, as the number one soldier of my intake. The same bloke that got arse-over-headed by the little "long hair" on Magnetic Island around fifteen months back and one of the blokes who was told not to get on the boat when we were going over to Vietnam.

'Foxy! Fuck, they got yur worken 'ere, ay?' I said, in surprise.

'Yeah, well someone's gotta doet,' he replied, sheepishly.

'Ow long yur been 'ere?' I asked.

'Aw, forra couple amonths now,' he told me.

'So wot am I 'ere for then?'

'Yur spose t' 'and in yuh black belt an' brass t'me so I can sign off onet,' he informed me.

'Yeah, well, I don't 'ave 'em on me t'day, an' no one told me I 'ad t'bring 'em in anyway. Iken bring 'em in t'morra, if yuh like.'

'Nar, its awright, I'll just sign off on 'em anyway,' he told me, and putting his head down he proceeded to do so as I stood there watching him. I noticed while he scribbled that his hands were shaking even more that mine were and he had not even been outside Australia.

'Yeah, right, OK then, see yur, mate,' I said, as I left him there to his demons.

Next, I fronted a Captain who told me, 'OK, we've finished

with you, youken go now, but remember you can't work for a month, cause if you get hurt doen so, we won't pay you compo. We'll send you the rest of your pay over thu coming months and your official discharge papers in thu mail in a little while. Right, now your free t'go — you're discharged.'

I was so high that I don't remember getting down to Parramatta train station. I was standing there in a daze with a grin so broad that it actually hurt my cheeks, when a little old bloke sidled up to me and said, 'They jus let you go outta thu Army, didn't they sonny?'

'They sure fucken did, 'ow'd yur know?' I said.

'I was there myself one day, son, an' I know just 'ow yur feel right now,' he grinned at me.

I was still floating when the train came in and I boarded it, but then I was brought right back to earth with a crash because as we swayed and rattled along towards Central I became acutely aware that the compartment was full of women, most wearing colourful scarves over their black hair and that everyone of them had brown eyes and was jibbering away to each other in a foreign language.

'Fucken Jesus,' I thought, *'I've just come back from a country where the women have brown eyes an' talk in a foreign language an' here I am in a carriage full a'women with brown eyes an' who are all talking in a foreign language, an' this is supposed to be my own fucken country; might as well have stayed where I fucken well was!'*

I took a train down to Kogarah and a taxi around to Pisani's to collect my trunk. Pisser was pleased to see me and, after spending a little time with him in his room going through some of the stuff from his childhood, we again went back into town with one of his brothers to meet up with my Dad as arranged.

I could see by the look in his eyes that the old man was extremely pleased to see me. We shook hands solidly. There was no hugging here; we Bishops didn't do that. We unloaded my trunk out of the Pisani boy's car, putting it into the boot of the light blue 1964 model *Humber* Super Snipe sedan with the white roof, which was the family car these days, and I said my goodbyes to old mate, George Pisani. They drove away and the old man and I turned to walk down the street towards Central Station to collect my carry-all bag from the lockers there. As I fell in with my Dad, I automatically got into step beside him and as we marched along that paved Sydney street together I thought, *'Yurken call me all thu names yuh fucken well like, Australia, but there's one thing yur can't take away from me. Like my old man here beside me, I am a Returned Digger and, on top of that, I'm an ANZAC.'* Of that I was so very proud, but little did I know at the time, I may well have been finished with the war, but my battles had only just begun?

* * *